The Lords of Human Kind

VICTOR KIERNAN is one of Britain's most distinguished historians. After a Fellowship at Trinity College, Cambridge, and a long period spent teaching in India, he joined the History Department of the University of Edinburgh, where he is now Emeritus Professor. The author of *European Empires from Conquest to Collapse*, *The Duel in European History*, *Shakespeare, Poet and Citizen* and numerous other books, he is also the translator of two volumes of Urdu poetry.

The Lords
of Human Kind

European Attitudes to Other
Cultures in the Imperial Age

Victor Kiernan

Serif
London

This edition first published 1995 by
Serif
47 Strahan Road
London E3 5DA

First published by Weidenfeld & Nicolson, 1969

British Library Cataloguing-in-Publication Data.
A catalogue record for this book
is available from the British Library.

Library of Congress Cataloging-in-Publication Data.
A catalog record for this book is available
from the Library of Congress.

ISBN 1 897959 23 0

Printed and bound in Great Britain by
Biddles of Guildford

In memory of Nazir Ahmad, a former Principal of Government College, Lahore, and of excursions to Dovedale, the Khyber Pass, the Oval, the tomb of Hafiz, and other places east and west.

'Pride in their port, defiance in their eye,
I see the lords of human kind pass by.'

Goldsmith, *The Traveller* (1765)

CONTENTS

Foreword   xi

Preface to the Serif Edition   xiii

1 Introduction
The Oldest Europe and its Neighbours   1
The Late Middle Ages: Contraction and Expansion   8
The Shape of Modern Europe   12
Europe and the World: The Seventeenth-Century
    Interval   16
The Eighteenth-Century Outlook   20
The Nineteenth Century: World Domination   23

2 India
Conquest and the Spoils   33
Impulses of Reform   37
British Isolation: Splendid or Perilous?   43
The Mutiny and its Effects   47
Rebuilding an Alien Power   53
Missionaries and Indian Religion   64
Imperfect Sympathies   70

3 Other Colonies in Asia
The British in Ceylon   79
The British in Burma   81
The British in Malaya   85
The Netherlands East Indies   91
French Indochina   95
Russia in Asia   101

4 **The Islamic World**
Turkey 112
Tourists in the Near East 119
Egypt and North Africa 122
Persia 126
The Oriental Scene: Despotism, Hubble-Bubble,
    Harem 135
Christianity and Islam 143

5 **The Far East**
China: An Illusion Fading 152
Celestial Empire and Foreign Barbarian 155
Foreign Residents in China 161
Estimates of the Chinese Character 165
Growth of Chinese Xenophobia 171
The Yellow Peril 177
Korea, Tibet, Siam 179
The Opening of Japan 181
Western Opinions of the Japanese 187

6 **Africa**
Africans in Europe 203
Africans in the Americas 205
The Slave Trade and its Suppression 210
Europeans in Western Africa 214
Europeans in Eastern Africa 221
Southern Africa: the Conflict of Races 229
Belgians and Germans 235
White Settlers 238
The 'Child-Races' and their Reaction 242

7 **The South Seas**
Free Love on Tahiti 255
Decorum on the Lewchew Islands 260
White Savages and Brown in the Pacific 263
Missionary Influence and Western Rule 267
New Zealand and the Maoris 273
Australia and the Aborigines 276

8 Latin America

Independence: White Man and Indian   286
Imitation Europe or New World?   294
Spanish America through European Eyes   302
Brazil and the Democracy of Races   308
Decadence and the Dictators   312

9 Conclusion   325

Index   339

FOREWORD

This book is concerned with the impressions and opinions of Europeans and non-Europeans about one another, their attitudes and behaviour towards one another, in the century or century and a half before the First World War, the epoch when Europe's importance in the world was greatest. It is a subject on which many very different works could be written, and no writer could claim more than a fragmentary knowledge of it. The materials drawn on here come from years of miscellaneous reading, not always well directed, unpublished papers from British and French diplomatic records, conversations with many people from many lands. The literature drawn on is predominantly English, and the only countries outside Europe that I have lived in are India and Pakistan. Britain, however, played the biggest part in the modern expansion of Europe, and its Indian empire was the most important single area of European contact with the world. The theme of the book was suggested to me by my friend Dr E. J. Hobsbawm. I have made some acknowledgements in the notes to other individuals, but in so wide a survey much must be owing in a more general way. Anyone who has the good fortune to belong to a large and sparkling department of history like the one at Edinburgh University is bound to pick up a good deal from his colleagues' daily talk. As to the errors and omissions that a work of this kind cannot be free from, the best apology any writer can make is Dr Johnson's – 'Ignorance, madam, pure ignorance'.

Edinburgh
15 February 1968

PREFACE TO THE SERIF EDITION

> 'For us, who happen to live while the World-Phoenix is burning herself ... Creation and Destruction proceed together.'
>
> Thomas Carlyle, *Sartor Resartus* (1838),
> Book III Chap. 7

The Lords of Human Kind was written half-way between the close of the Second World War and today, when it reappears in a landscape in many ways much altered. All kinds of new debates have sprung up about Homo Sapiens and his destiny, some of them running back to his first beginnings, the question of where he was born – in Africa, perhaps. Argument of a more acrimonious sort has raged over the final stages of the colonial empires, and their legacies. Wherever imperialists were determined to hold on to their possessions, directly or by proxy, the concluding scenes were likely to be more violent than any that had gone before them. Worst and longest drawn out were the French wars in Vietnam and then Algeria, and the American in Vietnam. One of their features was the regular use of torture, in Algeria 'the standard electric-shock treatment'.[1] Europe had prided itself on having left torture behind in the museums, or relegated to sensational novelettes about villains like Fu Manchu. Western relapses into barbarism helped to spread the practice over most of the globe, where it still flourishes.

Sadly, those who fought hardest for freedom have not been the best rewarded. Active struggle, Fanon hoped when Algeria rebelled, would have a purging, purifying effect, freeing a

nation from old bad ways and habits of mind. But since
independence the blighting effects of armed conflict there have
been more in evidence. From the most heroic of all such wars
in history emerged a Vietnam capable of beating off an
unprovoked attack from, of all countries, China; but economic
advance has been inadequate, and north–south fissures have
not yet been overcome. Of the Portuguese colonies, in
Mozambique the South Africans were able to foment and keep
going a vastly destructive civil war; in Angola they did the same
with American backing. In Guinea Bissau the leadership of
Amilcar Cabral raised high expectations among sympathizers
abroad.[2] But he was murdered in 1973; when freedom came,
and his brother Luis was made president, things quickly
deteriorated. After an army coup in November 1980 mass
graves of his opponents were discovered.

Among other newly independent countries India, the biggest
of all, has combined adherence to a parliamentary form of
government with state-promoted economic growth; but
population increase has ensured that poverty is still rampant.
Pakistan has had far less success in industrializing, in political
life none at all. Far Eastern colonies freed, or partially freed,
by the Second World War and its sequel, have had Japan as
pacemaker and the USA as custodian; they have done
formidably well economically, much less well otherwise. Africa
has fared worst. Most of it lacked the commercial and financial
skills which the Far East has always been familiar with.
Leadership has been poor, for one reason at least because
Britain, tutored by Cold War Washington, took steps to push
the ablest candidates out of the way before granting
independence, as too much inclined to Communism.[3] Financial
aid to former colonies has been inadequate, viewed as
compensation for wealth extracted by the former rulers, and
not always well directed. There has been much neo-colonialist
pressure, not excluding military pressure at times. It seems that
the Khmer Rouge, harassing the Vietnamese-sponsored
government of Cambodia, may have received arms from
America as well as from China.

Clichés from Western thinking about Asia have haunted
some Asian minds too. A bygone Shah of Gujarat, according to

Preface to the Serif Edition xv

one Indian historian, was 'fond of displaying the trappings of royalty and like many an eastern monarch loved magnificence and power'.[4] Indian historians are no longer guilty of such aberrations, but Pakistan's first dictator, Ayub Khan, could remark to a Western reporter in 1967 that Chinese representatives were usually easy to hold discussions with, though 'As oriental people they are affected by their emotions.'[5] To hear a Sandhurst graduate from the North-West Frontier talking in this strain might be simply quaint; a graver matter was the behaviour of West Pakistan officers and officials like him in East Pakistan (now Bangladesh), men to whom Bengalis were inferiors, virtually colonial subjects. Hence the movement for independence, which the government tried to suppress by brutality. In this sphere Iraq, with its persecution of Kurds and Shia Arabs, may be said to share the palm with Indonesia. There another dictator has followed up a huge massacre of opponents in 1965 with the seizure of Portugal's old colony of East Timor, and terroristic crushing of resistance.[6] To nearly all of these doings the enlightened West has turned a resolutely blind eye.

Arms are always available to well-disposed dictators, to strengthen armies whose sole purpose is to put down opposition. According to a recent Congressional report in Washington, 70 per cent of all armaments exported in 1994 went to the Third World, with a total value of £15.8 billion; France took the lead from the USA, now eager to catch up. Of American arms sales to the Third World in the past four years, another report tells us, 85 per cent went to non-democratic governments.[7] The enormous world trade in armaments feeds a horde of profiteers, and reeks of bribery and corruption at every stage. This has been so for a long time, and helps to explain the recommendation in the Covenant of the League of Nations that manufacture of arms should never be in private hands – a principle always ignored and long since forgotten.

Some special note deserves to be taken of a large category of the Third World's inhabitants, and the most hapless, the aboriginal peoples. These had fellow-sufferers in Europe, like the Lapps, pushed further and further into the Arctic by the Finns and others,[8] or the Highlanders as they used to be looked down on by Englishmen and Lowland Scots. 'Primitive races' were of only marginal interest to colonial governors. There were always frictions between them and the 'higher races' who often exploited them, and they seldom found a place in the nationalist movements and their gains. They had been forced into the least desirable homelands, jungle or hill. There were 'Montagnard' tribesmen in the hilly fringes of Vietnam, whom the Americans were able to make use of against the Vietnamese. In various parts of the world encroachment by the stronger on the meagre portion of the weaker, which has gone on time out of mind, is still going on; against the Indian populations of Central America, and by ranchers and gold-prospectors in the Amazon basin, or against 'tribals' in the Chittagong hills by land-hungry Bangladeshi settlers.

Here and there, behind an imperial screen, some clan as unknown to the great world as ignorant of it would be waging an obscure contest against those in power. In forest areas of British India officialdom professed to be protecting woodland from dwellers on its edges, who depended on it for materials to build huts and cook food. Really it seems they were often being shut out so that more timber could be sold to businessmen licensed to cut it down. It may be added that independent India is one of the few countries which have tried to make special provision for neglected peoples or castes, to help them to cope with change; sometimes to the discontent of better-off classes who feel that *their* opportunities are being curtailed, to make room for them.

An aboriginal people scattered across southern and western China, the Miao, many of whom had been compelled to retreat into the mountains, launched rebellions in 1735–36, 1795–1806, and 1855–72. A Chinese historian compares their fate to that of the Amerindians.[9] In October 1992, when the new possessors of the New World were celebrating the arrival of Columbus five hundred years before, there were mass demonstrations in protest by some of the forty million Amerindians. For them it was a disaster, portending massacre, degradation, enslavement; inflictions that have never ended, and in recent years may have been worst in Guatemala, home of the ancient Maya civilization, and in the Peru of the Incas. In the central square of Mexico City a large meeting denounced the imprisonment of six thousand 'Indians'. A strong enough impression was made to induce Latin American governments, and those of Spain and Portugal, to set up a fund for indigenous development; and the United Nations designated 1993 the International Year of Indigenous Peoples. Since then however there has been revolt in the southern Mexican state of Chiapas, largely aboriginal.

There have been successes of late in several countries originating from the British empire. There has been growing recognition (which a fresh discovery of Stone Age cave-paintings in France will strengthen) of what 'primitive' peoples have been capable of, in spite of narrow resources. In North America old tribal ceremonies have been reviving, and visitors have flocked to watch them and plumed themselves on being admitted to secret rituals.[10] This may often be simple curiosity, but there is also nowadays serious interest in the religious or philosophical conceptions of an ancient race. At the same time there has been a move towards a coalescence of scattered tribal grievances into something like a national movement, with intelligent organization, and complaints about old treaty rights and their violation, and lost territories, have won some rewards.

Most important materially in the USA has been a Supreme Court decision entitling Indian tribes on their reservations, as heirs to formerly sovereign nations, to set up gambling casinos, elsewhere banned by some states. They bring in fabulous profits; it is an odd experience to see white Americans flocking by the thousand to spend their money at Indian gambling tables – much as too many Indians have flocked to the white man's drinking haunts. An arrangement has thus been found which makes both sides happy; and at Green Bay in Wisconsin, for instance, on Oneida land, the enquirer is assured that the money flowing in is being sensibly invested in new schools, hospitals and community centres.

This implies a renewal of the collectivist spirit formerly animating Amerindian life, with all land belonging to the clan. White rule did its best to break this down, and privatize land and other property. Appeals to competitive self-interest only resulted in an ambitious, adaptable minority being skimmed off, leaving too many to sink into idleness and become derelicts. It was much the same in Canada, where a royal tour speech on 5 July 1973 deplored with unwonted frankness the poverty of the 'Native Americans', their scanty share in Canadian prosperity. Something has been won by them since then; and a dramatic alteration is now taking place in the status of their companions in misfortune, the Inuit or Eskimos. A vast Arctic territory is being handed over to them as their own homeland, whose mineral wealth they will be free to lease out. There are very few of them to confront the task of building a nation in such a wilderness; if they are even half successful, man's most optimistic hopes of mankind will be encouraged.

Australia's aborigines have been the only ones to be so labelled in common speech. Their criminal treatment for many years after the white man's arrival was deplored by Lord Lansdowne, Foreign Secretary, in the House of Lords on 9 May 1905, as likely to discredit the criticisms often made by Britain of misrule in other empires. His admission came in useful to Germany during the recriminations set off by the First World War.[11] Pots calling kettles black were a regular feature of the imperial scene. It was long believed, wrongly we now see, that these indigenous people were a dying race, who would soon carry their troubles away with them to a better world. This was a conviction shared by Daisy Bates, a remarkable woman who dedicated herself to benevolent work among them, not with any hope of improving them but simply to ease their passage. She reacted sharply to an incipient mutiny among some of her protégés, indignant at the white man stealing their land.[12] Their outcry has been taken up in recent years by a genuine movement, making claims for restoration of tribal lands and of sacred places bound up with tribal consciousness and unity. White Australians have been criticized by one of themselves for not caring about anything but a long enough lunchbreak to go surf-riding;[13] all the same, a new page is being turned.

Maoris were a better organized people, if somewhat too one-sidedly for warlike purposes. Their country was annexed, one of its historians observes, at a time when evangelical and philanthropic influences on colonial policies were at their strongest; but the good relations talked of did not materialize.[14] After the years of conquest there was some improvement, but too much of it appears to have been on the surface only, and lower down there have been familiar symptoms of the degeneration that sets in when a people is reduced to existing on the margins of a society in which it has little part. In 1994 a striking film, *Once Were Warriors*, showed a Maori woman trying to rescue herself and her family from a drunken brute of a husband. 1995 has seen an impressive act of contrition on the part of white New Zealand: restoration into Maori hands of a large tract of land, with a large sum of money to go with it, and an apology – to be signed, some suggested, by the Queen herself.

Empires have always set in motion a mixing up of peoples, languages, cultures. Much Afro-Asian blood must have entered the Roman empire, willingly or in chains, and deposited genes still circulating in Europe. Arab occupation of Sicily and Iberia brought numerous settlers, among them a large Jewish community. Massive reshuffling, outside Europe, was one consequence of modern imperialism, and left grave problems to former colonies, alien minorities like the Chinese in Malaya, the Indians in Ceylon, even, as in Fiji, a majority of outsiders. Now analogous difficulties have been visited on Europe itself, and on the USA. Armies withdrawing from the colonies have been followed by a host of migrants, obeying a medley of motives. It has been an unforeseen tit for tat, or rejoinder to colonialism; a new kind of invasion, sometimes legal, often not.

France forced its way into north Africa by years of war, and now has a strenuous anti-immigrant party protesting against the consequences. Even the good done by imperial rule now turns against the doers: their medical services have swelled population, but not resources. Britain has been equally unprepared. Whether or not it acquired its empire in a fit of absence of mind, that is certainly a faithful account of how it has acquired its sudden army of strangers. Yet such a situation is new only in its scale. As Osbert Sitwell said, Britain was for centuries before America 'the European melting pot'.[15]

North America is showing, more than Europe, a two-sided

development, an influx of hungry folk in search of jobs and food, and another of professionally qualified men and women looking for better rewards than they can expect at home, whether in Europe or in Asia. The former, the needy, are often repulsed, the latter welcomed. Canada has been more liberal than the USA, because still not adequately peopled; so that today in whole quarters of Toronto street names are in languages like Greek or Chinese. Both there and in the USA in recent years there has been much talk of 'multiculturalism', as preferable to the old insistence on all newcomers being fully assimilated. European countries face the same alternative. There are obvious merits in diversity, so long as all citizens have something to share in common. Without this it is too likely to mean, for some of them, a ghetto existence, with no culture at all that can have meaning in an alien environment.

Throughout this century reasons in favour of some kind of European union have been multiplying. There is something ridiculous in the thought of a small continent divided into a score of states, each with what is called a Defence Ministry piling up armaments for the benefit of manufacturers and exporters. Some practical beginnings of a coming-together were made not by the winners in the Second World War, as the League of Nations had been made by those of the First World War, but by the three defeated countries, France, Italy and Germany, with encouragement from America and from a neo-Catholic ideology. It was at the same time a re-establishment and consolidation of a badly-shaken capitalism, soon to enter on the most prosperous years of its history.

Part of the price that has had to be paid for this has been a jettisoning of older standards of conduct; a gospel, no longer veiled, of egotistic pursuit of wealth as the *summum bonum*, the only activity worthy of a man or woman of spirit; and with this a spread of financial and political corruption. Capitalism has always found generous room for bribes, perquisites, palm-greasing; but there must be limits beyond which it will cease to be viable. European 'sleaze' has been overflowing into other regions, and worsening similar maladies there. Until not many years ago Indians had a feeling that whatever its defects as a ruling power, Britain was strong by virtue of national character and honesty. 'Nation-building depends on character-building' became the watchword of the Jan Sangh party, and earned it much esteem.[16] Only Indians with eyes and ears tight shut can have any such impression of Thatcherite Britain today and its élite, 'the choice and master-spirits of the age', with one foot on a parliamentary bench and the other in the pork-barrel. Germany too used to be considered more trustworthy than most of its neighbours, but has been revealing itself as no better than the rest. American and Japanese businessmen and politicians have never been thought squeamish about breaking pedantic rules.

Union and mutual criticism may offer a kind of remedy. On the political side, constant harping on 'democracy', as a virtue not to be found in the USSR, has invested the word with a degree of reality. Spain and Portugal were obliged to abjure fascism in order to win admission to the European Union, as an unregenerate Turkey is trying to do. Eire has benefited from membership by being jerked forward some distance out of its clerical-conservative bog. England, so long accustomed to accuse others of backwardness, may benefit likewise, if it can close its ears to the siren songs of pseudo-patriots. Union can be recommended also as a counterweight to German preponderance, increased by Russia's eclipse. In one light European history since the Romans might be summarised as the steamrollering of Celts and Slavs by Teutons: in the west the Germanic conquest of Gaul and the British Isles, in the east the German and Austrian ascendancy over the fragmented Slav peoples.

But if there is to be a union of peoples, not merely of governments, the gravest impediment will be another sort of inequality, between classes, especially in countries like Britain where it has been growing steadily wider. On a bus in a London area where the working class has been got rid of to make way for dwellings fit for stockbrokers to live in, a City gent was heard asking a fellow-settler 'Are there any locals left where you are?' to which the reply was 'Yes, there are still a few savages.'[17] In Bosnia, 'ethnic cleansing' has been going on, in London social cleansing. Such divisions are a negation of civilized life, which must be a society of equals. A 'Startrek' parable of October 1986 carried us to a remote planet that was being reduced to ruins by hostilities between a dominant race and an inferior one, discontented and mutinous. Yet the only difference between them was that one had a face black on the left, white on the right, and the other the converse. It was an aim of my book to emphasize the kinship between prejudices of race and of class. There have always been individuals conscious of the lingering trauma of class division as a cleavage within the human family; artists and writers may have been more sensitive to it than others. It comes out very distinctly and recurrently in Thackeray's sketches of London life in the 1840s.[18] One of these shows us young working-class women gathering at Fenchurch Street Station at the start of a journey that will carry them to Australia, a long exile but in a land free from the divisive castes and snobberies that Thackeray lamented but could see no hope of removing.

All calculations about Europe's and the world's future must be deeply affected by what happens in Russia, and how soon it can find a new purpose instead of sinking into the happy hunting-ground of foreign capitalists that it was before 1917. All the conservative West had longed to see the Soviet Union and its great adventure running down, very much as in the nineteenth century, when the USA was a beacon-light for all Europe's democrats and radicals, its enemies hoped to see it broken up by civil war, and rejoiced to see it taken over by gluttonous machine-politicians. Yet it is well to remember that in both world wars Russia was on the same side as the West, and in the second bore the heaviest brunt of the fighting.

A British government memorandum of early 1918 discussed Russia and Turkey as 'the bridge between Europe and the East'.[19] As Trotsky was to write, 'Russia stood not only geographically, but also socially and historically, between Europe and Asia.'[20] A bridge is likely to be vulnerable on more than one side, and Russia underwent centuries of harassment by Mongols on the east, Turks to the south, Poles and Germans and Swedes from westward. It was a frequent gibe in later days that most of the Russian nobility was descended from foreigners, European or Asiatic. From Western example Russia learned empire-building, but it was wiser than its

Western compeers in not resorting to force to prevent the break-up of the Soviet Union. Only under a new capitalist regime did it go to war brutally to prevent the Chechens from seceding.

A Europe incorporating Russia would be a match for any other of the super-powers among which the world runs a risk of being partitioned, as old Europe virtually was among the half-dozen 'Great Powers'. It ought to see its mission now not as fomenting a senseless competition for first place, but as joining in all efforts towards disarmament and world unity. Tom Paine could think of himself long ago as 'a citizen of the world', and Tennyson could hail 'the Parliament of man, the federation of the world', though he too often slipped back into paeans to such exploits as the British conquest of Egypt, as more in line with a Poet Laureate's duties. This planet is too small to be safely left divided among jostling super-powers, each with a nuclear arsenal and an equally perilous tally of rabble-rousing demagogues.

Modern communication systems may seem to be preparing the way forward automatically. They bring us magically closer. Often indeed the miraculous vibrations seem to have no better work than to report the latest murder in Chicago or the tremors of ticker-tapes and gamblers' pulses. Little of a true meeting of minds may be conjured up by a British Airways advertisement showing the chief of the McLeod clan in Skye and the chief of the Caddo and Wichita tribe in Oklahoma beaming at each other in full rig. Yet television lends life to many happenings when the average imagination cannot; and an Anti-slavery Society representative could report in 1967 that the transistor radio was finding its way even into the sealed prison of the Eastern harem, bringing with it thoughts never breathed there before.[21] We can watch football or cricket matches going on anywhere, and competitive games and athletics have become a great career open to talents, where Africans, above all, have come into their own, and a Miss Goulagong has displayed some of the abilities of Australia's native race by winning the ladies' championship at Wimbledon.

Sex has perhaps been sufficiently demystified to be put in the same kind of entertainment category. Its magnetism seems always to have overleaped boundaries of nation or race. A rugged Yorkshire squire and naturalist, Charles Waterton, wont to explore South American jungles barefooted, was heedless of English prejudices when he visited the USA in 1824. He was meeting, he felt, 'an immense number of highly polished females',[22] a phrase suggestive of a butler burnishing the family silver, or a pasha's dream of the perfect seraglio. British troops ransacking Nana Sahib's palaces at Bithur during the Mutiny in 1857 came on heaps of affectionate letters from Englishwomen to a man named Azimullah Khan who had been Nana's agent in London.[23] Graham Greene touring Africa was struck by the charming colour of young African women, and 'the most beautiful *backs* of any race'.[24] Contrariwise, women in Thailand are reported to have expressed a preference for Americans, as more blonde and good-looking than their own men.[25] Social reasons too may be guessed, but if men and women are left to the guidance of Nature, the 'One World' we hope for may in not many centuries from now be inhabited by one race.

At the height of its missionary drive, in the years before 1914, the West could look to Christianity as the instrument for uniting the world, under its leadership; though it was signally failing to unite Europe. Its own belief in its religion has waned since then, but in the minds of America's Born Again Christians, Christianity itself is having a rebirth, as a twin to right-wing Republicanism. In Latin America well-endowed Protestant missions have been seconding the efforts of dictators, and the US corporations they protect, to counteract the 'liberation theology' of a progressive Catholic movement, and crush peasant resistance. Up and down the world a rapidly growing army of missionaries, estimated in 1995 at 100,000, is astir, most of them from the USA.[26] Many are at work in eastern Europe, helping, intentionally or not, to obliterate any traces of its socialist past. Albania, the latest country to open its doors, is overrun by missioners from both Christian sects and Muslim fundamentalists, with pledges of material aid to recommend their doctrines to a famishing people. Islamic fanaticism, like Christian, is well-funded, and with lavish supplies of arms from the USA and Pakistan it turned

Afghanistan into an even bloodier battleground than any of Born Again Christianity's in Central America. It is a relief to be able to turn to South Africa, as an afflicted country where Europe's Christianity has been its true self.

But in its homelands old dogmas and practices have lost their appeal, while that of the individual bringing a new message has grown. In 1919, in the revulsion from the First World War, D.W. Griffith made a film called *Broken Blossom*, incongruously anti-racist for the director of *Birth of a Nation*. In it an idealistic young Chinese Buddhist came to the West to save it from itself by preaching peace and harmony. He made no headway, and ended a suicide. The chief supplier of spiritual guides however has been Hindu India, with its wealth of myth and speculation, and a flexibility that allows anyone to take the stage with a doctrine of his or her own, and play the role of teacher, prophet, even divinity. There is something in this elasticity that American faith in free enterprise has found congenial, and some of the idle rich led the way in making a hobby of mystic orientalism. The Canadian humourist Stephen Leacock wrote an early story about a pair of burglars masquerading as holy men.[27] Since then some handsome fortunes have been made in the business, along with its stable-companion astrology; as no doubt they were in Rome when its conquests set loose a flood of Eastern mystery cults, and its own civilization, like ours, was on the wane.

Freakish ideas, mumbo-jumbo rituals, inspired seers, help to bring a remote unsympathetic heaven nearer, and testify to the West's declining faith in its own ability to exorcize its ills. India itself, racked like the West by tumultuous change, shows the same craving for supernatural assurances that its cherished past is not disappearing, that heaven and earth are still in their old places, even when everything seems to be upside down. One new cult, much favoured by successful families with modern education, was founded by a Sathya Sai Baba, who has been called 'Hinduism's most significant jet-age holy man'. He works miracles, claims limitless powers, and has promoted himself step by step to the rank of an incarnation of the supreme god Shiva. His secret it appears is an ability to infuse into others a 'fundamentally confident' attitude to life under unfamiliar stars.[28] Japan too has sprouted some new cults, or old ones refurbished; in 1995 one of them, the Aum Shinrikyo, has had an explosive dénouement. A melting-pot of superstitions is stirring; on the level of hocus-pocus, it seems, mankind finds it easier to come together than in more mind-taxing ways.

Fortunately the faculties of the mind have not been lulled to sleep altogether, but on many sides have been making genuine progress. It was an observation of Herbert Spencer that we often find our motives and actions incomprehensible to people of alien backgrounds, but constantly overlook our own difficulty in comprehending *them*.[29] But more and more of them have been making themselves comprehensible to others, and cultures apparently very simple have been revealing hidden depths. Africa, once analphabetic, has been learning, as India learned much earlier, to speak for itself, through scholars, novelists, leaders of its own. An example is Wole Soyinka, who has expounded the conceptions underlying mythic drama and tragedy in western Africa.[30] The world has made him Africa's first Nobel Laureate for Literature, his government has made it necessary for him to abandon his university chair in Nigeria and flee the country. Europeans have learned very much from one another, and are learning now from the rest of the world, which has been compelled to learn so much from them. There are no pure civilizations now any more than pure races. Japan sends out conductors to lead Western orchestras, as well as managers to set up factories.

In the lurid light of this century's wars and crimes, all over the globe, the profound Christian distrust of human nature is undeniably justified. Any region presuming to offer guidance to the others will do well to put strict self-examination first. Whether or not the 'civilizing mission' claimed by the West had much improving effect on other lands, it is high time now for it to set about civilizing itself. Europe can at least claim the merit of having brought the idea of socialism into a world where, in spite of many persecutions, it has found fertile soil. Europe will be giving another wholesome lead when it is seen to be steering towards a future of social justice and equal rights as well as international amity. The notion of lower races is not likely to disappear while that of lower classes, and an inferior sex, is allowed to persist.

V.G. Kiernan
Stow
22 August 1995

NOTES

(The place of publication of works cited, when not given below, may be assumed to be London.)

1. Maurice Larkin, *France Since the Popular Front. Government and People 1936–1986* (Oxford, 1988), p. 259.
2. See Amilcar Cabral, *Revolution in Guinea. An African People's Struggle* (1969).
3. Frank Füredi, *Colonial Wars and the Politics of Third World Nationalism* (1994), p. 222.
4. Ishwari Prasad, *The Life and Times of Humayun* (Bombay, 1956), p. 89.
5. *Observer*, 12 February 1967.
6. See Malcolm Caldwell, ed., *Ten Years' Military Terror in Indonesia* (Nottingham, 1975).
7. *Guardian*, 9 August 1995.
8. For a traveller's impressions, of a generation or two ago, see C.J. Cutliffe Hyne, *Through Arctic Lapland* (n.d.).
9. S.Y. Teng, *The Taiping Rebellion and the Western Powers* (Oxford, 1971), pp. 366 ff.
10. Ruth Adam, *Guardian*, 10 July 1971.
11. German Colonial Office, *The Treatment of the Natives and Other Populations* (Berlin, 1919), p. 57.
12. Daisy Bates, *The Passing of the Aborigines* (1938; new edn, 1972), pp. 200 ff.
13. Robert Hughes, *The Fatal Shore. A History of the Transportation of Convicts to Australia, 1787–1868* (1987).
14. K. Sinclair, *The Pelican History of New Zealand* (Harmondsworth, revised edn, 1980), p. 130. On the expropriation of Maoris from their lands, see Dick Scott, *Ask That Mountain: The Story of*

Parihaka (Auckland, 1975).

15. Osbert Sitwell, *The Four Continents* (1955), p. 52.

16. From a letter from my friend Dr P.D. Tripathi, 14 February 1969.

17. *Guardian*, 11 November 1987.

18. W.M. Thackeray, *Sketches and Travels in London* (1844–50; Gloucester edn, 1989), pp. 161 ff.

19. Cabinet Papers, CAB 24/39, January 1918, PRO. A copy was kindly given me by the late Mrs T. Brotherstone.

20. Leon Trotsky, *History of the Russian Revolution* (1930; London edn 1967), Vol. 1 p. 22; see also Vol. 3, Chapter 2, 'The Problem of Nationalities'.

21. BBC, 6 May 1967.

22. Charles Waterton, *Wanderings in South America* (1825; new edn, 1906), p. 184. See also Julia Blackburn, *Charles Waterton 1782–1865* (1989).

23. F.S. Roberts (later Field Marshal Earl), *Letters Written During the Indian Mutiny* (1924), p. 120.

24. Graham Greene, *In Search of a Character* (1961), p. 59.

25. BBC programme on Thailand, 2 April 1973.

26. *Observer*, 27 July 1995.

27. Stephen Leacock, 'The Yahi-Bahi Oriental Society of Mrs Rasselyer-Brown', in *Arcadian Adventures with the Idle Rich* (Toronto, 1914).

28. L.A. Babb, 'The Puzzle of Religious Modernity', in J.R. Roach, ed., *Indian 2000: The Next Fifteen Years* (Riverdale, Maryland, 1986), pp. 71, 76.

29. Herbert Spencer, *The Study of Sociology* (15th edn, 1889), p. 116.

30. Wole Soyinka, *Myth, Literature and the African World* (Cambridge, 1976).

1. INTRODUCTION

The Oldest Europe and its Neighbours

Man's most ancient ancestors have left their bones on three continents, and civilization seems to have begun where Asia and Africa meet, between the river valleys of Mesopotamia and Egypt, with Europe, Asia's extension, close by. Its outward mark was a society divided into classes and ruled by higher classes sometimes for the collective benefit, always for their own benefit. Several such societies were crowded fairly close together, learning from each other but also frequently at war, again for the benefit of their ruling groups; a feature that was to characterize most civilizations through most of history, and Europe's most of all.

During the first millennium BC three new civilizations were taking shape, which among them came to rule or influence most of Asia, and which through many changes have lived on to our own day – the Persian, Indian and Chinese. They borrowed from the older ones, in India from the Mohenjodaro or Indus Valley culture, that may have been in its prime about 2000 BC. They differed from them in being much larger, and in general further apart, which allowed each to feel itself, like every human being, the hub and centre of all things: China especially, the remotest, as Mohenjodaro had been earlier. Greece was also appearing, the first 'Europe' with which we can connect ourselves, although the earliest European settlements with some title to be called civilized now appear to go back much further than was thought until very lately. Greece lay scattered in small units from Asia Minor to the western Mediterranean – a distance about as great as from India's north to south tip. It floated on the sea, the others belonged to dry land. The permanence of these four, with least continuity in Europe and most in China, has been as striking as the failure since then of any radically new civilization to grow up, except in Central and South America and, by synthesis of older with new elements, in the Islamic world.

Linguistically Europe, Persia and northern India all belonged to an 'Aryan' or 'Indo-European' family that had spread out by migration or conquest, probably from southern Russia. Geographically Europe, western Asia and northern India form a continuum, separated from farther Asia by desert, mountain or sea. But linguistic affinities and whatever vaguer racial affinities may have gone with them counted for less than other factors. Persia was the least stable of the regions because it was in the middle, interacting with all the rest, and it was drawn (along with limited parts of Europe, India and China) into Islam, though it kept its distinct character. India too was subjected to recurrent interference, and defended itself passively by developing a uniquely tenacious social structure, caste cemented by religion, which is only being slowly eroded today. China, left more to itself except by barbarian assailants, evolved towards a more flexible society divided into classes, often racked by class conflict, but with a political structure as firm as India's social structure. In this and various other significant points the far west and far east of the Euro-Asian land-mass have had and still have more in common than either of them with any lands in between.

Europe has undergone far more change, particularly in the way of internal evolution, than any of the others, yet in each of its incarnations much has remained from earlier ones. Greece itself, moored close by the earliest civilization as Japan was moored off the coast of China, learned a great deal from Egypt, partly by way of Crete, and from Babylon. It had, however, a personality of its own, which its latest heirs or mortgagees like to sum up in the word 'freedom'. This is a word easier made into a parrot-cry than defined, and Westerners boast now of being free very much as not long ago they boasted of being white. Greeks, who invented democracy, were slave-owners when they could get hold of any slaves. Nevertheless their little republics, unlike the great empires and kingdoms of Asia, did harbour an independence of spirit, a right of individuals or groups to be heard, that elsewhere existed only at the lowly level of village or clan. This spirit was to recur throughout

European history in a multiplicity of forms, and helped to impart to it a restless changefulness. Europe's towns, the cradles of its civilization, began as separate city-states, and never ceased to be wholly or partially self-governing, small but complex political entities of a kind virtually unknown anywhere else in the world.

Greece grew conscious of itself by contact and contrast with Asia. Its citizens called everyone but themselves 'barbarians', as the Chinese also learned to do, but in a different spirit. They could not pretend to more wealth, knowledge, or refinement of living than the old civilizations of the East, towering like pyramids above their heads; but they could make a virtue of their own narrower means, untainted by corrupting luxury or extravagant pomp, and more positively of their civic institutions and the rationality and the disciplined courage in war that were both fostered by them. We still think of restraint, moderation, balance, as well as fortitude and patriotism, as qualities essentially Hellenic,[1] and modern Europe in contact with Asia has given itself credit for the same virtues. Then, as at every later stage, Europe cultivated its warlike prowess in conflict with Asia, as well as with itself. Greece beat off the Persian empire's attempt to swallow it up; Greeks employed by the Persians and Egyptians became their best soldiers; finally under Alexander Greece conquered both Persia and Egypt, and founded the Hellenistic kingdoms that stretched into central Asia and northern India. Striking experiments took place there in the fusion of diverse cultures, and it was only very slowly that they melted away into their Asian environment. We still often look at Asia through the eyes of those Greeks, or fancy we are doing so while really making them look through ours. In the nineteenth century triumphant Europe saw Alexander's army, carrying Western civilization into Asia, as its vanguard.[2] Governors and generals went out east with their heads stuffed with the classics, determined to find Asian rulers of the same breed as Xenophon's slippery satraps.

Rome built out eastward, as far as the head of the Persian Gulf, on Hellenistic foundations. It is within the ghostly frontiers of the Roman empire that a European still in a sense grows up and has his being – the empire, as Robert Louis Stevenson remembered it nostalgically far away in the Pacific, 'under whose toppling monuments we were all cradled, whose laws and letters are on every hand of us'.[3] In political structure it was a European power, ruling wide regions of Asia and Africa as well; it shared with and partly borrowed from its Greek teachers a conviction of representing civilization against barbarism, whether this barbarism was Gothic and primitive or Oriental and decadent. Rome like Greece grew through conflict with the non-European world and in resistance to it first displayed its strongest qualities. The great challenger in the early days was Carthage; from the heroic struggle against Hannibal the poet of the empire and its mission, Horace, later drew his conception of Roman valour and virtue. He was indignant at the soldiers of his own epoch captured by the Parthians, now masters of Persia, who, when Crassus was defeated in 53 BC, settled down there, married 'barbarian' wives, served in the Persian army.[4] He was indignant with them, in a modern phrase, for deserting their country and 'going native'.

Later on something like this befell Rome itself. Eastern trade and the wealth of the eastern provinces, as well as the death of the republic, drew the empire's centre of gravity too far eastward. There was trading with India, and through Arab and other intermediaries with China; Rome discovered, as Europe was to go on doing down to the late nineteenth century, that it had little to offer except its scarce silver for the goods of farther Asia, principally silk, that it coveted.[5] In the end the western half of the empire was left to fade into the backwardness of northern and western Europe; the eastern half, as the Byzantine empire, continued for another thousand years, but half-orientalized – 'barbarized' in the opposite sense – not distinctively 'European' as Greece and Rome at their best had been.

The West was left to make a new start, largely on new foundations and from a low cultural level. In the long run this shake-up proved an advantage, which China never experienced and Persia and India, through Muslim conquest, only in a restricted way. It ended a long era of technical stagnation, such as all these civilizations were liable to fall into through their own complexity and inertia. Rome lived on, its memory officially recognized in the 'Holy Roman Empire' started by Charle-

magne in 800 and terminated by Napoleon in 1806. It lived
on in some of the components of medieval feudalism, in vague
but therefore plastic and potent memories of senators, legions,
glories, and in the Christian religion it had adopted before its
fall. Christianity represented another blending of Europe and
Asia, as Hellenistic culture, in some devious ways its ancestor,
had done, but it was becoming practically a monopoly of
Europe, and part of Europe's essence.

This region as it took shape again in the Middle Ages was of
convenient size, big enough for diversity, small enough for
armies, traders and ideas to move about it. Byzantium was a
separate sphere, straddling Europe and Asia, with a separate
Greek Orthodox Church to which nascent Russia was linked.
The Levantine and north African fringes of the Mediterranean,
and for a long time Sicily and nearly all Iberia, were detached
after the seventh century by Islam. The Europe thus shifted
away north and west had an extreme breadth of less than two
thousand miles, rather less than India from north to south,
about the same as China from north-east to south-west. It was a
big peninsula jutting out from Asia, broken up and nearly surrounded by seas. It had no huge cavernous interior like Asia's
or Africa's, and always in one way or another looked outward.

More than any of the other civilizations this one was growing
as a congeries of separate political units, mostly quite small,
states that were also growing into nations. In Islam any national concept was completely overlaid by religious cosmopoli-
tanism; Persia held out, adopting a heretical Muslim creed of
its own, but was oftener than not under alien rule – Arab, Turk,
Mongol. China was in a sense a nation as well as an empire,
but because of its size only inertly; the smaller countries within
its radius, especially Japan, were also acquiring a kind of
nationhood. Europe had besides a peculiar social structure,
with a unique variant of feudalism in the countryside, and with
towns independent as in antiquity or at least autonomous. It
was held together and given a dim but pervasive sense of unity
by a common religion, organized thanks to its historic origins
in a Church of unique form (the very word 'Church' is hard to
translate into any non-Christian language): this, like urban life,
had its own autonomy, and collisions between Church and

State were frequent. This encouraged the growth of other permanent institutions, and of representative bodies – Estates, parliaments, city councils – that had scarcely any analogy in the rest of the world. The obverse of this freedom of privileged classes or corporations was the reduction of the rural masses to serfdom, which left them with less freedom than almost any peasantry in Asia or Africa. Republicanism in ancient Europe had leaned similarly on slavery, and the freedom of modern Europe was to rest on a dispossessed proletariat.

Periodically Europe, like Greece and Rome, was menaced by Asia. One danger lay in attacks by tribal hordes like the Huns and Avars. Some of these were repulsed, some absorbed like the Magyars settling in the ninth century in what was now Hungary. Early in the thirteenth century the biggest of all upheavals in inner Asia brought Mongol armies flooding through the Islamic countries into eastern Europe; one mass, the Golden Horde, stayed on the lower Volga and from there dominated Russia for two centuries. 'Hun' and 'Mongol' are still names that make flesh creep, and have been used in the twentieth century by Europeans as terms of abuse for one another. Still, the short-lived Mongol empire opened the route across Asia that Marco Polo and his fellow-merchants, and Franciscan missionaries, followed; the West caught a brief glimpse of farther Asia, after which China, or Cathay, faded into a dream.[6]

The other danger, more permanent and closer at hand, was the organized pressure of Islam. This last great religion and last new civilization of the Old World replaced Persia from the seventh to the nineteenth century as Europe's arch-enemy, the anti-Europe. These adversaries were worthy of each other's steel, and sharpened their steel, and occasionally their wits, on each other. No other religions have been so fanatical as Christianity and Islam, in their different ways, have been, and no other large societies so much addicted to war. They were next of kin, as well as neighbours; Islam had drawn on Christianity as well as Judaism and other sources, and its philosophy, military technique and material culture were Hellenistic or Byzantine as well as Persian.

They exchanged blows mostly at long range, across the dwindling Byzantine barrier; exchange of ideas was easiest in

Arab Spain, a transplantation of Asia on to European soil comparable with that of Europe in the time of the Hellenistic kingdoms on to Asian soil. Muslim Spain was a non-national, polyglot society made up of distinct races and communities rather than classes. Jews mediated between Muslims and Christians, and all western Europe learned much from the resulting brilliant culture. Most of what it learned belonged to its own past, however: ideas of Plato and Aristotle that the Arabs had preserved; Europe cared less for truly Islamic ideas or arts. Astrology and alchemy probably drew its attention most. If countries and civilizations were ready to accept one another's best, mankind would have got on more quickly.

In the Muslim world less civilized peoples came to the front, Moors or Berbers supplanting Arabs in Spain, Turks in Asia. The Turkish horsemen who poured out of central Asia to conquer first India and then Asia Minor, and finally south-east Europe and north Africa, were a remarkable stock, militarily and politically; but culturally, compared with either Arabs or Persians, they were philistines. Their advent paralleled that of the Normans in western Europe while the sophisticated Byzantines sank into decay. On each side the old strife of Asia and Europe was helping to bring the rude man of action to the front. To the Muslims the true Europe was still Rome, or Byzantium: Erzerum came by its name – Arz-i-Rum, the Roman land – because it once lay on the Byzantine frontier in the east. The barbarous Europe farther west, because of the prominence of French or French-speaking Norman knights in the Crusades, was 'Firangistan', or Frank-land. To this day 'Firangi' is a hostile term for European to Muslims as far off as India. Western Europe called itself in its vulgarized Latin lingua franca *'Christianitas'*, Christendom, and its enemies *'Pagani'*, paynim – a term that expressed its blank ignorance of their religion. It could not feel equal in splendour and wealth, and in fighting power not better than equal, to the East, so Christianity had to be made the most of as a badge of superiority. Later it began to use two 'national' names, and speak of Asiatic Muslims as Turks, or as Tartars: T'a-t'a, the Chinese name for Mongols (some of whom had become Muslim), turned into 'Tartar' by association with 'Tartarean', or hellish.[7] Some atrocity stories that originated in Crusading days went on knocking about Europe and did duty again in the propaganda of the Great War.[8]

The Late Middle Ages: Contraction and Expansion

In 1099 the Crusaders stormed and sacked Jerusalem; in 1453 the Turks stormed and sacked Constantinople, and turned it into Stamboul and Agia Sofia into a mosque. Islam had entered on a second great age of expansion, and seemed at last to have devised a military machine capable of crushing Europe. Not only had the Turks taken with enthusiasm to artillery, but for a while they revived the talent for naval war that the Arabs lost when they turned away from the sea into inner Asia. The Ottoman empire was organized for conquest, and pressed on north-west up the Danube valley until finally stopped before Vienna, and westward along the Mediterranean until stopped at Malta. Meanwhile the Turks continued to learn, though not quickly enough to keep up with the West. By moving their capital to Constantinople they partially westernized their empire, as the Romans had orientalized theirs by the same manoeuvre; it was, in a lesser degree, like the removal of the Russian government later from Moscow to St Petersburg. But Turkey's direct contacts were with areas of Europe not in the van of progress, first with decadent Byzantium, then with the Russian and Hapsburg realms.[9] Organized as the Turks were, their ability to originate new methods was limited; beyond a certain point they depended on borrowing. They had the accumulated resources of western Asia's past to live on, but western Europe after its long, obscure travail of the Middle Ages was ready now to move forward on its own, in a fashion the Turks were too far away to grasp.

France, it is true, with a freedom from prejudice – in spite of crusading ancestry – it often showed later, was prepared to seek diplomatic contacts with Turkey, as the enemy of its grand enemy Spain. Rabelais might humorously picture the Turks as a pack of droll savages,[10] but the French explorer Postel paid tribute to the good government of Sulaiman the Magnificent,[11] as the Europeans, not his own people, called him. To this extent Turkey might seem already in the sixteenth century to be taking its place in the European system, and there was no lack of merchants anxious to trade with it. Its most fanatical opponent was Spain, which had fought crusades of its own earlier on to dislodge Muslim power from its soil, and in the 1480s completed the process by conquering Granada. At the end of that century Islam and Judaism were both prohibited. Many Jews fled to the shelter of Turkey; a century of strained relations with a forcibly converted community of 'Moriscos' ended in their mass expulsion in 1609. It was an unhappy omen for Europe's future relations with Asia.

Spain itself in spite of this purging and purifying still looked half-eastern in manners and temperament, and it and Turkey were sinking in the seventeenth century into a curiously similar decline. But before this happened it was from Spain and Portugal that Europe, hemmed in on two sides by Islam, found new outlets and began its modern expansion. Portuguese voyages of discovery found a way round the southern tip of Africa in 1486 and across the Indian Ocean in 1497, thus circumventing the Turkish barrier between Europe and the farther East with its coveted spices and other wealth, formerly imported by way of Egypt. Partly the aim was the less materialistic one of striking a blow at Islam, an old enemy for all Iberians in a far more vivid sense than for Englishmen or Frenchmen. The Portuguese 'really hoped to find a Christian ally, perhaps even a black Prester John, in Africa or Asia';[12] there were old legends about Christian kingdoms far away. Europe's motives in going out into the world have often been very mixed. But once out in eastern waters the Portuguese started something like the corsair warfare that was developing in the western Mediterranean, plundering and levying blackmail and seizing on the carrying trade; though they also carried with them from land to land plants, crops, utensils, words, fertilizing as well as looting.[13] At this date western and middle Asia were familiar with gunpowder, and China built very large ships, but an art of naval gunnery was confined to western Europe and was its grand passport to the East. Manpower could be hired here and there, as by all Europeans later in Asia, and where governments were weak or careless the Portuguese occupied strong points and harbours like Goa and Diu on the west coast of India; India was reunited only in the later sixteenth century after long turmoil by the Mogul conquest, and never completely.

In 1492 Columbus discovered America. He too had been seeking the East, and America, unluckily for its inhabitants, happened to lie in his way round the world. Here there were no guns to face, not even weapons of metal; the coasts lay open, and the two organized empires, Aztec and Inca, were both new and oppressive; the invaders could go much further than occupying odd harbours, which in any case would have been useless. Mexico was taken from the Aztecs, with the help of their neighbours, before 1520, and Peru from the Incas in the 1530s. Neither Spain nor Europe ever lost the intoxicating memory of these two great realms overthrown in the twinkling of an eye by a handful of white men; it cancelled the triumphs of the Turks, and gave the West a perpetual confidence in its power and its future. Military victory was followed by spiritual. It was part and parcel of Spanish imperial policy to turn its new subjects into Christians of a sort, and they offered less resistance than the Jews and Moors lately baptized in Spain. Had the conquest of Mexico come before instead of just after the conquest of Granada and the abolition of religious freedom in Spain, a different attitude might have prevailed.

Spaniards in America, like Portuguese in Asia, showed how flimsy civilized habits of conduct were when customary restraints were removed. The primitive inhabitants of the islands first occupied were treated in such a way that they died out, like some races in other empires later on. That the native civilizations vanished must have been due to their own brittleness, compared with those of Asia, as well as to Spanish destructiveness. In the densely peopled areas like Mexico population fell catastrophically, mainly through the spread of foreign diseases.[14] Some churchmen in the colonies, led by Las Casas, and at home made honourable but on the whole ineffective efforts to protect the 'Indians' against the brutality of the settlers:[15] the first of many struggles of Christian missionaries and enlightened Europeans against the behaviour of unenlightened Europeans overseas. Gaps in the labour force soon began to be filled with slave labour from Africa; modern Europe has forged many links between other continents, of which this was the most sinister. Portuguese were the chief purveyors, and also brought Negroes into their own country, whose small manpower was overstrained. Thus while Moors were expelled from Iberia other Africans came in. By the middle of the sixteenth century a tenth of the population of Lisbon is said to have been composed of slaves from Africa, Asia and Portugal's American colony, Brazil.

It was an amazing demonstration of Europe's new daring and energy when the Spaniards began conquering the Philippine islands in 1565 with a small squadron sent across the Pacific from Mexico. A link was created between America and the Far East which had important effects especially through the introduction of maize and other new crops into China. But while Philip II was winning fresh territory he was losing the northern Netherlands, and his Dutch rebels soon forced their way into the Spanish and Portuguese preserves in Asia. In 1605 they inaugurated an empire of three and a half centuries by seizing the island of Amboina from the Portuguese. On another island, Banda, the inhabitants resisted, and were nearly wiped out.[16] It did not escape comment that the Dutch were no sooner gaining their own freedom at home than they were depriving other people of theirs, an inconsistency repeated by several European nations later on. But they were only doing to Asians what they were ready to do to their English neighbours, co-religionists and allies in their war of independence. In 1623 the English at Amboina were seized, tortured and killed.

England's East India Company had been founded in 1600. These two rivals represented a new imperialism, not in need of any crusading motives to nerve it for enterprises in continents now relatively familiar, or of any ideology beyond that of the counting-house. The Turkish threat to Europe was receding; besides, to Dutchmen and Englishmen, Spain and the Inquisition, not Turkey and the Koran, were the menace. They had no notion of spreading Christianity in Asia; these Protestants kept religion, business and politics in separate compartments. As the natives were going to be roughly handled in either case, it may have been better for Christianity not to be compromised, as it was in America, by getting mixed up in the matter. Anglo-Dutch power in the East Indies, until well on in the nineteenth century, marked the most sordid but least hypocritical phase of European expansion.

The Shape of Modern Europe

In the couple of centuries after 1450 Europe underwent a thorough stirring and shaking up, as if being plunged for rejuvenation into a cauldron of Medea. It was again a more radical transformation than any of the other big regions ever experienced, the stormy passage, full of changes good and ill, from medieval to modern. Internal pressures had slowly built up, and Europe's collisions with the other continents helped to release them. One facet of the process was the Renaissance. Revived memories of antiquity, the Turkish advance, the new horizons opening beyond, all encouraged Europe to see itself afresh as civilization confronting barbarism. But the Renaissance was an affair of aristocracy and intelligentsia, confronting also their own illiterate masses, and secularism was a false dawn in an age when the masses could still only act and be acted upon through religious feeling. Social crisis, the threatened breakdown of the whole feudal order, found expression in religious schism, the strife of Reformation and Counter-Reformation. Christianity was always the religion most given to schism and persecution, because Europe was the region most subject to change, growth, social tension. The old division between eastern and western, Greek and Latin Churches was promptly succeeded by a new division between Catholic and Protestant, broadly between south and north.

Class division and class consciousness, the driving-force of modern European evolution, were contained in and regulated by the national State, now fully developed in the West. Germany and Italy failed to coalesce into nations, and fell behind. A new type of government, absolute monarchy, managed the reorganization and modernization of feudal society, and then went on until overthrown by revolution: in the 1640s in England, in 1917 in Russia. This absolutism always differed from Asiatic monarchy, because it rested on other foundations; and even at the height of Bourbon power Frenchmen could feel that they were under a sort of 'constitutional', not merely arbitrary, régime. But it may be asked whether the monarchs' desire for unrestricted authority was not whetted by emulation of the Sultan, whom all Europe called 'the Grand Signior' much as the Greeks used to call the ruler of Persia 'the King'. Conversely, the more a Western people progressed the more it came to think of all personal despotism as 'Asiatic' and degrading.

Against its enemies, Muslim and Protestant as well as fellow-Catholic, Spain and consequently the Counter-Reformation which it championed received immense reinforcement from colonial tribute. Without this Europe might have emerged still further truncated by Turkish expansion, but more homogeneous. The tribute weakened Spain later on by inducing parasitism, and by strengthening all its conservative interests, Crown, nobility and Church, against the rest. It was then the turn of southern and south-western Europe to drop behind, while the north drew ahead. Russia and Sweden were both on the horizon, but the real growing-point was the north-west. The revolt of the Netherlands against Spain was also an early version of a bourgeois revolution, and in free Protestant Holland the explosive economic force of the coming age, capitalism, was maturing. England was moving in the same direction, and these two with northern France formed the vital area, a surprisingly small part of the continent as a whole, the truly 'European' area in terms of future development.[17]

National states in competition gave deliberate encouragement to the economic and technical progress that was ushering in industrial capitalism, with industrial revolution or mechanization to follow; the old cumbrous empires always stifled experiment. Protestantism changed and moved with the times, and helped to change the times, more than any religion had ever done. It was in this capacity to evolve that Europe was most unique. It grew less 'European' towards the east; or rather there were two dynamic Europes of the north, as well as the inert south and the Turkish south-east. How far Russia belonged to Europe was a question, as it has never altogether ceased to be. It had cast off Tartar overlordship in the fifteenth century and come together under the lead of Moscow, a defeat of Islam comparable with its expulsion from most of Spain long before. But Moscow lay four hundred miles further east than Stamboul, and morally often looked not less remote. 'Russia is a European State', Catherine the Great laid it down in her programme of government,[18] but this German woman might be taken as stating an aspiration rather than a fact. A French aristocrat of the next generation habitually thought of the Russians he saw as 'Tartars' or savages, though he could at the same time predict a brilliant future for them.[19] Many of the formative experiences of Europe had not been shared by this country: Rome, hierarchical feudalism, Reformation. It represented one of those borderlands, such as Macedon was to Greece, close to an elder neighbour in race and speech, but newer, cruder, and capable therefore on occasion of more rapid adaptation, of taking up ideas conceived but not carried out in the more advanced region.

Politically, untrammelled autocracy at one end of northern Europe contrasted with the early stirrings of modern politics, and their paraphernalia of parties, elections, newspapers, in the north-west. Socially, legal freedom here, with contractual relations and wage labour, contrasted with the serfdom still prevalent in the east – in Russia intensifying down to 1800, after being introduced by the ruling class under foreign tutelage to meet the costs of modernization just when more developed countries were moving away from it. Western armies, though not always navies, were manned by volunteers, often foreign professionals; eastern more by conscripts. Conscription goes logically with serfdom or slavery, and had died out along with it in most of Asia since ancient times. It spread from east to west Europe after the French Revolution (and thence later on to Asia), while industrialism travelled from west to east; a reminder that Europe's east was not a mere torpid hinterland, but had its own energy, its contribution to a future amalgam. It was on the cards, down to the defeat of the German army in 1918, that the future Europe would be more 'eastern' than 'western'. That this did not happen was due in good measure to the ability of the north-western area to draw on the resources of other continents, as Spain had done – though not without being coarsened and worsened in various ways in the process.

There were unifying influences as well. In military technology northern Europe was all one. Economically it was a compound, representing a division of labour. Serfdom was geared to a new 'feudal capitalism', producing surpluses of food and raw materials for sale to western countries in exchange for manufactures and luxuries. Western liberty and progress were buttressed on two sides by unfree labour, serfdom in Europe and slavery in colonies. In terms of sentiment, the break-up of the little Latin Christendom of old days into the *'Europe des patries'* was a stage in the growth of popular consciousness, and indirectly in the long run of European consciousness. Even in the course of fighting one another Europeans were recognizing their differentness from anyone else. As the sulphur and brimstone of the religious wars drifted away, there was a broader revival of the Renaissance consciousness of a common civilization, with rational, secular, scientific interests, much more vigorous though these might be in some countries than in others.

One aspect of the trend towards secular thinking was that colour, as well as culture, was coming to be a distinguishing feature of Europe. Part of the Christian world now lay beyond the Atlantic, but any kinship felt with it would be with Spanish colonists, as offspring of Europe, not with Indians as converts to Christianity. It was an important element in Europe's collective consciousness that its peoples all looked much alike. If Swede and Neapolitan differed, it was not more than northern and southern Chinese, less than northern and southern Indian, and there was every physical gradation in between. Between east and west physical though not social similarity was even closer. Europeans gave the impression, to themselves as well as to outsiders, of being one race. That Magyars or Basques spoke, like Turks, languages not of the European family was something Europe was hardly conscious of before the nineteenth century, and in any case counted for far less than physical appearance. In odd corners of the continent remnants of very primitive peoples could still be found; the Highlanders whom Dr Johnson met were nearly as alien to him as the Tahitians he read about. Yet a Highlander taught English and the minuet was at once European. Apart from a sprinkling of new African arrivals, only Jews and Gypsies, both of Asiatic origin, represented elements sometimes felt to be intrusive to Europe. In general all Europeans could intermarry, if not prevented by class or cult. Royalty always intermarried.

Europe and the World: The Seventeenth-Century Interval

While the new Europe discovered itself, most of the outside world it had discovered was being given a breathing-space. Spain and Portugal, the pioneers, were in decline by 1600; Holland and England were both small; all of them were chiefly occupied at home, and with Europe's incessant wars. The Thirty Years' War, and the conflicts of Louis XIV's epoch that followed, were European civil wars, and meant a respite for other continents, as the war of 1914–18 did later. They were, on the other hand, stimulating military science and spirit to a point where Europe would be crushingly superior to the rest when they did meet. A Brussels tapestry of the late seventeenth century depicting the Four Continents displayed Europe's emblems as a victory monument and a pile of pikes and guns, lances and drums.[20] At least its feuds meant, fortunately for itself and the world, that there would not be a united Europe going out to conquer the other continents. Napoleon brought this possibility near at one moment, Hitler at another.

Africa, the weakest, was not left alone. The Islamic lands had been drawing slaves from it for many centuries; like them Europe wanted not African territory but African men and women. They were wanted for all the parts of America where intensive cultivation was growing up, and most of all for the West Indian islands whose sugar plantations became in the eighteenth century the richest colonial prizes, much fought over by Britain and France. Elsewhere expansion was chiefly into the nearly empty spaces of northern Asia and America, whose accessibility carried the northern countries of Europe further into the lead. French, English and Dutch settlers were moving into north America above the limits of Spanish occupation. Russian explorers and trappers were drifting across Siberia towards the Pacific. Russia was the first country to open diplomatic relations with China – in Latin, of all languages, because there were Jesuits at Peking as interpreters.[21] A shipwrecked Japanese was brought to court to be scrutinized by Peter the Great.[22]

Interest in the outer world at large was nourished by travellers' tales, missionary reports, accounts from Spanish America and other colonies. One expression of such interest was the collecting of exotic curiosities. The Tradescant family collection now in the Ashmolean Museum had a printed catalogue as early as 1642, and included Red Indian hunting-shirts, Turkish slippers, Indian daggers. One has only to compare the cock-and-bull stories that Othello told Desdemona – and that Shakespeare may have taken as seriously as Raleigh took similar nonsense in America – with the matter-of-fact travel-tales of Defoe, to see how knowledge had accumulated in a little over a century. Othello had one foot in the world of Sinbad the Sailor, Captain Singleton in the world of the *Morning Post*.

Today when Europe is no longer in the lead it is tempted to think, or to agree with others, that the civilization it was incubating was no unique property of its own but a stage of progress that other regions were moving towards. India on this view would have had cotton-mills, Japan would have come by submarines, whether Europe had brought them or not. This is of course possible, but may be regarded as exceedingly unlikely on any time-scale of centuries rather than millennia. An intricate set of interacting factors is required to bring about any significant historical transition, and there is small sign anywhere else (most perhaps in Japan) of anything like the complex of material and psychological forces then at work in north-west Europe. No other part of Europe itself could have made an Industrial Revolution. It is even doubtful whether any Asian country would have modernized itself by imitation of the West, if not forced by the West to do so as India, Japan, China all in different ways were.

At some earlier points the meeting of Europe with other civilizations had been friendly and promising. Queen Elizabeth's contemporary Akbar, greatest of the Mogul emperors, was eager to meet English envoys or Italian missionaries, and hear their ideas. He was at the head of an empire strong enough to command respect, still expanding, and as a result self-confident, and interested in other people's religions and artillery. In Japan too, where Europeans – Portuguese, then Dutch and English – had been coming since 1542, Iyeyasu who in 1603 founded the new Tokugawa dynasty of Shoguns, or feudal overlords, had the same kind of omnivorous interest. But for many reasons the meeting of minds between East and West was broken off, or petered out. Missionaries in the Far East were, then as later, in close league with European governments capable of hostile designs. Most other Westerners had no ideas to offer, and few goods that the East wanted, so that they were always tempted to take what they could by force. Their irruption, and their firearms, worsened the disorderliness always endemic in Asia. This intermediate period was plagued by a vast swarming of pirates over the seas of the world, a state of nature on the waves, the result of wars and social dislocation and the endeavours of Europeans to break into one another's colonies. Western freebooters, or the half-caste Portuguese who infested the Bay of Bengal, rubbed shoulders, or exchanged broadsides, with Arakanese, Malay, Chinese buccaneers. Some Robin Hoods among them started a model settlement in the Indian Ocean which they christened Libertatia:[23] few joined them.

In addition, Asian governments were often less confident now, less inclined to expose their subjects' loyalty to foreign contagion. More receptive than India or China because smaller, and an island, Japan was likewise first and most vigorous in reaction. In 1637 began a savage persecution of missionaries and their numerous converts, and Japan was sealed off for two centuries, except for the small peep-hole of the Dutch warehouse allowed to remain at Nagasaki. It was to become a European gibe at the mercenary Dutch that they consented to humiliate themselves and perform the annual trampling on the cross that Gulliver narrowly avoided when he landed in Japan from Laputa.[24] With the Manchu conquest in the 1640s China came under alien rule, and the new government embarked at once on a policy of exclusion, actually depopulating a long stretch of the southern coast, ostensibly to repel pirates but really, it must be suspected, to keep the restive southern Chinese from contact with the outside. China was thus insulated, while its rulers, barbarians at the outset, turned back into the blind alley of inner Asia to subdue Mongolia and eastern Turkestan. A few Jesuits at Peking provided the sole point of contact, as the Dutch traders did in Japan; they were tolerated for their astronomy, useful to official calendar-makers, but the converts they made soon got into serious trouble with the authorities.

India was never under such effective control as China, and its rulers cared little about sea or coast; but with Aurangzeb in the later seventeenth century, before the Mogul empire fell into confusion, Akbar's open-minded eclecticism was abandoned in favour of narrow Islamic orthodoxy, anti-Hindu and impervious to any fresh ideas from outside. Turkey and the other great Muslim power, Persia, which had a national revival in the early sixteenth century under the new Safavid dynasty, were both most receptive when strongest; but both were soon drying up. Forced on to the defensive in Europe after a second failure to capture Vienna in 1683, Turkey began to be pressed back by Austria and Russia, and to fall into a more negative mood, a siege mentality. All in all, during the interval between Europe's first and later bursts of expansion Asia's biggest countries were curling up like hedgehogs, failing to realize how Europe's technology was going ahead and how much they needed to learn from it. Their failure was deepened by their increased isolation from each other, partly through their own introversion, partly because the seas were controlled by Western ships or flayed by pirates. No great merchant fleets came to India from Ch'ing or Manchu China, as they had come in the time of the previous Ming dynasty. Turkey and Persia, Persia and India, still had contacts, but these mostly took the form of forays with old-fashioned armies or, from Persia, of old-fashioned poets.

The Eighteenth-Century Outlook

Gulliver was a satire on how Europeans thought of and behaved to others, as well as on humanity as a whole. After his
homecoming the traveller was told that he ought to have noti-
fied the English government of all his discoveries, but he felt
no wish to enlarge European domination, too often merely 'a
free license given to all acts of inhumanity and lust' – starting
with a boat-load of pirates landing somewhere, killing some
people, setting up 'a rotten plank, or a stone, for a memorial',
and getting a free pardon for their services to the empire.[25]
What was known about the earlier history of the Spanish
American empire confirmed such criticism. Las Casas's book
on *The Destruction of the Indies* had been translated into many
languages, partly but not only for purposes of anti-Spanish
propaganda. Similar crimes were heard of from Bengal after
the fateful skirmish of Plassey in 1757 put it at the mercy of
the East India Company. Adam Smith thought of Europe as
the *magna virum mater*, the mighty mother of men, and of the
European character as uniquely capable of grand designs. That
the result of its conquests for the peoples subdued by it had
hitherto been unmitigated evil seemed to him too obvious for
argument.[26] Europe's crimes had indeed been, and were to be
again, as gigantic as its achievements, and some of them as unparalleled.

At home inside Europe, too, aggression and bloodshed were
too common. In the later eighteenth century thinking men were
in a chastened mood over the spectacle of its blighting wars,
which often seemed to have no reason but royal ambition.
Anti-war feeling grew in France and Europe after the Seven
Years' War of 1756–63, when Canada and the French foothold
in India were lost to Britain; and in Britain and Europe after
the War of American Independence, which brought on another
European conflict. The mood was strongest among the French.
They had no new possession like Bengal to make up for what
they had lost, and as their belated revolution of 1789 drew
nearer they were conscious of how far they had fallen, politically and economically, behind the English. Many of the most

perceptive travellers of the age were Frenchmen, whereas Dutchmen and Englishmen in Asia were apt to look at native peoples with boorish contempt or indifference.[27] Frenchmen could look at Asians as interesting foreigners, instead of looking down on them, because France owned no colonies worth mentioning in Asia until the later nineteenth century.

This was not unconnected with the fact that in Europe Frenchmen were the leading spirits in the Enlightenment of the eighteenth century. One feature of it was a willingness to recognize civilizations outside Europe as fellow-members of a human family, equal or even superior to Europe in some of their attainments. The *Philosophes* thought, or liked to think they did, as citizens of the world, bounded by no narrower frontiers than those of all humanity.[28] In material achievement Europe was not yet vastly ahead of the most advanced countries of Asia, though already further ahead than most men realized. Asia was known to have its barbarians, its illiterate masses, its swarms of beggars, but so had Europe. What these intellectuals of an aristocratic society were predisposed to look for and to admire was something resembling themselves, a class of men of enlarged minds and sympathies benevolently guiding ordinary mankind.

There was nothing of the kind in neighbouring Turkey, which was only too much like unreformed Europe, warlike and unintellectual. But far away in little-known China there did appear to be a class of enlightened men, occupying a higher station than in Europe – with power to direct and control, not merely advise, as intellectuals always feel they ought to have. On the strength of Jesuit reports from Peking, somewhat rose-coloured in complexion, the Celestial Empire was taken almost at its own valuation, as a model of how a vast region could be peacefully guided by a high-minded administration.[29] Tranquil and unwarlike, it made an attractive contrast with army-trampled Europe. Even its exports, tea, silk and porcelain, breathed the blandness and suavity of its supposed life.

In a more modest way China enjoyed a vogue in tea-drinking England too. When Goldsmith wanted to expound the creed of reason and benevolence he took as his mouthpiece an itinerant Chinese sage, who had seen many lands and learned 'to find nothing truly ridiculous but villainy and vice'. All civilization was one at heart, just as savages everywhere had only 'one character of imprudence and rapacity.[30] England was more concerned with India, and for a time the Brahmin was looked upon as a personage of the same order as the scholar-magistrate of China. Sterne was surprised to see a monk at Calais with a noble, lofty countenance – 'but it would have suited a Brahmin, and had I met it upon the plains of Indostan, I had reverenced it'.[31] Brahmins were supposed to be the repository of a profound philosophy; their learned language, Sanskrit, was being studied and vastly admired, and its affinities with the classical languages of Europe revealed. Lord Monboddo convinced himself that the Greeks got their language from Egypt, which probably got it from India.[32] It was only eight years after Plassey when Sterne saw his monk. As the occupation of India proceeded, familiarity bred contempt, both because the average Brahmin was not after all a very admirable being, and because his English masters were no longer in a humour to admire anything Indian. In Asia at large Englishmen rummaging in search of profits were coming to see it more crudely, but in some ways more realistically, than the French theorists. A novelist out to extol the hard-working bourgeois decried the lounging English aristocrat as one of a great fraternity of drones including 'the monks of every country, the Dervises of Persia, the Bramins of India, the Mandarines of China and the Gentlemen of these free and polished nations'.[33]

At the opposite end of the scale from the polished idler was the Noble Savage, another figure who haunted that age, and another compound of its open-mindedness and self-deception. It too originated in France, with Rousseau's essay of 1753 on Inequality, and it too suited the mood of a middle class pining for 'freedom', a Europe burdened with its own complexities. Commonly the ordinary man, in or out of Europe, was regarded as a born Caliban, only redeemable by paternal control. But perhaps on the contrary what he was suffering from was too much control, too much artificiality and class division. If so, man in his primitive condition might be expected to exhibit naturally the virtues that civilized men had to toil painfully for. The idea went through many metamorphoses, and Noble

Savages turned up in all sorts of places, like the lost tribes of Israel; at this stage the Red Indian was a favourite candidate. Another English novelist had a hero reared among Red Indians, though (like Tarzan) heir to a noble estate in England, who brought back with him from the forests their simple and natural good feeling.[34] Disillusionment soon crept in here too. Again Europe might partly have itself to blame, by its interference with other peoples; but at any rate primitive man was to prove as little able to resist European brandy as India or China to resist European batteries.

The Nineteenth Century: World Domination

Between 1792 and 1815 Europe was engrossed with the wars of the French Revolution and Napoleon, and most of it was cut off from the outer world. Russia went on foraging eastward, and Britain, to make up for the loss of its American colonies and its exclusion from Europe, had a free run of everyone else's colonies, besides pushing on in India. Britain thus got a long lead over all rivals, which it kept through the century. The wars were followed by a second and greater loss of European power abroad, the winning of independence by Spanish America and the peaceful severance of Brazil from Portugal. In this case too the absence of European unity was important. Three countries had helped Washington to defeat George III; and when Ferdinand VII of Spain begged for combined assistance against his rebels, and Alexander of Russia was eager to strengthen the Holy Alliance by giving it, Britain had its own motives for frustrating the scheme.

Europe had lost two empires, but the European race had lost nothing, and the other continents now seemed positively to invite attack. Their feebleness must have done as much as European ambition to cause fresh empires to spring up. Asia had to all appearance lost the faculty of self-renewal. Obstacles that retarded technology in Western lands like Spain were exaggeratedly present there: rigid ideologies and social patterns, governments suspicious of change, absence of a bourgeois middle class. Westerners impregnated with their new ethos of change, progress, energy, invested Commerce with the same divine right that monarchy formerly claimed, and were irresistibly tempted to resort to force. They could feel that by doing so they were doing right, as the French Revolutionary armies marching over Europe and carrying liberty on their bayonets had felt. To knock down decrepit régimes was to liberate peoples from the crushing burden of their past. In the first stage of European expansion Spain and Portugal thought of making a return to benighted regions for what they took from them, by giving them Christianity. Now there was again a feeling that expansion ought to have some ideal purpose, a goal beyond sordid greed, which came to be expressed in the phrase 'civilizing mission'. Backward lands would be given civilization, in return for the products wanted by Europe; Christianity might be part of it, though a subsidiary one. The idea of Europe's 'mission' dawned early,[35] but was taken up seriously in the nineteenth century. Turkey, China, and the rest would some day be prosperous, wrote Winwood Reade, one of the most sympathetic Westerners. 'But those people will never begin to advance . . . until they enjoy the rights of man; and these they will never obtain except by means of European conquest.'[36]

The idea was not entirely fallacious, but Europeans in Asia or Africa, like French armies in Europe, more than half falsified it by their other, more squalid motives. This happened all the more blatantly because often official Europe was preceded by private adventurers, rude pioneers of free enterprise, who hung on the skirts of decaying kingdoms or pressed into the wide areas where there was little settled rule. They might be under loose authority of distant governments, as in Siberia or on the American prairies; or bodies of men acknowledging some rough authority of their own like the Boer trekkers in south Africa. Some were individuals who took service with one faction against another, like the Frenchmen from Pondicherry who helped the last dynasty of Vietnam to get into the saddle, or the Americans employed in China against the Taiping rebellion, who dreamed of a principality of their own. Worst of all were the men under no kind of authority, successors to the buccaneers of the previous age. Piracy as a full-time profession was being left to Malays and other races, but these Europeans were pirates, traders, grabbers and settlers, by turns.

They spread far and wide, round Africa, among the Pacific islands, and gave the world a picture of Western civilization very much like the picture of Islam that Arab slave-dealers gave. Yet Europe's conviction of being the only really civilized region was becoming so strong that even its offscourings, these Ishmaels of the seven seas, carried it with them, and were fortified by it in their lawlessness. Whatever a white man did must in some grotesque fashion be 'civilized'. An opium smuggler, who could not help feeling shocked when he saw the 'shrivelled and shrunken carcasses' produced by the drug, landed on one occasion on Formosa with his men, had a fight, burned a village, plundered a junk, and removed its ammunition because 'there was no knowing how much they might yet require, before the natives were brought into submission to our superior civilization'.[37] Ruskin complained that some of the bigger men who had been selling opium at the point of the cannon were buying respectable estates in England.[38] At the end of the century the whole mob of adventurers had an apotheosis in King Leopold of the Belgians, building a private empire in central Africa with blood and iron.

India itself, the Mexico and Peru of the modern world, and the bridge between earlier and later imperialism, was acquired by a joint-stock company, whose morals before it was gradually brought under public control were not much better than the vagrant trader's with his glass beads and gun. It was a startling illustration of how haphazard, how unthinking, was Europe's approach to the world, in spite of the civilizing mission. Only by slow degrees was reckless plundering tempered by something closer to the better ideals of the Roman empire, so much a part of western Europe's education and consciousness. The conquest of India, spread over the century from Plassey to the Mutiny, was the main stride towards European domination of Asia, and most of the others followed from it. British power there radiated from India; other territories were taken with the help of Indian troops, often at the expense of the Indian tax-payer. Psychologically the effect was even greater. Wherever else the Briton went he felt and spoke as representative of the power at whose feet crouched a hundred million Hindus; he saw other 'natives' as so many crouching Hindus in different disguises.

So much of Britain's attention was drawn off to the East that from the fall of Napoleon in 1815 to the Anglo-French *Entente* of 1904 it was more often than not an absentee from European affairs, except for Palmerstonian games of bluff to amuse middle-class voters and, more seriously, engagement in the tangle of Turkish problems that were known as the Eastern Question. If Russia was sometimes held to belong rather to Asia, and Africa was humorously said to begin at the Pyrenees, Britain often appeared to belong to all the other continents more than to Europe; or appeared to itself, with its growing family of White colonies, a continent of its own. Empire meant for Britain a turning away from the rest of Europe as well as a turning towards the rest of the world. It was through most of the century Turkey's prop against Russia, and in 1902 it set a new precedent – followed later by Hitler – by an alliance with Japan.

France and Russia were Britain's chief rivals. Both looked alternately, as Spain had done, inward on Europe and outward on the world. Between Russia and Britain there was a trail of jealousies and recriminations from the Black Sea to the Pacific. Quarrels arose almost everywhere between France and Britain. Napoleon would have liked an empire beyond Europe too; after his Egyptian campaign of 1799 the East always fascinated him, as the grandest field of action for men like Alexander or himself. But he and France were faithful to the tradition of Louis XIV, and put Europe first. After Waterloo the French began to pick up crumbs in Africa for consolation; again after 1870, when Europe was bestridden by its new Colossus, the German army. Even then French interest in colonies had to be nursed by assiduous propaganda, chiefly by financial interests, and the old belief that power or influence outside Europe was something second-rate never entirely faded.

Hardly any European countries had significant connections, other than imperial, with any continent except America. Towards the end of the century, the 'age of imperialism' proper, a craze for annexations seized on everyone who had any chance, and Italy, Germany, Belgium all got shares, with the USA joining in. Individual businessmen were obviously doing well out of colonies; nations were easily tutored into believing (nearly always mistakenly) that they could do equally well, especially when they saw that all their neighbours believed it. The civilizing mission was now all the rage, whereas in earlier years it had often been rejected as too expensive. It was easiest of all to believe that what was good for Europe must be even better for the 'natives'. By now the white man had worked himself into a high state of self-conceit; but all through the century his reaction to any natives who tried to reject the blessings of civilized rule was that of Dr Johnson to the rebel Americans: 'They are a race of convicts, and ought to be thankful for any thing we allow them short of hanging.'[39]

Only those countries were able to cling to their independence that already had some national tradition and consciousness, besides some advantage of size or situation. Turkey had the rudiments of nationhood, partly from intercourse with Europe, though only at the end of the Great War did a true Turkish nation crystallize out of a lost Ottoman empire. Persia hung on precariously; but neither of these two made much internal progress, and practically all the rest of Islam, with its medley of peoples and its non-national structure, went under. It kept its identity by wrapping itself round and round in religion, as Hindu India under Muslim rule had done, thus falling still further behind. Africa, nibbled at from early in the century, was swallowed up entirely in the final scramble, with the exception of the ancient and mountainous kingdom of Abyssinia. It was in the Far East that nationality was best developed, and there modern nationalism could be grafted most successfully on to it, and modern technology adopted. Japan alone accomplished this in any radical way before 1914. China owed its survival partly to its vastness, though this helped to make it a slow and painful learner compared with Japan. But China's national unity was another factor, which delayed armed attack on it until 1839 when the conquest of India was almost at an end. In the Far East there was also the advantage that rival Western ambitions counteracted one another. Siam owed its survival to this.

In the course of their rivalries Europeans exchanged many hard words, and sometimes abused each other in order to please a non-European people. An Englishman in Haiti was indignant at the 'John Bull with the large and taloned hands, the creation of the French caricaturists'.[40] An Englishman in China, no admirer of that country, declared that China was 'certainly far more civilized than Russia'.[41] Russians deplored Britain's parasitic rule in India, directed as one wrote to 'profit and not civilization'.[42] They might all sympathize with one another's 'rebels'. But when it came to any serious colonial upheaval, white men felt their kinship, and Europe drew together. In 1857 its sympathies were mostly with Britain against the Indian sepoys;[43] it heard of course only of atrocities on one side. In 1900 there was united military action to put down the 'Boxers' in China. Above all, and very remarkably, despite innumerable crises over rival claims the European countries managed from the War of American Independence onward to avoid a single colonial war among themselves. (The Crimean War was fought partly in and because of Asia, and in the Russo-Japanese War Britain was a sleeping partner.) To this degree Europe had grown more solid than in its earlier days of chronic colonial wars, and better able to come before the world as one civilization.

Meanwhile, thanks in part to the resources it drew from other continents, it was able to expand in another way, building up its population to an unprecedented height without running into serious famines except at its two wretched extremities, Russia at one end, Ireland and Spain at the other. Facility of emigration was another safeguard, and the USA, free from Britain, attracted emigrants from all lands and became a second Europe instead of, like Australia, a second Britain. When its overseas members are counted in, it can be estimated that the 'white race' grew from about twenty-two per cent of the earth's population in 1800 to about thirty-five per cent in 1930.[44] In terms of wealth and power it grew by comparison with the rest infinitely more.

Of fourteen sovereign states in the Europe of 1914, excluding the Balkans, eight had – and a ninth, Spain, had until lately had – considerable possessions outside. In many indirect ways the entire continent shared, as Adam Smith had pointed out long before, in the colonial contribution to trade and wealth.[45] In the realm of knowledge, too, exploration and research in a dozen fields enriched the common stock. But though retarded nations like Spain or Portugal might plume themselves on belonging to Europe and sharing in its triumphant progress, grave inequalities within Europe, as well as between Europe and the rest, were being accentuated. As a class the rich grew richer far more quickly than the poor became less poor; as a nation France drew further ahead of Spain, Germany of Russia.

Europeans of superior countries thought of inferior Europeans and non-Europeans in not very different terms. Travellers described their journeys through Spain, before the railways, as if Madrid were somewhere near Timbuctoo. Stereotypes such as the Englishman's image of Paddy the Irishman, a feckless nimble-tongued fellow at whom one felt a mixture of amusement and impatience – or of the Italian as an organ-grinder with a monkey – provided ready-made categories for Burmese or Malays to be fitted into. And if the 'native' on occasion reminded the Englishman of his familiar Paddy, Paddy might sometimes remind him of the native. Lord Salisbury, the Conservative leader, supporting coercion in Ireland, said that Irishmen were as unfit for self-government as Hottentots.[46] Ireland was subject politically and economically to England, Italy through much of the nineteenth century to Austria. Down to 1918 a large proportion of Europeans occupied a more or less colonial status, differing only in degree from that of the Asian or African countries that were being annexed. There is a story of the Austrian representative saying to the Hungarian, when the Hapsburg empire was transformed into the Dual Monarchy in 1867, 'You look after your barbarians, and we'll look after ours' – meaning the Czechs, Serbs and so on. Treatment of these subject minorities was not always gentler than in colonies outside, and must have been roughened by the habits formed by Europe's ruling classes in dictating to the other continents.

It could be expected that unfree Europeans would have some fellow-feeling for the colonial peoples. Occasionally they did. Irish employees in Scotland Yard are said to have aided Indian nationalists to smuggle their literature.[47] But in general ignorance or indifference, or 'European' feeling, prevailed. Ireland took a share in the rewards by helping to conquer and manage Britain's empire. It was as a socialist, much more than an Irishman, that James Connolly denounced the empire and its war in 1914.

In the years of drift towards the catastrophe of 1914 nationalist movements against Europe were gathering up and down Asia, while others, and the socialist movement, struggled against the established order at home. At the zenith of its physical power in the world, Europe was at the nadir of its moral capacity to lead it, or even to reform itself.

NOTES

(The place of publication of works cited, when not given below, may be assumed to be London.)

1. See e.g. J. C. Stobart, *The Glory that was Greece* (4th edn, revised by R. J. Hopper, 1964), pp. 175–6.

2. cf. J. Abbott, *Sind* (Bombay, 1924), p. 25, on 'the unbridled enthusiasm for the tradition of Greece in Asia' in the nineteenth century.

3. R. L. Stevenson, *In the South Seas* (1896), p. 15 (Nelson edn).

4. *Odes*, Book III, no. 5.

5. See E. H. Warmington, *The Commerce between the Roman Empire and India* (Cambridge, 1928); M. P. Charlesworth, *Trade Routes and Commerce of the Roman Empire* (Cambridge, 1926).

6. See Sir H. Yule, *Cathay and the Way Thither* (ed. H. Cordier, Hakluyt Society, 1913–16).

7. 'Mawmetrie', or Mahomedanism, in medieval English was equivalent to idolatry, and the Romances showed as much ignorance about it as bloodthirstiness. (H. Bruce, *English History in Contemporary Poetry*, No. 1 (1914), pp. 33–6.)

8. H. D. Lasswell, *Propaganda Technique in the World War* (1927), p. 82.

9. My late friend and colleague Dr A. Geddes impressed me with the importance of this point.

10. *The Complete Works of Rabelais*, trans. J. Le Clercq (New York, 1944), pp. 216 ff.

11. Cited by H. Kohn, *The Idea of Nationalism* (New York, 1945), pp. 194–5.

12. A. Luttrell, 'The Crusade in the Fourteenth Century', in *Europe in the Late Middle Ages*, ed. J. Hale *et al*. (1965), p. 153.

13. On this better side of Portuguese activity see e.g. S. Murtaza Ali, *History of Chittagong* (Dacca, 1964), pp. 92–3.

14. See J. H. Parry, *The Spanish Seaborne Empire* (1966), pp. 213 ff.

15. See L. Hanke, *The Spanish Struggle for Justice in the Conquest of America* (University of Pennsylvania, 1949).

16. B. H. M. Vlekke, *The Story of the Dutch East Indies* (Harvard, 1946), p. 88.

17. See my article on 'State and Nation in Western Europe', in *Past and Present*, No. 31, July 1965.

18. The *Nakaz* or Instruction of 1767, Chapter 1, para. 6, in W. F. Reddaway, *Documents of Catherine the Great* (Cambridge, 1931).

19. Comte P. de Ségur, *Un Aide de Camp de Napoléon* (1873), pp. 288, 358, 360; *La Campagne de Russie* (1824), Introduction, and pp. 111, 149–50, 198–9, 250–51 (Nelson editions, Paris). Progressive Russians were sensitive to the imputation. 'We too are Europeans,' wrote S. Stepniak. 'For to be a Russian does not involve counting oneself an Asiatic ...' (*Nihilism as it is*: pamphlets, trans. E. L. Voynich, n.d., p. 63).

20. O. Sitwell, *The Four Continents* (1955), pp. 20–23.

21. M. N. Pavlovsky, *Chinese–Russian Relations* (New York, 1949), p. 102. Mongol had previously been used as the medium.

22. G. A. Lensen, *The Russian Push towards Japan* (Princeton, 1959), p. 29.

23. P. Gosse, *The History of Piracy* (2nd edn, 1954), pp. 200–201.

24. cf. the satirical picture of Dutch grovelling to Japan in Oliver Goldsmith, *The Citizen of the World* (1762), p. 314 (Everyman edn).

25. Jonathan Swift, *Gulliver's Travels* (1726), 'The Country of the Houyhnhnms', Chapter 12.

26. *The Wealth of Nations* (1776), Vol. 2, p. 192 (World's Classics edn).

27. I owe this point to my friend Mr A. Jenkin, of the British Museum, who can be turned to for guidance on almost any epoch of history.

28. See Alexis de Tocqueville, *The State of Society in France before the Revolution* (2nd English edn, 1873), Book III, para. 2.

29. See G. F. Hudson, *Europe and China* (1931), p. 317, etc.; L. Dermigny, *La Chine et l'Occident. Le commerce à Canton au xviiie siècle, 1719–1833* (Paris, 1964), Vol. 1, Chapter 1.

30. Oliver Goldsmith, op. cit., p. 10, and Pref.

31. Laurence Sterne, *A Sentimental Journey* (1768): opening section, on Calais.

32. W. Knight, *Lord Monboddo and some of his Contemporaries* (1900), p. 270.

33. Henry Brooke, *The Fool of Quality, or, the History of Henry Earl of Moreland* (2nd edn, 1767), Vol. 1, p. 157. I owe this, and the next reference, to Dr G. P. Tripathi of Patna University.

34. Robert Bage, *Hermsprong; or, Man as he is not* (1796).

35. H. Kohn, op. cit., p. 194, refers to the advocacy of a French presence in India by F. Charpentier, as early as 1664.

36. W. Reade, *The Martyrdom of Man* (1872), pp. 414–15 (Thinker's Library edn).

37. L. Anderson, *A Cruise in an Opium Clipper* (1891), Chapter 33. cf. the young Frenchman in Balzac's *Eugénie Grandet* (1833), who makes a fortune in the Indies by slave-trading and general wickedness.

38. John Ruskin, *Sesame and Lilies* (1865), p. 59 (1882 edn).

39. Boswell, *The Life of Samuel Johnson*, Vol. 2, p. 111 (Dent edn, 1926).

40. H. H. Prichard, *Where Black Rules White* (2nd edn, 1910), p. 328.

41. A. Little, *Gleanings from Fifty Years in China* (1910), p. 52.

42. Cited by P. Shastiko, 'Russian Press on 1857', in *Rebellion 1857*, ed. P. C. Joshi (Delhi, 1957), p. 334.

43. ibid., Part 3. Radicals, e.g. in Russia, sometimes sympathized with the sepoys.

44. Cited by C. Cipolla, *The Economic History of World Population* (1962), pp. 102–4.

45. *The Wealth of Nations*, Vol. 2, pp. 192–3.

46. J. L. Garvin, *The Life of Joseph Chamberlain*, Vol. 2 (1933), p. 239.

47. D. Keer, *Veer Savarkar* (Bombay, 1966), p. 49.

2. INDIA

Conquest and the Spoils

In the history of modern empires the British has far the most important place, and in the British empire India. The main patterns of all British colonial administration were formed there; and to the public, empire with all its romantic associations meant chiefly India. In fact the whole complex of relationships among continents and races was deeply influenced by the great and astonishing fact – as astonishing as the Spanish conquest of America – of the subjection of this country, with its immemorial culture and vast population, to a small land in the West, four or five months distant from it before steam shortened the journey. If the British had been driven out in 1857 the history of the world, not of Britain and India alone, would have gone differently.

Seen first at the height of their power, the Mogul rulers had impressed Europe strongly if vaguely with their splendour, whose memory passed into legend. A hundred years after they had dwindled to phantoms in the Red Fort at Delhi, a young lady in Scotland would write in her diary that a laird who was giving a ball and making a splash meant to 'act the Great Mogul'.[1] Dryden wrote a very unrealistic play about his contemporary Aurangzeb, who with equal unrealism was guiding the empire back into the old ruts that the cumbrous wagon of middle-Asian history had rumbled along for so many centuries. With Portuguese, English and French trading settlements on their coast India's rulers could have got to know far more than they did of Western resources, from which they were content to hire a few artillerymen for their wars. They were in touch with Turkey, Indian pilgrims went to Mecca, they could have sent missions to Europe itself. But the sea and the peoples of the sea had no place in the tradition they belonged to.

On the Western side there was not much more curiosity. The Portuguese had gone to sleep in Goa, the English worked out a routine of trade that satisfied them, and for the rest ate, drank, died – usually quickly – or went home. It was not their ambition that precipitated change, but the crumbling of Mogul authority, never complete in the south, and then the world-wide rivalry of England and France that helped to push both of them into the maze of Indian politics and wars, complicated by Persian and Afghan invasion. All the eighteenth and earlier nineteenth century was a time of confusion, raging in other areas long after Plassey and the establishment of East India Company rule over Bengal. A conviction was fixed in the British mind, unshakeable in later days, that India without British rule must fall a prey to anarchy and invasion.

To be bringing order out of such chaos could be regarded as justification enough for British conquest, if any were asked for; Order was from first to last the grand imperial watchword. In Bengal, where more than in any later acquisition it had to cover a multitude of British sins, there was added the idea of liberation, of downtrodden Hindus rescued from Muslim tyranny. Early inclination to think of Brahmins as wonderful creatures lent it a further persuasiveness. There were sterner struggles with the Marathas, and sternest of all with the Sikhs of the Panjab; both of these had a strong popular spirit, and they had long ago shaken off the Muslim yoke by themselves. But it had a permanent effect on the British that the peoples they first came in contact with, in the seaboard provinces, southerners and Bengalis, were so much less warlike than those of the north, where most of Indian political history had been made. Experience of Bengal in particular led to its inhabitants being considered extraordinarily spiritless and docile, and despised accordingly except by a man like the missionary Carey, who praised them as 'the most mild and inoffensive people in the world', sunk unhappily in superstition.[2] To a layman they were simply 'timid and cowardly'.[3] A Frenchman noticed the 'thorough contempt' of most Englishmen for them, as 'the tamest, and most pusillanimous set of men, on the face of the earth'. It was 1789, and he added: 'But beware!'[4] Much later than this Europeans were puzzled by their apparent passivity, 'that strange insensibility, which so strongly characterizes the natives',[5] and which gave Macaulay a purple patch for his essay on Warren Hastings.[6] A similar conception was carried over to India at large, aided perhaps by the fortuitous circumstance that ever since Columbus the term 'Indian' had been current in the sense of what the nineteenth century called a 'native', and had been applied to backward peoples, most of them easily subdued, all over the Americas and the Pacific.

Also because initial contact was with the south and Bengal, and Calcutta remained the capital until the removal to Delhi in 1911, Englishmen habitually thought of Indians in general as 'black'. Thackeray remembered coming to England as a child in the care of a 'black servant' from Calcutta.[7] It was customary for a long time to talk of the inhabitants as black, even up-country where skins were much fairer than in Bengal. After a mutiny in 1844 it came out that an English officer was in the habit of calling his men the *black soldiers*, 'which displeased the sepoys very much'.[8] Englishmen were already prone to this racialism as a result of long involvement with African slavery, and there was some coming and going in early days of planters, traders and troops, between the East and West Indies. An Indian environment was likely to magnify it, since Hindus themselves were acutely conscious of race, in the form of *varna* – colour, or caste – and Bengalis, largely non-Aryan in origin, attached an inflated importance to shades of complexion.[9] They called the European the *Gora*, or pale-face; the old British quarter of Burhanpur is still known as the 'Gora Bazaar'.

The later eighteenth century being the heyday of English slave-trading and slave-owning in Jamaica, English standards of conduct in India could hardly be elevated. Slaves were bought and sold for domestic service in Calcutta too. 'Europeans lord it over the conquered natives with a high hand,' wrote Trelawney, the friend of Byron and Shelley. 'Every outrage may be committed almost with impunity.'[10] Men were as completely emancipated from conscience or criticism as the Spaniards in their worst years in America. They went to India to make fortunes, and wanted to get home and spend them before they died of fever or debauchery. Those 'Nabobs' who did get home with their ill-gotten gains were welcomed for their money but detested for their insolence, and for the dissoluteness that was said to be infecting English society and even subverting the Constitution.

Yet this first and (except for 1857) worst chapter of British rule was also the time when Englishmen were most fully immersed in Indian life. They were few and scattered, and English wives still fewer. Their close social intercourse with Indians has often been sentimentalized in retrospect, and its abandonment regretted; but it was intercourse generally with the worst elements: tax-farmers, money-lenders, women of the sort that foreigners could stock harems with. The dreadful famine of 1770, which may have swept off a third of the population of Bengal, was in part man-made. This was no new thing in Indian history; and it may be supposed that the new masters, at once rulers and traders, and working through the agency of Indians accustomed to the old ways, picked up old tricks from them.

'The horrid scene that is now acting by the English Government in the East Indies,' wrote Tom Paine in 1792, 'is fit only to be told of Goths and Vandals.'[11] 'All their discourse,' we hear in 1793, on the other hand, of these Goths or Nabobs at Calcutta, 'is about the vices of the natives.'[12] By thinking the worst of their subjects they avoided having to think badly of themselves. Even years later when they were on better terms – sometimes too easy terms – with their consciences, Englishmen went on thinking of Indians as hopelessly demoralized by climate, or social habits, or ages of Oriental misrule, and therefore permanently in need of foreign tutelage. In 1820 one of them asked why this country with a fertile soil and 'a mild and paternal government' was so poor, and, shutting his eyes to any evils of taxation, found the cause 'in a natural debility of mind, and in an entire aversion to labour', which put the Indian at the mercy of the usurer.[13] 'It is but a too common practice,' another wrote a generation further on, 'to dwell upon the shortcomings of the natives of India, to enlarge upon their fraud, falsehood, or extortions.' Such charges were quite true, he admitted, but bank crashes and scandals in India proved that many Europeans gave way to temptation just as readily, and in full view of their subjects.[14]

It was easy to find targets for criticism in a land that had gone for two or three thousand years without a really drastic spring-cleaning. There had been Hindu reformers, Islam had done something, Westernism was doing something now, but a lot of the dust swept up merely settled down again in other corners. British conquest came at a time of moral as well as political enfeeblement, affecting both Hindus and Muslims. Hinduism in its more obtrusive aspects has usually repelled outsiders because, as a result of caste division, it kept the masses quiet with a ragbag of garish crudities, while reserving its esoteric subtleties for the initiated. Grotesque idols and superstitions had disgusted the Muslim invaders, and now disgusted the Protestant or agnostic British. Some features of Hindu social life were even more repulsive, most of all suttee – the burning of a Hindu widow on her husband's funeral pyre. This was one Indian institution that all Europe heard of, and must have helped to make even Jules Verne's countrymen feel that British power over India had some warrant.[15] The Incas are said to have justified their conquests by denouncing the barbarous customs of the tribes they subdued, and the Spaniards made a great deal of the human sacrifices they found in Mexico – as the Romans did long before of those of Carthage.[17]

Impulses of Reform

Gradually British rule grew from mere collection of *loot* (one of the words the English language owes to India) into an orderly, if still burdensome, administration. Things were changing at home, in the England of the Utilitarians, the Evangelicals, the Parliamentary-reform and anti-slavery agitators. Currents of change reached India more slowly, but little by little a regular civil service was being formed, with a strong corporate spirit and a sense of responsibility. Over it were men from the aristocracy. One of England's peculiarities was this class, no longer in power after 1832 but still active, useful in a variety of ways to the reigning bourgeoisie, and finding fresh pastures in the colonies. An earl sent out to govern was less likely than an upstart Nabob to be intoxicated by wealth and pomp. He might be dazzled by the glory of a war and another province annexed, like a Roman proconsul desirous of a triumph. But he might also be, as Dalhousie was, a man of energy and zeal for improvement, eager to employ talents that were ceasing to find employment in Britain. And a Canning could exercise some check on the frenzy for reprisals after the Mutiny in a way that no professional administrator could have done.

Under these dignitaries the run of officials belonged to the type of the *gentleman* who was evolving in Victorian England. An amalgam of the less flighty qualities of the nobility with the more stodgy of middle-class virtues, he had a special relevance to the empire, and indeed was partly called into existence by its requirements, made to measure for it by England's extraordinary public-school education. In India he was a rough diamond compared with his metropolitan self, less tainted by the vices that public schools were often accused of spreading from the upper to the middle classes, but roughened by life in outposts, coarsened by too much power. Hotels sometimes hung up notices requesting him not to beat the servants. All the same this English gentleman was to make a marked impression on the world, including India. Indians, groping from one epoch into another, have sometimes been more sensitive to the social standards he imperfectly embodied than Englishmen ordinarily are, and have been proud to have the title extended to them. A president of the National Congress in the last days of the British Raj was gratified when a Viceroy said at a banquet that the 'Congress leaders were gentlemen'.[18]

Reformers were finding their way to India by the 1820s and 1830s; their first task was to reform their own seniors. One earnest young man, C. E. Trevelyan, began by bringing to light the peculation indulged in by the head of his department, and was vilified for a while by nearly all the other English. 'Trevelyan is a most stormy reformer,' wrote Macaulay, whose sister he married. '... He is quite at the head of that active party among the younger servants of the Company who take the side of improvement.'[19] This active party wanted to sweep away medieval cobwebs with an iron broom. Most of its adherents were slower to grasp the need for a constructive programme, of irrigation for example, and even the sweeping away was done lopsidedly, with priority for what British interests were supposed to require. Old land-tenures were replaced by British laws inspired by competitive individualism, with the effect of ruining a good part of both the peasantry, accustomed to a semi-communal occupancy of village lands, and the old gentry. Where alteration of Indian custom for India's own benefit was in question, on the contrary, there was cautious prudence instead of peremptory decree. In the official view interference with his religion was the one thing that would goad the timorous Indian into rebellion; and practically any government action, outside the sphere of revenue sacred to British needs, could be construed as interference with religion.

A salient instance was suttee. Muslim rule in earlier times had discountenanced it, and British rule did the same, but not resolutely enough to satisfy reformers either British or Hindu. 'I have often beheld with regret the indifference which is generally manifested by my Country men upon this most important subject,' wrote 'Britannus' in 1820. An incident had just taken place, however, of two English officers interposing, at some risk from a crowd, to prevent a woman from being burned obviously against her will.[20] It was not the first, for there had been cases even in the seventeenth century of widows rescued by Englishmen, and 'very thankfull for ye saving of their lives'.[21] There were many vacillations of policy before suttee was prohibited in 1829.[22] In later years the same arguments were repeated for and against meddling with other time-honoured usages, like child marriage.

As early again as the seventeenth century an occasional Englishman had found fault with his countrymen for making no effort to preach the Gospel, in the pockets of territory they then occupied – 'although it be their secular interest as well as their spiritual to make as many of their subjects as they can of their owne Religion that soe they may be the firmer united to them'.[23] Britain, by contrast with Spain and Portugal earlier, felt no need of such support, and preferred the negative policy of non-irritation. The Company loudly disclaimed any design of converting India, and for a long time missionaries were banned; possibly because the 'Nabobs' did not want such people spying on them – some of them may have heard of Las Casas. Kiernander who came to Calcutta in 1758, the first Protestant missionary there, was a Swede; others who followed were

Germans; and William Carey, the first English missionary in Bengal, who came out in 1793, had to reside in the small Danish settlement of Serampore, now an up-river suburb of Calcutta where the college he founded still flourishes.

From there he could see across the Ganges the daily smoke of funeral pyres, and he believed that England was incurring a deep guilt by holding Bengal and not suppressing suttee.[24] Carey was a Baptist, a humble Northamptonshire shoemaker, and belonged to a missionary tradition tinctured with radicalism that went back to the Moravians and was an overflow of reform movements in Europe. He believed in the mission of Europe to carry civilization abroad; he was as firmly convinced as anyone in India that without the British the country would relapse into 'rapine, plunder, bloodshed, and violence'.[25] But he wanted to see Britain doing far more for India's good. He and his associates lived on equal terms with their converts; they had to persuade the high-caste convert to treat his low-caste brother as an equal.

That missionary activity came to be allowed, though not positively welcomed by authority, was one symptom of the new reformism. A letter to an editor from 'Christianus' argued that Europeans had a debt to discharge, having hitherto adopted native morality instead of imparting Christian principles: they had 'done everything but renounce the religion of their forefathers'.[26] 'Moderator' revived the old contention that Christianity would make more peaceful and loyal subjects.[27] Another symptom of change was a concern for education, one of the causes that Trevelyan had at heart. Here again Englishmen had to begin by educating themselves, and Fort William College at Calcutta, founded in 1800, was meant primarily to introduce them to Indian languages, laws, customs. It drew inspiration from the work of Sir William Jones, the judge and Orientalist who had lately started the Asiatic Society and translated *Shakuntala* – 'that celebrated and illustrious man', as the *Indian Observer* called him at his death in 1794, 'who has opened the long-hidden mines of Oriental literature, and displayed them to the European world'[28] – 'accomplish'd JONES', as a Cambridge man apostrophized him in a prize poem 'On the Restoration of Learning in the East'.[29]

There were some who wanted the College also to introduce Indians to Western knowledge, and enthusiasts could think of it as a University of the East, a lighthouse darting the ray of reason through Asia's old night. In every generation a handful of Englishmen made friends with Indians and worked with them for India's good, and one such was David Hare, a watchmaker forty years in India, who devoted himself to getting schools set up in Calcutta. With the encouragement of a few men like this there grew up in the city from 1815 the circle of Ram Mohun Roy, leader of a reforming, modernizing movement within the Hindu fold, who agitated against suttee, and showed a breadth of vision that extended to sympathy with Ireland and jubilation at the French Revolution of 1830.[30] He died in England in 1833. By that date higher education was running into the problem of the choice between English or Indian languages as the medium. Some of the vernaculars were looking up. It has been said that 'the foundation of Bengali prose was laid in the Fort William College';[31] Carey, who taught there, loved it. But the issue was settled in 1835 in favour of English by Macaulay's famous Minute.

Macaulay, who was president of the Committee of Public Instruction, held up the example of Russia, rescued from its ignorance by learning Western languages, and asserted that in works of information, at any rate, the superiority of European to Oriental literature was 'absolutely immeasurable'. In later days he was abused by Indian nationalists. No doubt he knew little about the wisdom of the East, and spent too much of his time at Calcutta reading Greek poetry; and he ought to have recollected that the Russian peasant was still at least as ignorant as he was before Peter the Great, and more cut off from the educated classes. Either decision would have meant loss as well as gain; but Ram Mohun Roy had come out strongly on the side of English, as Sir Saiyad Ahmad, leader of a similar modernizing movement among the Muslims half a century later, was to do.[32] The problem arose in other colonial countries, and Indonesians suspected that Dutch talk of an indigenous plan of education really meant a plan to keep Western knowledge hidden from them. In Great Britain itself one school of thought urged that patronizing Eisteddfods and keeping the

Welsh language alive must keep the Welsh people ignorant and backward. All Indian vernaculars were harmfully tied to their classical languages, Sanskrit or Arabic, whose professors were religious obscurantists. The Indian mind had walled itself up inside such a prison that only a new language could give it a ladder of escape.

Some Bengalis revelled in English literature and Western ideas for their own sake; a bigger number wanted to learn English, as under Mogul rule they had learned Persian, to qualify for posts in government service. This Western-educated class, or a good part of it, was prepared to admire Britain, the bringer of light to the East, more fervently than that country has ever been admired, except by itself, before or since. A section went so far in snobbish imitation of English ways, some even adopting Christianity, that they grew 'denationalized and hyper-westernized'.[33] This 'Young Bengal', led till his death in 1831 by a Eurasian, Derozio, was a somewhat freakish trend, whose manners and tight pantaloons lent themselves to ridicule both English and Indian.[34] Such extravagances were for a time inevitable; but what was really only a fringe of the 'Bengal Renaissance' gave the whole of it a damagingly eccentric look; and it lacked a solid programme. Others were developing the new Bengali literature that culminated at the end of the century in Tagore. Ram Mohun had been discriminating in his welcome of the West, and from the outset there was a critical current as well as admiration. After about 1840 this was swollen by impatience for admission to higher government posts. In 1833 the Act revising the East India Company Charter had made government service rather easier to enter, but the British wanted a supply of assistants or clerks, not colleagues. In 1851 a number of groups joined to form a 'British Indian Association', which in 1853, when the Charter was again up for renewal by Parliament, presented a petition about jobs and other grievances, even asking for an Indian legislature.

British Isolation : Splendid or Perilous ?

This, four years before the Mutiny, marked the emergence of a relatively mature, modern-minded class, though one mostly confined to western Bengal and the three 'Presidency towns', Calcutta, Bombay and Madras. Britain could take some credit for it, and could, had it wished, have begun to collaborate with it. But few even of the reformers had any such wish: their motto was that of the benevolent despots in Europe – 'everything for the people, nothing by the people'. Any new governing class or nation, even when it sets out to remould its subjects, is partially remoulded by them, because it is impelled to adopt the same postures as its predecessors in order to command the same respect with least effort. India had always been ruled from elephant-back, and Englishmen quickly learned to ride the high elephant themselves, striking oriental attitudes at first unthinkingly, later – with Disraeli and his empress and his durbars – deliberately.

There was the same refusal to contemplate anything like a partnership with the other chief class of Indians genuinely willing to admire and work with the English – the sepoy officers. Indian regiments were doing most of the work of conquering India for the English; Indians were employed before 1857 in all branches, including the artillery; they could appreciate both the military equipment of the West and the 'discipline of the wars', the leadership that England brought. Those in the 'Bengal Army', biggest of the three Presidency forces, were not Bengalis, but 'Hindostanis', men of the Gangetic provinces northward from Bengal towards Delhi, which abounded in professional soldiers and martial traditions. Most even of the rank and file were Hindus of high caste. Between sepoy officer and Bengali intellectual there was scarcely a point of contact, a fact which allowed their rulers to look down on both all the more comfortably. Officers who might come from families of note could only rise very slowly to a modest rank, and were treated as unceremoniously as English corporals, their loyalty taken for granted as purely mercenary. Lord Combermere, when commander-in-chief from 1825 to 1830, was exceptional in his approach to them: he 'holds levees for them', Bishop Heber's wife wrote home, 'enquires into their histories and seems to consider them as his equals, instead of despising them'.[35] If his example had been oftener followed the Mutiny might not have happened. One who followed it was Lord Auckland, when governor-general. At the end of a tour in 1838 he held a reception for the Indian officers of his escort, and performed the old feudal ceremony of presenting betel-nut to each. Their gratitude was pathetic. 'G. is quite of opinion', Lord Auckland's sister noted, 'that there is too much neglect of meritorious natives, and that it is only marvellous our dominion over them has resisted the system of maltreatment.'[36]

There had in fact been occasional mutinies, sometimes ending in ringleaders being blown from the mouths of cannon – a style of military execution that told its own tale about this new empire. One mischief was that Indian troops might be put in charge of raw cadets from England, young louts given to vicious pranks and duelling.[37] A better type was coming out in the decades of improvement, in the army as among the civilians, a truly English jumble of habits older and newer. 'Subaltern', who published his journal of a campaign in the Panjab, came of a respectable church-going family – was famishing for promotion and prize-money, or plunder – felt shocked at scenes of carnage, quickly consoled at the prospect of medals – played cricket and the flute, scribbled verses, did his duty, and was not overly interested in Indians, who were *niggers*, or Sikhs, who were *rebels*.[38] Auckland's sister met with one English major in Indian uniform – 'everything most theatrical' – which scarcely suited his figure, but did go with his fatherly relationship with his squadron-leaders. 'He doats on his wild horsemen.'[39] But these were irregulars, outside army convention. General Outram as a young officer was 'sincerely attached' to the primitive Bhil tribesmen whom he organized for service in the hills.[40]

The aristocratic streak in these English rulers made for an aloof and chilly manner, and Indian environment stiffened it. They came to think of themselves, it has been remarked, as a caste, infinitely above all the rest.[41] If Hindus complained of being looked down on, they could always be reminded that their own treatment of one another, especially of untouchables, was worse. In Britain itself something like a caste mentality among retired Anglo-Indians reinforced social divisions already deep. A book was written about the castes of Edinburgh, one of them consisting of the Scottish capital's numerous pensioners from India.[42] 'Brahmin' came into use to mean a nob, someone boasting pedigree and blue blood.[43]

European life in India was lived as far as possible apart. There was no intercourse with the inhabitants, someone said in 1812, except in a small way at Calcutta where it was confined to the lowest Europeans and native-born Portuguese; and whenever he came on drunkenness or insolence among Indians he put it down to such contacts.[44] The Presidency towns were all European creations, and each was really from the start two distinct towns. At Calcutta, 'the city of palaces', the English occupied stately homes round the wide green space of the Maidan, and never went near what they called the 'Black Town' if they could help it. Wherever else the British settled it was in new suburbs, the civil or military 'Lines', well outside the old Indian cities which were in any case too congested and too little amenable to sanitation.[45] An Englishman's bungalow was very much his castle, standing in a large walled space or 'compound', a miniature of the squire's park, where he could be out of sight or sound of any Indians but his own underlings.

Britain had many enemies, but India was so divided that most Englishmen felt safe in their splendid isolation. They rejected any but strictly official contacts with Indians, a critic wrote in 1815, 'from the false idea, that it is *inconsistent with the dignity of their status*'.[46] Young men were too apt, an experienced senior wrote privately in 1848, to think it 'unbecoming of us to pay any regard to popular feeling'.[47] The Honourable Company was so thickly wrapped up in its cloak of dignity that to the protected kingdom of Oudh, shortly before the annexation that was one of the starting-points of the Mutiny, it was 'a terrible myth'; the very ignorant imagined it as a huge dragon issuing from a den in some strange land. 'All, high and low, go in awe of "Koompanny Bahador".'[48]

There was always a platoon of pessimists who felt uneasy

about this state of affairs. As a rule they argued from a conservative standpoint, not as advocates of an approach to the
common people or to new sprigs like 'Young Bengal'. They
took for granted that a foreign government could only tax the
masses, it could have no moral contact with them except
through their own hereditary leaders. It was perilous, they
maintained, to sweep away all old families of note and wealth,
leaving no buffer between government and people. Several wit-
nesses recorded in the famous Fifth Report of 1812 dwelt on the
government's 'extreme unpopularity' with the land-owning
classes, which had lost much under it, and wished that posts
in the services had been reserved for the 'native gentry', to
attach them to its interests.[49]

Against this there were two objections. One was that of pride
and prejudice, confidence in the Englishman's ability to do
without any assistance from Indians except those he hired as
drudges. The second, felt more by reformers, was that the
'native gentry' were stragglers from bad old days, feudal relics
to be cleared away for the sake of progress. Sir John Malcolm
was the most judicious spokesman of the case for taking them
by the hand. He united arguments of prudence with a desire
for progress. England, he thought, could guide the upper classes
towards reform, and through them the country, by slower but
safer methods than those of the iconoclasts. His Scottish birth
may have helped to give him both a respect for feudal rights
and some freedom from prejudice against Indians as Asiatics.
Early in his career, in 1799, he was pointing out how sepoy
loyalty might be undermined by the 'cold, confined, and de-
pressive' tone of British officers, and on campaign, all through
the day's march, he made a point of conversing with Indians
of every sort.[50] When he drew up instructions for his staff in
Central India in 1821 he called on them to go beyond cold
civility and display real fellow-feeling. Englishmen as individuals had no sweeping advantage over Indians. He was not for
adopting Indian habits, and pointed out that rich Indians who
adopted European ways only forfeited the respect of their
countrymen without winning that of the foreigner;[51] what he
wanted was that each should take the other on his merits. In
1828 he warned the India Board of the harm being done by 'an

overweening sense of our superiority' and the exclusion of Indians from all positions of trust.[52]

This led on to the question of whether it was wise to continue annexing territories still under Indian rule. Motives for annexation were a blend of philanthropy, stirred by the evils of native despotism, and greed, excited by the Company's chronic need for more revenue. Malcolm saw that between them they did not make good sense. He was 'sickened', he told a governor-general, Bentinck, by the 'mawkish morality' that wanted Britain to intervene against abuses in native states, when there were often more crying abuses in British provinces.[53] Undoubtedly in the period before 1857 when annexation was in vogue, the evils of princely rule were luridly portrayed – as in Knighton's account of Oudh in its final phase of imbecility[45] – and those of British rule were left in the shade. Yet in 1842 the peasantry of Bengal was said to be 'trembling on the remotest verge of human misery and brutalization', while responsible Englishmen knew nothing of how it was being preyed on by their native agents.[55] And this was largely the outcome of the creation by the Permanent Settlement of 1793 of an artificial class of big landlords, more rapacious than the older sort who were got rid of in other provinces. A few years later a writer drew attention to the contrast between the peasantry of British India at large, 'ground down to the lowest possible condition, physically and morally debased', and the foreigner ruling over them 'in all the luxury of Eastern splendour ... the yearly income of one of these tillers of the soil will be smoked in cheroots by a junior civilian in a week'.[56]

The Mutiny and its Effects

Richard Burton, who did not like Indians (he liked very few of the innumerable peoples he met on his wanderings), pointed out a few years before 1857 how ignorant Britons were of Indian feeling, and of how Indians hated them.[57] The early, unwholesome mixing had been succeeded by no better relationship, except among a few individuals; the changes that British rule was bringing about went far enough to antagonize many interests, not far enough to create many new interests as a support. The revolt that Burton foresaw was the first massive revolt of Asia against Europe. It was a rising of soldiers, led or abetted by old feudal groups, and aided by peasants, and it had some early tinge of an Indian national feeling: the army represented both the great religious communities. Englishmen had chosen to rely on India being divided against itself, rather than attached to them, and now there seemed an end to 'that antagonism of the Asiatic races, which', the historian of the Mutiny frankly declared, 'had ever been regarded as the main element of our strength and safety'.[58] They were saved by other divisions, even more than by their own better organization and gunnery. For the most part the rising was confined to the old Hindostan, and the Sikhs of the newly-conquered Panjab proved eager to serve their new British masters against their old Muslim enemies. None the less the sudden discovery by the British of their true position after so many years in India was a shock, which helped to unbalance them.

It was a contest on both sides of heroism and, as usual in such wars, of atrocities. After victory there were savage reprisals. For the first time on such a scale, but not the last, the West was trying to quell the East by frightfulness. 'History shudders,' wrote G. O. Trevelyan, nephew of Macaulay, who went to India a few years later to make inquiries, 'at the recollection of the terrible "Spanish fury" which desolated Antwerp in the days of William the Silent; but the "English fury" was more terrible still.'[59] Some of the facts that have come down to us almost stagger belief, even after the horrors of Europe's own twentieth-century history. Nothing worse was ever done against Negro rebels in the Americas. Public opinion in England could not be a restraining influence; it was in one of its two grand fits of hysteria of that century – the other coming on in the Boer War. In the folk-memory of India these things lingered for many years.[60]

Let us rule by virtue, one of the more idealistic Englishmen wrote during 1857, 'and we shall reign over these poor Asiatics with infinitely greater security and more power than if we had in India the whole grand army of Napoleon'.[61] Robespierre in the midst of his reign of terror dreamed of a reign of virtue.

When revenge was satisfied the prime need of profit from India remained, and necessarily took precedence. And the old sleepwalker's certainty of the British there, the carefree assumption that they knew what was good for the natives and that the natives, like children with nasty medicine, would learn to be thankful, was gone for good. India was never forgiven for what it did in 1857, still less perhaps for what it exasperated the English into doing, or allowing to be done, which most of them before long ceased to speak of, and would very likely have been glad to stop thinking of. The bitterness that India had always felt was now felt on both sides, and the gulf had become impassable.

Trevelyan felt the change sadly. He gave the British official credit for incorruptibility, and for more devotion to duty than ever before, a 'fire of zeal which glows in every vein' – 'but that duty is no longer a labour of love'. There had been a time, he believed, when some Englishmen had not been afraid to call Indians their friends, and would have been ashamed to call them *niggers*.[62] This opprobrious term was brought back into common parlance by the Mutiny. Writing in 1857 Karl Marx quoted from an Englishman's letter in a newspaper: 'Every nigger we meet with we either string up or shoot.'[63] It went on being used by Europeans among themselves after coming to be officially discouraged in public. In a collection of sketches of life in a small station the author jocularly catches himself in a slip of the pen when he speaks of its well-paved streets being a pleasure 'to the niggers – I mean to the Oriental gentlemen – whose duties attract them to Kabob'.[64]

The worst mischief of the 'damned nigger' mentality deplored by Trevelyan[65] was that it ruled out a new approach to the newer, more progressive sections of Indian opinion. After the Mutiny the East India Company was abolished at last, and India given an empress instead, a more rational administrative structure, and, with railways, the basis for a more modern economy. During the crisis the Bengali intelligentsia was torn between fear that rebel success would mean relapse into another dark age, and disgust at British ferocity. It tried to rally behind Canning, the governor-general, as a moderate.[66] Its behaviour went unthanked, in the then mood of the rulers.

'Young Bengal' – still their uncomplimentary name for the whole class – was dismissed by one of them as 'remarkable generally for conceit, disloyalty, and irreligion'.[67]

One reason for the failure of education to bring about a meeting of minds was the way it had developed since Macaulay. What was wrong with it was not the English medium but the content, far too literary and academic. It was the same or worse in England, where fossilized universities and public schools went on teaching young gentlemen to compose imbecile verses in dead languages and to ignore science and technology as undignified; but there games, and the prospect of active careers ahead, were a partial corrective, and schoolbooks were quickly forgotten. Indians lacked this, and if they took greedily to their new learning it was partly because it had much in common with their old. They were meeting new philosophers, Rousseau or Mill, and new poets, instead of old ones; Shakespeare had an astonishing effect; but none of this had any direct connection with the country's practical problems, and abstract ideas left mind and muscle disastrously separated as they had always been in India. The result was not calculated to win the hearts of Englishmen, mostly philistines who tossed Rousseau and Shakespeare to India with careless indifference, as good enough to teach clerks. Their respect was bestowed more readily on an Agha Khan, who understood racehorses: 'Perhaps that goes pretty far towards pleasing the British residents,' wrote an opponent of his bitterly.[68] A later Agha Khan was to win far more hearts in England with his horses than Tagore with his verses. And while Indians, unlike Britons, are excellent linguists, few had opportunity to gain a colloquial, as they did a literary, mastery of English, and their way of talking sounded comical to Englishmen. England was a country where the educated classes derived perennial entertainment from the faulty speech of the uneducated. 'Babu Jabberjee' became a stock figure of fun.[69]

There was a great deal of prejudice in the British attitude to educated Indians, but not prejudice alone. Behind any academic defects lay the legacy of all that was amiss in an old, degenerate society. An individual like Ram Mohun Roy could shake it off swiftly, and prove that there was a reservoir of pent-up mental and moral energy in the old India whose release was England's true, but imperfectly fulfilled, mission of liberation. A whole class could not shake it off so soon. In 1866 a Hindu from the south discussed its problems in a candid lecture at Benares. He had unbounded faith in Western knowledge and principles as Asia's salvation. 'A man that has received a thorough English education is fit for everything that is good and laudable.' He had only one serious grievance against the British, that 'they look upon us as beings of an inferior order ... Does not this sort of conduct ... tend to demoralize us and to estrange us?' At the same time he confessed that Indians were already demoralized by their own past. 'We lie; we steal; we deceive; we commit rape ... and then early in the morning we bathe in the Ganges, whose filthy waters wash away our sins.'[70]

This was precisely what Europeans said, in and out of season. The **most** open-minded of them were often repelled by what they **saw, in** Bengal particularly, even now when suttee was a thing **of the** past. There Britain had brought new light, but also a new darkness in the form of a vicious landlordism that was fast reducing the countryside to a worse than Irish condition; and between intellectuals and landlords there were unhealthily close ties of class and family. Trevelyan deeply regretted that 'the habit of sneering at our dark fellow-subjects is so confirmed in some people, that they lose sight of sense and logic';[71] but he himself felt baffled. Physically these better-off Bengalis struck him, as they struck all Englishmen brought up on a cult of the athletic, as disgustingly flabby – 'the most helpless, feeble set of beings in the universe'. Morally too they appeared very lax, deficient in 'the earnestness of purpose which a Briton carries into his business, his pleasures, even his vices'.[72] They were of course Hindus, and a lack of any sense of a lie being something to feel shame for had always been a Muslim reproach against Hinduism, as it was now a British reproach. 'Unfortunately,' wrote Trevelyan, too sweepingly, 'this want of truthfulness leavens the whole being of the Bengalee ... the mass of Bengalees have no notion of truth and falsehood.'[73]

It made a singular impression on him, as it well might in the land of the Permanent Settlement, to hear a schoolroom commenting with Johnsonian orotundity on *The Deserted Village*.[74]

This aptitude of the Bengali for Western literature and thought was amazing, but he asked himself whether it was more than skin-deep; and added, with insight: 'In fact, it may be doubted whether he knows himself.'[75] A man or a people can only know themselves through the test of action, and Bengal, absorbing at second-hand so much of the experience of another continent, had as yet no experience of its own to serve as touchstone either of what it read or of its own soul. A polygamous young man bloated with messy sweets, declaiming tirades from *Julius Caesar* while his peasants starved, was certainly an incongruous spectacle. He might really love both his sweets and his Shakespeare; every nation and class suffers from its own peculiar form of schizophrenia; only the ordeal of action could teach him what he was really born for. A sharper vision of truth and not-truth would come with the emergence of a collective ideal and duty, a public cause, such as Europeans had always had, if they were seldom worthy of it. The national movement and its demands were to reveal what part of the seed of new ideas had fallen on fertile or on stony soil. There was a rehearsal in 1859–60, when agitation against abuses on British-owned plantations swept the province and roused the intellectuals, giving them for the first time something serious to declaim about. As to physical courage and endurance, one Bengali revealed unexpected reserves before long by exploring forbidden Tibet alone, in disguise, as a secret agent of the Indian government.[76]

The royal proclamation of 1858 promising free entry on merit to all government posts was hailed at first as a pledge of alliance with a new India. But statues of Queen Victoria were to multiply faster than jobs for Indians in the higher civil and military grades. Disappointment over this was one of the starting-points of a decade of agitation in Bengal, leading to the National Congress movement that began in 1886, with independence gradually becoming its goal.[77] If for Indians concessions to nationalism meant first and foremost more jobs, for Englishmen they meant fewer jobs. Hence there was a professional incentive to the latter to convince themselves and British opinion that an Indian, however well-trained and intelligent, could never have a character equal to real responsibility.

The old type of nominated civil servant was bitterly resentful of the new type of Englishman, the much-derided 'Competition-wallah' now coming in through public examination; the thought of having to make room for Indians as well was unbearable. The Briton was always finding fault with his Indian subordinate or colleague for not having manliness and independence enough. His own overbearing behaviour was more likely to snuff out these qualities than to foster them, and he was not free from a tendency to think of colour, rather than culture, as the true index of worth.

Still, India's narrow specializations of caste and community really had hindered the all-round development of mind, body and character that a gentleman and an efficient district official was supposed to have. India was running true to its old self when Bengalis took to English literature, Parsees to English commercial methods, and Panjabis, who cared for neither, to English bayonets, and all three moved further away from one another than they had been before. Bengalis spreading over India in the lower and middle cadres of the administration often earned unpopularity in other provinces, through both friction over jobs and clashes of temperament. It was easy for a long time to dismiss nationalists as a small selfish minority. Most of them were higher-caste Hindus, not free from an ancestral disdain for the mass of their countrymen, Hindu or Muslim. Only British obduracy compelled them, from the early years of this century, to turn to the common people and think of a mass movement and a struggle instead of painless adoption of the élite into the British framework. It was no use 'licking the boots of the English', said a distinguished Bengali scholar who had seen them at close quarters. 'The English are afraid of fighting . . . entreaties do not move them in the least.'

Rebuilding an Alien Power

Meanwhile the Raj had been rebuilt on other foundations. In 1857 isolation had proved more dangerous than splendid, and the arguments of men like Malcolm against it became irresistible. But whereas Englishmen earlier had felt impatience at

India's unwillingness to change, now they were in a mood to feel disquiet at the eagerness of some Indians for change. Like the reform programme earlier, the reconstruction programme was one-sided and too largely negative. Pillars of Indian society would be preserved, and encouraged to stand still. The remaining princes would be allowed to survive, as Malcolm advocated, but not left to their own devices, to work out some modern relationship with their subjects – instead they were placed under imperial guarantee, and their States built into the British fabric as buttresses of conservatism. Political progress in them was ruled out; and in British India, thus shored up, any really searching reform could be comfortably postponed.

Rulers of the kind lately vilified as Oriental tyrants were now eulogized as the natural leaders of their people. Leaving a third of the country under princely rule could be speciously represented as a concession to Indian feeling; and if, as was increasingly the case, conditions were worse there than in British India, nationalists could be invited to contemplate the consequences of self-government. This plan of utilizing puppet rulers may have owed something to Dutch practice in Indonesia; in turn it may have helped to decide French or Russian administrators to adopt similar policies. It was copied in other parts of the British empire, and was in fact a hallmark of all the later imperialism.

Most of the surviving princes were Hindu, but among the land-owners, who shared their feudal mentality, were a good many Muslims, like some of those *taluqdars* of Oudh who, reprieved from confiscation after the Mutiny, took care thereafter to be loyal. With official patronage they could take the lead in the Muslim community, which, having fallen far behind the Hindu, could not hope to catch up without government aid. More forward-looking Muslims quite agreed about this. Their leader Sir Saiyad Ahmad had the same unquestioning regard for Western knowledge and its channel, the English language, and for British administration, as the Bengali Hindus had formerly had. In a speech in 1867 he thanked God for rescuing India from slavery by sending it a government founded on 'intellect, justice and reason'.[79] In practice this came to mean better relations between government and a Muslim élite than between either of them and Hindus. Once the 'liberator' of Hindu India from Muslim oppression, Britain was now the 'protector' of Muslim India against Hindu economic domination. Insensibly there crept back – in the end more intensely than anyone had desired – the communal antagonism so alarmingly absent at first in 1857.

In the army the British contingent had been greatly strengthened, and given sole charge of the artillery; the sepoy forces were rebuilt, with the Panjab, split among Muslim, Hindu and Sikh, and politically inert, as the chief northern recruiting-ground. Very few Indians were admitted to commissioned rank; but the British officer, drawn from an army undergoing changes at home too, developed a closer relationship with his men, and campaigns outside India favoured the growth of an *esprit de corps* that both could share. They helped also to fashion an 'Indian Army' which even nationalists could take a certain pride in, and which independent India has taken over with little change beyond substitution of Indian officers. Britons were free to consider its successes their own, since it was an article of faith that native troops could learn to be good soldiers only by virtue of European training and leadership. For them as for the British rank and file the officer wore the air of a superman, born to command the lower race as well as the lower class. To this day a junior Indian officer has to establish himself in the eyes of his men by comparison with the still lingering image of the departed Briton.[80]

Between the recruiting-districts and the army there grew a hereditary attachment. The official category of 'martial races' was not fictitious. Panjabis or Rajputs did have fighting traditions that Bengalis or Gujeratis lacked. Practically the whole Pakistani army today is drawn from areas of the western Panjab and the adjoining Frontier province that the old Indian army drew on. To the government the essential point was that these martial races of the interior belonged to pre-industrial societies of feudal landlord and peasant, blissfully untouched by the political ideas that the big cities were breeding. Simple, manly fellows, they were far more congenial to it than the Bombay *bania* or shopkeeper-moneylender, or the voluble Bengali *babu* or clerk, or the Madrasi lawyer, heir of a long line of Brahminical logic-choppers; all of whom the villager despised or feared as instinctively as the Englishman did. Officers or district magistrates could think complacently of Sikhs and Jats under their charge as a bold peasantry, their country's pride. 'To know the simple, unsophisticated tiller of the soil in the village is to love him,' wrote a Scot who went out in 1905. 'He is wonderfully contented despite his illiteracy, poverty and low standard of living.'[81]

An old general, to whom the only thing that made India bearable was the 'shootin'', spoke warmly to Somerset Maugham of his *shikaris* – 'except for their colour pukka white men'.[82] Very likely they returned his esteem. A civilian was not as a rule so null and void, but he too preferred the guileless rustic, the faithful domestic, the army veteran, stock characters in the neat little play with a happy ending to which he liked to reduce life: the Englishman in the colonies was, revealingly, a great one for amateur theatricals. He was not fond of townsmen in general, and the educated sort who were getting above themselves in particular. The mental stiffness or indolence that went with his physical and moral energy disinclined him to put himself on a level with men who might well be cleverer and better-informed than he was. He had small desire to hobnob even with the most staunchly loyal, except for an occasional shoot in their forests. The fashioning of conservative alliances was not his affair; he left high policy to the Serene Highnesses at Calcutta and London, and continued to occupy in his own sphere the splendid isolation that the Raj could no longer indulge in.

It was not surliness alone. Britons were still few, and their ability to control a vast population, whether for good or for ill, depended more on moral ascendancy than on physical force. There is a picture in one of Kipling's stories, sublime in its way, of a solitary Englishman quietly riding towards a town seized by an outbreak of mob passions, not doubting for a moment that at his appearance the angry waves will be stilled.[83] This enormous confidence rested partly on a record of success in arms, almost unbroken save for 1857 and then almost miraculously recovered. But it owed much also to the studied remoteness of the English, as of a race more than human in civil as in military life, capable by divine warrant of that art of government, that 'mystery' which rulers, as James I held, must keep strictly to themselves. Men being what they are, all leadership of men or command over men, whether by Napoleon or by a deputy-commissioner at Ambala, must be half charlatanism. A Cambridge lecturer coolly turning over the fossil bones of history could afford to doubt whether the size of Britain's empire really proved any 'invincible heroism or supernatural genius for government'.[84] Practical men knew better. 'For a century,' wrote a former cabinet minister in 1892, 'the Englishman has behaved in India as a demi-god ... Any weakening of this confidence in the minds of the English or of the Indians would be dangerous.'[85]

For a demi-god to begin abdicating his power is still harder than for a dictator. For him to be civil and chatty with ordinary beings is too much to ask. In public the Englishman had to be perpetually on his dignity, wearing what was half a naturally supercilious expression, half a mask. In private he had to be able to relax, to groan at the vile weather and the worse politicians at Westminster, to drink his own health as often as he felt it required. He had therefore to keep Indians, except servants, at a distance. No man is a hero to his fellow-club-member. Then, at an age (it came to be fixed at fifty-five) long before senility, his service ended and he vanished abruptly to England. India never saw the giant old and feeble.

This detachment was not without its value for India as well as for the rulers. All India's governments had been too personal, too much a matter of *sifarish* or backstairs influence. So had Europe's, but the West was learning now to think in terms of an administrative machine dealing impersonally with objective facts. In Asia, in spite of some valiant efforts by righteous Muslims, the concept of equality of rights before the law was virtually unknown. Englishmen picked it up more readily in some ways in India than they did at home, where a minister taking office in mid-century was still expected, like Lord John Russell, to remember his relatives while not forgetting his friends. Among Indians they had no relatives and no friends. Government as a machine without sensibility, incapable of yielding to the generous impulse that makes a man in office happy to oblige his acquaintances at the expense of the public, was uncongenial to Indians, and its foreignness made it still more distasteful. And it could of course perform no more than a bureaucracy can perform. Only the tidal wave of a great popular movement could renovate India fundamentally, but that was not yet a possibility. In the meantime a bureaucracy that often blundered and was always expensive, but seldom gave way to favouritism or caprice, was – as Indians have been willing to admit – useful for propelling the country out of feudalism into modernity, for draining the political marsh and creating solid standing-ground. In the princely States the alternative, the old ways, were plainly in view.

Harmfully as the rulers were cut off from Indian life, this was a much lesser evil than the kind of intercourse that existed in the days of the Nabobs. Memories of those depraved times lingered among Englishmen; the moral they drew was not so much that their forefathers had wronged India, but that the unwholesome, decadent East had blighted the native virtue of Englishmen too intimately acquainted with it. In a novel of these later, more austere days (by a woman) an old hand puts a newcomer on his guard against the quicksand waiting to swallow him. 'Oriental life has an irresistible fascination for some natures; the glamour, the relief from convention ... the lure of attractive and voluptuous women, idleness, ease, luxury, *drugs*! I could tell you of an officer who went crazy about a beautiful Kashmeri ...'[86]

Such Delilahs, luckily for British morale, were less easy to meet with in life than in novels. Godlike aloofness was greatly facilitated by the absence of Indian women from the social scene. Since Roman times Europe had allowed women of all ranks a latitude unique among the higher civilizations. In England it had gone further than in most of Europe, in India it was more severely curtailed than in most of Asia. The Englishman could excuse his stand-offishness when it began to come under criticism, by arguing that he brought his wife and daughters into the drawing-room and the Indian did not. In later years the Hindu was to use exactly the same argument against the Muslim.

A Miss Walker was an ornament of the royal harem of Oudh

in its last days, and another Englishwoman had married into a respectable Muslim family and written an intelligent book about Muslim life.[87] But these were very rare cases; and while in Indonesia a certain number of white men continued to have legitimate native wives (far more had concubines), in India there was very heavy pressure of opinion against any such unions, as well as against irregular ones, and corresponding prejudice against their offspring.[88] Aristocratic dislike of the *mésalliance* had weight; but in any case Indian women of good status were quite inaccessible. A Muslim lady could not even be seen, a Hindu lady could not marry a Hindu of different caste, to say nothing of a foreigner; and neither, until near the end of the epoch, began to learn English or come by any modern education.

Intermarriage could have promoted good feeling with only a very few Indians, at the cost of illwill and suspicion among many more. But the taboo on it did have the bad effect of worsening the tinge of racialism always present in the British make-up. When the Englishman turned his back on the invisible Indian beauty, as on a poisonous orchid or a sour grape, he was in a way turning his back on India altogether. His wife, whose susceptibility to the ravages of the climate was notorious, was less uneasy about him because he ostentatiously avoided all Indian society. It may be surmised that a broad moat between the races helped the white paterfamilias also to feel easy in his mind. There were other too well-known effects of a hot climate; young Indian men were often handsome, in a raffish Italian style; they were believed by prudish Victorians to be inordinately, unnaturally lascivious.[89] Altogether, the peace and quiet of the family were safer if Indian company was excluded from the spacious bungalow. And the peace and quiet of the empire were safer if the bungalow set a good example to the barracks; for Tommy Atkins to go wandering among women would foment endless rows, and undermine discipline.

Another acquaintance of Somerset Maugham, the Prince of Berar, son and heir of His Exalted Highness the Nizam, complained of not being allowed to set foot in the fashionable Yacht Clubs of Bombay and Calcutta.[90] Good understanding with the princes was strictly a matter of political convenience. Much later, one year before independence, Gandhi's son was refused admission to a European restaurant at Shillong.[91] Apartheid carried so absurdly far helped to stiffen the self-esteem of the British, wilting in the later decades of the Raj, and, still more, to bind together their upper and lower ranks, especially the ruling caste and the common soldier. Racialism is always in one aspect a spurious leveller of class distinctions. Mogul emperors married Rajput princesses; for an English viceroy to do so would have been more disgraceful and unthinkable than for him to marry an English parlour-maid. The indispensable Tommy Atkins got a poor share of what Britain made out of India, but as a white man he had the privilege, for what it was worth to him, of seeing all Indians from Highness to sweeper officially regarded as his inferiors.

We have scant record of how he felt about this, or about the rest of his existence in India. In later times he was not stuck there for good, awaiting death or discharge, as in the old Company army. But the royal army too was recruited from Ireland, the Highlands, and the poorest classes in England, whose refuge from pauperism it was in youth as the workhouse was in age. The soldier suffered more than his comfortably lodged superiors from a climate that only wealth or electricity can make tolerable. In the post-Mutiny decade sixty-five of every thousand European soldiers in Bengal died or were invalided out each year.[92] He was more or less illiterate, and his notions of this strange land where he strangely found himself must have been as bizarre as his versions of Indian names, with Siraj-ul-Daulah, villain of the Black Hole, refracted into Sir Roger Dowler, and Shah Shaja'-ul-Mulk into 'Cha sugar and milk'. Most of the time he must have accepted the attitude to Indians of those above him as natural and proper. In 1857 official Anglo-India, itself wild enough for revenge, could not help feeling amused at his simple conviction that all blackies, down to the most harmless-looking, ought to be knocked on the head.[93]

Children everywhere slip through some of the entanglements of grown-up conduct. Tommies on the walls of Lahore Fort would exchange good-humoured abuse with the urchins playing below at bat and ball.[94] An Indian novel shows us some of them through the admiring eyes of a sweeper-boy cleaning their latrines, to whom they were in a rough way much friend-lier than his own high-caste countrymen.[95] Unable often to afford a wife, the private soldier also saw more than his betters usually did of Indian women, chiefly in the army brothels; but whatever secrets he and they shared with one another they have carried with them into a longer exile.

It was a dominant fact throughout that there was no big resident population of non-official Europeans. When the Company lost its commercial monopoly in 1813 private individuals were able to enter more freely: not usually intending to lay their bones in India, though some families did stay, but to make money and go back home. Friends of India like Carey hoped that their presence would be helpful to Indian progress, as men like Livingstone hoped in Africa. Missionaries were prone to the mistake of fancying other Europeans as well-meaning as themselves. In some directions the settlers in India were useful; they started newspapers, criticized the bureaucracy, helped to generate something like a political atmosphere for Indians to breathe. But their own interests came first with them, and only accidentally coincided with Indian interests; and what official-dom lacked in friendliness towards Indians was very far from being made good by settlers.

Their two leading categories were merchants in the ports and planters. In feudal Asia commerce was not the most admired vocation, and so far as skill at it went Indian traders were admittedly, as one writer said, 'possessed of great sagacity and foresight'.[96] Foreigners could not pretend to more sagacity, but they could put on airs to raise them above the vulgar associa-tions of trade, and aped the demeanour of the officials who set the social tone. Planters on their estates were dealing with Indians of the most unlettered kind, and their standards of conduct had been formed too much by the American slave-plantation. Like Shylock they assumed that anything the law did not explicitly forbid, they might do cheerfully; unlike Shy-lock they had a hand in making the law. Indigo was their first love, and gave them an unsavoury reputation. Charges against them of flogging and otherwise maltreating peasants were found by the authorities in 1810 to be undeniable;[97] but the evils went on.

The Mutiny prompted the thought that British power – if not Indian progress – would be firmer if there were more Europeans. A Select Committee recommended a more liberal policy of admission, as in Ceylon; it heard complaints that officialdom – 'as it were, the nobility of India' – resented outsiders and tried to keep the door shut.[98] The idea was to attract men with capital, not labourers and the like for whom there was little room and whose presence would have defaced the image of the ruling race. Capital could not make up for want of other desirable attributes, and the civil servant was not merely snobbish in looking down on those who came: most of them were not *gentlemen* morally any more than socially.

Trevelyan found these two classes on opposite sides of every question, and in their attitude towards Indians the settlers vastly the worse of the two. Any notion of a British duty to India they dismissed as 'execrable hypocrisy'.[99] The official class as well as the public at home was, he thought, a good deal ashamed of the frenzy of 1857, but the settlers not at all: they were still talking about all natives or niggers with 'rabid ferocity'.[100] Decent mutual respect between the races, the most that in his opinion could be hoped for, was 'simply impossible' while the settlers behaved as they did.[101] He was at first the guest of indigo planters, but was shaken by the violence of the 'anti-native journals',[102] and realized that the whole plantation economy 'had become an instrument of intolerable oppression'.[103] An inquiry had to be held, and the evidence laid before it 'proved the horrible tendency of the existing system'.[104] Trevelyan might have noticed more than he did the activity of progressive Bengalis in making the inquiry fruitful.

Planters had strong backing at home, and officials disliked them more than they interfered with them. After what had been brought to light about indigo, evils of a similar kind were allowed to gather round tea, which from the middle of the century was becoming the biggest commercial crop, pioneered and always mainly controlled by British capital and management. Suitable land for tea-growing lay in remote hill areas, the Assam valley being the best, where labour was scarce. Recruitment of 'coolies' from other parts of India formed a murky chapter in the history of the 'indentured labour' system which in many parts of the colonial world replaced the slavery that was being abandoned. Workers were easiest to procure from poor regions of hill or jungle like Chota Nagpur, where primitive, often aboriginal, communities eked out a bare existence. Native contractors got hold of them, frequently by trickery, and a great many perished on the way to Assam before any government regulation was imposed.

Planters could prevent coolies from going away before finishing the terms of years they bound themselves to, and employed bands of ruffians to maintain discipline, as big Indian landlords did on their estates; an instance of the level at which East and West were too apt to learn from each other. While tea-drinking refined English manners at home, tea-growing in Assam hardened and brutalized. In 1866 the Commissioner of Assam started some prosecutions, and expressed surprise that such 'cold-blooded revolting cruelty' could be perpetrated.[105] From the 1880s Indian newspapers were agitating against the abuses. It was another of the issues that brought educated Indians to defend their humbler countrymen, and to feel disillusionment over Britain's civilizing mission. Isolated and ignorant, a great proportion of them women, the workers were learning to defend themselves. In 1884 when a new manager who had 'made himself unpopular by excess of zeal' caned one of them, 'the coolies retaliated and beat him severely'.[106]

When modern forms of industry began British capital led the way, but with equally little desire to set a humane example. On the contrary it combined, as Western industry in the other continents usually did, the harshness of Europe's own industrial revolutions with the harshness of feudalism. It was content to point out that in Indian-owned enterprises, most of them smaller and less efficient, conditions were worse still. This was true for instance on the Bihar coalfield, which like the tea districts drew on easily exploited labour, including men and women of backward tribes like Bhuiyas or Manjhis. They were enrolled and dragooned by native 'sardars' or gang-bosses, who squeezed money out of them on every pretext while the European owner or manager looked no further than his ledger. For such workers the cheapest living conditions were judged suitable; as late as 1939 an inquiry committee's report described company housing as 'the merest pretence of housing, incredibly dark, damp, ill ventilated, filthy, with no privacy or sanitation'. Few collieries employed personnel officers, and the report emphasized the 'deep cleavage between the ranks and supervisory grades', here as in Indian industry at large.[107] This cleavage reproduced that between government and people in the political sphere, with the gang-bosses and contractors performing in their smaller way functions not unlike those of the feudal landlords and princes.

Missionaries and Indian Religion

In one of Quiller-Couch's novels an East India Company man of the old days was suddenly gripped by remorse when on the point of sailing for home with his pile. He left the ship disguised as an old Indian beggar, was helped ashore by a light-hearted kick from an English seaman by way of good-bye to India, and spent the rest of his life as an ascetic in a cave in the hills.[108] No real Nabob, no planter, or mine-owner, is known to have succumbed like this. But Britain in the nineteenth century made as great a profession of Christianity as any European country, partly because it had the biggest empire; since then the two attributes have passed together to the USA. India thanks to its tormented past was the most religious country in Asia; Indians still make conversation about God as Englishmen do about the weather. Here was one meeting-point of interests, if an awkward one, and on the whole the contact between the two countries strengthened the religious proclivities of both.

Conservative Anglo-Indians after the Mutiny could forget their sins of omission or commission by putting the blame on indiscreet proselytizing, which they said had made Hindus and Muslims feel that their religions were under attack. Others argued on the contrary that British rule ought to have won allegiance by showing itself far more Christian than it had ever done. The Quaker journal, *The Friend*, which protested that 'The cry for indiscriminate vengeance is a disgrace to a Christian nation', called for wider promotion in India of both Christianity and commerce.[109] Even the best of Victorians were over-ready to regard these two as parallel roads to human felicity.

Missionary work was resumed, but under the long shadow of the gallows of 1857. Neither before nor after this date were conversions numerous. It was an accepted axiom that Muslims were impossible to convert, and Hindus were not much more malleable. Converts came mostly, as they had done from Hinduism to Islam, from the humblest classes, and a good many of them were Catholic: they were thus doubly cut off from official Anglo-India. But whatever their status they would not have been taken much notice of: no familiarity with the Bible, any more than with Shakespeare, could alter the fact that a native was a native. Here again standoffishness had its good side; it deterred the growth of a multitude of 'rice-Christians' dependent on government patronage and serving as auxiliaries of British power, like a section of the Catholic minority that was growing in French Indochina. In a more roundabout way missionaries did bring the government some aid and comfort. Their work's disappointing results made them feel, and through them the public at home, not precisely that Christianity was too good for Indians, but that Indians were too bad for Christianity, and, *a fortiori*, for self-rule.

Preachers whose sermons fell on such deaf ears could not help forming a darker view of Indian nature than the optimistic Carey, convinced that only official obstruction stood between the country and conversion. We have a picture of his heroic contemporary Henry Martyn, who went out from Cambridge in 1805 and died after many wanderings in 1812, preaching at Cawnpore to an audience of holy men disfigured by self-inflicted deformities, whose repulsive exterior was 'but a faint emblem of their inward depravity and moral vileness'.[110] Unpromising material indeed for an Anglican congregation; but men who identified Christianity with civilization and morality always saw things in these black and white terms, the West robed in light, the East clothed in darkness. One of them tersely summed up the Hindu character as '*obsequious, deceitful, licentious, and avaricious*', adding that the worst hardship of missionary life was having to dwell among a people 'destitute of all that is good, and distinguished by almost all that is evil'.[111] Another in a survey of the spiritual condition of Calcutta hinted at indescribable depths of wickedness among some of the Hindus there.[112] At the end of the century a missionary bishop was still laying it down that 'The Hindu is inherently untruthful and lacks moral courage'.[113] This was to ignore very much, including all the changes under way in the past hundred years; and the more condemnatory the missionaries grew, the fewer converts they were likely to win.

As the vision of a Christian India faded, effort was attracted more into social service, educational and medical work. This was invaluable, but it too brought Indians before the foreign eye in an unfavourable light. Panjabis were far from being the feeble shiftless creatures that 'inhabitants of Eastern lands are supposed to be', a Scottish Church mission allowed, but they were scandalously 'indifferent and apathetic' about health, or their children's welfare; 'they are essentially a dirty people, and have a great abhorrence of soap and water'.[114] India's faults, like Cassius's, were set in a notebook, learned and conned by rote, to cast into its teeth; there was less alertness to faults of the imperial power, whose shelter alone made it possible for missionaries to preach at all. Some foreign workers may have been more sensitive to these British failings, but were not in a position to call attention to them; German Lutherans, for instance, living among the abjectly poor and sharing their poverty in order to reach their hearts,[115] in a way that no British family could respectably do. It may have helped them with the Indians to be known as not British. Carey had been a radical, but preoccupied with evils of Indian society; his successors took no great part in protests against conditions on British-owned plantations or in British-protected States. The other clergy, those of the official establishment, of course took for granted that with statues of Queen Victoria on every hand things must be as well as in this bad land they could be.

Where all this was leading in the later years can be seen epitomized in an Englishman still remembered in Kashmir for his fifty years' work there as pioneer of modern schools, Canon Tyndale-Biscoe. The contrast could hardly be more complete between Carey the shoemaker and this country gentleman who went out a century later. He personified what was coming to

be called 'muscular Christianity', and made little distinction
between the superiority of his religion and that of his nation or
race. A firm upholder of all constituted authority, he had no
sympathy with Indian nationalism, and not much with the un-
rest of the Muslim majority in Kashmir, though he could not
help seeing how it was tyrannized over by the Hindu prince
and selfish Hindu minority to whom British policy had abandoned the Valley. Modern schools would benefit directly only
the well-off minority, and cynical Englishmen told Tyndale-
Biscoe that it was a mistake to teach them, because 'an educated thief is more dangerous than an uneducated one'.[116] It was a
sombre Kashmir that he went into, where ten thousand coolies
were yearly conscripted to carry supplies over the 'death road'
to Gilgit in the far north, and where an official could be seen
torturing extra money out of a peasant with iron hand-
squeezers.[117] But his faith in God and the British Raj, under
whose joint countenance these enormities took place, never
wavered. He put them down to the foulness of human nature,
and his remedy was to fashion a new breed of MEN (he writes
the word often in capitals), by character-building discipline and
manly sports, a small devoted band ready like Arthur's Knights
'to set wrong right, to defend the weak against the oppressor;
in short, knight-errantry'.[118]

Such a man would see the bad side of Indian life more clearly
than the good, and be repelled most of all by the ill-treatment
he saw of women and of animals. Perhaps men of all nations
are stung most keenly by criticism of their behaviour to their
women, and an old judge once lost his temper with Tyndale-
Biscoe and retorted that women were worse off in England.[119]
He had not been there, or he might have produced cogent evidence about how mill-hands and match-girls fared. The Canon
could hardly know much about them. His relatives were Army
and Navy men, and visits to other parts of the empire made
him glow with pride. 'Thank God for the British Navy!' A
brother of his had been in it as a midshipman, and helped to
chase Arab slave-dealers: he then settled in Rhodesia, dug for
gold, fought the Matabele and the Mashona, and 'developed a
great affection for the African'.[120]

At bottom Tyndale-Biscoe's was a pessimistic philosophy;

and pessimism about India as a land too overburdened by its past for any regeneration, afflicted by woes that British rule could do no more than put some check on, was deepening among Englishmen of the more conscientious kind in the later years of the Raj. They were seldom aware of the contradictions between imperial self-interest and good intentions, but nationalism was putting them on the defensive. Those who were really trying to plough a small furrow in a land that seemed all stones and misery toiled on doggedly, in something like the spirit preached there ages before by the Gita, devotion to duty without thought of success or reward.[121]

One Indian reaction to Christian or Western strictures was to fall back on the claim of an inborn gift of spirituality, above vulgar material concerns. It supplied an excuse for lack of material achievement, and, to conservatives, for neglect of social reform. This morbid reaction helped to give Europe its semi-comic picture of the Hindu perpetually gazing at his own navel or climbing up a magic rope. More positively Christian pressure, which converted few Hindus or Muslims, led many to increase their efforts to put their own religious houses in order. On one side this revivalism meant an ominous growth of fanaticism; more healthily it gave new life to traditional charities, and colleges and hospitals were founded in emulation of those run by the missions. It even inspired Hinduism to renew its own activity abroad, after an interval of many ages. Vivekananda visited England in 1895 and 1896, travelled in Europe, and before his death in 1902 made neo-Hindu philosophy known there and in America.[122] Western life, he once said, was gay on the outside, tragic within: Eastern life gloomy on the outside, inwardly carefree because it knew the universe to be only a divine plaything.[123] He was himself half-Western, in being social worker and reformer as well as saint; he was also a patriot, who, as his English disciple and biographer Sister Nivedita records, had a struggle to reconcile his mysticism with 'his love of his country and his resentment of her suffering'.[124]

By that time Christian certainties, in many of the less muscular minds, were growing blurred, partly through finding themselves confronted with the certainties of other faiths. A few Europeans in India had always felt the attraction of its philosophy; not always laudably, as in the case of the man who was angry with Carey for attacking suttee and wanted to see this upstart rolled in the dust by some learned – and aristocratic – Brahmin.[125] A Colonel Oswald who was out with a Highland regiment took up with some Brahmins and turned vegetarian, but subsequently joined the French Revolution.[126] Sir George Everest, who was there from 1806 to 1844 and rose to be surveyor-general and give his name to a mountain, went out at the age of sixteen, got into close touch with Indians and their thinking, and came home at last convinced that Christianity had no truths except those common to all creeds.[127] His niece Mary Boole credited the Indian mind with an intuitive perception of mathematical as well as spiritual principles.[128] It was out of such notions that Theosophy arose. Some critics accused it of pandering to reaction by being too tolerant of Brahminism and by expecting India to be rejuvenated by its own ancient doctrines, destitute they maintained of any ethical sense, any message of righteousness. 'It is this,' said one, 'more than anything else, that keeps back the Hindus from attaining the place in the world that their intelligence and ability fit them to occupy.'[129]

Yet Theosophy in its curious way, strengthened by a number of women less tied (like the suffragettes) than their men to hidebound opinions, did provide a meeting-ground of East and West, political as well as moral, at a time when the two were so far apart that only a species of flying carpet could bring them together. The Labour Party growing in England before 1914 might have been expected to provide a more rational and effective contact; but on India, then and later, it had scarcely anything different from the older parties to say.[130] Mrs Boole's advice to India – to treat its British rulers as a set of noisy children, and ignore them except when they interfered with its sacred things[131] – was not very helpful; but Mrs Annie Besant was actually beginning to play a considerable part as a leader of the Indian national movement. She had been a feminist and a socialist for years before coming under the spell of Mme Blavatsky, the Russian adept initiated in Tibet, and was never completely carried off her Anglo-Saxon feet by the balloon of the higher mysteries.

Imperfect Sympathies

Indian philosophy, whatever its merits, and most Indian sculpture, painting and architecture, were very old; and Europeans were free to think of this country as one that, like Greece, had once been great but had long ceased to create. Some new stirrings of genius, in Urdu poetry or the Bengali novel, went unnoticed. Still, the same Forbes who wrote on Rajput history[132] was also in 1864 the first president of the Gujerati Sabha (Society), founded to promote the literature of the province and its study. In scholarship the work of the Asiatic Society went on, adorned by a line of distinguished orientalists. Not all Englishmen were philistines, and they left behind them a vast body of research into Indian history, geography, sociology, linguistics. By these investigations they were revealing India to itself, as well as to the world, giving Indians a tangible motherland to belong to in place of the shadowy Bharat of legend.

Indians were soon joining in the task, but here too there were obstacles to co-operation, especially in the field of history. Like the Muslim conquerors before them the British were bound to see Indian history from a standpoint of their own; and when Elliot a few years after the Mutiny planned his monumental collection of records it was avowedly with the design of showing Indian readers how barbarous and bloodstained their past was, and how fortunate they were to have been redeemed by Britain's intervention.[133] With the rise of nationalism his work was vehemently assailed as a falsification of Indian history, calculated to embitter Hindus against their former rulers, the Muslims.[134] National sentiment crystallized round opposite assertions of past grandeur and prosperity, sometimes as subjective and inaccurate as anything in the British version. Forced to seek support among the masses, nationalism was under the usual temptation to rely on emotion instead of on a programme of social reform for their benefit. There was even some turning away from the Western intellectual tradition because of its association with foreign rule. Spaniards in the same spirit had rejected the enlightenment carried into their country on Napoleon's bayonets.

No people is easily understood, and India had always been a separate world, hard for any outsider, Eastern or Western, to penetrate. It was a freakish destiny that brought it and England together. 'Of all Orientals,' wrote the censorious Burton, 'the most antipathetical companion to an Englishman is, I believe, an East Indian.'[135] Not all Britons felt this hostility, but nearly all felt the strangeness. 'Two races could scarcely be more alien from each other than the English and the Hindus,' said Seeley.[136] A temperamental affinity could be felt with the chivalrous Rajput, the sturdy Panjabi, the idol-hating Muslim; but these Indians were mentally the most stuck in the mud of the past, while the nimble-minded southerner, readiest for a jump into the present, seemed in all other ways the most un-European. G. O. Trevelyan saw more of Bengalis than of any others, and despaired of comprehending them. 'Their inner life still remains a sealed book to us.' To them, he conjectured, Britons must be a special race of demons, with an aptitude for fighting and administration, but 'foul and degraded' in their habits.[137] In Bombay about the same time an English newspaper warned its readers not to lose sight of 'the fact of our dense ignorance of the inner and instinctive feelings and modes of thought among large classes of the native community'.[138]

Of what Englishmen were to Indians born a generation later, much can be gleaned from the autobiography of Nirad Chaudhuri, among all modern Indians one of those most fully saturated with European ideas. Growing up in a village of eastern Bengal, he and his boyhood friends were aware of Britain as of something immeasurable, 'like the sky above our head'.[139] They took an intense interest in the Boer War, with minds divided between hope of British victory and defeat.[140] (A British sea-captain at Penang was told by way of a joke how loyally the Chinese there had felt during the war – 'pig-tailed, slit-eyed fellows talking of "we Britishers – our defeats – our successes"' – and commented briefly: 'D—d cheek.'[141]) A few years more and Chaudhuri's generation was feeling 'an immense elation' at the Japanese victory over Russia,[142] as Asians did wherever a national movement was alight. In Calcutta he saw Indian spectators habitually beaten and knocked about by the police when crowds flocked to gape at British military or naval displays.[143] In Tsarist Russia, with the same primitive exhibition of strength, spectators at a coronation would be thrashed or ridden down by the Cossacks.[144] Indians knew less about Cossacks, and the English were chronically nervous about Russian propaganda – Tsarist, later Soviet – and how India would act when the long-expected Russian invasion came.

Indian habits often seemed, not to Englishmen alone, Indian oddity; and the educated class was awkwardly suspended between two worlds, at home in neither. Arnold Wilson as a young cadet, priding himself on getting on well with Persians and Arabs, was stumped by Indians. He tried to make friends with two on shipboard, who always wanted tea when everyone else was having coffee and were 'very self-conscious and rather apt to take offence at quite imaginary rebuffs'.[145] Collectively Indians had suffered too many real rebuffs, and the consciousness of not being masters in their own country was festering. A few individuals struck up friendships, of an odd sort as often as not, like the one between E. M. Forster, an exceptional Englishman only temporarily in India, and the eccentric little Maharaja whose private secretary he became – nominally an ally, not a subject, of the Raj. Forster was in India shortly before the Great War, and again shortly after. Writing home in 1921 he lamented that England was having to pay now for 'the insolence of Englishmen *and* Englishwomen out here in the past ... English manners out here have improved wonderfully in the last eight years. Some people are frightened, others seem really to have undergone a change of heart. But it's too late.'[146]

NOTES

1. *Parties and Pleasures. The Diaries of Helen Graham 1823–1826*, ed. J. Irvine (Edinburgh, 1957), p. 212.

2. G. Smith, *The Life of William Carey* (1909), p. 45.

3. A. F. Tytler, *Considerations on the Present Political State of India* (1815), Vol. 1, p. 270.

4. Preface by Raymond in 1789 to his translation of the *Seir-Mutaqherin* of Ghulam Husain Khan (Calcutta, n.d. (1903)).

5. H. Boyd, *The Indian Observer* (1798), p. 365.

6. T. B. Macaulay, 'Warren Hastings', in *Critical and Historical Essays* (8th edn, Edinburgh, 1854), Vol. 3, pp. 235–7.

7. W. M. Thackeray, *The Four Georges* (1855): 'George the Third', para. 2.

8. A. N. Barat, *The Bengal Native Infantry* (Calcutta, 1962), p. 247.

9. See on this N. C. Chaudhuri, *The Autobiography of an Unknown Indian* (1951), Book II, Chapter 4.

10. E. J. Trelawney,*The Adventures of a Younger Son* (1831), p.57 (World's Classics edn).

11. *Rights of Man* (Part 2, 1792), p. 146 (ed. H. B. Bonner, 1907).

12. G. Smith, op. cit., p. 60. A Briton home from Bengal described its people as 'Hottentots' but without their virtues (*The Asiatic Journal*, Vol. 1, 1816, pp. 537–9).

13. *Selections from Indian Journals*, Vol. 2, *Calcutta Journal*, 1820 (Calcutta, 1965), pp. 363–4.

14. J. Capper, *The Three Presidencies of India* (1853), p. 474. The habit of defending British rule by painting India in the darkest colours showed itself strongly again in the last days of the Raj; see K. Mayo, *Mother India* (1927), and B. Nichols, *Verdict on India* (1944).

15. See Jules Verne's *Around the World in Eighty Days* (1872), Chapter 14, where a rajah's widow is rescued by the resourceful Frenchman, Passepartout.

16. Spaniards boasted of having cured their Indians of human sacrifice, idolatry, sodomy, etc. See e.g. L. Hanke, 'More Heat and some Light on ... the Conquest of America', in *Hispanic American Historical Review* (Vol. XLIV, No. 3, August 1964), pp. 296–7.

17. On the Incas see T. J. Hutchinson, *Two Years in Peru* (1873), Vol. 2, p. 224, citing Garcilaso; on the Romans, B. H. Warmington, *Carthage* (Penguin edn, 1964), p. 25.

18. Maulana A. K. Azad, *India Wins Freedom* (Bombay, 1959), p. 107.

19. Letter of 7 December 1834, in Sir G. O. Trevelyan, *Life and Letters of Lord Macaulay* (1876), Chapter 6.

20. *Selections from Indian Journals*, Vol. 2, p. 95 and pp. 85 ff.

21. John Marshall's Notes on India (1670): Harleian MS.4,254, British Museum.

22. These vacillations in one province are described in K. Ballhatchet, *Social Policy and Social Change in Western India 1817–1830* (Oxford, 1957).

23. Memorandum with Dr H. Prideaux to Archbishop of Canterbury, 27 March 1665, in S. A. Khan, *Sources for the History of British India in the Seventeenth Century* (Oxford, 1926), pp. 324–6.

24. G. Smith, op. cit., pp. 78, 145, etc.

25. ibid., p. 234.

26. *The Asiatic Journal*, Vol. 1, pp. 111–13.

27. ibid., p. 417.

28. H. Boyd, op. cit., p. 295.

29. Extract in *The Asiatic Annual Register*, Vol. 7 (1805). The prize of £100 had been offered by a clergyman at Calcutta.

30. See Iqbal Singh, *Rammohun Roy* (1958).

31. J. C. Ghosh, *Bengali Literature* (Oxford, 1948), p. 100.

32. J. M. S. Baljon, *The Reforms and Religious Ideas of Sir Sayyid Ahmad Khan* (3rd edn, Lahore, 1964), pp. 53–4.

33. J. C. Ghosh, op. cit., p. 113.

34. Amit Sen, *Notes on the Bengal Renaissance* (Bombay, 1946), pp. 155 ff.

35. R. H. Cholmondeley, *The Heber Letters 1783–1832* (1950), p. 334.

36. Emily Eden, *Up the Country* (1866), pp. 122–3 (ed. E. Thompson, Oxford, 1937). A. Barat speaks of the 'gradual, yet marked worsening in the relationship between the European officers and their sepoys over the period of 1796 to 1852' (op. cit., p. 79).

37. A. Barat, op. cit., pp. 75 ff.

38. *Leaves from the Journal of a Subaltern* (Edinburgh, 1849), pp. 25–6, 140, etc.

39. E. Eden, op. cit., p. 76.

40. L. J. Trotter, *The Bayard of India* (1909), p. 38.

41. A. L. Basham, *The Wonder that was India* (Indian edn., Bombay, 1963), p. 481.

42. J. Heiton, *The Castes of Edinburgh* (Edinburgh, 1859). Chapter 12 is on 'Our Retired Indians'. 'With no high caste originally of their own (we admit exceptions), they have gone to get one among a people of castes' (p. 159).

43. Like the genteel London gathering 'Of highest caste – the Brahmins of the ton', in Byron's *Don Juan*, Canto 13, stanza 83. The late Mrs Subbarayan told me an anecdote of Ramsay MacDonald when premier saying to her at a dinner that his son was 'engaged to a Brahmin'.

44. *Fifth Report from the Select Committee on the Affairs of the East India Company* (1812), Vol. 1, pp. 706–7.

45. cf. *Patrick Geddes in India*, ed. J. Tyrwhitt (1947). pp. 19–21.

46. A. F. Tytler, op. cit., Vol. 1, p. xv.

47. Major-General Sir W. H. Sleeman, *Journey through the Kingdom of Oude in 1849–50* (1858), p. xxxiv.

48. W. Knighton, *The Private Life of an Eastern King* (1855), p. 122 (ed. S. B. Smith, Oxford, 1921).

49. *Fifth Report*, Vol. 1, pp. 758, 769.

50. J. W. Kaye, *The Life and Correspondence of Major-General Sir John Malcolm* (1856), Vol. 1, pp. 95–7, 102. It is noteworthy that the *Life* appeared one year before the Mutiny.

51. Sir J. Malcolm, *The Political History of India from 1784 to 1823* (1826), Vol. 2, App. 8.

52. Sir J. Malcolm, *The Government of India* (1833), p. 57.

53. ibid., p. 163.

54. W. Knighton, op. cit.

55. 'The Rural Population of Bengal', in *Calcutta Review*, Vol. 1 (3rd edn, Calcutta, 1846), pp. 189–91.

56. J. Capper, op. cit., p. 478.

57. R. F. Burton, *A Pilgrimage to Al-Madinah and Meccah* (1855), Vol. 1, pp. xii, 37–40 (Bohn Library edn).

58. J. W. Kaye, *History of the Sepoy War* in India (1865), Vol. 1, p. 565.

59. *Competition Wallah* (2nd edn, 1866), pp. 244–5; cf. pp. 342 ff. See also R. C. Majumdar, *The Sepoy Mutiny and the Revolt of 1857* (2nd edn, Calcutta, 1963), Book II, Chapter 5 : 'Atrocities'.

60. See P. C. Joshi, 'Folk Songs on 1857', in *Rebellion 1857*, ed. P. C. Joshi (Delhi, 1957), pp. 271 ff.

61. H. T. Lambrick, *John Jacob of Jacobabad* (1960), p. 346.

62. G. O. Trevelyan, op. cit., pp. 124, 238, 240.

63. Article of 4 September 1857, in Karl Marx and Friedrich Engels, *The First Indian War of Independence 1857–1859* (Moscow edn, 1959), p. 93.

64. Captain G. F. Atkinson, *'Curry and Rice'* (3rd edn, n.d.), 5th sketch.

65. G. O. Trevelyan, op. cit., p. 218.

66. See B. Ghose, 'Bengali Intelligentsia and the Revolt', in P. C. Joshi, op. cit., pp. 119 ff.; and S. B. Chaudhuri, *Theories of the Indian Mutiny 1857–59* (Calcutta, 1965), pp. 120 ff.

67. M.R.Gubbins, *An Account of the Mutinies in Oudh* (1858), p. 84.

68. *A Voice from India. An Appeal . . . by the Khojahs of Bombay . . .*, by a Native of Bombay (1864).

69. 'F. Anstey', *Baboo Jabberjee, B.A.* (1897).

70. Lingam Lakshmaji Pantlu Garu, *The Social Status of the Hindus* (Benares, 1866), pp. 20, 35, 28.

71. G. O. Trevelyan, op. cit., p. 49.

72. ibid., p. 218.

73. ibid., p. 221.

74. ibid., pp. 50 ff.

75. ibid., p. 331.

76. Sarat Chandra Das. See his *Narrative of a Journey to*

Lhasa in 1881–82 (Calcutta, 1885), and the edition by W. W. Rock-hill (1902); and my article on 'India, China and Tibet in 1885–86', in *Journal of the Greater India Society*, Vol. XIV (1955).

77. See on this period Hira Lal Singh, *Problems and Policies of the British in India 1885–1898* (Bombay, 1963).

78. R. C. Dutt, cited in I. M. Reisner and N. M. Goldberg (ed.), *Tilak and the Struggle for Indian Freedom* (Indian edn, Delhi, 1966), pp. 260–61.

79. J. M. S. Baljon, op. cit., p. 71. For some less formal Muslim Indian impressions of the British and of Europe, see M. Mujeeb, *The Indian Muslims* (1967), pp. 491 ff.

80. I was told this by Colonel Prabjinder Singh, an old student whom I had the pleasure of meeting again in 1965. On the rebuilding of the army after 1857 cf. F. G. Hutchins, *The Illusion of Permanence. British Imperialism in India* (Princeton, 1967), pp. 176 ff.

81. D. Clouston, *From the Orcades to Ind* (Edinburgh, 1936), p. 21.

82. Somerset Maugham, *A Writer's Notebook* (1949), pp. 264–5 (Penguin edn).

83. I have failed to trace this story, and can only say that Kipling either wrote it or ought to have written it.

84. J. R. Seeley, *The Expansion of England* (1883), p. 342 (2nd edn, 1895).

85. Sir C. W. Dilke and S. Wilkinson, *Imperial Defence* (revised edn, 1897), p. 80.

86. Bithia Mary Croker, *In Old Madras* (1913), p. 11 (Tauchnitz edn).

87. Mrs Meer Hassan Ali, *Observations on the Mussulmans of India* (1832). She met her husband in England, and returned there after twelve years in India.

88. cf. the degraded status of the two Eurasians in George Orwell's novel, *Burmese Days* (1934), Chapter 10.

89. See e.g. A. F. Tytler, op. cit., Vol. 1, p. 296. The idea is luridly developed in K. Mayo, op. cit.

90. Somerset Maugham, op. cit., pp. 255–6.

91. Sudhir Ghosh, *Gandhi's Emissary* (1967), p. 69.

92. G. O. Trevelyan, op. cit., p. 179.

93. J. W. Sherer, *Havelock's March on Cawnpore* (1857), pp. 108, 151–2 (Nelson edn, n.d.).

94. A reminiscence of my friend Dr Nazir Ahmad of Lahore.

95. Mulk Raj Anand, *The Untouchable* (1935).

96. A. F. Tytler, op. cit., Vol. 2, p. 351.

97. R. Reynolds, *The White Sahibs in India* (1937), p. 173 and n. 3.

98. Report of Select Committee on *Progress and Prospects* ... of *European Colonization and Settlement in India* (1859) p. iii.

99. G. O. Trevelyan, op. cit., p. viii.

100. ibid., pp. 263, 255. cf. 256, on 'a Reign of Terror' directed by some of these 'low Europeans' in a big town.

101. ibid., pp. 349–50; cf. the brutal episode of which Trevelyan was a witness, p. 352.

102. ibid., p. vii.

103. ibid., p. 265.

104. ibid, pp. 365–6.

105. S. K. Bose, *Capital and Labour in the Indian Tea Industry* (Bombay, 1954), p. 72.

106. Cited ibid., p. 89.

107. Report of the Labour Committee, 1939.

108. A. T. Quiller-Couch, *Hetty Wesley* (1903), Prologues to Book I and Book III.

109. Editorial, January 1858. I owe this reference to my colleague Mr W. H. Marwick, a member of the Society of Friends and a student of its history. On Quaker interest in India in that epoch see J. H. Bell, *British Folks and British India Fifty Years Ago* (Manchester, n.d.).

110. Mrs Weitbrecht, *Missionary Sketches in North India* (1858), p. 401.

111. J. Smith, *The Missionary's Appeal to British Christians on behalf of Southern India* (1841), pp. 149, 153.

112. J. Mullens, Foreign Secretary of the London Missionary Society, *London and Calcutta Compared* ... (1868), p. 53.

113. H. H. Montgomery, *Foreign Missions* (1902), p. 35.

114. Rev. J. F. W. Youngson, *Forty Years of the Panjab Mission of the Church of Scotland 1855–1895* (Edinburgh 1896), pp. 18, 275–6.

115. G. O. Trevelyan, op. cit., pp. 296–7.

116. *Tyndale-Biscoe of Kashmir. An Autobiography* (n.d.), p. 79.

117. ibid., pp. 126, 255–6.

118. ibid., p. 240.

119. ibid., p. 119.

120. ibid., pp. 250–51.

121. Like Alden, in E. Thompson's novel *An Indian Day* (1927), p. 247 (Penguin edn).

122. See the collection of lectures given by him on his return from the West: *From Colombo to Almora*, ed. F. H. Müller (Madras, 1897).

123. Sister Nivedita (Margaret E. Noble), *The Master as I saw him* (1910), p. 139 (4th edn, 1930).

124. ibid., p. 59. The temple dedicated to Vivekananda is one of

78 India

the sights of Calcutta today, and was designed architecturally to symbolize the unity of religions.

125. G. Smith, op. cit., pp. 250–51.

126. J. A. C. Sykes, *France in Eighteen Hundred and Two* (1906), pp. 70–71.

127. Mary Everest Boole (Sir George Everest's niece), *The Psychologic Aspect of Imperialism* (1911), pp. 16–17.

128. ibid., p. 5, etc.

129. E. S. Oakley, *Holy Himalaya* (Edinburgh, 1905), p. 12.

130. See G. Fischer, *Le parti travailliste et la décolonisation de l'Inde* (Paris, 1966), and my article on this work in *New Left Review* (London), No. 42, 1967.

131. Mrs Boole, op. cit., p. 36.

132. A. K. Forbes, author of *Ras Mala*, on the history of Gujerat (1856).

133. See Sir H. M. Elliot's Preface to *India's History as told by its own Historians*, ed. J. Dowson, Vol. 1 (1867).

134. For a balanced view of this see S. H. Hodivala, *Studies in Indo-Muslim History* (Bombay, 1939), Preface.

135. R. F. Burton, op. cit., Vol. 1, p. 37.

136. J. R. Seeley, op. cit., p. 213.

137. G. O. Trevelyan, op. cit., pp. 345, 347.

138. *Bombay Times and Standard*, 9 May 1861, cited in *A Voice from India* (see note 68).

139. N. C. Chaudhuri, op. cit. (Indian edn, Bombay, 1964), pp. 100–101.

140. ibid., p. 108.

141. J. J. Abraham, *The Surgeon's Log. Impressions of the Far East* (1911), p. 88 (18th edn, 1933).

142. N. C. Chaudhuri, op. cit., p. 107.

143. ibid., pp. 297, 313.

144. M. K. Waddington, *Letters of a Diplomat's Wife, 1883–1900* (1903), letter from Moscow, 22 May 1883.

145. Sir A. Wilson, *S.W. Persia* (1942), p. 14.

146. E. M. Forster, *The Hill of Devi* (Penguin edn, 1965), p. 153.

3. OTHER COLONIES IN ASIA

The British in Ceylon

Ceylon came to Britain at third hand; the Portuguese and then the Dutch had settlements on the coast, which were taken over during the wars of 1793–1814. A Crown Colony was organized in 1801, and occupation was extended from the coast over the whole country: in this and other ways Ceylon evolved like British India, but more rapidly because it was smaller and had been brought under European influence earlier. The ruler of the old kingdom of Kandy, now seized, was accused of being a tyrant; a stock pretext, which even to some Europeans looked 'ridiculous', on a par with the hackneyed argument that we must 'show our spirit'.[1] A revolt in 1817–18 in protest against the annexation was something like a miniature 1857.

Plantations, secondary in India, here quickly came to dominate the economy: first coffee-growing, later tea. Ceylon's availability coincided with the crippling of planters' profits in the West Indies by the abolition of slavery: 'men's attention was then turned from West to East'.[2] From the late 1830s a boom was in full swing, and drawing speculators like a gold-rush. Many of these were, as a governor, Lord Torrington, complained, 'of the very *worst* class of Englishmen', bound to 'lower and degrade our *caste* and character in the eyes of the natives'.[3] Evidently Anglo-Indian notions were filtering into Ceylon, in spite of its separate political status. Besides the fortune-hunters from outside, officials and judges and chaplains were neglecting their duties to get rich quicker by taking up shares of the lands granted away to planters. Most of these were forest lands in the hilly interior; all the same Sinhalese feeling was antagonized, and in 1848 this and other grievances led to an agitation and some minor disorder. Demoralized officials were thrown into a panic, and harsh repression followed.[4] This, however, led to a parliamentary inquiry, and some improvement. Much was due to an Irishman, Christopher Elliott.

one of that small number of really valuable European settlers who went to the colonies. He was a radical who had led a campaign for representative government in Ceylon, and in 1848 championed the popular cause. He had friends in London who could raise questions.[5]

Thereafter several factors made for easier relations in Ceylon than in India, as a result of which to this day an educated Indian going to Ceylon finds Europeans less standoffish, more part of local society, than he has known them at home.[6] There was no North-West Frontier, no Russian menace, and no large contingent of military men with their heavy-dragoon mentality. Buddhism was an easier religion to get on with amicably than either Hinduism or Islam. There was also a Christian community of Eurasians, a legacy of the Portuguese and Dutch, which retained a better status than the similar one in India, and has grown into one of the most thoroughly westernized communities in Asia. To some extent it formed a link between Europeans and Sinhalese. In addition there was a minority of Tamils, immigrants of ancient date from south India. A minority is always likely to be more adaptable to new ideas and methods, and Tamils were readier than Sinhalese to pick up English and therefore came – like Bengalis in India – to occupy a big proportion of the lower posts in government service. Some even became Christians. Their dependability helped to smooth the way for the rulers, at the cost of worsening relations between them and the majority community, to the detriment of independent Ceylon later on.

A second and quite distinct class of Tamil immigrants was coming in by 1850. Peasants with land of their own had no desire to work on the plantations, which like those of Assam had to import coolie labour from outside. By the end of the period over half a million had come, about one seventh of the island's population. An isolated, self-contained area like Ceylon or Assam was ideal for the development of the plantation system, as revolutionary an innovation in Asia as industrial capitalism in Europe, and requiring a still stronger element of compulsion to get it going and keep it going. A captive workforce was under the thumb of employers virtually identical with government and police. As in Assam, inquiry into what was happening on the plantations was belated. In 1917 it was discovered that nearly all the workers were in a chronic state of indebtedness, though the village headmen and other contractors who supplied them did well.

Servants and labourers too were often Indian rather than Sinhalese; it was a rough sort of Tamil that Englishmen learned to speak, in the imperative mood to which most European speaking of Asian languages has been confined. They might come to feel a liking for these useful and unpretentious folk; Sinhalese by comparison were peasants living their own lives, or elegant dawdlers with a turn for the arts and for the politics and speechifying of nationalism that finally spread from India into this quiet haven.

The British in Burma

'The expedition to Rangoon is accused of having acted with great severity,' Sir Charles Grey wrote from Madras during the first war between Britain and Burma in 1824–5, 'and it is certain that the whole population have the greatest horror of us.'[8] Resistance was unexpectedly stiff, and Rangoon and Lower Burma were not occupied until the next war in 1853. Then a new great port, one of the more attractive blendings of eastern and western life, grew up round the towering gold Shwedagon Pagoda, symbol of a continuing Burmese tradition. Rangoon began to supplant the old-world capital at Ava, and then near-by Mandalay, as the centre of Burmese life and culture, including its flourishing drama; audiences took a nostalgic pleasure in plays about free Burma.[9]

Timber and ruby interests, and the motive of forestalling the French, now established in Vietnam, combined to bring about the annexation of Upper Burma at the end of 1885. Annexations at this date, and in face of European rivals, had to be explained and justified rather more carefully than in previous epochs; in fact this culminating stage of imperialism was one of the forcing-houses of modern propaganda, the science of blackening enemies and whitewashing friends, before it reached full growth inside Europe in 1914–18. King Theebaw was portrayed, more elaborately than the King of Kandy in 1815, as a most bloodthirsty and unbearable despot. The Oriental tyrant was a familiar stereotype by now, with which any Asian ruler could be identified when it was desired to get rid of him instead of to make use of him. The Black Hole of Calcutta had joined the battle of Hastings as one of the few titbits of history that all Britons knew. Government at Mandalay was purely arbitrary, said the *Imperial Gazetteer* of India in a very captious account of Upper Burma.[10] Theebaw inflamed a native savagery with strong potations, said another English writer. 'A monster, reminding us of Nero or Caligula, had appeared on the throne of the Golden Foot.'[11] It was stated in Parliament that six thousand citizens of Rangoon had petitioned for intervention.[12]

A missionary who knew Theebaw as a schoolboy recalled him as 'a quiet, inoffensive, docile lad',[13] and Fielding Hall in his celebrated book on Burma was to sum him up as 'young, incapable, kind-hearted': his administration was to be sure very bad, but then it affected most of the country very little.[14] However, in 1885 indignation at his crimes, real or imaginary, precluded any policy of keeping a puppet monarchy. Commissioner Bernard, who would have liked a protectorate, was accused of 'an extraordinary predilection for Burman ideas and sentiments', unworthy of an Englishman.[15] Mandalay was taken with ease, and a Lower Burman who went there to see how people felt about the change found them not too hostile, though uneasy at the prospect of their country being flooded, as Lower Burma already was, with Indian immigrants.[16] Britons were jubilant. The haughtiest conqueror has moods of regret that he is not loved, and Burma was hugged as a consolation for India. 'This absolute conviction that the Burmans are eager to be annexed,' one enthusiast wrote, 'is exhilarating ... at last we have discovered a reasonable and reasoning population which has an enlightened sense of their own interests.'[17]

It was an amiable hope that sprang eternal in the empire-builder's breast. But though the capital might submit, in the countryside a guerrilla resistance broke out and lasted for years. The common man has often proved more patriotic than the upper classes in face of foreign invasion, in modern Asia as in Spain in 1808–14 or France in 1940–45. People did not after all seem to have been so unhappy under their old régime, an officer was sorry to find, 'and gave no evidence of rejoicing at our coming'.[18] The enthusiast soon had second thoughts; the campaign was having a brutalizing effect on the British troops, and the government at home had to act to restrain excesses. 'One grows sceptical as to the tranquillizing effect of military executions.'[19] He sought comfort in the idea that those resisting were not patriots but *dacoits* or brigands, taking advantage of the confusion. Others who recognized 'some faint tinge of patriotism' in the opposition convinced themselves that it was quickly degenerating into mere anarchy.[20] The army professed to be confining its punitive operations to bandits and their friends – 'villages which harboured them were destroyed, cattle were carried off and crops impounded'.[21] These were elastic terms of reference. Outlaws were an established part of society in all this area of the world, and their adventurous habits qualified them to make the sort of contribution that Spain's contrabandists made against Napoleon. Even from a merely professional point of view they had reason to prefer the old lax ways to rigid European control. Fielding Hall looked back on the struggle as a genuinely national movement of the common people, 'a passion of insurrection'.[22]

By 1910 or so there was a national movement of more sophisticated type, hastened by the proximity of India; but it did not prevent relations, especially with Burmans of the higher classes who had taken less part in the resistance, from acquiring a more free and easy tone than in India. This came about partly because Burmans were more free and easy among themselves, unburdened with caste distinctions. Buddhism as in Ceylon had helped to mould an amiable national character. It did not oblige women to be kept in seclusion, and they won Western appreciation from the first. One of the Border Regiment's souvenirs of the occupation campaign was a big photograph of a bevy of 'Burmese Dancing Girls', too faded alas for their charms to be recognizable today.[23] There is a story of the German Crown Prince on a visit to India scandalizing his hosts by missing a banquet to keep a rendezvous with a Burmese princess.[24]

By contrast with the misery that was and is India's most eye-catching feature, Burma with its surplus of rice had a comfortable air; it was 'the difference between simplicity and squalor', someone remarked.[25] And as in Ceylon, Indian immigration made other contrasts more visible. This was not a plantation economy, but one of small peasant rice-fields, and here Indians formed in general not a rural proletariat but a middle class of retailers and moneylenders: a middle class of the new hybrid kind that grew up in the colonies, combining Asian usury and Western property-law to squeeze profits out of unsuspicious cultivators. Necessary as some of their functions were, like those of Jews in old Europe, they were heartily disliked by the Burmese and despised by the British. Relations between these two benefited by Europeans being less obnoxious to Burmans than Indians were.

Educated Burmese could get into government service, or took refuge in their arts, especially the art of living, or of *dolce far niente*. And the example was contagious. Englishmen began to discover that in Burma one could enjoy leisure, not merely kill time when off duty. They had been in the habit of denouncing Burmese laziness, but the time came when some of them began to think it sensible and refreshing. They themselves were supposed to love freedom, but to a Burman the life of industrial Britain would seem mere slavery. He was 'absolutely enamoured of freedom'.[26] Hall put highest among many attractive qualities his 'light-heartedness' and 'tolerance', his not wanting to meddle with anyone else's inclinations.[27] To men from the grimly earnest West it was a revelation to see human beings still able to enjoy the passing moment, free from care or ambition. It appealed the more because the West itself was changing, empire-building mellowing into coupon-clipping, the craggy type of mid-Victorian brought up on Samuel Smiles and Carlyle into a contemporary, a cousin however many times removed, of Wilde and Beardsley.

There was a medley of small non-Burman nationalities, also with attractive qualities. Shan hillmen were described as generous, open-hearted folk. 'They certainly possess consciences' (a virtue clearly not attributed to all Asians), and 'a refinement of their own'.[28] Missionaries took to these hillmen, whose prim-

itive cults or very diluted Buddhism were less resistant to conversion than the great religions of the East always were. These
backward tribes, as in India the lowest castes, provided the
bulk of converts, Karens the greatest number. Along with
Christianity they could adopt in a generation a modern outlook
which they might feel put them ahead of the plainsmen, formerly their masters – though Burma had once been part of a
Shan empire. Since independence the country has been plagued
by a running quarrel between Rangoon and the separatist
Karens, as India has by a quarrel between Delhi and the Nagas
and other Christianized hill-folk of neighbouring Assam.

The British in Malaya

Sir Stamford Raffles, who started Singapore on its way in 1819,
designed it to be a challenge to the narrow selfish exclusivism
of the Dutch in Indonesia, a testimony to Britain's new-found
faith in free trade as the bringer of mutual understanding, as
well as prosperity, to the world. He took a warm interest in the
peoples among whom he was thrown, and was remembered as
a champion of native rights.

Singapore had to gather a population, and was bound to have
a great future, an observer wrote in 1837, because it lay 'in the
centre of myriads of active nations'.[29] The West was setting up
a variety of melting-pots in Asia, not all of which melted very
successfully. But settlers came to Singapore chiefly from China.
Most of them were southerners, not much in love with their
own government, who brought with them a mistrustful attitude, and their notorious Secret Societies. These both gave them
protection and exposed them and others to racketeering. In
Siam, where the Societies also spread, it was reported that 'the
Government appears to be powerless against them'.[30] At Singapore inscrutable Celestial and inscrutable Englishman were
brought face to face, each trying to out-stare the other. Both
understood business, and prosperity grew, if not mutual understanding, at least for the minority of Chinese who became rich
and for the British residents whose showy carriages and expensive style of living struck visitors: no wonder they were

always complaining that fortunes were harder to make than they used to be.[31]

Before long they wanted more room, and the long narrow Malay peninsula hanging down towards them from the north was temptingly close. Two of its nearest harbours, Malacca and Penang, were added to Singapore to form the Straits Settlements, which became a separate Crown Colony in 1867 and promptly developed a small local imperialism of their own, embarrassing at times to the home government. This had the backing of wealthy Chinese citizens, and two great merchants, Kim Chin and Whampoo, helped to convince a new governor from Australia, Sir Andrew Clarke, that expansion was the right policy.[32]

As late as 1874 no maps or handbooks of the peninsula existed.[33] Current notions about Malays were drawn chiefly from their depredations in the Archipelago. Some of them, of the piratical sort, had been messmates of Trelawney when he was in these waters early in the century, and played their part in the wild scenes of rapine and buccaneering and slave-dealing that fill his pages. Malays had already won the reputation of being 'the most fierce, treacherous, ignorant, and inflexible of barbarians'. He himself thought better of them: they were 'true to their words, generous to prodigality, and of invincible courage' – a chivalrous race, 'devoted to war, and to its inseparable accompaniment, women'.[34] Decades later it was necessary to contradict reports that all Malays were pirates or savages, forever running amuck and knifing one another.[35] Their homeland was depicted as being in a frightful condition of misrule or chaos, the mass of its cultivators in a state of slavery. Debt-slavery was indeed prevalent, here and in Siam, and the British public had learned to react sharply to the word, little as the reality might differ from indentured labour on a British plantation.

Government consisted of petty rulers, who dignified themselves with preposterous titles like 'Sultan of China', and whose business consisted of petty wars with each other. What they manifestly stood in need of was civilizing British influence. The Maharaja of Johore, closest to Singapore, felt it early, and could be described as quite Anglicized.[36] 'It may be taken for granted,' someone wrote, 'that amongst the more enlightened Malays there is a disposition to welcome the English.'[37] Since the only satisfactory test of enlightenment was a disposition to welcome the English, his dictum could not easily be disputed. Everything prescribed a policy of control through whatever rulers might prove amenable: geography and jungle, shortage of troops, the precedent of the Native States in India, and after 1885 the difficult pacification of Burma. It was to be effected through a Residency system, on Indian lines, and was initiated by the despatch of a Mr Birch in 1875 to the troubled State of Perak. Birch knew little Malay, but 'dashed into Perak like a Victorian rationalist schoolmaster', freeing slaves and interfering with feudal imposts right and left.[38] Naturally he was soon set on and killed, and a punitive expedition followed.

There were a few protests in England, some of them from men with a traditionalist respect, like Sir John Malcom's in India, for rulers and prescriptive rights – Clarke by contrast was or had been 'a strong radical'.[39] Sir P. Benson Maxwell published a pamphlet in 1878 that deserves a place in the record of dissent from the barbarism of civilization. 'English Governors in the East fall into a moral atmosphere which sadly distorts their mental vision,' he asserted.[40] Rival claimants to petty thrones in Malaya solicited British aid, and officials seemed really to believe in 'a divine mission to improve the Malays'. Public and Parliament never troubled to study what was happening. 'If a town is shelled in some distant land . . . or some hecatombs of natives are slaughtered, up we throw our hats and rend the air with cheers for the gallantry of our troops or tars . . . But nobody asks about the rights and wrongs of the matter.'[41]

Clarke himself in later years condemned 'useless, expensive, and demoralizing small wars', only serving to dazzle the public and win medals.[42] In Malaya no prolonged fighting was required. Rulers had much to gain from British support against their own disorderly vassals, and in this feudal society there was no danger of the popular resistance met with in more democratic Burma. Moreover, Burma was a nation, and Malaya, like most of the Islamic lands, was not. Swettenham, its outstanding English administrator, could claim that by 1900 'the friendship and active co-operation of the people themselves' had been secured.[43] This really meant the friendship of the Malay aristocracy, a class of similar stamp to the land-owners favoured or created by the British in India. The British had little need to interfere with ordinary Malays, because as in various other colonies the hard labour of development was shouldered by newcomers. But landlords had more incentive to rackrent tenants, and peasants had more facilities for becoming enmeshed in debts to Indian moneylenders and Chinese shopkeepers.[44]

Most Chinese started as indentured labourers, who were brought in mostly for the tin-mines, but astonished the other races, as they often did, by their resilience and versatility. South Indians were employed on the rubber plantations, and to some extent on public works. The Indian góvernment was understood to be keeping a fatherly eye on them; what probably gave them better protection was that in rapidly developing Malaya they, unlike the Assam tea-coolies, could run away from plantations and look for other work. Forty thousand 'deserted' in 1915 alone, which tells its own tale about conditions. The benefits of the new order – advertised as one of the most brilliant successes of colonialism[45] – were very unequally distributed, and it rested on a balance of races which as in all such conglomerate societies came to feel towards each other the hostility that elsewhere rival classes feel. After 1945 this would lead to the British partnership with the Malay aristocracy against the Chinese.

Within these limits an Englishman like Swettenham, who understood how much knowledge of and sympathy with a people are needed to reach its 'innermost heart',[46] could take a keen interest in Malay arts and ways of living. The curiosity Raffles had felt about the history and culture of this part of the world revived, and other Europeans, and soon Asians, joined in contributing to the miscellaneous stock that accumulated in the Journals of the Straits and Malayan branches of the Asiatic Society. Search for knowledge as well as profits was spilling out from British India into new realms.

Malays had spread far and wide over the Archipelago, carrying with them and carried on by their Islamic faith, and were

often to be met with as conquering groups levying tribute on
more primitive or less warlike peoples. In this situation both
the good and the bad qualities of a nobility of the sword, which
on the mainland marked the ruling class, were likely to be
common property among them. They had 'all the quiet ease
and dignity of the best-bred Europeans', the naturalist Wallace
observed during a lengthy stay in the Archipelago, along with
'a reckless cruelty and contempt of human life'; in intellect
they seemed 'rather deficient . . . incapable of anything but the
simplest combinations of ideas'.[47] These traits could be seen in
full flower in Borneo, where the Dyak aborigines were being
preyed on and pushed into the hilly interior by Malay coastal
squatters and their chiefs, headed by a sort of sultan.

Europeans sympathizing with the weaker side might well
feel that their interference was called for. Britain should see
itself as the chosen people in this part of Asia, urged one
writer.[48] Arguing in favour of a British establishment in Borneo,
another declared that 'The Malays, with proper management
may, in my opinion, be rendered a very superior race in many
respects to some of the natives of Hindostan.'[49] What a 'crown
of glory', George Borrow wrote, to 'carry the blessings of civilization and religion to barbarous, yet at the same time beautiful and romantic lands . . . Yet who has done so in these times?'
Only one man, he believed – Rajah Brooke.[50]

Undoubtedly Brooke stands out among the Europeans who
were adventuring alone through strange lands. First employed
in Borneo by the sultan against a Dyak rebellion, and rewarded
in 1841 with the principality of Sarawak in the north of the
island, he endeavoured to protect the Dyaks from oppression
by Malay robbers and Chinese traders. Disgusted by the
rapacity of the Malay chiefs and their followers, he thought
the simple Dyaks far the better people of the two. His naval
friend Keppel agreed with him in liking these hill-folk whom
the Malay rajahs looked on 'much in the same light as they
would a drove of oxen'.[51] Wallace stayed with Brooke during
1854–6, and saw that the Dyaks looked up to him as a supernatural being.[52]

Brooke himself was sometimes taxed with high-handedness
in dealing with natives, but his principle, which as a lone hand

unlike the juggernaut of empire he was free to adopt, was that they ought to be approached as equals. 'On this point,' he wrote, 'most Europeans are grossly wanting ... When we desire to improve and elevate a people, we must not begin by treating them as an inferior race; and yet this is too generally the style of our Indian rulers, with a few brilliant exceptions.'[53] Brooke ran into many problems, and all through the 1850s and until his death in 1868 he was trying to persuade the British government to assume responsibility for the defence of Sarawak, while respecting the rights of its people, by whose will he claimed to hold power. He would like to stay on as 'a friend and adviser of the Natives', he told the Colonial Office. After his death his nephew, striking what he may have judged a more persuasive note, took credit for having helped to turn these natives into 'quiet and obedient subjects'.[54] The British government boggled at the awkward precedent of treating a Briton as an autonomous ruler, and only in 1888 took charge of Sarawak foreign relations.

It felt no awkwardness about allowing a group of British investors to assume sovereign powers or impersonate the chosen people in the adjoining North Borneo territory. This was built up by a Chartered Company, much as the Indian empire had been. We have some graphic detail of the preliminary spadework through the eyes of one J. D. Northwood who had investments in Borneo. He arrived when a rebellion of the Murut tribe was being suppressed by a small mercenary force the Company had collected, one of a number of private armies of that epoch. It was 'a miscellaneous gathering of Asiatic ruffians of all kinds, officered by a few Europeans'. Paying his first call at Government House, the newcomer found some of the recruits, Dyak head-hunters, smoking Murut heads on the tennislawn. Proceeding to his plantation he discovered that hundreds of the coolies working on it had just died of fever. He was not there to look for any crown of glory, but this gave him pause. 'Dividends of one hundred per cent appeared in a new and horrid light.'[55] Fresh supplies of coolies could always be got, and rubber plantations multiplied briskly. To leave 'pacification' of such wild areas to unofficial agencies often suited European governments, which could disclaim responsibility for any incidental blemishes. Misgivings did arise in England about the doings of the British North Borneo Company, but it had Gladstone to defend it in Parliament.[56] It was a speciality of his to make dirty linen look as if it had been washed in public.

The Netherlands East Indies

The rest of Borneo fell to the Dutch empire, still expanding through the century in sometimes acrimonious competition with the British. Brooke predicted this in one of his first letters from Sarawak: if Britain were not more active the Dutch would step in, 'and then farewell hope; for Dutch rule, with respect to natives, is a palsy, and death to British manufactures'. 'Is the English lion for ever to crouch beneath the belly of the Dutch frog?'[57] These two empires differed widely in their views of colonies and of colonial peoples; the British watchword was *laissez-faire*, while the Dutch, with no industrial revolution to overthrow the maxims of an earlier capitalism, clung to monopoly, restriction, regulation. There was no doubt that they knew how to conjure immense profits out of their plantation-economy, and this compelled admiration; they passed in Europe for the most scientific of all colonial managers.

An Englishman disillusioned with his own industrial society might conclude that the patriarchal sway of Holland was better for its subjects. In some areas at least they seemed to Wallace 'well fed and decently clothed', whereas Britain instead of taking native peoples as they were was trying to modernize them all at once. 'We demoralize and we extirpate, but we never really civilize.'[58] More often, and too truly, Dutch rule was seen as a peculiarly remorseless, undeviating, phlegmatic exploitation. Free from all romantic illusion, this oldest of bourgeois countries reckoned silk-worms, pepper-plants, peasants, all as items in a balance-sheet. Starting only a century after the Spaniards and Portuguese, it united their simple belief in the native having been created for the benefit of his European master with the northern efficiency of the later empires. Adam Smith commented on the 'savage policy' of the Dutch in cutting down spice plants to keep up prices, and cutting down with them the population of some of the 'Spice Isles' or Moluccas.[59] Recalcitrant islanders were cleared out to make room for plantations worked with slave-labour from India or China. When Captain Cook was there he noticed that Europeans were seldom executed for any crime, natives promptly impaled or broken on the wheel[60] – a mixture of the penal barbarities of Asia and Europe.

Holland's method of extracting tribute was to collect spices and other crops, from the mid-eighteenth century chiefly coffee, and ship them to Europe to be sold for its own benefit. Cultivators were compelled to grow quotas and hand them over, in later days receiving a fixed price in return. In the half-century after 1830 the method was brought to perfection under the title of the 'Culture System'. The more land was devoted to cash-crops for sale abroad, the less remained to grow rice for the swelling population. Rumours leaked out and gave rise to criticism in Europe, to which for a long time the Dutch public turned a deaf ear. Even with private planters forcing their way in against the old official monopoly, the empire retained much of the character of a State-capitalist enterprise, profitable to the whole nation. The nation was content to leave things to the permanent officials, with whom the States-General, though it was after 1848 the ultimate authority, interfered very little[61] – even by comparison with Parliament and the British empire.

It might be wondered how these officials were able to wring such tribute for so long out of so many people, some of warlike stock. Dutchmen at Batavia in the eighteenth and early nineteenth century always looked swag-bellied gormandizers even beside the average run of overfed Europeans in Asia, victims self-fattened for the fevers that decimated them. Holland had been a warlike nation only in the first century of its independence, and even then only on the sea. After that it no longer had a navy on the scale of Britain's, and it was a small land with few reserves of manpower. Being rich, however, it could hire foreign soldiers, Scotsmen or Germans at home, Balinese or Amboinese in the Archipelago for use against other islanders.[62] Dutch strength lay very much in the fact that this empire was a conglomerate of countless peoples and languages, without much in common, though the slow drift of Malay blood and Muslim faith over Indonesia continued. Java, the heart of the empire, was predominantly Malay, but it too contained sundry minorities.

Nevertheless, to the Dutch the necessity of some local buttress of their power was obvious earlier than to the English in India, and this could only mean the standard imperial policy of alliance with the old ruling class against the people. Initiated by the Company, it was inherited by the Crown when Indonesia was restored by Britain in 1815. Part of the empire consisted of vassal states, and even the part directly ruled, increased as time went on by further annexations, was really under a dual control. In India after 1857 the princes were an auxiliary force held in reserve, their territories entirely distinct from British India. In Indonesia the two authorities, native and foreign, worked side by side, or hand in glove. A district was under the joint charge of an Assistant-Resident, a Dutchman, and a Regent, the most prominent local notable.

This had diverse consequences. On social relations between the two races the effect was, within a narrow sphere, an equalizing one. It was impossible for rulers who depended so heavily on the native aristocracy and its hereditary influence to look down ostentatiously on all 'natives', as the British did in India. Intermarriage was not disreputable; a mixed population continued to grow, and Eurasians, if not fully on a par with Europeans, were not publicly rejected. Other factors worked in the same direction. A republic until 1814, Holland had a small old aristocracy, but this was not aped by the administrative middle class nearly so much as in British colonies. Women in Indonesia, moreover, were not strictly fenced off by religion and convention. Many outlying areas were still pagan, and Islam had had neither time nor energy to impose stern orthodoxy on the carefree manners of its converts. Latitude in matters of sex made for something similar in the related department of clothing, and in social life generally. English visitors were astonished not only by the status of native wives and their offspring, but by the sight of Dutchwomen wearing a comfortable costume of sarong and loose jacket, instead of the sweltering Western dress with which Englishwomen in the tropics stiffened their pride and soured their temper.

This kind of contact had its value, but one far outweighed by other results of the partnership between colonialism and feudalism. How bitter these could be for the poor, Holland and Europe learned from what may be the most startling book ever written by a European about a colony – the novel *Max Havelaar*, published in 1860.[63] Among the thousands of officials who worked in the colonies a good many must have felt at times as its author did, but very few spoke their thoughts aloud. This book threw a beam of light into the darkness visible of official reports and figures whose false optimism – as the author repeats – was meant to avoid disturbing the equanimity of official superiors. It described a scene of oppression due even more to the native rulers than to the foreign. Holland required its pound of flesh, or coffee, but to the demands of the rajahs for the peasant's plough animals, or his tiny savings, or his unpaid labour on their own lands, there were no bounds. They were men of the same type as the Malay chief everywhere, only with the old chivalrous temper sunk into parasitic ease. A conscientious officer might wish to check the plundering, but he was a small man, and the Regent, with his claims of birth and his more permanent position, might be upheld by the higher authorities against him. It was one of the less bad sides of British racialism in India that this at least was unlikely to happen: any English civil servant's word, like that of a policeman at home, would be taken against that of any two thieves, whether rajahs or not.

Max Havelaar was written just after the Indian Mutiny, in the hope that a revelation of what was going on would avert an upheaval in Java, as it might have done in India. It did help to bring about the changes and improvements introduced later in the century. Regents were brought under closer supervision, before being discarded altogether. Dutch rule took on a paternalistic flavour, and set about organizing welfare, in certain directions, as scientifically as it organized profit. Higher education was not part of this. Because of the alliance with feudalism, there had been little need for the kind of intelligentsia that the British made use of in India, and in these later days there was a fear of letting in too many modern ideas. Indian nationalism was a warning that the Dutchman could not fail to heed, and gloomy Englishmen were inclined to think his views on colonial education sensible. 'He does not yearn to elevate the native to the bomb-throwing standard of British India ...'[64] For want of leaders a national movement was slower to develop in Indonesia; no concession was made to it until 1916, when a purely bogus local Assembly was started.

In the 'Outer Islands' contract-labourers from Java or foreign countries suffered the same hardships as in other colonies; and fighting was still going on in the years before 1914 to complete the conquest of Sumatra, which was proving rich in mineral resources. Achin, the centre of resistance, had defied the Dutch for many decades. They met there 'an enemy ready enough to fight and who fought under skilful guidance', wrote a British military expert, who also observed what perfect conditions the dense jungle afforded for a guerrilla struggle.[65] It was an omen of other jungle wars that the West was to condemn itself to in Asia.

French Indochina

Hardly anyone had a good word to say for the fragments left in Asia of the two oldest colonial empires. At Timor, Wallace deemed the Portuguese régime a 'most miserable one ... All the Government officials oppress and rob the natives as much as they can.'[66] In the Philippines there were sporadic risings against the Spaniards, swelling after 1872 into a national movement. When the islands were annexed by the USA in 1899 after the war with Spain, resistance to foreign rule was put down more effectively. But in the second half of the nineteenth century a new empire was making a place for itself in south-east Asia, and France coming forward as Britain's neighbour and rival in the great Indochinese peninsula as Holland was in Indonesia.

Siam survived as a buffer between British Burma and the eastern part of the peninsula – Laos, Cambodia, Annam or Vietnam – which became French. In terms of historical evolution the dividing-line was rather between Annam furthest east, along the coast, and all the rest. Annam belonged to the 'Far East' proper, along with China, Japan, Korea, all of which have been making the great stride into the modern world while the rest of Asia westward to Stamboul has by comparison failed to shake off the dead weight of the past. French economic interests, and French influence, both attraction and repulsion, centred here too.

French imperialism even in its earlier career inside Europe had two aspects, the arrogance as well as the enlightenment of the Great Nation. Pushed outwards from Europe after 1870, it was often in a worse, not a better, mood. The old confidence had been crippled, and there was a straining after national greatness instead of an easy consciousness of it. All the European nations were being radically altered, and not always improved, by industrialism and the other changes they were going through, and by their dealings with the other continents. In old books the French are so frequently described as a polite, cheerful, good-natured people, that they really must once have been like this; just as the Germans must once have been a guileless, kindly, unworldly folk. Trelawney praised the 'urbanity and equality' of the French colonial official and contrasted it with the 'doglike surliness of the rude and stiff-backed Englishman'.[67] The disaster of 1870, more humiliating than 1815, followed by the Commune, conscription and drilling for the next war, and Stock Exchange imperialism, all helped to bring about a deep transformation in the Frenchman.

Saigon and the southern tip of Annam were seized before the fall of Napoleon III; the capital Hue and the reigning dynasty were not brought under a French protectorate until 1883, and in the northern province of Tonking there was fierce resistance, aided in 1883-5 by China. Annam like all the Far Eastern lands had been a nation for ages, even if it was often torn, as on the eve of French conquest, by internal faction and peasant revolt. French 'pacification' was carried out in Tonking, largely by the ruffians of the Foreign Legion, that incongruous vehicle of the civilizing mission, with a brutality that an English observer described as 'a disgrace to the Christian world';[68] by the time his book came out the British army was killing prisoners in Burma as the French army had done, more massively, in Tonking. Each Western country was in the habit of thinking itself over-indulgent with troublesome natives, too sparing of the wholesome severity that its rivals understood the need for. An ex-soldier from Tonking whom W. S. Blunt talked to in Paris exclaimed against his government's folly in sending armchair philosophers to run the colonies, who fancied that all men were brothers – it was the English in India who were realistic – '*en agissant avec des brutes il faut être brutal*'.[69]

There had been a time, corresponding with the British optimism about India before 1857, when Frenchmen hugged the idea of civilizing colonial peoples so completely that they would be 'assimilated' to European standards. This was an idea that marked them off from both British and Dutch. Britain was prepared to give some of its subjects Western knowledge, Holland to give some of them Western husbands: France proposed to give them in addition Western souls, to translate them into Frenchmen. This conception had a complex background. Louis XIV taught France to think itself the teacher of Europe, and from long before his day it had been absorbing other nationalities – Breton, Flemish, Basque, German – into itself, making Frenchmen out of aliens. French nationalism was developing for several centuries before 1789 under the aegis of the Bourbon monarchy, whereas the Dutch were historically republican and the English virtually so since Charles I; even after 1789 France reverted three times to monarchy, and a fourth return after 1870 was on the cards. Kings are less prone than demagogues to racialism, being indifferent to what their subjects look like so long as they pay their taxes. Monarchy also promotes respect for Culture, as one of its own badges: this traditional respect, blighted in England by centuries of creeping capitalism and philistinism, France found it natural to transpose into an imperial setting. The French theatre had once dazzled Germany, and now French companies went out regularly to dazzle Saigon, and to enable Frenchmen to think of Annam and Cambodia as new provinces of France, taking the place of those lost in Europe.

In another sense France was, thanks to 1789, socially more modern and democratic than Britain. A Briton of low degree could become rich, but he could not become a gentleman It went logically with this that a British colonial subject could

not rise in the scale of humanity beyond a certain point. In
France anyone who accepted the established order of society
could rise by his talents to any level; similarly a colonial subject who accepted French ascendancy could be lifted up by it
and shake off all his clogs. It was one further inducement to
accept him as a fellow-Frenchman that France was suffering
from a low birth-rate, while its European rivals increased and
multiplied.

Whether or not Frenchmen ever really thought of Galliciz-
ing whole native peoples, in practice only minorities or élites
could ever be given the necessary polish. And this meant that
an Annamite, who could only become really civilized by ceasing to be an Annamite, would be cut off from the mass of his
people, and these would be left leaderless – like Slovenes in the
Hapsburg empire with all their educated class turned into
Magyars. In principle, on the other hand, the British attitude
acknowledged that an Indian could grow into a civilized Indian, and at some remote date be able to run his country himself.

But the ideal of assimilation soon wilted under contact with
the realities of colonial profit-making. On the whole the
French record in Indochina was mediocre, like most of the
officials responsible for it, men with poor pay and prospects,
bored with their duties.[70] There were of course some material
improvements, in water-control for instance. Formal slavery
was suppressed. But throughout south-east Asia there were
many informal shades of servitude in the old societies, peonage or serfdom or forced labour;[71] and inevitably European
enterprise took advantage of this, fitting its own greeds into a
ready-made mould. On the big French-owned plantations, as in
Assam, horrid abuses came to light from time to time, and the
government showed 'extraordinary timidity' in dealing with
them.[72] Here too, coolie labour was recruited partly from
among backward tribes, like the Moi; and here too, foreign
rule brought with it an unpopular influx from neighbouring
lands, chiefly India and China. Indochina could be numorously
called a Chinese colony administered by Frenchmen. It was not
rare for Chinese who started as pedlars to end with bigger
fortunes than French businessmen.[73] Usury was the special

affair of the Chettis, a moneylending caste from south India who got control of much of the fertile southern rice-land.

Similar realities pervaded other colonies too, and by the 1890s French administrators were looking for an alternative to the ideal of assimilation. This was worked out chiefly in Indochina and transferred to the empire at large.[74] Instead of old ideas and institutions being swept away to make room for new ones, it was argued now that they should be preserved and utilized, and this could be presented as recognition of the right of a native people to evolve on its own lines. De Lanessan, one of the pioneers of a new strategy of indirect rule in Indochina, talked of Annamites as a people with a mature culture of their own, whom France should accept as partners in the work of civilization.[75] This sounded well, and might be sincere, but in practice the French, like the Dutch and British, were irresistibly pushed into alliance with the old parasitic ruling classes. Three puppet monarchies, the land-owners, and other 'notables', were fitted into the French framework, and tied to French rule by a bond of common interest; while the village commune, the institution of most value in the old society, disintegrated like its counterpart in India under the pressure of new economic forces.

For assimilation into French enlightenment a kind of second-rate substitute, more suitable for the common herd, was provided by Catholicism. Voltaire did not talk atheism before his servants, for fear of having his spoons stolen; the Third Republic was vigorously anti-clerical at home, but very willing to employ its clerical opponents in the colonies, as a sop and also for the sake of their soothing influence there. Religious prejudices in the Far East being fairly mild, as well as sexual taboos – the two always influencing each other – it was feasible to work up a body of support for French rule by converting a substantial minority; though the rise of the Sects, with their bizarre hotchpotch of religious and other fragments Western and Eastern, revealed how imperfect Franco-Annamite harmony was even on this level. Protection of Catholic missionaries and converts had been the original pretext for the French entry; and an official who in the early days of French rule was heard complaining of the Church as a law unto itself admitted that the clergy had been extremely useful to army intelligence during the conquest, and even marched at the head of the columns.[76] The spirit of the Counter-Reformation stirred once more in this militant Christianity. Kept alive all these years by the mission Orders, like the spirit of feudal France marooned in Quebec, it now joined forces with its successor, the civilizing mission of modern imperialism.

Modern communications, available as they had not been in the first century of British India, might have been expected to cancel distance and strengthen France's moral hold, but their effect was the opposite one of accelerating a new nationalism. The early resistance had hardly been stamped out before a new movement of independence was under way, which the authorities tried in vain to suffocate by the same violent methods, sometimes applied by the same Foreign Legion. Individuals lucky enough to reach a college in France found there, and could love, the true French culture they had been told about; but in their own country they saw little enough of it. There, perhaps, as much assimilation of Frenchmen to native ways took place as the opposite process; to opium-smoking, for example. A Briton who smoked opium in India would have been guilty of a derogation only less unpardonable than a native wife; he could drink unlimited whisky to float him through his dusty years of exile, because whisky was not a native product. It was another odd differential that John Bull, the strange convolutions of whose conscience have never been fully anatomized, did not sell Indian opium to his own Indian subjects; he dumped it on the Chinese, for whose vices he was not responsible. Envious of his opium profits, and more logical, the French made opium a government monopoly in Indochina and sold it to the public for revenue. In the 1920s three quarters, at a guess, of the French themselves were partakers.[77] In pipe-dreams they could still be the philosopher-kings of the Utopian colony of French official theory.

Russia in Asia

The Comte de Ségur, a prisoner of war of the Russians in 1807, thought he recognized among them (the upper-class Russians he conversed with, that is) an overweening pride of which one cause was a long-standing sense of superiority over neighbouring Asia.[78] This sense must have been all the more gratifying because it made up for inferiority to western Europe. In Asia a Russian could feel that he represented Europe. The reactionary historian Pogodin had a scheme for the whole European white race to join in conquering and civilizing Africa.[79] Later in the nineteenth century, Pan-Slav ambitions inside Europe were balanced by a rival philosophy, that of the *Vostochniki* or 'Easterners' who saw Russia's future lying in Asia.[80] To them race meant less than to a Slavophil like Pogodin. They would on ocasion, hoping to win Asian confidence, emphasize the strain of Tartar blood that the oldest families of the aristocracy absorbed when Russia lay under the Golden Horde.

In any case the governing class had very mixed origins, and was held together by common interest and allegiance more than by blood. Pushkin wrote a story, *Peter the Great's Negro*, about his own ancestor, the Tsar's African protégé. A swarm of chieftains from the Caucasus were allowed to call themselves Princes, whereas the sole peerage ever conferred on an Indian, in the late days of the Raj, threw the House of Lords into transports of indignation. A Russian general boasted to a British journalist that a regiment of Russian soldiers was commanded by a Turkoman chief who had once fought against Russia, whereas after a century of British rule no Indian officer was trusted with any such command.[81] The journalist might have retorted that Russian soldiers could be put under anyone, because they were peasants who until yesterday had been serfs and were still treated like serfs.

All Britain's colonies were far away beyond the seas; it had a marked psychological effect that even Ireland – like France, and unlike Wales or Scotland – was divided from England by water. The Tsarist empire was contiguous with the homeland,

and stretched away from it in one continuous mass. It was as if England and India and Canada had lain side by side, and been racially less discordant than they were. Siberian tribes, if primitive and odd-looking, were more or less fair-skinned; while of the empire's two southward appendages, Caucasia and Central Asia, the first was inhabited by peoples of European type – among whom a future dictator of all the Russias was born in 1879 – the second by Turki peoples, men who when they conquered India in the Middle Ages were almost as conscious as the British were of their lighter colour.

The Russians drifted into the vast near-emptiness of Siberia by a simple continuation of their older expansion over the surface of European Russia. Westerners who hated or feared the Tsarist government and army could admire the pioneering qualities of the Russian peasant, a migrant by old instinct, and they were struck by his willingness to mix with other peoples. Sometimes Russians were thought to have a special faculty for assimilating smaller peoples by complete physiological absorption.[82] When Siberia came into use as a penal settlement area other elements were introduced. Escaped criminals sometimes (as in Tasmania) turned robber and preyed on the natives.[83] Some of the scattered tribes were more able than others to hold their own, trading furs for the white man's goods. In Yakutia all the others seemed mere 'naïve savages' compared with the Yakuts, who had long been dispossessing the weaker Tunguses; and a political exile early in the twentieth century noted that Cossacks settled there for some generations had 'undergone a process of strong Yakut assimilation'.[84]

In another tribe this exile, Zenzinov, observed 'an incredible fusion of Christian and heathen beliefs and rites', priest and shaman as it were arm in arm.[85] Mixtures of creed, as well as of race, were spreading about the world: the sects of Indochina were only one case. Ordinarily St Petersburg might not bother its head about who was assimilating whom in Asia, but it had fits of anxiety about the loyalty of its subjects, and for want of anything better might decide to ensure it by inducting them willy-nilly into the Orthodox Church. We hear of Buryat Mongols being rounded up and pitched into streams, as the quickest baptism, like sheep being dipped. These Mongols were more advanced than the Siberians, and their history provides some neat examples of interaction between races.

Cossacks first met them in 1629, and made friends with the *noyons* or aristocracy, who exploited their poor clansmen and the near-by forest tribes. The poor resisted the Russians, and some were enslaved. By the end of that century the poorer Russian colonists were rebelling against their own governors, and were being joined by the discontented Buryats. Some liberals implicated in the Decembrist conspiracy against Nicholas I in 1825 were banished to this region, and made a sympathetic study of Buryat culture, which caused the Mongols themselves to think more highly of it. (A Frenchman's novels about heroic Turk conquerors in medieval Asia helped to ignite Turkish nationalism in the late nineteenth century.[86]) In 1905 Buryats were ready to take part in the revolutions sweeping over the empire.[87]

Perennially threatened with revolt at home, Tsarism had to make some appeal to popular feeling, and could do so most readily – with the aid of the Church – by crusades against the old Turkish foe, Russia's enemy in Asia as well as Europe. Russians pressing into Muslim Asia could feel that they were revenging their former subjugation by the Golden Horde, a memory invoked once again by Soviet writers during the struggle against the equally barbarous Nazis. By the late eighteenth century they were forcing their way into the Caucasus. A worse obstacle than Turkish resistance proved to be the confederacy of Muslim tribes high up in Daghestan. These hillmen, thanks to the tribal solidarity still intact among them as well as to their rocky fortresses, held out much longer than any of the organized but decrepit Muslim States to the east. Their leader for nearly three decades was Shamil Bey, a mullah or religious personage, whose lieutenants were a band of *murids* or disciples. Europe heard of him intermittently as a wild hero whom Byron might have admired; when finally captured he was treated fairly liberally, his exile sweetened with a pension. He died in Arabia, his holy land.

In Transcaucasia Russians could bask in the southern sunshine they were always supposed to be pining for – the vision that swam before the tipsy eyes of the runagate embezzlers in

Kataev's novel: 'mountain slopes, cliffs, "shashlik", Circassian girls, wine of Kakhetia in large jars – in a word, a symphony of sensations!'[88] Up in the hills the Russians, as quick as other empire-builders to see the advantage of 'setting Asians to fight Asians', lost no time in enrolling Ingush and Osietin tribesmen in their ranks. To the south, Georgians and Armenians and Azerbaijanis had been engaged in perpetual feud; the Armenians especially, many of whom remained under Turkish rule, did stand in need of the protection that Russia professed to be bringing. There was a strong commercial class among them which could look for opportunities elsewhere in Russian Asia: this empire like the rest was profitable to others besides its masters. Much of the trade of Russian Turkestan fell into Armenian hands.[89]

Central Asia was a dismal anarchy of petty despots, the strongest of them Uzbegs related by language as well as religion to the Ottoman Turks. Whether from climatic or moral desiccation, or both, a culture once the pride of the Islamic world was in gloomy stagnation. Very little was known about it outside, even in Russia.[90] Fanaticism made Bokhara and Samarkand nearly as inaccessible as Lhasa. One or two British explorers made their way there from India, Burnes to be well received in 1832, Stoddart and Connolly to be murdered in 1841. Vambéry, the Hungarian traveller, penetrated Central Asia in disguise early in the 1860s. He depicted Nasrullah Khan, the late Emir of Bokhara, as an embodiment of all the country's degeneracy, an unredeemed tyrant kept going by a swarm of spies, reactionary clergy, and executioners.[91] The Russians pushing on across the steppes[92] made the most of such reports, which helped them to appear in the light of rescuers. The Khanate of Khiva was likewise 'weighed down by the most coarse and unbridled despotism', and its inhabitants, by the testimony of nearly all travellers Russian or foreign, were full of 'treachery, mendacity, cruelty and rapacity';[93] the capital was thronged with miserable slaves brought in by the savage Turkoman raiders out on the steppes.

In 1867 a new province of Russian 'Turkestan' was organized; next year a treaty was forced on Kokand which reduced it to vassalage, and a similar one offered to Bokhara but re-

jected under pressure from the clerical bigots. Brought to heel
by the annexation of much of his territory including Samarkand, the Emir was then glad to join hands with the Russians
in putting down his fanatics.[94] This was the start of a partnership that lasted till the Revolution put an end to Emir and Tsar
together. Khiva was dealt with in the same fashion in 1873.
It had fended off more than one Russian attempt in earlier
days, but its people now proved – according to the victors –
nothing but 'ordinary Central Asian cowards' when firmly
tackled.[95] Militarily the Russians were having 'extraordinary
success' in Central Asia, because their opponents faced them in
pitched battles, in one of which 40,000 men were routed by
3,000.[96] It was typical of such archaic and unpopular régimes
to be able to fight only in this way, very ineffective compared
with the guerrilla resistance of some other countries. Here the
best fight was made by the Turkomans of the steppes, who
were crushed ruthlessly.[97] Russian practice in such cases was to
break the will to resist by ferocious means, promptly exchanged
for amiability once the enemy gave in. Englishmen were inclined to feel a sneaking respect for the method. It was an instinctive one with half-feudal Russia, where the rich flogged the
poor with knouts but addressed them as 'brothers'. In turn the
habit of quelling barbarians in Asia reinforced feudal instincts
at home, and the ferocity of the Whites in the civil war after
1917, whose infection spread to the Bolsheviks, must have
owed something to it.

A few Britons felt that Russia's advent in Central Asia must
be welcomed as putting an end to intolerable conditions.[98] But
it was anathema to most of them, who saw it as a threat to
India. On their side Russian empire-builders like others could
give themselves a better conscience by sympathizing with the
unhappy lot of the inhabitants of rival empires. A Russian
officer wrote that India was being destroyed by the poisonous
plant of British rule. 'Sick to death, the natives are waiting for
a physician from the North.'[99] Not many outsiders were allowed
to go and see how the physician's own patients were faring.
The British officer and traveller Burnaby managed to reach
Khiva in 1876 and had an audience with the Khan, whom the
Russians had portrayed as a regular monster. Burnaby, ex-

pectably, saw him in a more amiable light.[100] While at Khiva he wondered whether the barber who was shaving him was bigot enough to want to cut his throat.[101] A few years later, tempting fate once too often, he was killed by a Muslim devotee in battle far away in the Soudan.

An American diplomat Schuyler, less prejudiced against the new dispensation, was one of the few who were allowed to make a tour of inspection. He annoyed the Emir of Bokhara by shaking hands with him too vigorously: the potentate's hands were shaky, from aphrodisiacs it was presumed.[102] Schuyler's impression was that the common people had been hopeful at first of the Russians, but now had to pay heavier taxes for little improvement. Slave-trading was being pushed out of sight rather than suppressed.[103] He heard people asking 'How are the Russians better for us than the Khokandians? They also take away from us our daughters and our wives, and also love presents ...'[104] The men sent out to Turkestan were the dregs of Tsarist officialdom, and glaring cases of misconduct came to his ears.[105] By 1913 a Russian apologist may have been justified in saying that things were better under Russian than under native rule, and that most Bokharans would have preferred direct annexation.[106] He admitted grave defects, which might make the whole region unreliable in case of another war with Turkey.[107]

Civilization, however shoddy, has to be paid for, and Central Asia paid with cotton to supply mills in Russia. When Witte, the later finance minister and ardent 'Easterner', visited Turkestan in 1890 he could not help seeing that the peasantry was suffering because the government was taking too much of the available water for cotton.[108] It was the familiar colonial phenomenon, the sacrifice of food crops to cash crops. There was a rising in Farghana in 1898 of poor folk and of peasants pushed off their farms. Another aspect of Western civilization was conscription. This was not imposed until 1916, when the white man was anxious to share some of his burden with anyone he could. Kirghiz steppe-dwellers then rebelled and, like some French soldiers who mutinied in the same year, were massacred.

Besides the official arrogance that Lenin deplored as one of the legacies of the Tsarist empire to the Soviet Union, there was a chauvinism of the ordinary Russian. Wars with Turkey fomented it; and the long-continuing migration of the Russian peasantry eastward could be called 'a kind of Russian people's imperialism'.[109] It was overrunning great areas of steppe, pushing nomads like the Kazakhs off their land.[110] Former inhabitants were being displaced rather than exploited. In some districts the immigrants formed an urban working class surrounded by a native peasantry. Yet a possibility of fraternization remained, stronger than in any settlement areas of other empires. There was more mingling in the same jobs, at the same standard of living; son or grandson of a peasant serf, the Russian was little accustomed to habits or comforts much above what his new neighbours were used to. If political consciousness touched him, the thought of brotherhood with the colonial masses, an abstract one to Western socialists, in a place like the Baku oil-field could be felt as a living reality.

NOTES

1. 'Hermes', in *The Asiatic Journal*, Vol. 1 (1816), pp. 105–8.
2. L. C. A. Knowles, *The Economic Development of the British Overseas Empire* (1924), p. 215.
3. K. M. de Silva, 'The "Rebellion" of 1848 in Ceylon', in *Ceylon Journal of Historical and Social Studies*, Vol. 7 (1964), p. 154.
4. ibid., pp. 164–5.
5. ibid., pp. 151, 167–9.
6. I owe this observation to my friend Mr S. N. Chib, lately Director-General of Tourism at Delhi.
7. L. C. A. Knowles, op. cit., pp. 183–4.
8. R. H. Cholmondley, *The Heber Letters, 1783–1832* (1950), p. 320.
9. Maung Htin Aung, *Burmese Drama* (1937), p. 111.
10. 2nd edn (1885), Vol. 3, p. 213.
11. Col. W. F. B. Laurie, *Our Burmese Wars and Relations with Burma* (1880), pp. 401, 387.
12. *Hansard*, 3rd Series, Vol. 293, Col. 1,830 (1884).
13. Dr J. E. Marks, *Forty Years in Burma* (ed. Rev. W. C. B. Purser, 1917), p. 218.
14. H. Fielding Hall, *The Soul of a People* (1898), pp. 52, 83 (1928 edn).

15. G. Geary, *Burma after the Conquest* (1886), p. 5.

16. Taw Sein Ko, *Burmese Sketches* (Rangoon, 1913), p. 49.

17. G. Geary, op. cit., p. 6.

18. ibid., p. 293.

19. ibid., pp. 234, 237.

20. Sir C. Crosthwaite, *The Pacification of Burma* (1912), pp. 13–14.

21. Colonel C. E. Callwell, *Small Wars. Their Principles and Practice* (War Office, London, 3rd edn, 1906), pp. 147–8.

22. H. F. Hall, op. cit., p. 53. Chapters 5 and 6 are on the struggle, which he saw himself; it spread as he points out into Lower Burma.

23. In the regimental museum, Carlisle Castle.

24. Lord Hardinge, *My Indian Years 1910–1916* (1948), p. 19.

25. R. Grant Brown, *Burma as I saw it, 1889–1917* (1926), p. 46.

26. H. F. Hall, op. cit., p. 106. Treatment of animals was one way in which Burma shone by contrast with India (Chapter 19).

27. ibid., p. 225. A man like Hall was exceptional no doubt in any colony; and George Orwell's novel *Burmese Days* (1934) is a reminder that many Europeans in Burma, especially commercial agents in small stations like the one depicted, were as rabid as any in India. Orwell served from 1922 to 1928 in the Police, during the post-war worsening of relations all over the Indian empire. My friend Dr Shwe Tin of Rangoon agrees with me in thinking that the novel shares his characteristic excess.

28. Mrs L. Milne, *Shans at Home* (1910), pp. 117, 140. cf. W. C. B. Purser, *Christians in Burma* (1911), p. 39, on the eagerness of poor hill-folk to learn what the missionary could teach.

29. R. M. Martin, *History of the British Possessions in the Indian and Atlantic Oceans* (1837), p. 167.

30. Consular Report from Bangkok, 1882.

31. J. Thomson, FRGS, *The Straits of Malacca, Indo-China and China* (1875), p. 62.

32. Lieutenant-General Sir A. Clarke, 'The Straits Settlements', in *British Empire Series*, Vol. 1, India (1899), p. 460.

33. See my article 'Britain, Siam, and Malaya: 1875–1885', in *Journal of Modern History*, Vol. XXVIII, No. 1 (1956).

34. E. J. Trelawney, *The Adventures of a Younger Son* (1831), pp. 353–4, 357 (World's Classics edn).

35. Major F. McNair, *Perak and the Malays* (1878), pp. 22, 239.

36. ibid., p. 207.

37. ibid., p. 415.

38. Sir R. O. Winstedt, *Malaya and its History* (n.d.), pp. 66, 68.

39. Dictionary of National Biography.

40. Sir P. Benson Maxwell, *Our Malay Conquests* (1878), p. 40.

41. ibid., pp. 10, 51, 111.

42. Sir A. Clarke, loc. cit., p. 452.

43. Sir F. Swettenham, *Footprints in Malaya* (1942), p. 81.

44. J. S. Furnivall, *Colonial Policy and Practice* (Cambridge, 1948), p. 336.

45. L. C. A. Knowles, op. cit., p. 473.

46. Sir F. Swettenham, *British Malaya* (1906), p. 134 (1929 edn). See generally Chapter 7.

47. A. R. Wallace, *The Malay Archipelago* (1869), p. 448 (1890 edn).

48. F. S. Marryat, *Borneo and the Indian Archipelago* (1848), Conclusion.

49. H. Wise, *A Selection of Papers relating to Borneo* (1846), p. 49.

50. G. Borrow, *The Romany Rye* (1857), p. 162 (1905 edn).

51. Captain Hon. H. Keppel, *Expedition to Borneo of H.M.S. Dido* (2nd edn, 1846), Vol. 1, pp. 246–7, 260; Vol. 2, pp. 201, 206. cf. Brooke's letter of 10 December 1841 in *Rajah Brooke and Baroness Burdett Coutts*, ed. O. Rutter (1935), pp. 29–31.

52. A. R. Wallace, op. cit., pp. 68, 71.

53. H. Wise, op. cit., p. 24.

54. C. J. Brooke to Lord Clarendon, 28 April 1869, in Foreign Office 72.843, Public Record Office, London; and see earlier correspondence in this volume.

55. J. D. Ross, *Sixty Years: Life and Adventure in the Far East* (1911), Vol. 2, pp. 181–3.

56. P. Knaplund, *Gladstone's Foreign Policy* (New York, 1935), p. 117. The British North Borneo Company was formally incorporated in 1882 and authorized by Charter to administer the territory acquired from the Sultan in 1878 by a syndicate (which included Keppel); it continued to do so even when the territory became a British protectorate in 1888.

57. H. Wise, op. cit., p. 2.

58. A. R. Wallace, op. cit., pp. 73, 197.

59. *The Wealth of Nations* (1776), Vol. 2, pp. 248–9 (World's Classics edn).

60. *Captain Cook's Voyages of Discovery* (Everyman edn), p. 107. This relates to 1770.

61. D. K. Fieldhouse, *The Colonial Empires* (1965), p. 326.

62. B. H. M. Vlekke, *The Story of the Dutch East Indies* (Harvard, 1946), p. 108.

63. 'Multatuli', *Max Havelaar* (1860; trans. W. Siebenhaar, New York, 1927). See in particular pp. 53–4, 115 ff., 201 ff., 222.

64. J. J. Abraham, *The Surgeon's Log. Impressions of the Far East* (1911), p. 237 (18th edn, 1933).

65. C. E. Callwell, op. cit., pp. 32, 103, 127.

66. A. R. Wallace, op. cit., p. 151.

67. E. J. Trelawney, op. cit. p. 243.

68. C. B. Norman, *Tonkin, France in the Far East* (1884), p. 304.

69. W. S. Blunt, *My Diaries* (1891), p. 51 (1932 edn).

70. A comment on the French colonies at large, by C. Southworth, *The French Colonial Venture* (1931), p. 25.

71. See B. Lasker, *Human Bondage in Southeast Asia* (Institute of Pacific Relations, 1950).

72. V. M. Thompson, *French Indo-China* (1937), p. 148.

73. See C. Robequain, *L'Indochine française* (Paris, 1935), Chapter 3.

74. See D. K. Fieldhouse, op. cit., p. 319; P. Renouvin, *La question d'Extrême-Orient, 1840–1940* (Paris, 1946), p. 262.

75. J. L. de Lanessan, *L'expansion coloniale de la France* (Paris, 1886), p. 542. He was Governor-General from 1891 to 1894.

76. J. D. Ross, op. cit., Vol. 2, Chapter 32.

77. H. A. Franck, *East of Siam* (New York, 1926), p. 23.

78. Comte P. de Ségur, *Un Aide de Camp de Napoléon* (1873), p. 398 (Nelson edn, Paris n.d.).

79. N. V. Riasanovsky, *Nicholas I and Official Nationality in Russia, 1825–1855* (University of California, 1959), pp. 159–62. Pogodin was strongly pro-British during the Indian Mutiny. Just before this, during the Crimean War, Western propaganda had made a point of the Asiatic infusion in the Russian governing class; see e.g. J. Harwood's novel, *The Serf-Sisters: or, The Russian of To-day* (1855).

80. See A. Malozemoff, *Russian Far Eastern Policy, 1881–1904* (University of California, 1958), pp. 42–4, etc.

81. W. T. Stead, *Truth about Russia* (1888), p. 151. In early days it had not been unknown for British troops to be under an Indian officer.

82. W. D. Foulke, *Slav or Saxon* (2nd edn, New York, 1899), pp. 21–3, 27, 29.

83. G. Borodin, *Soviet and Tsarist Siberia* (1943), p. 61.

84. V. Zenzinov, *The Road to Oblivion* (1932), pp. 50–52.

85. ibid., p. 190.

86. The novels of Léon Cahun; see Sir H. Luke, *The Old Turkey and the New* (new edn, 1955), pp. 153 ff.

87. G. D. R. Phillips, *Dawn in Siberia* (the Mongols of Lake Baikal) (1942), pp. 54 ff., 90–92, 113, 116–17.

88. V. Kataev, *The Embezzlers* (trans. K. Zarine, n.d.), p. 227.

89. V. Baker, *Clouds in the East* (1876), p. 309. The Russian conquest of Transcaucasia was partly instigated by a Russianized Georgian, Prince Tsitsianov, who was made commander-in-chief in 1802.

90. 'Nowhere is so much ignorance of Central Asia displayed as in Russian society ...' (*Khiva and Turkestan*, trans. from Russian by Captain H. Spalding (1874), p. 7.)

91. A. Vambéry, *History of Bokhara* (1873), p. 366. See also on his hazardous explorations *The Story of my Struggles* (Nelson edn, n.d.), Chapter 4.

92. See Sir O. Caroe, *Soviet Empire* (2nd edn, 1967), pp. 72 ff.

93. H. Spalding, op. cit., pp. 209, 190–92.

94. A. Vambéry, *History of Bokhara*, pp. 414–15.

95. H. Spalding, op. cit., p. 194.

96. C. E. Callwell, op. cit., pp. 104–5, 190.

97. O. Caroe, op. cit., p. 79, quotes General Skobolev's dictum : ' 'in Asia the duration of peace is in direct proportion to the slaughter you inflict upon the enemy ...'

98. e.g. H. Spalding, op. cit., pp. vii–viii; W. W. Hunter, *A Life of the Earl of Mayo* (1875), Vol. 1, p. 268.

99. Captain Terentiev, cited by F. Burnaby, *A Ride to Khiva* (10th edn, 1877), p. vi.

100. F. Burnaby, op. cit., p. 308.

101. ibid., p. 101.

102. E. Schuyler, *Turkestan* (New York, 1876), Vol. 2, pp. 83–4. At Bokhara the chief minister told him that now the Russians had Khiva they would soon take the city of England (Vol. 2, p. 68).

103. ibid., Vol. 2, pp. 233–4, 311.

104. ibid., Vol. 2, p. 225.

105. ibid., Vol. 2, pp. 220, 247, 249, 350–51. cf. A. Krausse, *Russia in Central Asia, 1858–1899* (1899), pp. 136, 139–40; and D. K. Fieldhouse, op. cit., p. 336 : 'Russia never developed a trained corps of professional colonial administrators.'

106. A. Woeikof, *Le Turkestan russe* (Paris, 1914), pp. 197, 327.

107. ibid, pp. 330, 336.

108. *The Memoirs of Count Witte*, trans. A. Yarmolinsky (1921), pp. 33–4. cf. M. Ilin, *Men and Mountains*, trans. B. Kinkead (1936), on the buying up of irrigated land by Russian firms.

109. W. Kolarz, *Russia and her Colonies* (1952), p. 3.

110. D. K. Fieldhouse, op. cit., p. 337.

4. THE ISLAMIC WORLD

Turkey

At the two ends of Asia two old empires maintained their independence, with reduced territories, through the age of European expansion. China was a riddle, but Turkey in a sense even more so, because it lay partly in Europe, and the question had never been settled of whether Turkey was, or might become, a European entity. The 'Eastern Question' that haunted Europe through the nineteenth century and down to 1914 was in effect the same. Turkey was weakening, its Christian subjects in the Balkans were rebelling, some of the Powers wanted to despoil it: others – in turn France, Russia, Britain, Germany – wanted to preserve it under their own tutelage, and therefore to supply it with a kind of certificate of European naturalization. What stands out from the confused record is the very subjective character of Europe's opinions about the Turks, always biased by political interest, and more often than not oblivious of whether Turks wanted to be Europeans or not.

Katib Chelebi, the Turkish essayist of the early seventeenth century, had judicious views about men's need to familiarize themselves with other societies.[1] Yet he himself displays little knowledge of other lands, and scarcely alludes to Europe; and the hairsplitting scholastic debates he censures among his contemporaries reveal how the Turkish intellect was failing to develop, at bottom because Turkey, like Spain too merely military and religious, was failing to grow economically and technically. Its mentality was turning defensive and static; by the end of that century it was no longer a menace to southern or eastern Europe. To the northwest it and its Moorish auxiliaries had never been more than a nuisance, if an unpleasant one. There were Turkish prisoners in 1626 at peaceful St Ives in Cornwall, and long after the corsairs ceased to haunt the English Channel they lurked in wait for trading ships in the

Mediterranean. Public appeals for money to ransom captives from 'their fierce and tirannous dealing'[2] were frequent. In 1662 the Dean of Lincoln Cathedral was writing to Archbishop Sancroft about this laudable purpose,[3] in 1670 the Earl of Bedford was subscribing £5.[4] A century later released or escaped prisoners on their way home were still a recognized object of charity.[5]

By the later eighteenth century Europeans could contemplate Turkey with more detachment. Religious excitement had ebbed on both sides. Turks were familiar figures, only outlandish enough, like Muscovites or Hebrideans, to look picturesque. Turkish costume made an attractive fancy-dress at carnival time. George II dressed up as a sultan at a Hanover fête in 1740, with one of his mistresses as a sultana.[6] The real Sultan was a despot, but absolute monarchy was the form of government admired by most of the leaders of thought in Europe. Shakespeare had talked of the cruelty of 'stubborn Turks and Tartars',[7] but both names were taking on the half-playful overtones they still have today; unlike *Hun*, the name of a vanished race, still terrific because only existing for imagination. The drums and cymbals of the janissaries, that once appalled Europe, were incorporated into its orchestra; a 'Turkish Rondo' could be the most graceful of compositions. Pasha Selim in Mozart's *Il Seraglio* was a true man of the Enlightenment, a devotee of reason, resisting more successfully than Count Almaviva the temptation to abuse his power over a woman.

Mozart's 'Albanians' in *Così fan tutte* had no difficulty in winning a pair of young Italian hearts. There is a reminder here that in physical aspect Turks might be indistinguishable from Europeans; they had been mixing with peoples of Caucasian stock since long before their irruption into Europe. The reigning dynasty had practically no Turkish, and some European, blood. Murad III's favourite wife, the mother of his eldest son, was a Venetian; Mahmud II in the early nineteenth century had a French mother. Western renegades were still turning Turk, and many such men achieved prominent positions, as in the army during the Crimean War when the most successful commander was Omar Pasha, a Croat from Hapsburg territory.

So far as all this went, it should not have been harder to think of Turkey as part of Europe than, today, as part of that more nebulous region, 'the West'. Turks, however, were a minority in their European provinces, and the Ottoman empire had a long tail of non-Turkish dependencies stretching away into Asia and Africa. If Europe's proximity tended to jerk it forward, Africa's, with the steady tribute of Negro slaves, always dragged it back. In the opening crisis of the Eastern Question in 1791,[8] when Pitt risked war with Russia in order to protect Turkey and with it (according to British strategic theory) the overland route to India, he had to argue that Turkey was deserving of help and protection. Opponents strenuously denied this. Turks were a people 'wholly Asiatic', declared Burke. 'What had these worse than savages to do with the Powers of Europe?'[9] A milder version of his thesis, expressed some years later, was that 'there will always be some boundary, to European cultivation of intellect', and that natural frontier was the mind of Turkey.[10]

Turkey was repeatedly involved in the turmoil of the Revolutionary and Napoleonic wars, most dramatically by General Bonaparte's conquest of Egypt in 1798. Turbans were for a time the rage among ladies in Paris, and the most colourful section of the First Consul's guard was his squadron of Mameluke cavalry. The Turkish ambassador in Paris at this time seemed to a young Irish lady 'of very imposing aspect, majestic in his air, and beautiful in his features', though capable of fits of rage in public. He and his suite spoke good French, and adapted themselves wonderfully to French manners: they were as assiduous with ladies 'as if their own were not slaves'.[11]

Turkey, however, had no part in the general peace-settlement of Europe in 1814–15, and during the next decade the Balkan risings started, first with the Serbs and then the Greeks. The Sublime Porte was baffled. It knew nothing about nationalism; it had always been tolerant, if contemptuous, of other faiths, and until near the end non-Muslims were never conscripted into the army, as Muslim and other colonial manpower might be into a European army. Too confused and distracted to stick to any line of policy, it alternated between fits of torpor and

fits of violence. Massacre became, not in the European provinces only, part of the routine of administration. The struggle
in Greece during the 1820s was peculiarly atrocious on both
sides (rather like the Indian Mutiny with the roles reversed),
and Western sentiment about Greece as the cradle of European
civilization, and Byron's death at Missolonghi, helped to fix
public attention on it.

No governments were eager to assist Balkan rebels. They
had too many similar rebels of their own, in Ireland, Poland,
Catalonia, Italy, Belgium. None of them had any feeling that
it was wrong, or undignified, to leave Europeans under Asian
rule; and the Balkan nationalities looked scarcely more civilized than their masters. 'The Ottoman empire was an essential
part of the balance of power in Europe,' Wellington affirmed
in Parliament during the Greek struggle.[12] Ultra-conservative
after 1815, the Tsars thought instinctively of the Sultan (and
of the Shah, likewise plagued with malcontents)[13] as a brother-
monarch. But even they could not forego for ever the popularity that would accrue to them from crusades against the
infidel. Most of the Balkan Christians belonged to the Orthodox
Church, so their sufferings made a special appeal to the Russian people. Religion was three quarters of the ordinary Russian's patriotism, and nine tenths of the Turkish peasant's. The
Crimean War of 1854–6, when both Tsar and Sultan were
under heavy pressure from their fanatics, was almost a war of
religion strayed out of its proper century.

Official England continued to adhere to the policy of bolster-
ing up the Ottoman empire. It was coming to have far bigger
stakes in Asia than in Europe, and unlike Russia it had (until
shortly before 1914) no designs on Turkish territory in Asia.
Also the Sultan's informal status of Caliph or leader of all
Muslims made it worth while in Muslim India to give publicity
to Britain's protection of Turkey. A ludicrous resemblance can
be detected between this propping up of the Commander of
the Faithful by Britain, assisted in the Crimean War by France,
and the propping up of the Holy Father by a French garrison
after 1848 in Rome. Both policies had bitter critics. Middle-class
England took religion more seriously than its government did.

Bright in 1854 recalled Burke's words of 1791, and denounced as bad even for the Turks themselves 'the miserable and lunatic idea, that we are about to set the worn-out Turkish Empire on its legs'.[14] A cartoonist caught a more plebeian facet of British opinion in his Crimean War drawing of a jolly Jack Tar, pipe in mouth, taking a ride about the hills on the shoulders of a Turkish soldier, with another tied behind him on a rope as a spare mount.[15]

A cartoon of 1877, after Britain had risked war to protect Turkey once again from the Russians, drew an opposite picture – Disraeli on a tightrope with a fat smirking Sultan squatting on his shoulders.[16] Massacres of Bulgars and Armenians revived half-forgotten memories of older Ottoman savagery, and the phrase 'Unspeakable Turk' was repeated. Gladstone talked fiercely in his Midlothian election campaign in 1880 about how the Turks ought to be cleared out of Europe altogether, bag and baggage, bashaw and bashi-bazouk; as he was then in opposition no doubt his stirring words ought to have been taken in a Pickwickian sense only. Abdul Hamid II, Sultan from 1876 to 1909, was known in England and denounced in sermons as Abdul the Damned. Among the figures of Victorian pantomime were sultans with huge moustachios and scimitars,[17] and the man in the street probably thought of Abdul Hamid as one of them. He concentrated on keeping the Asian provinces intact, and played on his attributes as Caliph. In this sense the empire towards the end was growing more instead of less Asiatic.

Imperial calculations decided official England not to see too many motes in the Turkish eye, but various factors assisted it. There had never been war between the two countries. Turkey's religion was bad, but to good Protestants not much worse than the Catholicism of Spain or Naples. Its government was bad, but not very much worse than Russia's. In time of war its army always commanded respect, as the British did, not by cleverness at the top but by doggedness down below. A young Anglo-German serving as a volunteer in the defence of Plevna in 1877 – the Sevastopol or Verdun of the Turkish army – was deeply moved to see 'to what heights the sons of a proud and devoted nation can rise'.[18] Its empire had once been resplendent, and an

Englishman such as Burton could feel an admiration for it, and something like admiration for some of its methods. Like Tsarism in Asia it had rough and ready ways of making itself felt by disorderly subjects. England could not do quite the same, Burton admitted, but might learn from them at least the value of a 'just, wholesome, and unsparing severity', calculated to infuse 'fear instead of contempt'.[19] From unsparing severity to massacre is only a few imperial strides.

Altogether, to Englishmen of army and empire affiliations Turkey seldom appeared so unpleasant as to Nonconformist or Radical. Another phrase was in vogue, 'The Turk is a gentleman'. As a conquering race Turks had acquired much of the temper and outlook of an aristocracy, and the more so, as a people, because they had no hereditary nobility to monopolize these attributes. They disdained all base mechanical employments leaving them to Greeks, Jews and such underlings. Their own chosen existence was divided between spirited action and leisured repose. To Kinglake, himself a man of imperial views, Greeks, including those now independent, were about as 'oriental' as Turks, and sometimes less attractive, full of those habits of petty fraud and greed that Turks were notably free from. As a gentleman the Turk might be said to be standing by his convictions, clinging to his dignified indolence even now when the bailiffs were gathering round his door; a sturdy refusal to change with the times that must have touched nostalgic chords in a Europe where the old ruling classes were being seduced by the moneybags into City directorates or alliances with Jewish heiresses.

On the other hand there could be no denying that Turkish administration, even when not oppressive, was corrupt and inefficient. One Russian envoy smoothed his path by collecting private information about the ministers he had to deal with, and threatening to reveal it to their sovereign.[20] Britain was able to gauge the results of Turkish rule by seeing them in a number of areas taken over from it: the Ionian islands, Cyprus, Egypt. In Cyprus the old régime had been 'a curse to the people and a curse on the land'. Commissioner Wauchope gave the new one a good start by hanging a Turk for murder, a procedure heretofore unheard of.[21] In Egypt after the occupation in 1882

British officials felt they were wrestling with the outcome of 'centuries of unremitting misrule'.[22] It has to be added that in both cases the new authority came under criticism for continuing the flogging policies of its predecessor.[23] But if the Ottoman empire was to be kept going it would obviously have to pull itself together, and Englishmen were forever vexing the dull ear of the drowsy Turk with admonitions of the need for reform and progress; admonitions that after 1857 their Indian princes were usually spared. The man who talked loudest and longest was the Great Elchi or ambassador Stratford Canning, and he found it, as he told his brother, 'uphill work. Such roguery, corruption, and falsehood and deep anti-social selfishness . . .'[24] He was a man equal to thirty hours' deskwork at a stretch, but to activate Turks was beyond even his energy.

Like twentieth-century Americans these Englishmen overlooked the difficulty in Asia of reform without revolution. England had almost forgotten its own revolution. About what kind of reform was called for there was not much clarity. Parliaments and elections were the cure-all of British philosophy, but realists judged them beyond the capacity of Spaniards, let alone Turks, and were in no haste to introduce them in India. What they wanted to see at Stamboul was a modernized, efficient autocracy, something very much like a governor-general's at Calcutta. This might not seem too much to hope for. After all this empire did hang together for nearly five centuries after the capture of Constantinople, a long time by either Eastern or Western clocks. Nearly every Asian monarchy during the nineteenth century threw up some ruler who tried to reconstruct it, and at Stamboul this ruler was Mahmud II. In 1826 he put an end to the usurpation of power by the praetorian corps of janissaries by having them massacred. Foreign envoys hastened to congratulate him on this statesmanlike *coup*. In 1839 there was issued the *Khatt-i-Sherif*, or imperial rescript, tracing a programme of reform.[25] But the inertias of the old order were too heavy. Subsequently the Young Turk party tried to push things forward. Few of them cared about parliamentarism, as liberals in the West fancied. They were 'by no means friends of European civilization', Nubar Pasha the Egyptian politician remarked to a German diplomat in 1877; 'they wished to re-

construct Turkey ... with the material resources of civilization, but in the spirit of the past'.[26] This was exactly what the
ruling élite in Japan was doing, as some of the Young Turks
must have been aware.

What was possible in Japan might not be practical politics
in Turkey, with its unwieldy size and unyielding religion. In
days gone by it had borrowed from a Western technology still
elementary, but now an Asian country had to learn a great
deal more to survive. Gunpowder had been a novelty congenial to the Turk; steam was a different matter. A foreigner
at Stamboul in mid-century noticed his distaste for the steam
paddle-boat lately introduced, as a threat to the good old
ways: 'Every paddle-wheel which churns the waters of the
Bosphorus, produces, by its revolutions, others almost imper-
ceptible, but no less certain, in his social and political state.'[27]
Karl Marx on the Bosphorus would have been visited by the
same thought. Wherever modernity spread, the true Turk
seemed to vanish, a later observer wrote;[28] he seemed to be
doomed to extinction by poverty, the effects of conscription,
and the 'inconceivable spread' of syphilis.[29] Modernism had
many aspects, and the East had a heavy price to pay for what
it learned from the West.

Tourists in the Near East

Well acclimatized in Europe in the eighteenth century, in the
nineteenth tourism was spreading to the Near East. Italy and
Spain were growing humdrum, and it was time to go farther
afield in search of the glamorous medley of rags and ruins that
the tourist had learned to expect. Antiquarians studying ruins
seriously helped to make Greece a stepping-stone. One of these,
Gell, stumbled on the chronic paradox that a lax despotism like
the Turkish allowed a surprising degree of 'personal liberty,
both of word and action'. Mentally all was darkness, he added,
except where European residents had 'awakened some sparks
of intellect'.[30] Byron had a vivid sense of the romance of the
East when, dressed for the occasion in a 'staff uniform, with a
very magnificent sabre', he stood face to face with Ali Pasha

of Janina among the wild Albanian mountains. The Pasha's foreign physician, who had some Latin, was their interpreter; it was often by such roundabout means that East and West exchanged thoughts. They have not often confronted each other in the persons of two such men, both fated to perish before many years were past not far from where they now stood. Ali, whom his young friend well knew to be 'a remorseless tyrant, guilty of the most horrible cruelties', was very civil. Byron liked all the Albanians, as a warrior race and the handsomest in the world, with plenty of bad qualities but no mean ones.[31]

It was another dramatic confrontation when the author of *Eothen* abruptly appeared before a pair of Bedouin in the desert and without a word seized their water-flask and took a deep drink: their first sight possibly of a white man, 'and for this ghastly figure to come swiftly out of the horizon, upon a fleet dromedary'[32] might well make them gape. The West has found a certain pleasure in astonishing the East with its unexpectednesses and eccentricities. When Kinglake and an officer returning overland from India passed each other in the desert, stiff and silent on their camels, with a slight nod,[33] each must have felt agreeably conscious of how they were mystifying their attendants, denizens of the garrulous East.

Kinglake was one of the last Romantics, seeking between desert sands and stars the visionary world that in the West had faded into common gaslight. He journeyed in search of impressions, not of Blue Book facts, and was the most brilliant of all English travellers at catching them. *Eothen* taught a generation of tourists what to see, or to fancy they saw. When Thackeray was invited in 1844 by the P. & O. Company to join a Mediterranean cruise everyone on board was struggling for the ship's copy.[34] Thackeray by contrast was an unromantic midVictorian, whose concern was with the march of progress and common sense, and whose dislike of squalor and ignorance was never lulled for long by any amount of picturesqueness, whether in Turkey or in Ireland. Two universes were close together when Thackeray watched the Sultan of the day, Abdul Mejid, on his way to the mosque, looking like a young French *roué*, with a clever dissipated face, almost too enervated by the pleasures his mother and courtiers kept him plunged in to be able to sit on his horse.[35] Thackeray and his party felt they were contemplating 'the last days of an empire', borne down by 'weakness, disorder, and oppression'.[36] He too counted on steam, 'the civilizing paddle-wheel', to sweep the old rottenness away.[37]

His very minor but not unamusing brother-novelist Albert Smith was there a few years later, an energetic solo traveller with a knapsack of his own designing; another matter-of-fact chronicler, who laughed at the tourist eye that saw romance in every kind of dullness and dirt as the Scottish wizards 'turned cobwebs to tapestry'.[38] He laughed too at the ghoulish tales of heads chopped off and palace charmers sewn up in sacks and thrown into the Sea of Marmora. Improvement was coming in, he thought, chiefly because foreigners were being employed, like the Mr Taylor in charge of the gun-foundry who 'gave the Turkish workmen a good character for intelligence and a wish to oblige'.[39] The higher classes, from the Sultan down, were in European dress, surmounted by the new-fangled fez. To Burton this westernizing meant degeneracy, not progress, and he derided 'the pert and puny modern Turk in pantaloons, frock coat and Fez, ill-dressed, ill-conditioned, and ill-bred, body and soul'.[40] Peoples long sunk in stagnation like Turks or Spaniards decay most thoroughly at the top, and it was the governing class, not Mr Taylor's workmen, who were putting themselves into pantaloons.

About that same time a young Englishman named Whittall, with an ancestry of merchants settled at Smyrna, was starting a business career of fifty years in Turkey. At the end of it he modestly confessed that he had no more than an imperfect understanding of the country, along with a good deal of liking for it. He went all over the interior, not as most visitors did only from one semi-foreign port to another. 'The Oriental mind is so very differently constituted to ours that it is impossible to fathom it completely at all times.'[41] We are always more or less in the dark about all our fellow-creatures and about ourselves, but it is among foreigners that we grow conscious of our ignorance. Whittall knew of a respectable Turk who, when the Greek revolt was inflaming popular feeling against

Greeks in all the provinces, rescued several from being lynched, at the risk of his own life.[42] It is a consoling memory to set against the fearsome slaughter that flared up over and over again until the cancered empire finally collapsed.

Egypt and North Africa

Egypt broke away from the empire early in the nineteenth century, under its governor Mehemet Ali, an Albanian of humble birth, and its Turkish upper class. Stirred up by Bonaparte's brief tenure, and in need of resources to enable it to challenge Stamboul, Egypt was the theatre of a thorough-going experiment, the first in all the East, in westernization by decree. Mehemet Ali built a new army of Albanian mercenaries and Egyptian conscripts, drilled by foreign officers. One of these, the Frenchman Sève, embraced Islam and went by the name of Sulaiman Pasha.[43] Mehemet also tried to build a modern industry based on State monopolies. Three young men he sent to Britain to study at the Nasmyth engineering works did very well there, and one later went back to marry an English girl and start a business.[44] In both his military and his economic ambitions Mehemet bore a resemblance to Peter the Great; he was likewise an inexorable despot and flogger.

There was much debate among foreigners, sharpened by rival interests, as to whether the new Egypt was a *bona fide* imitation of Europe, or a grotesque travesty of it. France chose to regard Mehemet, as it had formerly done the Turks, as its protégé, and took him to what a nation editorially calls its heart. Englishmen were always less pleased than Frenchmen to see natives dressing up. 'Can you tell me what all this row is about,' asked one of Kingston's midshipmen, 'between us and these wide-breeched, red-capped niggers, the Egyptians?'[45] The reason was partly that Palmerston detested Mehemet, though Sir John Bowring whom he sent on a mission of inquiry in 1837–8 formed a different opinion of him. He tried to get the Pasha to abolish slavery, a stumbling-block to any goodwill from Britain; but black slaves from Egypt's colony of the Soudan formed part of the revenue.

Egypt failed to get beyond a certain point, which may be proof that no similar attempt in Turkey or any other country with the same historical foundations could succeed. The cost to the scanty population was crippling. On the surface, by the time tourists began to arrive, there was bustle and newness. Thackeray found Alexandria looking 'scarcely Eastern at all',[46] and the Nile at Cairo lined with foundries and steam-mills as well as palaces. As at Stamboul he felt no regrets for the past. He had no magicians or exotic dancing-girls to regale his readers with, he admitted, but instead was delighted to meet with honest British enterprise, along with 'manliness, bitter ale and Harvey Sauce', novelties that the forty centuries looking down from the Pyramids ought to be better pleased with than General Bonaparte 'running about with sabre and pigtail'.[47] Burton dissented. 'The land of the Pharaohs is becoming civilized, and unpleasantly so . . .' He was disgusted with a host who sat on chairs, ate with a fork, and talked European politics.[48]

The man who knew the country best was Lane, who went there first in 1825, plunged into native life, and in 1836 produced his encyclopaedic account of Egyptian life and manners. No admirer of Mehemet Ali, he found much to like in his subjects: a general cheerfulness, hospitality, unusual temperance and frugality, scrupulous cleanliness among the higher classes, and the lower not less clean than in Europe.[49] In point of intellect they seemed to him better endowed than most; unfortunately their faculties were eroded by the influence of climate, religion, and oppression.[50] No one could help seeing the oppression of the fellah or peasant by the Turk whose Western fripperies he had to pay for. Thackeray had 'a sickening feeling of disgust' at the brutal treatment of these Egyptians, 'a tall noble handsome race', by their masters, and all their masters' hangers-on, the Negro slave worst of all. 'The whip is in everybody's hands.'[51]

Impenetrably disguised as Abdullah the Mecca-bound pilgrim, Burton could hear Egyptians talking as frankly about Europeans as Europeans did about Egyptians; and he knew everything about the East, except perhaps that he knew nothing about ordinary men anywhere. It was to him 'unintelligible' that even Egyptians employed for years under European

roofs should have 'the liveliest loathing' for Western ways. All
foreigners were detested, except that 'somehow or other, the
Frenchman is everywhere popular'. (Englishmen have always
found this unintelligible.) Yet Burton managed to believe that
Egypt longed for Western rule, and wanted it hot and strong.
'This people admire an iron-handed and lion-hearted despotism; they hate a timid and a grinding tyranny.'[52] In reality they
had developed a sullen kind of passive resistance of their own,
'refusing to pay their taxes until they have been severely
beaten';[53] in the Mameluke and Ottoman times there had been
not a few peasant revolts.[54]

Yet their reputation with Westerners continued to be one of
servility, and in the British epoch this had a malign effect on
methods of administration. One of those who worked them out,
Colvin, quoted with approval Milner's verdict on 'a nation of
submissive slaves, devoid of the slightest spark of the spirit of
liberty', and likely long to remain so.[55] The longer the better, a
candid European bondholder, for whose benefit the peasant
was being taxed and sometimes flogged now, might have
added. Colvin saw no anomaly in the fact that in 1882 Egyptians banded round Arabi Pasha to resist the British occupation. 'Then, as now, politically blind, they followed blind
leaders', instead of waiting for true Hampdens or Washing-
tons to appear to them.[56] By this date any Afro-Asian people
really had only a choice between blindness or slavishness, and
whichever it chose the Western response was the same.

Tripoli remained Turkish until seized by the Italians in 1911
after the bombardment that often served as baptism into Western civilization; the rest of Muslim north Africa, the *Maghrib*
or West of the Islamic world, had drifted away from the Ottoman empire, only to follow the same downward course and
end in the maw of the French empire. It was an unsavoury
region where African savagery seemed to blend with Muslim
fanaticism, especially in the interior, which was a chaos of
tribal war, blood-feud, slave-raid, and the wild rituals of Dervishes and Marabouts, outlandish superstitions varnished with
Muslim orthodoxy. It might well seem marked out by Providence for European knowledge and laws to blow through like
fresh air.

So the French thought when they entered the field in the 1830s. Their first objective, the port of Algiers, was easily taken, but pushing inland into Algeria they ran into desperate resistance, tribal and religious. Its leader Abd-ul-Qadir earned a measure of respect by his long, exciting struggle, much like Shamil Bey's at the same period in the Caucasus; and the story of the French lighting fires to suffocate Algerians hiding in caves was often told. Browning put one of his dramatic monologues into the mouth of a follower of Abd-ul-Qadir,[57] but it is a stilted exercise in rhyme, very different from the poetry that he and many others wrote in praise of Italy's struggle for freedom. In the pacification of so nightmarish a land even French ruthlessness could seem justifiable.

To a British officer inspecting the country in 1857 it appeared that the conquerors were getting on quite well with the inhabitants. 'The French certainly have the knack of this kind of thing'; he contrasted it with the rudeness of the British that offended their Turkish allies in the recent Crimean War.[58] France was far closer geographically to Algeria, and could feel more intimately connected with it, than Britain with any colonial region. No English writer made a character like Daudet's 'Nabob' – a French profiteer from north Africa, drawn from life – the central figure of an important novel.[59] In the Kabyle mountains resistance had continued: this officer watched the final phase of the conquest there, and like others gave very high praise to the Berber hillmen for a defiance 'almost unparalleled for temerity and audacity'.[60] He judged them, moreover, a far more orderly and industrious people than the loafing Moors of the plains.[61]

In north Africa even ramshackle Spain, looked down on by Europe for its backwardness, could pretend to a civilizing mission, with the approval of a radical like Emilio Castelar[62] as well as of pushing generals and of the Church. General O'Donnell, premier in 1859 picked a quarrel with Morocco and led a campaign in person. It was a bungled affair, but served to make him Duke of Tetuan and allow Spain for a histrionic moment to recapture the elation of bygone crusades. Morocco instead of heeding the warning went back to sleep, and presently the French came.

In the Arab lands eastward from Egypt the West saw one more illustration of the blighting effect of Islam, and of Turkish misrule: two words as regularly coupled as 'feudal anarchy' or 'female depravity'. Interest was keenest in the desert tribes, scarcely under any rule, and supplying material for the perennial argument about man in his natural state. They inspired opposite feelings, both of them strong in Burton, that man of contradictions who believed in empire and order but hated tameness and sameness. Much that he saw in the Arabs on his surreptitious way to Mecca repelled him; hereditary 'greed of gain and revengefulness', 'the screaming Arab voice, the voluble, copious, and emphatic abuse, and the mania for gesticulation'.[63] Any such mannerisms were liable to awaken in taciturn upper-class Englishmen the same distaste that noisy Latins did. Yet he had an instinctive sympathy with the Bedouin spirit of chivalry and contempt for manual labour; 'there *is* degradation, moral and physical, in handwork compared with the freedom of the Desert'.[64] The West suffered from a chronic misgiving as to whether all the discipline and the toil it imposed on itself and its bondsmen were not a worse vanity than the curling pipe-smoke of the East.

Persia

England failed to conquer Afghanistan, and thought it in consequence, as Englishmen thought Scotland in the age of Bannockburn, intractably barbarous. Afghans, it was true, when not fighting invaders were fighting one another, and in no gentle style. A Scotswoman who did medical work at Kabul in the early years of this century and described the scene in the form of a novel chose as its hero no Afghan but a Panjabi, who had risen to be minister and who was, as she saw him, toiling to bring order out of chaos and old night.[65] No British woman in India would have made an Indian (except a religious saint) the hero of a book; only beyond the Khyber Pass was such a friendship possible.

Farther east yet the last new Islamic kingdom of traditional

pattern came into existence in the 1860s in Kashghar when
an adventurer named Yaqub Beg made himself master of eastern Turkestan, which had revolted from China. Because of
the Anglo-Russian rivalry in middle Asia a good deal of
curiosity was felt about him.[66] He and his son met foreign representatives with a 'studied expression of gravity', 'an air of
self-conscious dignity';[67] their visitors were more likely to be
impressed by Yaqub's calibre as a disciplinarian, and one
Englishman declared appreciatively that he had never seen a
population more 'quietly-conducted' or 'submissive-looking'.[68]
Before long the infant State was overthrown, not by the Russians, whom Yaqub feared, but – to add ignominy to the decline and fall of Muslim power in Asia – by the Chinese, themselves tottering towards collapse.

But the Muslim country apart from Turkey that touched
Western imagination was Persia. Europe's oldest extant drama
is called *The Persians*; this was the people that had sought to
conquer Greece, had defeated Roman legions, and sacked Delhi
a century before the British sacked it, after ruling north-west
India twenty-two centuries earlier. To Shakespeare Isfahan
had not seemed impossibly remote, at any rate from Illyria.[69]
Comparative philology was showing that old Persian was akin
to Greek. So was Sanskrit, but Indians were of much darker
complexion, as Persians like Turks had always been very conscious: in Persia the European was among people who often
looked very much like himself, in other words looked handsome,
well-built and intelligent. It was realized that in matters of
culture Persia had been, even when politically weak, the *grande
nation* of the entire Muslim East; from its capital, as from
Paris, polite letters and polished manners spread on every side.
Now in the West too Persian miniatures were collected, Persian poetry was translated, Hafiz was spoken of in the same
breath with Horace, Goethe wrote imitations of him; in 1854,
five years before Fitzgerald's version of Omar Khayyam first
dawned, Tennyson was struggling to learn Persian and taxing
his eyesight over the elusive script until he saw Persian letters
'stalking like giants round the walls of his room'.[70] Omar
Khayyam was a revelation to England: it put into exquisite

words the doubts lurking behind the façade of religious faith, the weariness of effort and empire that beset the devotees of work, competition and power.

Yet Persia like the rest had fallen on evil days, and those who saw it from within were more conscious of decrepitude than of the qualities that had made it great. It was caught between the Turks to the west and the Uzbegs and Turkomans to the east and north, and at home Persians were often at odds with a medley of tribal minorities. A Turki dynasty, the Qajar, was reigning in the nineteenth century. One ruler, Nasr-ul-Din (1848–96) got himself known in Europe by making a tour and publishing his journal of it. A woman who saw him in London disliked his 'coarse bad face'[71] but he was the Shah who tried to give the country a new lease of life by incorporating in the old framework as much modernism as it would hold – which was not enough. At the theatre at Berlin in 1873, during an interval in an 'extremely wearisome' ballet called *Sardana-palus* put on for his benefit, he was seen plying Bismarck with a stream of questions. 'He is thirsting for information,' a German noted, 'and prides himself on being the Peter the Great of Persia.'[72]

Persia's growing feebleness, and then by 1914 its oil, made it another cockpit of rivalries, which sharpened the eyes of political visitors. There was also some quality of the Persian air, even now, that whetted observation and literary faculties, and many of the accounts written about the country retain their interest. Last in the eighteenth century to arrive was Sir John Malcolm, sent from India on a mission in 1800 when Persia was becoming a counter in the French wars. He was making a careful study of the country and its 'extraordinary inhabitants', he reported from Shiraz. 'The men appear to me all poets.' Officials were not too poetical to embezzle funds extorted from the public for the mission's transport. The Shah was chiefly concerned to inquire how many princes there were in the English royal family – in his own they were legion – and how they were treated.[73]

Eight years later there arrived young James Morier, the diplomat who was to publish in 1824 the best-known and wittiest of all descriptions of Persia, *Hajji Baba of Ispahan*. He was

born with an oriental spoon in his mouth, his father being consul at Stamboul. His novel stamped its picture of Persia on
the Western mind for the rest of the century. It was a marvellously graphic delineation of an Eastern régime and society
with one foot in the grave, an Arabian Nights comedy where
the fishmonger of yesterday might be the minister of today and
the bastinado'd jailbird of tomorrow. Under thin disguise
Morier brought in the ministers of the day, and the Shah, Fath
Ali, whose stupendous beard still deluges us in his portraits, so
it is scarcely surprising that the book was banned in Persia for
a century. It left out, of course, many things little in evidence
at that low ebb of Persia's chequered fortunes, including the
consciousness of a proud national tradition that, once acquired,
no nation ever seems altogether to lose. Out of such resources a
regeneration of Persia by the Persian people was to have its
painful beginnings before the end of the century; something
that could no more have been guessed from *Hajji Baba* than
the Spanish struggle against Napoleon from *Gil Blas*.

E. O'Donovan was in north Persia in 1879–80, as *Daily News*
correspondent. He was a resourceful and well-armed traveller,
but he found the going hard, and his impressions were almost
unrelievedly dismal. The frontier town of Astarabad that he
entered by, a neat enough little place today, on the edge of the
Caspian, was then 'full of hopeless dirt and neglect', and part
of the area inside its crumbling ramparts was jungle infested
by wild boars.[74] Teheran was nondescript, 'a strange mixture of
the Eastern and Western styles'. He witnessed a royal procession there, coachmen who looked more like scullions driving
the harem favourites in old coaches, with apes and baboons
capering about them.[75] Hajji Baba in London found public ceremonial equally ridiculous, no doubt.[76] Local governors had
carte blanche to take what they could, and at one place where
O'Donovan heard 'sad tales of misgovernment and extortion'
a merchant had lately been buried up to his neck in a dungeon
with ice packed round his head as a persuasive.[77] At Kuchan,
north of Meshed, the governor was a Kurdish chief, who honoured the traveller with a banquet in semi-European style. A
long table was set out in his courtyard with snowy cloth and
French as well as local wine and arrack; but just as the Irishman

was constructing a Kurdish pun on mushrooms, which were being eaten, the bench opposite him gave way and the emir and his officers rolled together on the ground, where they 'kissed each other with fervour, swore undying devotion, and seemed in no wise inclined to resume their positions at table'.[78]

Above all O'Donovan depicted a general state of insecurity, a government energetic in robbing its subjects but impotent to protect them. He joined a caravan of pilgrims making for the holy shrine at Meshed five thousand strong, with an armed escort and a four-pounder gun. On the premises of the courteous governor there he was shown a heap of Turkoman heads, stuffed with grass, that were dumped in a cellar. Payment for these marauders' heads represented a regular part of a frontier commandant's income.[79] Readers at home might well conclude that to such a land, with clocks centuries behind Greenwich time, there could be no greater blessing than the Union Jack. This was the conclusion reached by W. S. Blunt, later an uncompromising anti-imperialist, when he travelled in the East in the 1870s and viewed the misery of countries like Persia: surely England had 'a providential mission' to set them right, he thought – until he saw India.[80]

E. G. Browne went out from Cambridge in 1887, a young scholar destined to be the leading Western authority on Persian literature. When he wrote his *Year among the Persians* he had no political moral to point, or hint, yet his colours were about as gloomy as O'Donovan's. Before long he met an uncle of the Shah, that eager questioner of Bismarck, who as governor of Shiraz for four years had cut off seven hundred hands, and walled men up alive.[81] It is at Shiraz that the tomb of Hafiz stands amid its enchanted rose-gardens. Browne had an eye for the plebian wretchedness that underlay patrician refinement, the shocking conditions for instance in which the famous Persian rugs were made.[82] He thought it quite understandable that common people objected to the railway and tramway contracts that would enrich only the ministers who gave them and the foreigners who got them. Europeans tended to suppose 'that the interests of the Shah and of his subjects are identical, when they are in fact generally diametrically opposed'.[83]

In religious debate Browne was upset by a 'dreadful' note

of passion, still more by the sight of heretics of the new Babi sect being executed.[84] We may interpret this *odium theologicum* as a twisted outlet of embitterments and frustrations in Persian life. When these could be forgotten there was much more in social intercourse than the traditional Persian fine manners. Dinner-parties had a charming unrestraint, and scintillated with brilliant talk. This realm of wit and fantasy, this escape from the plane of base reality to that of poetry and opium pipes, so fascinated Browne that when summoned back to his university he had to make an effort to uproot himself from his 'dreamy speculative existence'. Teheran on his way back looked depressingly Westernized.[85] How stolid suburban Cambridge looked one can only guess.

Curzon's book on Persia came out in 1892, a few years before he was made Viceroy of India. He saw Persia in Churchillian fashion, as an arena where the mastery of Asia was to be decided; he prepared for his tour with Churchillian thoroughness, turning over all the two or three hundred books in European languages.[86] Probably none of them did more to fix his ideas than *Hajji Baba*; in 1895 he wrote a foreword to a new edition of the novel, recommending it as a still faithful inventory of the 'unchanging characteristics of a singularly unchanging Oriental people'.[87] His concern as he rode about the country filling his notebooks was with facts about Persia's trade, resources, politics, just as later on he was passionately interested in India, but not much in Indians, mere clay to be moulded on the potter's wheel of empire. The poverty he saw made him fear that the people would do nothing to resist a Russian entry; they could not be worse off. 'A Persian is a coward at the best of times.'[88] He agreed with an estimate that population had sunk from ten to six millions between 1850 and 1873, through famine and cholera;[89] he might have reflected that Ireland had been undergoing a similar fate. He thought well of the Shah, but disapproved of his erratic enthusiasms, for example for buying skates or bicycles and making his grandees career about the park on them.[90]

Sherlock Holmes must have been in Persia about the same time, crossing the country on his way back from Tibet before he 'looked in at Mecca',[91] and it would be instructive to have his opinion of Persian police. It was not long before Persia was being crossed by another traveller well known to the novel-reading public, 'Pierre Loti', who started from the Gulf and made his way northward over the massif to Teheran and the Caspian. A naval officer and an aesthete, he was a combination less eccentric in France than he would have been in England. Absorbed in exotic suggestion and sensation, he tells us brilliantly how Persians looked, not how they lived; his most lyrical flight is about the vacant ruins of Persepolis that had haunted his imagination from boyhood.[92] By the end of the century the West was experiencing a certain drying-up of human sympathies and concernments. Where he came closer to earth Loti was thinking either about Persian women or, equally as a good Frenchman, about British villains. When Europe's national hatreds, its equivalent of the theological hatreds of Persia, exploded in 1914 France and Britain were to be allies, but solely by diplomatic accident. Loti was coming from India, and commiserated with the unhappy Hindu groaning under British rule (now directed by Curzon). And while Englishmen found Persians in dread of invasion by France's ally Russia, Loti found them indignantly anticipating aggression from Britain, and determined to sell their lives dearly.[93]

For Loti, Persia's charm lay in not being the noisy bustling vulgar West, but an idyllic survival from older ways. He wanted its inhabitants to harmonize with his own sentiments, to feel happy because they had no thumping machinery around them. In the towns, all blank windowless walls except in the jostling bazaars, he was too much a European not to be chilled by the absence of life, especially after sunset, and too much a Frenchman not to suffer gnawing curiosity about the women, invisible in their mantles. At Isfahan he foolhardily bribed a tradesman to let him climb a ladder and peep over a garden wall. He beheld three ladies engaged, as Persian ladies should be, in gathering roses. '*Je les espérais plus jolies . . .*'[94] In this city he was refused lodgings, as an infidel outlander, by a hostile mob, and charitably taken in by Prince D., the Russian consul-general, and his wife, the only resident Europeans, whose establishment gave him 'European comfort in an Oriental setting'[95] – an ideal union that Isfahan today offers to all travellers with purses. Nearing the frontier he felt that European proximity was spoiling his innocent Persians, making them tipsy, impudent, thievish.[96] It was part of Europe's changing mood by this time to wonder more often whether its influence on other people was not doing them more harm than good.

Wilson – the later Sir Arnold – was in southern Persia in the seven years before 1914, and his letters and diary bring before us a young cadet from India full of interest in his surroundings and brimming over with devotion to the Curzon-and-Kipling imperial ideal then at its apogee. Persians were feeling the attraction of other Western ideals, and a struggle for constitutional reform and an elected Majlis or parliament was under way. It became a struggle also to defend the national independence against Britain and Russia, suddenly turned allies. In the abstract Englishmen might believe in parliamentary government for all, but oil, then as now, mattered more than ideology. They always wanted to have it both ways, however, and liked to think that their new Russian friends got on better with Persians only because Persians thought them 'no better than themselves', whereas they recognized England as on 'a different plane of civilization'.[97]

'I like Persians, of all classes,' Wilson wrote, 'even nomads and robbers: they are ... easier to work and live and play with than Indians ...'[98] This was probably the feeling of most Europeans who knew the two countries. Because they had kept their national existence, Persians did not suffer from a humiliating sense of inferiority, and sometimes looked down on Indians for their tame submission to the foreigner. But Wilson had no patience with their political aspirations. 'The *majlis* will not work,' he wrote positively, 'it has no roots.' He dismissed Browne, who was writing in England in defence of the constitutionalists, as a well-meaning 'visionary'.[99]

Asia was always wrong, when it copied the West and when it did not. Nationalism in India helped to prejudice empire men against popular movements in neighbouring countries; and they were apt to be very distrustful of politicians even in their own countries as wiseacres and windbags. Politicians in Persia were for Wilson, who saw half the truth about them, 'charming French-speaking frock-coated grandees' imposing on gullible foreigners.[100] He liked the frank Bakhtiari tribesmen who were being enlisted by the oil company as guards. They might look like 'stage assassins',[101] but were untainted by the nonsense of politics and asked no sophistical questions about British intentions. Increasingly empire men found common ground with both feudal potentates and with hill-folk and desert-dwellers, as against the townsman who had got more education than was good for him.

W. H. Shuster was an American, employed with four others in 1911 to straighten out Teheran's tangled finances. It was a time when some Americans still thought hopefully of helping to make a better world, rather than an American world, and Shuster was an idealist. His job would have been a hard one at the best, but his worst obstacle was the Russian determination, acquiesced in by Britain, to prevent reform. In the same fashion, he might have recollected, Catherine the Great blocked reform in Poland in order to paralyse the country until it was ready for partition. He admired the courage of the Majlis party, whose leaders, all men from the upper classes, were winning national support.[102] He as well as they were being vilified by the Russians, as W. S. Blunt noted sympathetically in his diary.[103]

When Russia dropped out of the Great War after the Revolution a British force entered western Persia from Iraq to counteract the advancing Turks there and in the Baku oilfield. It was led by General Dunsterville, Kipling's Stalky, a personification of the empire spirit at its full maturity, with all its virtues and all its limitations. He too had taught himself what to expect in Persia by reading *Hajji Baba*,[104] and was sure the new politics need not be taken seriously. There was no real patriotism,[105] so no good army could ever be formed; conversely it was very easy to organize an intelligence service and take Persian breath away by well-timed displays of information. British officers had acquired a flair for secret-service work, so much a part of colonial administration. Dunsterville saw the wealthier classes at their worst when famine raged at Hamadan. While he did his best to provide relief work on the Indian model, they remained perfectly callous to horrors that would have appalled anyone 'not endowed with the wonderful

apathy of the Oriental'. Well-fed mullahs ordered the execution of wretches driven by hunger to cannibalism.[106]

His logic contained no way of escape for the Persian masses
whom he pitied, except foreign rule. For them to rise against
their tormentors would make things worse. Revolutionism of
every shade, Bolshevik or Persian, plebeian or aristocratic, was
for him synonymous with anarchy, social dissolution, moral
collapse. A revolutionary was quite literally a degenerate, a
creature without human instincts. His only good word for the
Russians streaming homeward from the front was when they
saved the English from being ambushed by Persian irregulars:
'even the revolutionary soldiers proved themselves to be "white
men" in this matter.'[107] At the end of the war there floated
before men like Dunsterville or Curzon, who became Foreign
Secretary, an afterglow of the old idea of Britain's mission, the
vision of a grand Pax Britannica stretching from the Mediterranean to India.[108] It was a vision that Britannia no longer had
strength to turn into reality; and its intended beneficiaries
might have wondered why a country which had just lost a
million men in a war nobody knew the meaning of should be
offering to bestow Peace on the tranquil East.

The Oriental Scene: Despotism, Hubble-Bubble, Harem

Kinglake set out on his travels to contemplate 'the splendour
and havoc of the East'.[109] His phrase summed up a dual conception of fabulous wealth in the midst of once-great cities in
decay and once-proud nations in tatters. Men who talked about
the Orient had in mind as a rule what was then called the 'Near
East' and is now, grown somehow less familiar and more distant, the 'Middle East'. In other words it was the Islamic world,
from Morocco to Turkestan, the realm of minaret and muez-
zin, bashaw and bulbul, camel and veil and palm. It was the
East that Christendom had known for ages, fought a hundred
wars with, and in earlier days learned a good deal from, though
it preferred now to think itself the heir of Greece and Rome
alone. Conscious of this Old World at his elbow, the Westerner
felt his identity by contrast with it: it was his shadow, his

antithesis, or himself in dreams. He felt in it as Curzon did a 'wonderful and incalculable fascination'.[110]

The Arabian Nights enshrined this spell and formed one of Europe's grand passions. Here was a vista of life comic and irresponsible, and by turns romantic, mysterious, sinister. To its own denizens a realm of necessity or destiny, to Western fantasy this Orient was one of freedom, where man could expand beyond all common limits, with the unlimited power that Napoleon dreamed of there, unlimited luxury, palace and princess, magic and adventure; all those inordinate things that orderly modern man had to renounce and live as if born, King-lake wrote, with a bit in his mouth. If, as we are now told, our dreams are necessary to our mental equilibrium, Europe's collective day-dream of the Orient may have helped to preserve it through the century when it was leading humanity's plunge into the unknown.

The East appeared absolved from ordinary laws of rationality because it knew no civil law except the caprice of the stronger. A European, even if not encouraged to think himself 'free' as Englishmen were, expected to be decently, sensibly governed under some fixed code, as Prussians were. It was some consolation to him to reflect that if he had little freedom the East had no security, that society there, with no stable ranks or dignities, was a haphazard whirligig of ups and downs, entertaining in fiction but unbearable in fact. Beckford's novel *Vathek* of 1787 may be seen as an orientalized version of the old Faust legend that Goethe rediscovered in the same age of violent change, as the Elizabethans had done in theirs. It drew on the forbidding aspects of the East, the violence of the arbitrary will released from any curb, when this was looked at seriously instead of comically. When a Greek secretary of a Turkish embassy suddenly disappeared it was assumed at least half-seriously that he had been strangled and his head sent to Stamboul.[111]

Rulers like Mehemet Ali accused of tyranny might have protested that every government in Asia was condemned as either detestably cruel or nervelessly feeble. They might have said too that Westerners in the East, private individuals as well as colonial officials, were not always slow to adapt themselves to its arbitrary ways. Its inhabitants had to be dealt with high-handedly, it was often alleged, because that was what they were used to, as its horses were used to ponderous bits and saddles. 'The practice of intimidation thus rendered necessary is utterly hateful to an Englishman,' Kinglake wrote,[112] but he was a greenhorn, and he discovered that Lady Hester Stanhope, domiciled in Syria, met her requirements by employing a band of fierce Albanian retainers, who 'inspired sincere respect amongst the surrounding inhabitants', to levy contributions on them. She instructed him that 'a downright manner, amounting even to brusqueness', was the best way with orientals, and that no Englishman got on so well with them as 'a good, honest, open-hearted, and positive naval officer of the old school'.[113] Readers at home came naturally to feel that colonial government must be run on the same no-nonsense lines to inspire respect.

That all Eastern government was hopelessly corrupt, as well as arbitrary, was a tenet not very incorrect, and not confined to empire men. A Prussian who had worn uniform as well as a socialist, Engels studied Asian armies and criticized them scathingly. No efforts of foreign instructors to lick the Persian army into shape could make head, he wrote, against 'the cupidity and corruption of the Orientals' and 'Oriental ignorance, impatience, prejudice'.[114] Another part of common opinion was that the East was senile and worn out, the West brisk and youthful. Kinglake could scarcely credit even the authorship of the Arabian Nights to 'a mere oriental, who, for creative purposes, is a thing dead and dry – a mental mummy'.[115] In Anstey's novel *The Brass Bottle* the Jinn whom the hero unluckily liberates, a being 'at once so crafty and so childlike, so credulous and so suspicious',[116] is an epitome of the Westerner's Oriental. He is very old and far behind the times, having been shut up in his bottle by Solomon, and he has a plethora of old saws and adages to illustrate the obvious. In popular mythology and the cinema Orientals have continued to converse in sententious proverbs, revealing thereby their inability to say anything original.

Such threadbare wisdom might be respectable enough when it fitted in with sound conservatism. Dunsterville knew his Sa'adi, and held that Persians could find all the guidance they needed in their own poets, without turning to any Bolshevik ranters. 'They look feebly for enlightenment to the West, when all that we have worth knowing, except modern science, we have got from the East.'[117] Most of what the West had been learning in the past century was a sealed book to its Stalkies, who could find the East congenial because its ideas were even more old-fashioned than their own.

Europeans uneasily conscious of the price they were paying in never-ending instalments for their boasted progress saw other redeeming features in the down-at-heel East. Loti recalled the noise, the ugly scuffling life, that enveloped Europe's railway-stations, and rejoiced that Persia had been 'spared by the scourge of progress', left in 'happy immobility'.[118] Eastern ability to stand aside from time, to bask in the passing moment, was often envied. Societies which leave sordid labour to slaves, women, and donkeys will be rich in leisure, if in little else. The Arabic term *kaif* found its way into Western dictionaries: it denoted something there was no Western word for, what Burton called 'the pleasant languor, the dreamy tranquillity, the airy castle-building', Asia's counterpart of Europe's restless ambition.[119] Thackeray ran into a London acquaintance who had settled in Cairo for the sake of 'an indulgence of laziness such as Europeans, Englishmen at least, don't know how to enjoy', 'a dreamy, hazy, lazy, tobaccofied life'.[120]

Europe's active sectors were not ready yet for leisure, but they were studying comfort, and this was a department of life that well-to-do Muslims (unlike well-to-do Hindus) were neither too idle nor too indifferent to cultivate. All Turks drank coffee, as all continental Europeans did, and Muslim Asia and Britain were the two borrowers from China of tea. Kinglake found it 'a glad source of fellow-feeling between the Englishman and the Asiatic'.[121] Another aid to well-being was the Turkish bath, which the Turks had received from the Romans and now restored to Europe as the more intellectual Arabs received and restored Aristotle. No traveller who meant to write could afford to miss the Hamam at Stamboul.[122] Carpets too the East brought to perfection, because it sat on them. 'We are going to have a *Turkey*!!! carpet in the dining-room,' Dorothy Wordsworth wrote to a friend. 'Ottomans' entered French drawing-rooms in the eighteenth century, 'divans' were in the smoking-rooms of all Europe in the nineteenth. Sherlock Holmes kept his tobacco in a Persian slipper, and children ate Turkish Delight. But it was at bedtime that the East really seemed to make itself comfortable. If the East half envied, half despised the West's diurnal activity, the West had the same mixed sensation about the East's nocturnal existence. Beardsley's drawing of Ali Baba was a wonderful evocation of the pampered Oriental as Europe saw him, plump, sensual, cynical, heavy of thigh and jowl, with narrow eye and spirited moustache and begemmed turban.[124] A Muslim was a man with or in pursuit of four wives, and with a taste for having women about him that were fat, who in pious hours licked his lips over the rewards promised him in paradise –

Harems well stocked, and banquets every day.[125]

His women had no souls; what could they do in such a paradise even if they got there?

Translations were being made for connoisseurs of old Arab and Indian manuals on sex and on aphrodisiacs, some of which first began filtering westward in the days of the Crusades.[126] It was plausible to allow the East, with its licence and its leisure, an advantage over the West in these matters at least. A French savant recommending Turkish stimulants in 1686 argued that 'the greatest passions of Orientals are those which they hold towards their women'.[127] A hot climate was often said to make both men and women more 'libidinous' than they were in the chilly north.[128] Scott's pseudo-oriental heroine Zarah, whose mother was a native of an 'Eastern clime', owed to it her 'fierce torrent of passion' and her confused ideas of morality, as well as to an irregular upbringing in a strolling circus.[129] Lane extolled the Ghazawee entertainers as 'the finest women of Egypt',[130] and the Cairo belly-dancer was to succeed the Indian nautch-girl as a stock figure of the Westerner's Orient.

Nothing would go right in Turkey, Palmerston once priggishly told a Pasha, until polygamy was abolished. *'Ah! milord,'* rejoined the Pasha, *'nous ferons comme vous, nous présenterons l'une et nous cacherons les autres.'*[131] In practice, while the ordinary man in the East could only afford one wife, the man of means in the West indulged himself with a plurality of women. He divided his life as it were into an Occident and an Orient, the latter being the sphere of the illicit, the fleshly, the old Adam, where Old Testament patriarchs and Turkish pashas disported themselves side by side. Goldsmith's London beau was 'strongly prejudiced in favour of the Asiatic method of treating the sex ... it was impossible to persuade him, but that a man was happier who had four wives at his command, than he who had only one'.[132] Boswell communed with himself in the same simple arithmetic with his usual frankness. That celebrated beauty Miss Gunning had 'as fine a seraglio figure as I could wish to see', he notes. At the theatre 'I could not help indulging in Asiatic ideas as I viewed such a number of pretty women'.[133] At service with Dr Johnson in Lichfield cathedral he reassured himself about some recent peccadilloes as simply 'Asiatic satisfactions, quite consistent with devotion and with a fervent attachment to my valuable spouse'.[134] Johnson himself was not a stranger to day-dreams about a harem, and the same was true in private it may be supposed of many a strait-laced middle-class Victorian who took a stoical pride in his monogamy as part of the self-discipline and self-denial that made him the backbone of his country and of civilization.

The harem image appealed to an instinct of possession and domination as well as of mere pleasure. In Christian convention a man talked of his *mistress*, but it was agreeable at times to think of himself, like his Turkish neighbour across the Danube, as *master*. An earlier generation of Europeans in the East, the Nabobs among them, did adopt its domestic arrangements. A Frenchman of the later eighteenth century who had been robbed in Arabia of his precious collection of manuscripts sought consolation by collecting a harem in India instead; a hobby 'so luscious and fascinating in theory, but so irksome and cloying, as well as dangerous in practice'.[135] Some tried it in later years, like the acquaintance Kinglake met at Smyrna, a man of roving fancy who had dropped anchor there because on any whim he could 'give orders to his slave-merchant for something in the way of eternal fidelity'.[136]

Most travellers were content with speculation. When Thackeray's party cruised by the grated windows of the palace at Stamboul, close enough to hear 'whispering and laughing behind the bars – a strange feeling of curiosity came over some ill-regulated minds . . .'[137] By the 1850s, so true is it that money opens all doors, tourists were being shown round the interior when the inmates were absent.[138] Baron Munchausen enjoyed the unusual distinction of having been shown round in their presence, by the Grand Signior himself.[139] Byron's Don Juan went one better by making free with some of these inmates,[140] and Scott's court dwarf Hudson, who had been a captive on the Barbary coast, bragged of 'wild work' in the Moroccan emperor's seraglio.[141] Here was a Western fantasy at the opposite pole from that favourite of opera-writers, the 'escape from the seraglio', where the Western hero rescued the heroine from her gilded cage. A more modest but less fanciful exploit was that of a Frenchman in Russian service who visited the harem of a Crimean chieftain, disguised as a European lady. He had a ticklish time 'among so many beautiful women, very scantily clothed', and very inquisitive about his costume.[142] Stay-at-homes had to make do with what imagination could supply. Odalisques multiplied in the art galleries. There was a vogue of *poses plastiques*, and tableaux such as 'The Sultan's favourite returning from the bath' were popular.[143] In *Vanity Fair* an Eastern traveller with a black servant devises a charade at Steyne House concerned with a Turk, a slave-merchant, and the unveiling of a ravishing slave-girl.[144]

To Thackeray the East was fully as vicious as it was comic, and in Cairo he picked up revolting rumours about harem life,[145] which may quite well have been true of some rich mansions but cannot have been more typical of Cairo than the wicked Lord Steyne's conduct of London. Wives there may have been as much open to censure as husbands. 'Innumerable stories of the artifices and intrigues of the women of Egypt have been related to me,' writes Lane.[146] Burton thought them rather too well protected by law; he was long enough in the East to imbibe some of its notions about how women as well as men ought to be governed. 'The fair sex is so unruly in this country, that strong measures are necessary to coerce it.'[147] Suspicions of dark doings in the depths of the seraglio were liveliest at Stamboul. In a novel by the Hungarian writer Jokai a high official fled from the capital and up the Danube to save his life from persecution and his daughter from being seized on.[148] In 1880 questions were asked in Parliament about a female said to have escaped from the Sultan's palace and been given up by the British embassy – this was denied – to be strangled.[149]

In its treatment of its own working-class women, to say nothing of those employed in the mills it built in Asia, the West had not much to boast of; but one of its commonplaces was that Eastern women aged quickly because of over-work as well as climate. They were 'complete beasts of burden', said Byron in Albania.[150] Here was another reason for thinking of the East as a place where, in the words of Mustard Pott the retired bookie in Wodehouse, 'women are kept in subjection and daren't call their souls their own'.[151] Feminists were indignant over their lot, and the spectacle may have helped to set them thinking about the far from complete liberty and equality of women in the West. Lady Psyche in Tennyson's *Princess*, lecturing on the history of woman's hard usage, having denounced the Salic Law

> And little-footed China, touch'd on Mahomet
> With much contempt.[152]

Western man, on the contrary, uneasy about the emancipation of women going too fast, had fits of wondering, like Burton, whether the domestic discipline of the East might not have something to be said for it. Turks 'manage these things better than we do', declared Byron.[153] 'You ought to live in the East,' the cynical uncle in Goncharov's story tells his love-lorn nephew. 'They still tell women whom to love there, and if they disobey, drown them.'[154] Schopenhauer defended the Oriental view of the inferiority of women as far more rational than the Gallic, chivalric woman-worship of the West, which only spoiled women and made Asia laugh, as Greece or Rome would have laughed.[155] Germany was coming late on the scene, resentful of French pretensions, half inclined to turn away from time-honoured European standards it had taken no part in framing.

While Europeans meditated about invisible Eastern beauties, Easterners were intrigued by the novel visibility of Western beauties. Persian painting was infected with Western sex-appeal in its vulgarest forms, which can be studied in Fath Ali Shah's collection of pictures of dancing-girls and female acrobats, one of them standing on her hands.[156] The greatest hit of a Western circus at Stamboul in 1849 was a young lady who flew round the ring on a horse in a very scanty dress.[157] For amateurs with money the West had richer treats. One of the brilliant Cora Pearl's lovers was a Khalil Bey, an old gentleman who turned up in Paris in the 1850s and astounded even the Second Empire by his lavish style of living and loving.[158]

Christianity and Islam

To the age of faith Mahomed had been Anti-Christ; to Voltaire's the arch-fanatic, for the cult of reason formed itself against the background of Turkish as well as Spanish and Italian un-enlightenment. Then he was the hypocrite, the wily impostor. Carlyle in his 1840 lectures on Heroes set out to free him from this charge, and historical scholarship moved in the same direction. But 'Mahomedanism' as practised continued to provoke dislike or derision more often than not. Reformation and purification had begun, with the Wahhabis in Arabia, but were making slow progress in most lands, and there was still a load of primitive superstition as well as another load of fossilized scholasticism. A great deal was heard about wild Dervishes, the fanatical warriors of the Soudan who killed Gordon, or the 'dancing dervishes' who performed on Fridays at Stamboul, gyrating like tops in their conical hats. To that downright Englishman Albert Smith they looked 'inexpressibly sly and offensive', and he longed to 'hit them hard in the face'.[159] Another tourist attraction of Stamboul was the noise of the 'howling dervishes'.

Englishmen and other Europeans in the nineteenth century had a peculiar combination of rationalism and piety, two things each needful to them at home and still more in their empires, but liable to fall out, as they did over Moses and geology and that other 'Eastern Question', the age of the earth. Here again, like Voltaire's generation, they benefited by being able to set their enlightenment against the dark backcloth of the East. When Curzon dismissed 'the sterile nonsense that passes for philosophy in the East',[160] he was giving vent to the same robust scepticism that the eighteenth century felt towards Europe's own outworn creeds and orthodoxies. Such men could tuck their respectable Christian beliefs, along with any doubts they might have about them, into the back of their minds, and feel up-to-date and rational by spurning the absurdities of less progressive regions – Spain, Africa, Islam.

Unreconciled to loss of empire, Muslims clung the more unshakeably to their religion and their anti-Christianism as the badge of what they had once been and dreamed of being again. At Medina in 1853, when war was blowing up between Russian and Turk, Burton heard talk of how the frightened Tsar was offering submission and vassalage to the Sultan, but the Sultan was insisting on his accepting Islam also, and proclaiming a jehad, and an Arab contingent was to be formed, and the spoils of Europe awaited the true believers.[161] Muslims above all who had fallen under infidel sway, as in India, were resentfully turning their backs on the new world and retreating into an inner world of dream and dogma. Colonial governments were so careful not to intrude on it that missionaries complained of their work being held back and hampered in countries like the Soudan, and especially where Muslim rulers were being preserved, as in northern Nigeria or some of the Indian States.[162] Conversion of Muslims was admittedly so arduous that there was no great eagerness to attempt it. As late as 1925 an Anglican commission pointed to the 'startling' fact that of five thousand missionaries in India scarcely one hundred were making Muslims their quarry.[163]

The consensus of opinion was that Islam was hopelessly sterile and stationary, that its devotees had walled themselves up in a mental prison from which they could neither escape nor be rescued. Oriental fatalism was an obtrusive symptom. Controversy between free will and predestination was one of many things the two religions had shared; now the West, by launching on its career of Progress, had plumped for free will, and in the mirror of the East it could see the image of what it had escaped from, the stupor and paralysis of the human faculties. Stories were told of Turkish soldiers who neglected to take cover because there was no sheltering from the destined bullet, or from the Pen that wrote down whatever was to happen before the creation of the world.

Politically all this might serve Europe well, as in India. And Europeans might be willing to admit that in the very primitive corners of the world where Islam was still spreading, it was an improvement on the old paganism. Winwood Reade welcomed its advent in odd parts of Africa on this ground.[164] More unaccountable was the conversion to Islam of one or two Europeans, including a British peer – who might as easily have been expected to sprout wings and turn into a fairy, like the peers in *Iolanthe*. Lord Stanley of Alderley made himself the spokesman of Muslim feeling in India and Malaya. On his estates in Wales, where Anglicanism and landlordism were coming under fire together, he continued to be 'an ardent supporter of the Church of England'.[165]

NOTES

1. Katib Chelebi, *The Balance of Truth*, trans. G. L. Lewis (1957), pp. 29–30.

2. R. Hakluyt, *Voyages* (Everyman edn), Vol. 3, p. 40. cf. the sad experiences in the later seventeenth century recorded in *Adventures by Sea of Edward Coxere*, ed. E. H. W. Meyerstein (Oxford, 1945), pp. 54 ff.

3. J. H. Srawley, *Michael Honywood, Dean of Lincoln (1660–81)* (Lincoln, 1950), p. 19.

4. G. S. Thomson, *Life in a Noble Household, 1641–1700* (1937), p. 362.

5. *Boswell for the Defence, 1769–1774*, ed. W. K. Wimsatt and F. A. Pottle (1960), p. 125. Special certificates were furnished to such men in Scotland.

6. W. M. Thackeray, *The Four Georges* (1855): 'George the Second'.

7. *The Merchant of Venice*, Act 4, Scene 1.

8. See M. S. Anderson, *The Eastern Question* (1966), Chapter 1.

9. John Bright quoted this passage in his speech in the House of Commons on 31 March 1854.

10. Sir W. Gell, *Narrative of a Journey in the Morea* (1823), p. 217.

11. *An Irish Peer on the Continent*, ed. T. U. Sadleir (1920), under dates 3 January and 14 February 1803.

12. Lord Eversley, *The Turkish Empire* (3rd edn, 1924), p. 270.

13. N. V. Riasanovsky, *Nicholas I and Official Nationality in Russia, 1825–1855* (University of California, 1959), p. 219.

14. See note 9.

15. *John Leech's Pictures of Life and Character*, from *Punch* (n.d.), p. 117.

16. Reproduced in R. S. Lambrick, *A Historian's Scrapbook* (1932), p. 60.

17. J. W. Sherer, *Havelock's March on Cawnpore* (1857), p. 323 (Nelson edn, n.d.).

18. Captain F. W. von Herbert, *The Defence of Plevna, 1877* (1895), pp. 233–4 (1911 edn).

19. R. F. Burton, *First Footsteps in East Africa* (1856), pp. 14–15 (Everyman edn).

20. W. T. Stead, *Truth about Russia* (1888), p. 274. The Russian was Ignatiev.

21. W. Baird, *General Wauchope* (Edinburgh, 1900), pp. 58, 64.

22. Sir A. Colvin, *The Making of Egypt* (1906), p. 383 (Nelson edn, n.d.).

23. See W. Baird, op. cit., p. 60; George Bernard Shaw, Preface to *John Bull's Other Island* (1906).

24. Letter of 5 February 1843, in S. Lane-Poole, *The Life of Lord Stratford de Redcliffe, K. G.*, p. 21 (one-volume edn, 1890).

25. See Sir H. Luke, *The Old Turkey and the New* (new edn, 1955), Chapter 3 : 'The Era of the Tanzimat'.

26. *Memoirs of Prince Chlodwig of Hohenlohe Schillingsfuerst*, trans. G. W. Chrystal (1906), Vol. 1, pp. 200–201.

27. A. Smith, *A Month at Constantinople* (1850), pp. 53–4.

28. Sir J. W. Whittall, *Frederick the Great on Kingcraft* (1901; second part is on Turkey), pp. 186–7.

29. ibid., p. 166.

30. Sir W. Gell, op. cit., pp. 211, 220.

31. Letter of 12 November 1809, in *The Letters of Lord Byron*, ed. R. G. Howorth (Everyman edn), pp. 25–7.

32. A. W. Kinglake, *Eothen* (1844), Chapter 21.

33. ibid., Chapter 17.

34. W. M. Thackeray, *Notes of a Journey from Cornhill to Grand Cairo* (1845), p. 118 (1888 edn).

35. ibid , pp. 127–9.

36. ibid , pp. 147–8.

37. ibid., p. 109.

38. A. Smith, op. cit., p. ix.

39. ibid., pp. 57, 90.

40. R. F. Burton, *A Pilgrimage to Al-Madinah and Meccah* (1855), Vol. 1, p. 99 (Bohn Library edn).

41. J. T. Whitall, op. cit., pp. 164–5.

42. ibid., p. 157.

43. See on this Frenchman W. Connely, *Count D'Orsay* (1952), pp. 429–30, 439.

44. *James Nasmyth, Engineer*, ed. S. Smiles (new edn, 1885), pp. 271–3.

45. W. H. G. Kingston, *The Three Midshipmen* (2nd edn, 1873), Chapter 7. These Egyptian soldiers surprise them by their dogged courage.

46. W. M. Thackeray, *Notes of a Journey*, p. 255.

47. Ibid., pp. 271–2.

48. R. F. Burton, *A Pilgrimage*, Vol. 1., pp. 17, 35.

49. E. W. Lane, *An Account of the Manners and Customs of the Modern Egyptians* (1836), pp. 267, 269–70 (1890 edn).

50. Ibid., p. 255.

51. W. M. Thackeray, *Notes of a Journey*, p. 292.

52. R. F. Burton, *A Pilgrimage*, Vol. 1, pp. 110–12.

53. E. W. Lane, op. cit., p. 273.

54. A. N. Poliak, *Feudalism in Egypt, Syria, Palestine, and the Lebanon, 1250–1900* (1939), p. 66.

55. A. Colvin, op. cit., p. 27.

56. Ibid.

57. 'Through the Metidja to Abd-el-Kadr' (1842).

58. H. M. Walmesley, *Sketches of Algeria during the Kabyle War* (1858), p. 116.

59. L. Daudet, *Le Nabab* (1877).

60. H. M. Walmesley, op. cit., pp. 259 ff. cf. Engels on the Kabyles: 'the bravest, most tenacious, and most wary skirmishers the world ever saw' (*Engels as Military Critic*, ed. W. H. Chaloner and W. O. Henderson (Manchester, 1959), pp. 89–90).

61. H. M. Walmesley, op. cit., pp. 18–23, 118.

62. There are several essays on this theme in the collection by E. Castelar, *Recuerdos y Esperanzas* (Madrid, n.d.).

63. R. F. Burton, *A Pilgrimage*, Vol. 1, p. 247, Vol. 2, p. 17.

64. ibid., Vol. 2, p. 10; cf. p. 118.

65. Lillias Hamilton, *A Vizier's Daughter* (1900).

66. See my article 'Kashghar and the Politics of Central Asia, 1868–1878', in *Cambridge Historical Journal*, Vol. XI (1956).

67. H. W. Bellew, *Kashmir and Kashghar* (1875), pp. 300, 357.

68. ibid., p. 237.
69. *Twelfth Night*, Act 2, Scene 5; Act 3, Scene 4.
70. Hallam Lord Tennyson. *Alfred Lord Tennyson* (1897), Vol. 1, p. 374.
71. M. K. Waddington, *Letters of a Diplomat's Wife, 1883–1900* (1903), p. 302.
72. Hohenlohe Schillingsfuerst, op. cit., Vol. 2, p. 91.
73. J. W. Kaye, *The Life and Correspondence of Major-General Sir John Malcolm* (1856), Vol. 1, pp. 123, 126, 133.
74. E. O'Donovan, *Merv* (1883), pp. 52, 54.
75. ibid., pp. 79 ff.
76. See *The Adventures of Hajji Baba of Ispahan in England* (1828), James Morier's less entertaining sequel to his earlier novel.
77. E. O'Donovan, op. cit., p. 73.
78. ibid., pp. 114 ff.
79. ibid., pp. 130, 139.
80. W. S. Blunt, *Secret History of the Occupation of Egypt* (1907), pp. 9, 12, 59, 62. He visited southern Persia in 1879.
81. E. G. Browne, *A Year among the Persians* (1893), p. 107.
82. ibid., p. 441.
83. ibid., p. 90.
84. ibid., pp. 270, 517.
85. ibid., pp. 535, 551.
86. G. N. Curzon, *Persia and the Persian Question* (1892), Vol. I, pp. vii–viii.
87. ibid., Vol. 1, p. ix.
88. ibid., Vol. 1, pp. 219, 277. cf. A. Vambéry, *The Story of my Struggles* (Nelson edn, n.d.), p. 187, on 'the unexampled cowardice' and disorganization of the Persian army; he reckoned one Turkoman worth ten Persians.
89. G. N. Curzon, op. cit., Vol. 2, p. 492.
90. ibid., Vol. 1, pp. 397–9.
91. See 'The Empty House', in *The Return of Sherlock Holmes*.
92. 'Pierre Loti', *Vers Ispahan* (1904), p. 119 (Nelson edn, Paris, n.d.).
93. ibid., p. 80, etc.
94. ibid, p. 216.
95. ibid, p, 183.
96. ibid., p. 274.
97. Sir A. Wilson, *S. W. Persia* (1942), p. 287.
98. ibid., p. 197.
99. ibid., pp. 89–90.
100. ibid., p. 95.

101. ibid., p. 52.

102. W. M. Shuster, *The Strangling of Persia* (1912), pp. 175–6.

103. W. S. Blunt, *My Diaries* (1932 edn), e.g. pp. 618, 786.

104. L. C. Dunsterville, *The Adventures of Dunsterforce* (1920), p. 13.

105. ibid., pp. 153–4.

106. ibid., pp. 80, 110.

107. ibid., p. 54.

108. See A. P. Thornton, *The Imperial Idea and its Enemies* (1959), p. 184.

109. *Eothen*, Chapter 1.

110. G. N. Curzon, op. cit., Vol. 1, p. 12.

111. T. U. Sadleir, op. cit., 14 February 1803.

112. *Eothen*, Chapter 24.

113. ibid., Chapter 8.

114. 'Persia and China' (May 1857), in Karl Marx and Friedrich Engels, *On Colonialism* (collected articles, Moscow, ?1960), pp. 111 ff. Unlike Curzon and Vambéry, Engels did not accuse the Persians of cowardice. As to corruption, Shuster had to admit that even tried patriots succumbed to Persian habit once in office (op. cit., p. 3).

115. *Eothen*, Chapter 6.

116. 'F. Anstey', *The Brass Bottle* (1900), p. 218.

117. L. C. Dunsterville, op. cit., pp. 91–2.

118. Loti, op. cit., p. 94.

119. *A Pilgrimage*, Vol. 1, p. 9.

120. *Notes of a Journey*, pp. 303–4. cf. A. Vambéry, op. cit., p. 129: 'A prominent feature of the Oriental character is an extraordinary serenity and an easy-going, contemplative turn of mind.'

121. *Eothen*, Chapter 12.

122. E.g. W. M. Thackeray, *Notes of a Journey*, p. 124; A. Smith, op. cit., pp. 73 ff.

123. September 1813; see M. Moorman, *William Wordsworth: The Later Years, 1803–1850* (Oxford, 1965), p. 230.

124. No. 117 in *The Best of Beardsley*, ed. R. A. Walker (n.d.). It belongs to 1897.

125. P. G. Hamerton, *Poems* (1859), pp. 185–9: 'Al Jannat' (Paradise). cf. Voltaire's Sultan in *Zaïre* (1732), Act 1, Scene 2:

> '*Je sais que notre loi, favorable aux plaisirs,*
> *Ouvre un champ sans limites à nos vastes désirs . . .*'

126. A. H. Walton, *Stimulants for Love* (1966), Chapter 2.

127. ibid., p. 109.

128. E. W. Lane, op. cit., p. 274.

129. Sir W. Scott, *Peveril of the Peak* (1822), Chapters 47 and 49.

130. E. W. Lane, op. cit., p. 348.

131. Sir M. E. Grant Duff, *Notes from a Diary, 1851–1872* (1911), p. 206.

132. *The Citizen of the World* (1762), p. 267 (Everyman edn). Europe has also, however, thought of homosexuality as a prevalent vice of the Muslim East.

133. *Boswell: the Ominous Years, 1774–1776*, ed. C. Ryskamp and F. A. Pottle (1963), pp. 55, 65.

134. ibid., pp. 293–4.

135. Raymond, preface to translation of the *Seir-Mutaquerin* (1789; new edn, 1902).

136. op. cit., Chapter 5.

137. *Notes of a Journey*, p. 131. For earlier impressions of the palace at Stamboul see N. M. Penzer, *The Harem* (1965).

138. A. Smith, op. cit., p. 97.

139. R. E. Raspe, *Baron Munchausen. Narrative of his Marvellous Travels* (1785), Chapter 9.

140. *Don Juan*, Cantos 5 and 6.

141. *Peveril of the Peak*, Chapter 36.

142. *Memoirs of the Comte de Rochechouart, 1788–1822*, trans. F. Jackson (1920), p. 119.

143. P. Fryer, *Mrs Grundy. Studies in English Prudery* (1965 edn), p. 273. In the eighteenth century 'Turkish beauties' was a cant phrase for buttocks (ibid., p. 40).

144. W. M. Thackeray, *Vanity Fair* (1848), Chapter 51. cf. Chapter 9, 'The King's Harem', in W. Knighton's book on Oudh before its annexation, *The Private Life of an Eastern King* (1855).

145. W. M. Thackeray, *Notes of a Journey*, pp. 278–9.

146. E. W. Lane, op. cit., p. 236.

147. *A Pilgrimage*, Vol. 1, p. 175, n. 1.

148. M. Jokai, *Timar's Two Worlds* (English edn, Edinburgh, 1930).

149. *Hansard*, 3rd Series, Vol. CCLV, Cols. 1,572, 1,842 (1880).

150. *The Letters of Lord Byron*, p. 26.

151. P. G. Wodehouse, *Uncle Fred in the Springtime* (1939), Chapter 14.

152. 1847; part 2.

153. Cited in P. Quennell, *Byron in Italy* (1951 edn), p. 257.

154. Goncharov, *The Same Old Story* (1846), trans. I. Litvinova (Moscow, n.d.), p. 191.

155. Essay 'On Women', in *Selected Essays*, ed. E. B. Bax (1926). He thought Hindus and even Hottentots more sensible than Europeans about women.

156. See the collection in the Victoria and Albert Museum, London.

157. A. Smith, op. cit., pp. 87–8.
158. W. H. Holden, *The Pearl from Plymouth* (1950), p. 98.
159. A. Smith, op. cit., p. 108.
160. G. N. Curzon, op. cit., Vol. 1, p. 493.
161. *A Pilgrimage*, Vol. 1, pp. 291–2.
162. See Report of Commission VII of the World Missionary Conference, 1910: *Missions and Governments* (Edinburgh, n.d.).
163. *The Call from the Moslem World*, preface by Right Rev. S. Donaldson (1926), p. 25.
164. *The Martyrdom of Man* (1872), pp. 234 ff. (Thinker's Library edn). G. Simon, *The Progress and Arrest of Islam in Sumatra* (1912) complains that the active spread of Islam, in regions like central Africa as well as Indonesia, is the Christian missionary's worst obstacle (p. xxii).
165. Dictionary of National Biography.

5. THE FAR EAST

China : An Illusion Fading

It was a very long process, quickening in its later stages, that turned the fabled Cathay of Europe's half-buried memories into a solid, humdrum China pervaded by an aroma of night-soil. When modern contact began in the sixteenth century the last native dynasty, the Ming, was failing; in the seventeenth it was supplanted by the Manchu conquest, and an imposing edifice of government rebuilt, much as India had been reorganized a century earlier by the Mogul conquest. Catholic missionaries like Verbiest who were the first to see the new Ch'ing régime formed on the whole a high opinion of it, and of the traditional Chinese culture with which it quickly identified itself.[1]

This high estimate lingered on in the eighteenth-century conception, inspired by the Jesuits at Peking, of Chinese government and society as the perfection of what humanity was capable of, with true benevolence above and grateful obedience below. In China, the American scientist Count Rumford said appreciatively, men of intellect instead of feudal aristocrats were in control.[2] In pre-Revolutionary France this rosy vision harmonized with the mood of a politically retarded middle class; an instance of how deviously history works, and what far-fetched nourishment, including myth or illusion, has contributed to man's growth. Voltaire recognized that materially China had fallen behind the West,[3] but to his generation the supposed moral miracle, the reign of reason, and the freedom from Europe's desolating wars, far outweighed this.

With 1789 the French bourgeoisie turned from daydream to action, and its field of action was Europe. In China Europeans were *Fo-lang-ki*: Firangi, Franks, that old name of Crusading days carried to the Far East by the ubiquitous Arab;[4] but Englishmen, not Frenchmen, were leading the new Western crusade into Asia. Their dream was a different one, not of Celestial harmony but of limitless markets and profits; it was to turn out equally deceptive.

Among Englishmen practical dealings with China began early to breed scepticism about its model civilization. When Commodore Anson was steering for China after many ocean hazards, he and his officers looked forward eagerly to 'the advantages of an amiable, well-frequented port, inhabited by a polished people and abounding with the conveniences and indulgences of a civilized life'.[5] Arrived on the coast in 1743 he was piqued by the wooden indifference of the swarming boatmen to him and his ship, and told himself that the Chinese had received 'extravagant praises';[6] though to look for the fine flower of the Chinese mind off Canton harbour was as unreasonable as to look for the English mind in Wapping. When some mandarins came aboard in the Canton river they made a better figure, displayed interest, and impressed their hosts, men of a hard-drinking Europe, by drinking a great many glasses of wine before finally taking themselves off none the worse. By the time Anson left, however, he was disgusted with the greed and duplicity and general conduct of 'this celebrated nation, which is often recommended to the rest of the world as a pattern of all kinds of laudable qualities'.[7]

At home in England opinion fluctuated. Dr Johnson in 1778 referred to all 'East-Indians', or Asiatics, as 'barbarians', 'You will except the Chinese, Sir?' inquired Boswell. 'No, Sir,' replied the Doctor, and would allow them no accomplishment beyond pottery.[8] There was not very much information to go on, for China was proving surprisingly hard to get to know better. By the kind of topsy-turviness that came to seem normal in the Far East, peaceful shopkeeping China was a much harder market to get into than warlike Turkey. There was a long epoch, starting from the 1750s, when foreigners were cooped up in a corner of one port, Canton, and allowed to trade only with the 'Hong' group of authorized Chinese merchants. An embassy led by Lord Macartney in 1792, another by Lord Amherst in 1816, failed to induce Peking to agree to regular diplomatic and commercial intercourse. Eventually the West resorted to force, and the Opium Wars of 1840–42 and 1856–60, with France joining Britain in the second, inducted China into what Europeans were wont to term the comity of nations.

Of all the official personages who knocked on China's barred door during this long epoch Macartney was the most intelligent and open-minded. He was a good representative of the European enlightenment, and he knew India and could compare China with it as well as with Europe. He did not forget, when he encountered ridiculous customs in China, that others flourished nearer home;[9] and he was conscious of his countrymen's besetting sin of contempt for the rest of mankind, and noticed that while other foreigners at Canton mingled socially with the Chinese, the British kept aloof.[10] His early impressions were uniformly favourable. Some officials seemed frank and able; ordinary people looked well-built and healthy.[11] Chinese character as exemplified by the mandarins soon began to strike him as 'inexplicable'. Yet even after the failure of his mission at the capital he retained a good opinion of leading ministers.[12] To the skill and success of Chinese agriculture he always paid tribute.[13] Of China's armed strength his estimate was realistic and low. Two British frigates could paralyse the entire coast; indeed, so shrewdly did he see through the imposing façade that he thought it might collapse of its own weight during his lifetime.[14]

A good many aspects of China continued to compel admiration. With all the shortcomings that were discovered, it remained different from any other region where the Westerner was setting his foot. Its painting became better known, its poetry began to be known. In a more practical field, irrigation, a Frenchman could rate its achievements higher than anything the West had to show.[15] Its government could be praised by an American as at least 'far superior to other Asiatic countries'.[16] In its competitive examinations for civil-service entry it was ahead of Europe.[17] For a heathen country all these attainments were remarkable, an Englishman admitted.[18] Another, an authority on India, said that while most Asian kingdoms were stationary because they were barbarous, China stood still by deliberate policy.[19]

But this was the point where respect for China commonly ended. A philosophy of standing still was not one that the age of Progress could sympathize with. Not only impatient businessmen fumed; China was becoming for the West at large the archetype of obstructive conservatism. Spain, or the Austrian empire, could be talked of as the China of Europe. But for the ancient Greeks, declared Shelley, Europe might now be in the same 'stagnant and miserable state of social institutions as China and Japan'.[20] Marx yielded to no Manchester trader in his scorn for China's 'hereditary stupidity', and spoke of the paradox of a country that only an opium trade could arouse from slumber.[21]

Celestial Empire and Foreign Barbarian

It was not easy for foreigners in China to grasp what the country really thought about them, and why they were making so little headway. One simple fact they could never bring themselves to face was that the goods they brought for sale, with the exception of their smuggled opium, were not wanted. At first the barrier seemed to be mainly linguistic. China was one of the very few countries that had forbidden foreigners to learn their language, and before pidgin English sprouted interpreters or go-betweens had to be looked for among Chinese at Macao who had picked up some Portuguese. Less imperfect conductors of ideas became available when some Europeans, diplomats or missionaries, succeeded in learning Chinese; but as often happens, greater understanding brought more disagreement, not less.

When the Jesuits constructed globes and wanted to explain political geography, Chinese bureaucrats refused to look at them,[22] just as the Catholic priest refused to look through Galileo's telescope for fear of seeing something in the sky that ought not to be there. To pretend that other countries do not exist is one way of getting on with them, until they begin shooting. Europe was confronted with a China more than usually conservative, partly because of the Ch'ing dynasty promoting neo-Confucianism to make itself more acceptable and its subjects more tractable. It was a factor in the condition of Asia at large that much of it was under foreign or semi-foreign rule when Europe arrived. What had appeared so solid to Voltaire was really a precarious equilibrium of Manchu ruling caste, Chinese officialdom, and people. Its Confucian ideology belonged to an agrarian society, and had failed to adapt itself to commercialism. The mandarin steeped in his ancient classics looked down on the trader with a superciliousness that galled China's own moneyed men, as new winds began to blow across the sea, as well as Westerners.

Confucius taught his adepts to think of themselves as Superior Men, exerting a moral authority over the commonalty by force of character. Nations pick up many of the attitudes and habits of their rulers, and China thought of itself as a Superior People looked up to by all around. It was a secular equivalent of the Islamic disdain for unbelievers, and a ludicrously close counterpart of Europe's own self-esteem. For ages China had diffused culture over an empire, and over a wide circle of other lands closely attached to it like Korea, or less closely like Tibet, or distantly like Burma, or politically not at all like Japan. That China was the Middle Kingdom, the one truly civilized realm, was as much an axiom to its inhabitants as it had been to medieval Europe that the earth was the centre of the universe.

An explorer saw tribal folk near the Burmese border treated like dirt.[23] Among the vast rebellions that convulsed China in that century one was in this far-off region of half-aboriginal Yunnan, another in the half-alien north-west. A Chinese escorting another traveller in the western mountains talked of the local hill-folk, a fine-looking race, as 'wild men', because their New Year was a different day from China's. Some of them, he added, lived exclusively on wine.[24] The most ridiculous Western notions about 'natives' could hardly outdo this. Another wayfarer, down in the south when French troops were over-running Tonking just beyond the border, met a functionary posting on his way to look into the conduct of an unruly frontier tribe – the French.[25]

In this one must suspect some deliberate make-believe meant to reassure the man in the street that the world was still a Chinese world. Responsible officials even in Macartney's time had been quite aware that England was a big and distant nation.[26] It gave Westerners a good conscience – opium and all –

to be able to assert that they only asked China to treat them as equals; but from the Chinese point of view this was a monstrous impertinence. As late as 1873 a Censor was indignant at the practice of foreigners when drawing up treaties of putting their rulers, those 'puny hobgoblins or petty monsters', on the same footing as the Son of Heaven.[27] It had even been regarded as objectionable that foreign dignitaries should be carried in palanquins on the shoulders of Celestial coolies.[28]

Europeans of the diplomatic or armed services might have been expected to get on better with the Manchu ruling group than with its Chinese underlings. Occasionally they did. Sir John Davis, who became British plenipotentiary in 1844, thought the Manchus he was dealing with in the government humane and moderate, the Chinese cruel and treacherous.[29] But the Manchus did not form an aristocracy in the European sense: indeed the absence of such a class almost everywhere in Asia except Japan was one of the stumbling-blocks in the way of mutual respect. Japan's nobility translated itself readily enough into a standard five-decker peerage, but Chinese honours, outside the official table of ranks, were more elusive. 'Marquis' Tseng, an early and respected representative in Europe, and not a Manchu, was the only individual who came to be known familiarly to foreigners by a non-royal Western title.[30] Manchus were shadowy palace figures, or ordinary officials, or princelings mass-produced by polygamous households, or Bannerman of the old and now farcical army. That they were often called 'Tartars', the military men especially, helped to invest them with a flavour of unpleasantness.

One way, then, of looking at China was to pity it for being under alien domination, and to blame its obstructiveness on the Manchus. The majority of office-holders were Chinese, but symptoms could be detected among them, by Macartney for instance, of impatience against the less polished but more powerful Manchus. But it was not easy to trace a general line of division, and the Chinese mandarins were not better liked as they came to be better known. Their own position was awkward; it was they who were most exposed to and embarrassed by Western pressure, and then by the displeasure of the Manchu Court on one side and of the Chinese public on the other side if they gave way to it. As time went on this pressure began to reopen the old sores of the Manchu conquest and make rulers and people more conscious of their differences.

Macartney came away feeling that the Chinese people and their mode of life were on the whole sound, their government rotten. By the time of the first armed clashes foreigners were dubious about the people being good, but certain of the government being bad and the people downtrodden, in need therefore of liberation by the West. This note was often sounded during the Opium Wars, to which it lent a more edifying character. Emancipation could not be called aggression, and Britain was still busy, until the Mutiny, emancipating India from its bad old rulers. At Canton in 1841 the British posted placards saying that they had no quarrel with the common man, only with the wicked government.[31] This cut little ice. Yet Western principles of administration and justice really had something to offer beyond the best Asian standards, and the degenerate Ch'ing régime was now falling well below these. When the British temporarily occupied Canton between 1858 and 1861 they were on their best behaviour, and did it seems win public confidence.[32] But they had not come round the world merely to win friends, and the Chinese could not expect to be saved from themselves gratis.

The opening of China was mainly a naval operation, and appropriately a naval man concerned in it, Captain Osborn – one whom Lady Hester Stanhope would have warmly commended – left on record the plainest statement of its philosophy. There was a good deal in this philosophy, with its self-righteousness and its conviction that what Europe wanted must be good for China, that marked its descent from an older spirit of religious war and conquest. All efforts of Westerners to come to terms with China failed, Osborn wrote in his book on the second war in 1860, 'simply through their not being able to think as a Chinaman thinks'.[33] This feat he evidently had accomplished, and was able to announce that 'force rather than argument, necessity rather than conviction, is the only rule by which a Chinaman can be made to agree with a European'.[34] Osborn saw clearly enough that the West had become dependent economically on the world and therefore must make the world dependent politically on it. 'We cannot exist without tea and silk; we want that huge market of four hundred millions ...'[35] But between them and us there need be no antagonism. 'No! our enemy – that is, the enemy of British Progress in China – is he who stands between us and these creatures – the burly, obstinate, over-fed mandarin', thanks to whom 'squalor, hunger, and misery seemed the general condition of the lower orders'.[36]

Britain's task then was to break down 'the unrighteous walls of monopoly which bar out four hundred millions of men from European civilization and God's truth'.[37] (We need only read Cadre for Mandarin, seven hundred for four hundred, and American for European, to make a jump of a whole century.) British bombardments had been too mild, not too rough: 'with those who misunderstand forbearance, humanity is, in my opinion, a weakness.' 'They are only Asiatics ... treat them as children; make them do what we know is for their benefit, as well as our own, and all difficulties in China are at an end.'[38]

That Asians and Africans were children, to be firmly dealt with for their own good, was a very common assumption. Victorians held that to spare the rod was to spoil the child, and sent their sons to schools where flogging held first place in the curriculum. They were not likely to spoil natives by neglect of the same discipline. And if Chinese were mere infants they could not know how to liberate themselves from their bad old masters by any efforts of their own. Yet the second Opium War coincided with the climax of the Taiping rebellion, the greatest revolutionary upheaval in the history of Asia before the twentieth century. Over a wide area of central China peasants and artisans had taken arms against their sea of troubles; and here was a challenge to the West to decide whether it really wanted to see them set free or not.

Both the causes and the aims of the upheaval were complex, and for long after this date the West had only the haziest understanding of the structure of Chinese rural society. In the earlier stages of rebellion there was both interest and sympathy, strengthened by some Christian borrowings in Taiping ideology. There was also contempt for a Chinese government that was begging for foreign help against its own subjects at the very time when the foreigners were attacking China. All the same, such intervention as took place was on the government side. Disorder was bad for trade. American and other mercenaries played a part; it was a British officer, 'Chinese Gordon', who organized the most effective of the anti-rebel forces that were being raised.[39] Victory set the landlords free to massacre rebels or suspects by scores of thousands, and order and opium profits revived. A man like the God-fearing Gordon could not, any more than General Dunsterville in Persia, endorse revolutionism or class war. He could feel for oppressed Asians, but Asians after all were children. The Mutiny in India in 1857–8 was bound to colour British feeling about China too.

The old régime never learned to use Western arms and training effectively against foreign aggression, but they were more easily used against its own subjects, at home or in colonies like Chinese Turkestan. Thus contact with the West bolstered up the old China in one way, while undermining it in another, and as in Turkey obsolete institutions were artificially prolonged In the end the result would be a social explosion of unprecedented violence. Meanwhile undulations of opinion about China continued. For some years after 1860, with diplomatic relations forced on Peking and the West feeling entitled to its gratitude, there was an appearance of recovery. In Tonking during 1883–5 Chinese troops for the first time made a fair showing against Europeans. 'China has learned much from the conflict, and comes out of it stronger than ever before,' wrote an observer.[40] For the next ten years China was often thought of as a worthwhile ally for Britain against Russia. But with radical reform at the bottom frustrated, no radical improvement could take place at the top. In 1894 China's new-style military and naval forces fared very poorly against Japan, and one more Chinese myth evaporated. 'A more hopeless spectacle of fatuous imbecility . . . it is impossible to conceive,' was one Briton's trenchant comment.[41]

Foreign Residents in China

Englishmen like Osborn were often resentful of the way Russians or Americans criticized them for bullying China, and then stepped in to share the proceeds. About 1860 Russians suspected that Englishmen were maligning them in order to please the Chinese.[42] Mutual candours like this must have given the Chinese some new thoughts about Europe. Dissensions continued, but on the whole the 'concert of the Powers' was better preserved here than in Europe or anywhere else, down to near the end of the century when imperialist rivalries intensified everywhere and in China the 'battle of the concessions' raged. Even then the Powers could sink their differences and combine against the Chinese people, as they showed when the Boxer rebellion broke out in 1900, though no longer against the Chinese government. Solidarity was felt still more by the unofficial Western communities growing in the 'Treaty' or open ports. Despite steamships and Suez Canal the Far East was far away, and white men felt they must stand together. Before 1895, one resident wrote later on with regret for good old days, 'we were all something of a happy family'.[43]

In diplomacy and in commercial investment alike Britain led, and its behaviour towards China, which set the tone for others, was determined in many ways by the fact of its being the grand imperial nation, with the second biggest country of Asia firmly in leash. When Macartney was in China in 1792 British India was still only a few provinces, and the plan he had heard ascribed to Clive of seizing Chinese territory seemed to him midsummer madness.[44] By the date of the first Opium War the conquest of India was nearly complete, and the attitude to China correspondingly more hectoring. Possession of India had also two practical consequences affecting China: it gave Britain opium to sell, and sepoy troops to use.

There was carping criticism of the opium trade by Quakers and others at home, and when Kingston's three midshipmen found their ship ordered for duty in the first Opium War two of them felt misgivings: the whole business looked to them 'very ugly'. Their better-informed leader had to clear it up. Opium was bad, to be sure, but so were the Chinese, who had broken a treaty, and if this went unpunished Britain would be leaving them 'to sink into the extreme of barbarism, towards which they appear to be hastening'.[45] On their part the Chinese were said to have thought of India as the most barbarous of all realms, 'a land of monsters, deformities and wild animals'.[46] If so they now had reason to think of it as a land of wild men too, for the sepoys employed in British operations were not always kept under control. It was admitted after the attack on Canton in 1841 that some were guilty of acts of rape, which helped to provoke violent popular feeling.[47] So undoubtedly were British soldiers and sailors too, but it would seem that the unfamiliar appearance and dark complexion of the sepoys sharpened resentment against them.

Some Britons in China had been in India first, and brought a nabob mentality with them. All Britons were apt to think imperiously. A naval officer employed by the Chinese government was indignant at being expected to follow its instructions – 'the notion of a gentleman acting *under* an Asiatic barbarian is preposterous'.[48] Long before this, in the old days at Canton, a dinner given by some Chinese merchants to their foreign acquaintances was followed by a play in which an English naval officer strutted fiercely in a cocked hat, exclaiming *God damn*.[49] British businessmen formed the majority of the foreign residents. A British writer saw them as a 'fine race of men, open-handed and generous, full of courage and enterprise';[50] an American missionary-doctor at Chefu saw many of them as narrow-minded and ignorant, though he met with better ones too.[51]

Inevitably the apartheid firmly established in India was transferred in a great measure to China. Everyone has heard of the 'Dogs and Chinese not admitted' notice in the park. Here again European women, forbidden entry by the Chinese authorities in early days, helped to keep the foreign community aloof from the people among whom it lived. Macao's sadly run-down condition could be regarded as proof of the evil results of intermarriage, which the Portuguese had favoured. In Hong Kong the position of the Chinese as subjects under British rule increased British haughtiness. Bowring in 1858 observed that 'the separation of the native population from the European is nearly absolute; social intercourse between the races wholly unknown'.[52] Decades later a visiting journalist noticed among the residents 'a distinct abhorrence for the Chinese. They speak of them as if they were beasts.'[53]

Sheltered in their own settlements behind extra-territorial rights, not amenable to Chinese justice – which though fallible was not always worse than their own treatment of Chinese unable to protect themselves – foreigners lived a life of their own, for the most part banal enough. Any notion at home in Europe that they were mingling in and getting to know Chinese society was, someone who knew them well wrote, 'altogether a mistaken one'.[54] 'As to anything like social intercourse with the inhabitants of the country,' another reported, 'the thing is quite unknown, even in the faintest sense of the term.'[55] At first forbidden to learn Chinese, foreigners now seldom troubled to do so though, as in other lands, the Germans who appeared on the scene showed more alacrity than Britons. The average resident went through his Far Eastern years conscious of the aliens around him only as beggars, or rioters, or servants, and spent his lengthy leisure hours grumbling in his club at everything Chinese because he was not getting rich fast enough. Yet it was these 'self-elected exponents of the ideas and methods of European civilization'[56] who represented Europe to China; and it was the same Old China Hands, strutting and fretting their hour at Shanghai and then heard no more, whose fantasies represented China to Europe.

A few were drawn to Chinese studies, and made contributions, more modest than in India because China had always written its own history and collected its own literature. And there were always a few who succumbed to the spell that many visitors to China in later years have found it hard to resist. Compatriots did not fail to note the symptoms of decadence in these few, the 'mental transformation' of those who studied the language and underwent its insidious influence.[57] Men thrown on their own in outposts were most liable to the infection, like the character in Somerset Maugham's novel who after twenty years had come to agree with China that 'the

Europeans were barbarians and their life a folly', and was
actually married to a Manchu lady.[58]

One badge of superiority of Europeans in the Far East was
their religion. Britons felt themselves to be peculiarly the pioneers of Christianity as well as of trade. To his fellow-countrymen
General Gordon was the exemplar, and they made a great
deal out of the episode of his losing his temper with a Chinese
commander who violated the pledge given by Gordon to some
captured rebels:[59] it pointed a fine contrast between Christian
gentleman and soulless Asian. But on weekdays the businessman left religion to the poor and rather despised missionary.
The latter found fault with his 'cold neutrality' about the saving of Chinese souls;[60] it was his own savings that he was concerned about.' Worse than indifferent, positively anti-mission-
ary, one commentator said, was the type of merchant who left
his business to his comprador or native agent, and divided his
time 'between the club, the race-track, and various other places
of amusement'.[61]

Yet sometimes the missionary was able to influence the
Old Hand's brusque style of dealing with disaffected Chinese.
British and French missionaries were not without their own
share of the imperial outlook. Their reports brought China, like
India, before the Western public in an invidious light. China
had not even a recognizable religion of its own, such as Islam
and Hinduism were; there seemed to be only a wretched rig-
marole of superstitions, centring round ancestor-worship, a
'degrading slavery' which could with some force be said to
mark a country looking backward instead of forward.[62] In early
days the Jesuits had been willing to adapt Catholicism to
Chinese notions: the resulting 'Chinese Rites controversy' within the Church was a forerunner of controversy in British India
and other colonies about whether education ought to be given
in Western or Eastern forms. Later missionaries were in no
mood for any such compromises. At the end of the century
Catholic priests secured the status of Chinese officials, in order
to be able to protect and otherwise advantage their converts.
They always had close relations with their own protector, the
French government, and for its legation at Peking were, some-

one remarked, 'the best Intelligence corps in the world'.[63] A body of converts might prove as useful to France in China as in Indochina.

A fair trickle of them came in. Chaotic conditions made some Chinese willing to look either for rice, or for a new spiritual foundation, wherever they could find it. Socially and intellectually too conversion could be an escape from the cramping confinement of the old China, which many of its own people wanted by now to shake off. It was the missionaries who were bringing books and translating books, not religious ones alone. As in India they turned more as time went on to social service, and did valuable work especially in medicine. In education, however well-meaning, they were bound to represent the thinking and bring the books of a bygone generation, instead of what was really modern and stimulating in Western thought.[64]

Estimates of the Chinese Character

Much of the West's questioning about this unique country crystallized round prominent individuals. Some of these belonged to the Tsungli Yamen or Foreign Office which the Chinese had been compelled to set up, but which they made use of only for evasion and obstruction. China was having to play for time, though unluckily doing very little with the time it gained. One of the notables here was Wen-hsiang, whom a broad-minded foreigner described as 'an exceedingly shrewd, intelligent, and, as far as Chinese nature permits it, honest man'.[65] As the old order crumbled the individuals who came to the front were not likely to be of the most honest sort. The two most in the Western eye towards the end of the century were the dowager empress and virtual ruler Tzu Hsi, who began as a lowly Manchu concubine in the palace and worked her way up by intrigue, and the high Chinese functionary Li Hung-chang. Many strange and some bloodcurdling rumours about Tzu Hsi percolated from the recesses of the Forbidden City. She was said to practise archery, and even to take boxing lessons from an old eunuch.[66] Li came to be regarded as the champion of modernizing policies, but there was disagreement as to whether he was a patriot or merely one of the old gang smart enough to scent new opportunities for filling his own pockets. Opinion settled, correctly, on the second view. A woman biographer thought him 'the most entertaining man' she had ever met, but also one of the most corrupt.[67] When he visited Russia he gave some trouble by his contemptuous tone to the Emir of Bokhara,[68] one of those barbarians of inner Asia whom the Chinese had always looked down on.

Foreign opinion ran to bold and sweeping generalizations about Chinese in the mass. There were obvious regional differences among them, and it was a saying that the Cantonese were the Irishmen of China. Still, by and large the Chinese looked a formidably homogeneous people, and could be summed up collectively as 'John Chinaman'. A modern Chinese scholar has remarked that the result was 'a constant, unintelligent elaboration of the Chinaman *as a stage fiction*'.[69] To this day, curious discoveries about him by the Old China Hands find their way afresh into print. We hear that if a Chinese fell into the water, his countrymen never tried to pull him out; and that they judged foreigners by their 'outward behaviour'.[70]

'Chinaman' itself, a designation much disliked by Chinese when they learned English (still more its shorter form 'Chink'), conveyed a suggestion of wiliness or artfulness, which might be engaging, as in Bret Harte's playful verses,[71] or in the cricketing parlance of recent years, or might have a more unpleasant flavour. It lent itself to epigrams like Halliday Macartney's after a tour in 1873, 'the Chinaman is a low animal'.[72] Often the foreigner was beset by irritating doubts about whether it was artfulness or simple-mindedness that he had to deal with. When buying land for a building or railway he might have to pay extra as compensation for injury to the local dragon.[73] Did these stolid farmers really believe in dragons, or were they gammoning him? People would promise vaguely to do things in 'the time it takes to drink a cup of tea', and *tomorrow* might mean anything;[74] yet there was an astuteness about many of them which suggested that they knew very well what time of day it was.

China looked 'inscrutable' because foreigners blindfolded themselves, but also because of the habitual self-command of an old, civilized, overcrowded nation, the exact reverse of the spontaneous children of nature whom the West met with in some other lands. Even those who were seriously trying to explore the Chinese character felt baffled. Archdeacon Gray found it highly contradictory. There were grave faults, yet the Chinese were a 'courteous, orderly, industrious, peace-loving, sober, and patriotic people'.[75] All these epithets turned up frequently, except the last. Chinese businessmen stood out from the first. 'In their buying and selling they are verie subtill,' wrote Mendoza in the sixteenth century.[76] Their commercial instinct never flagged, wrote Michie in the nineteenth, 'continuously converting objects and opportunities into cash'.[77] At Hong Kong they were soon outstripping their European competitors.[78] What was more, these dealers, unlike the officials, had a fund of honesty that shone by contrast with Levantine or South American standards – often by contrast with European, for adulteration of cloth and other wares to be dumped in distant markets was common practice. A maxim current in the Far East was that Japanese were clean but deceitful, Chinese dirty but honest. Someone who claimed to know both laid it down that a Chinese in business was as much smarter than an Armenian as an Armenian than a Jew, but once he made a bargain he would stand by it at any sacrifice. 'Yes, sir; John Chinaman is a gentleman.'[79]

It was common ground too that the labouring classes had sterling virtues. British manufacturers, Lord Elgin warned them in 1859, would have to strain every nerve to provide cheaper cloth than 'this industrious, frugal and sober population' made for itself in its spare time, and it was a 'pleasing but pernicious fallacy' to suppose that only obstructive mandarins robbed them of eager customers.[80] The energy of the Yangtze boatmen, said an Englishman in Szechuan, he had 'never seen equalled by man or beast elsewhere, and could not have believed to be possible'.[81] Another river community, living in *sampans*, seemed to a lady a good deal more civilized than the squalid bargees she remembered in England.[82] The craftsman's deft fingers and quickness to learn new skills were often extolled. In 1872 the first steam-frigate was launched at Shanghai, practically all the parts having been made there under supervision of a handful of foreigners. In that year the thought occurred to someone that these patient toilers might one day supplant the British workman, always nowadays going on strike.[83] Upper-class Westerners impatient of the 'laziness' of their own working classes saw more and more to commend in the diligent Chinese. 'Work all day and 7 days a week is the usual rule throughout China',[84] and its inhabitants seemed positively to love work, as an American observed, and laboured with 'untiring patience, unfailing good humor', though little originality.[85] Why could not Western workers apply themselves to making profits for their employers in the same spirit?

Much as they might love work, China's poor were often obviously overworked by their masters, as harshly as some of them were to be before long in the foreign-owned steam mills of Shanghai. Other painful or disgusting impressions assailed the visitor from a Europe busy with reforms in its own public health, sanitation, penal codes. Sets of pictures illustrating Chinese punishments and tortures were in vogue, and helped to people the Western mind with ideas about the Chinese as masters of refined cruelty. Health, or rather disease, was appalling, as it was in all Asia and was only just ceasing to be in Europe, where what was significantly known as 'Asiatic cholera' was a scourge until well on in the century. A redeeming point was that China's common-sense materialism ensured a ready welcome for Western medicine and surgery, and these were soon 'winning golden opinions'.[86]

To Westerners apprehensive about their own social problems Chinese society might look, in spite of peasant revolts, enviably close-knit; and its 'unexampled stability' could be ascribed, with some reason, to its firm unit, the family.[87] Yet the Chinese family had in miniature the faults, the tyrannies, of China as a whole. It was part of the psychology of the situation that Westerners with qualms of conscience about how they were treating the Chinese should deplore the way Chinese men treated women, just as they deplored the treatment of the masses by the mandarins. Foot-binding was the one flagrant instance in which this self-complacent civilization behaved more brutishly than the rudest barbarians on its fringes. In Western eyes it damned upper-class China as suttee damned

India. An English resident wondered how any parent could bear to live under the same roof with an infant girl undergoing the eighteen painful months of the process of crippling.[88] This was an old and indigenous custom, not adopted by the Manchus; the shaven head and pigtail had been imposed on the Chinese by the Manchus as a badge of allegiance. They made men look as ridiculous as women with bound feet looked pathetic. But humanity in all climes has had a knack of making itself look ridiculous to its neighbours. The denizens of Britain began by painting themselves blue, and have gone from strength to strength.

China's misery was great, and a good part of it, like India's, self-inflicted. There were in all probability far more Chinese than ever before in history, struggling for bare existence. By comparison with this, any extra hardship brought by foreign guns or opium could be deemed a trifle. Another thought that foreigners were tempted to console themselves with was that in this race, schooled by aeons of suffering, physical sensation was mercifully blunted; that Chinese were more or less impervious to pain, as well as inscrutable. In other parts of the world too it was a habit of the 'higher races' to take comfort from supposing that the 'lower races' did not feel things as sensitively as they did. Anglers like to suppose that fish have no feelings.

Westerners and Chinese had their first modern contact outside China, in the Philippines and then in Java, and seldom in a way to promote amicable relations. Some Chinese had been kidnapped as slaves; among those who went abroad voluntarily – as among Europeans – there was a proportion of malcontents, outlaws, rough customers. Well into the nineteenth century Chinese pirates infested the Yellow Sea, like the Malay and European pirates in the Archipelago. To foreigners they were a fearsome tribe, and Kingston's readers must have felt for his midshipman struggling in the waves under the glare of 'half a dozen hideous Chinese faces with flat noses, grinning mouths, and queer twisted eyes'.[89]

At the same time demand for Chinese labour to develop colonies for the white man was reviving. It was felt from the late eighteenth century, well before the suppression of African slave-trading gave it a further stimulus.[90] Energetic measures were resorted to, not always much different from the kidnapping of older times. China was so overpopulated and wretched, it could be comfortably assumed, that its people must be glad to be removed by any methods to anywhere else. Many thousands were recruited in the ports, by fair means or foul, and shipped off to the West Indies, the South Seas, Peru, Malaya, as 'indentured labour' under contract for a term of years. This 'coolie trade' flourished for decades, and was known among practitioners as the 'pig trade'. 'Pig-dealing' by the firm of Syme, Muir & Company caused a riot at Amoy in 1852.[91] On the emigrant ships riots were fairly common, and a traveller crossing the Pacific in a liner with eleven hundred Chinese homeward bound from America saw hoses and steampipes trained on their quarters all the time in case of trouble;[92] a small epitome of relations between the two races.

While foreigners forced their way into China, Chinese immigration was prohibited in some British territories, in terms offensive to Chinese self-respect; in the USA, in 1888, more tactfully.[93] But in various quarters Chinese and Britons, the earth's two great migrant peoples, jostled together, the white man always top dog. English ships had begun employing Chinese as well as Indian or 'lascar' seamen during the French Revolutionary wars, and since they were cheap and plentiful this went on through the century. On a big ship they led a ghetto life in a separate hold, where opium was surreptitiously smoked. Opium accompanied the Chinese everywhere, helping to kill some of them but to keep others alive in exile and servitude, and the opium-dens of Singapore, or London's Chinatown, had a sinister repute.

In white countries like America or Australia, Chinese settlers had a precarious footing, and might be set on by mobs. In the tropical colonies they were indispensable, and those who survived and stayed soon began to work their way up economically; though this too might make their position perilous in the long run, as local peoples began to resent their presence as well as that of the white man who brought them. First-generation immigrants were nearly all men, and homosexuality was another vice often charged against them; but before long they won the reputation of making good husbands to women of more races than any other men could – a faculty related perhaps to their omnivorous approach to food. Taken all round, these Chinese abroad impressed Europeans by their tenacity of life and ability to prosper under every handicap. In every society or people there is a smothered reserve of energies and aptitudes, which may come to light in individuals cut adrift from it. China's history had been long enough for a very large reserve to be accumulated. Europeans liked to give themselves the credit and take for granted that it was the escape from bad Chinese to good colonial government that allowed the emigrant 'to develop into something like a new being'.[94]

Growth of Chinese Xenophobia

For a country to invent gunpowder and waste it on fireworks was, to martial Europe, an enigma. In the Opium Wars the Chinese seemed to be as destitute of patriotism – an attribute Europe thought of as its own monopoly – as of decent weapons. Apparently people in other provinces cared nothing about what was happening. These astonishing Celestials 'never have indigestion, nor public spirit',[95] wrote an Englishman who must have suffered from both. There is not much to choose between such a conviction and the popular Chinese notion that Europeans had webbed feet.[96]

They did have other features that the Chinese may have found distressing, from protuberant noses to obstreperous women. It was in the elemental form of detestation of foreigners that public spirit first unmistakably revealed itself, though this was linked from the first with discontent against the state of things inside China. It had more potent causes than mere antipathy. Macartney had been conscious of no widespread xenophobia, even if he suspected the government of circulating anti-foreign propaganda.[97] Ordinary Chinese might look down on foreigners, but it was the West that taught them little by little to hate foreigners. Even on Osborn's admission it was guilty at times of 'an unjust and violent abuse' of its power.[98] One among countless incidents occurred in 1862 when a French cook was killed at Canton and ninety-six Chinese massacred in return. As always, sexual resentments entered powerfully into the hatred that was being stirred up. The rape of Chinese women that accompanied all foreign attacks led to a belief that Christianity was a religion of debauchery, and that missionaries practised magical means of enslaving women.[99]

Europeans all round the world were surprised when they were not liked, and theories were expounded to account for their unpopularity in China. One was that it was all worked up by cantankerous members of the *literati* or educated class, from which the mandarins were drawn, in the same way as labour troubles at home were all the work of agitators. Whatever the cause, the accepted cure was coercion. Englishmen as usual reproached themselves for their foolish leniency, and complimented Frenchmen, Russians, or Germans on their greater realism. Experience taught that 'the Chinese were friendly and reasonable under a firm hand', but England was always forgetting the lesson and relapsing into illusions.[100] Force was the only language understood in China, exclaimed a visitor indignant at being insulted in the streets of Peking even when riding with the British minister and his escort.[101] Conciliation was no use in Asiatic countries, echoed a legation attaché; 'they understand the iron hand much better than the velvet glove', and when two men molested him he hit one on the nose and kicked the other, on the principle that 'half measures are of no value with barbarians'.[102] An American diplomat noticed that a visiting Prince Henry of Prussia, a man of naturally courteous disposition, deliberately put on out here a rough, harsh demeanour.[103]

This rise of a modern nationalism out of simple dislike of bullying strangers began with the fighting in Tonking and the French acts of aggression along the Chinese coast. Western countries in that age were always ready to play Jupiter and hurl thunderbolts, but one day in 1884 foreigners gathered on the Shanghai Bund to watch the news as it came in by telegraph of the murderous bombardment of Fuchow had an unwonted sensation of the Chinese, not the French, being the heroes.[104] Clearly this war either proved the existence or marked the birth of 'real patriotism'.[105] Coolies at Hong Kong refused to load French ships, the governor reported, whereas in 1860 it was easy enough to hire Chinese labourers for Britain's war against China: since then telegraph-wires and newspapers had been fostering an unfamiliar national spirit.[106] 'The people to a man detest and despise us,' wrote another Englishman.[107] It began also to dawn on the Western mind that Chinese might turn into good soldiers. 'What will happen,' Kipling asked himself on a visit a year or two later, 'when China really wakes up?'[108]

Defeat by Japan in 1894 proved that if the nation was waking up, the government was not. Yet a traveller far inland up the Yangtze was taken aback at the bitterness of the public reaction to Japan's peace terms.[109] Foreign appetites were encouraged by China's weakness. The Russians pushed into Manchuria, and Germany, a newcomer, tried to turn the northern province of Shantung into a colony. China seemed on the point of collapse, and its economy too was being disrupted by the influx of foreign goods, which railways were now coming in to accelerate. Facile belief that the Western presence must be good for China was fading; Europeans grew more cynical or realistic as the world struggle for empire intensified, and cared very little whether it was good for China or not.

In fact, one dissentient remarked, they seemed to think it nothing short of criminal for the Chinese to want to keep control of their own resources.[110] This man spent nine years in China and was in ten provinces without once meeting with real discourtesy,[111] which suggests that other foreigners brought trouble on their own heads by their behaviour. Against these new barbarians China was building a new Great Wall, of hatred. Wherever they went they were saluted with cries of 'foreign devil'; the reputedly pro-foreign Kung, Sixth Prince in the dynastic table, was nicknamed in Peking 'Devil number six'.[112] Residents at Fuchow – a town notorious for its 'mobbing propensities'[113] – suddenly saw placards announcing that a day had been chosen for them all to be killed.[114]

Bitterness understandably fastened on missionaries and their converts in particular,[115] and they often reacted in the same retaliatory spirit as the foreign layman. A work written by one of them at the time of the Boxer rising, which began with attacks on missions, accused the Western ministers at Peking of slackness, of being 'dazzled by the glamour of an Oriental court', and complained that after the murder of one missionary only 'some few scapegoats were decapitated'.[116] Curzon was not alone in censuring men like this writer for irresponsibly dragging their governments into quarrels with the Chinese, and for being too ready to call for gunboats to back them up.[117]

For the governing classes of China to come to terms with Western knowledge was more difficult because they were living under the threat of social revolution. After the Taiping rebellion their strongest impulse was to retreat into the past, to hide from reality behind Confucian texts and teachings[118] that might conceivably keep the Chinese people quiet for a while longer, but could not possibly quieten the impatient foreigner. In the 1890s, after the defeat by Japan, a new kind of reformism emerged within the old order. Its gospel was a book by the scholar and high official Chang Chih-tung, of which by 1900 a million copies were said to have been sold.[119] He had better arguments than the old ones to prove the inferiority of the West, such as the Western curse of pauperism; on the other hand he denounced mandarins of the old school as 'befuddled, ignorant, slippery nepotists'. He wanted China to hold fast to its traditional philosophy, with Western knowledge added.[120] But for the old order to make this fusion and transform itself from within was an impossibility, even when as happened in 1898 a young emperor, Kuang Hsü, put himself at the head of the reformers, rode a bicycle, bought a gramophone, and tried his hand at the piano. He was promptly snuffed out by Tzu Hsi, returning to power with the reactionaries, and the West shed few tears over his fall. It derided China for not making progress, but did not really want it to make progress except in Western leading-strings.

The Boxer rebellion of 1899–1900 was in a sense the result of this failure. Literate minority and illiterate majority were breaking apart, and the masses falling back on primitive instinct and old-world patterns of peasant revolt. It was an outburst of passion in northern China against both government and foreigners, but was skilfully diverted by the Court so that its weight fell on the latter. Its wild rituals and superstitions, its talismans to ward off bullets,[121] revealed to them more nakedly than they had ever seen it before the face of this other, rustic China, which in normal times the polite Confucian culture covered like a mask. This primitivism made the outbreak all the more bewildering, and invested it with a grotesque, horrific character. Stories that reached Europe aroused the same kind of sensation as those from the Soudan of the Mahdi a few years earlier, or those about the Mau-Mau in Kenya half a century later. Panic exaggerated them; a conqueror's uneasy conscience easily generates belief that his victims are nursing monstrous plots and revenges against him. Once seen as sedate well-regulated citizens, then as badly brought up children, the Chinese people were seen now as demons, just as they saw Westerners. Thus the West came round again to the point of view of the Spanish officer at Canton three centuries earlier who wrote to his superior at Manila that China was Satan's own country, and every man in it had a devil inside him.[122]

What made things worse still was the fanatical courage of the rioters. At the outset agitation could be dismissed as an affair of 'a few ill-conditioned and irresponsible outlaws', but before long there was the 'almost incredible sight' of bands of peasants hurling themselves against modern weapons without a sign of fear. Here was proof of 'much less cowardice and much more patriotism or faith' than the West had dreamed of.[123] China had been reproached with having no patriotic spirit, now it was showing far too much. On the other side the boasted superiority of the white men showed up poorly under the strain. In the siege of the Legations most of them were 'absolutely distraught', and the heads of missions wasted their time in mutual recriminations.[124]

They took their revenge afterwards by reprisals of the kind that had followed the Indian Mutiny. In the joint expedition that put down the rising Europeans and Americans and Japanese all took part, the British with an Indian contingent once more, under a German commander. It was one of the very few such international operations of modern history, and provided a model for the war of intervention against Bolshevik Russia eighteen years later. There was little pretence of carrying the 'civilized warfare' of the West to the Far East. The allies vied with one another in fierceness, the Kaiser giving the watchword with his speech exhorting his troops to make Germany's name a terror. A German diplomat, Baron von Ketteler, who was more 'offensive in his manner to the Chinese'[125] than most Europeans, had been killed. Murder and rape were accompanied by wholesale looting.[126] Peace terms imposed on China in 1901 were 'humiliating and crippling',[127] the culmination of a century of abuse of Western strength.

'The history of China, ancient and modern,' two experts wrote, 'is a series of paroxysms; its keynote is bloodshed and famine.'[128] They might have said much the same, and Americans often did, about the history of Europe. But the conclusion was obvious, and many were now drawing it. 'Whatever our rivalries and jealousies,' a Mr Parker declared, 'we Europeans, including even Russians, are all imbued with the one spirit of humanity, justice, and progress, summed up in the word "Christian"; and this is none the less so though half of us may be atheists, freethinkers, and Jews.'[129] This elastic Christianity now called for each Power to take over an area of China and rule it for the people's good. Britain should not try to hinder the Germans from taking Shantung. They would not, Parker a trifle unexpectedly hoped, exploit it 'in a grinding selfish way' as the Dutch did Java.[130]

European concord, whether in the spirit of Christ or of the Kaiser, did not last long. Dissensions among the allies during the campaign may have convinced them that any long-term understanding was beyond them.[131] Four years after the Boxers came the war between Japan, with Britain as sleeping partner, and Russia. There could be no peaceful partition of China. In addition there may be truth in a Chinese view that Boxer defiance, though crushed in 1900, compelled the West to think in terms of controlling China through Chinese puppets, instead of directly.[132] The Manchus were now little more than puppets, but too feeble to be of much use; their swarm of princes were 'besotted and effeminate creatures'.[133] In 1911 the dynasty fell and a new era of civil strife, that of the 'warlords', opened. It might have been fatal to China if Europe had not fallen just then into the hands of its own, much more destructive, warlords.

The Yellow Peril

Out of the ill-starred and chaotic encounter between West and
Far East grew the idea of the 'Yellow Peril'. It was a cloudy
though persistent one. Dislike had been spreading between the
two sides far more than knowledge. When Li Hung-chang came
back from his world tour he could truthfully say that responsible Chinese were not more ignorant of Europe than Europeans of China;[134] at St Petersburg, according to Witte, hardly
any of the leading men, including the Foreign Minister, knew
anything whatever about the Far East.[135] But some impressions
had been growing very strong. With all their failures the Chinese were perceived to be a remarkable people, bound to count
in the world sooner or later. This could help to recommend
partition, as not only profitable but prudent; it could be made
an argument by missionaries that if China was some day going
to be a great power it had better be turned into a Christian
power,[136] though the spectacle of Christian Europe scarcely
suggested that this would make much difference. Kipling toyed
with the thought that the grand imperial experiment might
have gone better here than in India – that Britain had 'conquered the wrong country. Let us annex China.'[137] In the
depths of China's humiliation after the Boxer rising a British
general was impressed in spite of himself even by the ordinary
Chinese conscripted by the invaders for forced labour. 'The
"cat" soon brightens their ordinarily dull faces when they
don't wish to understand,' he remarked tolerantly. 'As a matter
of fact they are just about as intelligent a race as you could
find in any part of the globe. The Chinaman grows on you, at
first I thought he was a horror ... Our officers of the Chinese
Regiment swear by him.'[138]

China might turn into a menace in two ways, economically
and militarily. If modern industry were forced on the Chinese,
it was said, these toiling myriads would flood the world with
their products.[139] It was a hair-raising prospect, and one writer
confessed to feeling grateful that 'after all, the dénouement
is not likely to crop up in our time'.[140] But already 'the number
of foreigners able to make a living in China is daily diminishing',

it was complained,[141] and it was these foreign residents, the most immediately threatened, who did most to prejudice public opinion at home. In military terms, after the Tonking war 'people saw visions of Chinamen overrunning the world';[142] twenty years later the danger that seemed more pressing was that one foreign country might gain sole control, as Britain had done in India, and draw on China's gigantic reservoir of manpower to build an army of high quality and staggering size. If Britain had China, said one pipe-dreamer, 'we could raise in twenty years an army that would hold the world at bay.'[143] A Tsarist army with inexhaustible Chinese reserves would be a Russian steamroller indeed. As early as the middle of the nineteenth century prophecies of Russia dominating China and then using China to dominate the world could be heard. Before the end of the century an American was predicting that Russia would seize China, then India – 'and then Asia will begin the conquest of Europe'.[144]

China was often thought of as a vast ant-heap, and soldier-ants were exactly what the vast over-drilled armies then coming to full growth required. Similar fears were in the air about a huge black army. Europe before 1914 sometimes felt that it was becoming too civilized, or physically enervated, to fight in good earnest; if so, future wars would have to be transacted with native cannon-fodder officered by Europeans, like armies of robots thrown against one another half a century later in science-fiction.

But the natives might not always be content with the role assigned to them. An Englishman engaged with the Boxers clung to a conviction that at a pinch 'two thousand Aryans are worth a hundred thousand Chinese'.[145] This required a robust faith in Aryan blood, especially when four years later Japan defeated Russia. During the Boxer crisis one of Tzu Hsi's vain efforts was an appeal to the Mikado for Asian unity against the West. If such a combination ever took shape the West might very well expect the tables to be turned on it. Fears like these were taken up by the Kaiser, who devised a cartoon representing a warlike archangel summoning Europe's nations to repel the Far East, symbolized by a Buddha-figure floating menacingly towards them.[146] It was not hard to recognize under this Germany's ambition to lead, or dominate, Europe, but William II himself may have taken it quite seriously – at the same time as he proclaimed himself protector of Turkey and Islam against Europe. On the eve of the Great War he was never tired of saying that a European war would be 'utterly foolish', and that 'the coming antagonism is between the Asiatics and the Western peoples'.[147]

In the minds of many ordinary people to whom the Yellow Peril brought vague alarms, it meant the thought of China's enormous population, already spilling over by millions into other lands. Europeans cradled in small cities and nation-states might well be sensitive to the vertigo of numbers. To them Asia had always stood for an overwhelming multitude of beings, only to be counteracted by superior skill; the word 'horde' that had come into the European languages from the steppes of central Asia signified a mass of creatures on the move, less human than animal, a blind menace. It is a wholesome instinct that warns man against the obliterating multiplication of mankind. There *were* too many Chinese, there *were* coming to be too many people in England. In however grotesque a form, the 'Yellow Peril' was one of the starting-points of the recoil of civilization against the nightmare of human fecundity that has become its greatest peril, mentally even more than economically.

Korea, Tibet, Siam

Exploration was in progress in the scattered borderlands of China, impeded sometimes by Nature, sometimes by man. By the early years of this century the West had some acquaintance with Manchuria, Mongolia, Chinese Turkestan or Sinkiang. Korea, the 'hermit kingdom', was being opened up from the early 1880s, and something learned about its culture as well as its more marketable resources. A German consul, Möllendorf, was one of the first to master the language.[148] International rivalries leading towards Korea's annexation by Japan in 1910 drew a good deal of attention to it; comments were as discordant as the temperaments of visitors. One was gratified to find even in the peasants, superstitious and over-burdened with taxes as they were, 'an amazing sense of the beautiful in nature.'[149] Better-off Koreans had, for an English scout, 'an eminently respectable well-to-do appearance'.[150] Curzon dismissed Korea as 'one of the dirtiest and most repulsive countries in the world'.[151]

Tibet remained a mystery longer; a British invasion in 1905 kicked the door open for a while. It was a challenge to daring explorers as one of the most nearly impossible lands to get into or out of. It also drew a few Buddhist pilgrims, one of whom, a Japanese monk, has left us an account of his long stay in a monastery to weigh against Western reports.[152] Tibet's 'image' in the West evolved in the opposite direction from China's. Instead of being first idealized and then despised, Tibet was realistically seen as a wretched land of feudal barons and serfs, balanced by droves of idle monks and their preposterous god-king; only later was it romanticized into a Shangrila, a haven of peace and quiet watched over by philosopher-priests until Communist China laid rude hands on it and abolished serfdom. Primitivism had come to be admired as an alternative not to civilization and its maladies, but to socialism; it was restful to conservative minds in the West to contemplate a country whose people still felt a childlike confidence in their governors.

By 1857 Siamese envoys were to be seen at London nightclubs,[153] and their royal family, imposing in size if no more, found its way into the *Almanach de Gotha*. In Siam the king who recognized the need to study the outside world, in the hope of survival between hungry England and thirsty France, was Mongkut. He taught himself English, and was always in a flutter of activity, but like similar rulers elsewhere in Asia he had too few helpers, and was himself too deeply embedded in the old ways to be able to emancipate his country from them. We have a window into his palace and mind, thanks to a governess from Wales who worked there, the celebrated Anna.[154] His son Chulalongkorn, who succeeded him in 1868, toured Europe and published some unpretentious travel-notes.[155] On Court life in his reign we are again well informed, thanks to a British doctor who spent some years there.[156]

As in many parts of the world, the common people seemed

more attractive than the decadent ruling class. A British survey in 1885 praised them for several virtues, not least that of being 'submissive to authority in a degree that must render them excellent subjects'.[157] Here was a quality uniquely calculated to win European approval. It did not at that date appeal so strongly to Americans, and Townsend Harris, who was at Bangkok before becoming the first resident American envoy in Japan, went away disgusted with 'this false, base and cowardly people', among whom every man grovelled to his superiors and made his inferiors grovel to him.[158] But an English diplomat who came to Bangkok from Tokyo was equally disgusted with official life, a compound of sloth, corruption and deceit. 'There are so many abuses of every kind to fight against that my soul is weary.'[159] As between Siam and Japan, the two small Far Eastern countries that escaped losing their independence, it looks nowadays a matter of 'pre-ordinance and first decree' that one was to vegetate, the other to shake the world. Yet Sir Harry Parkes, that battering-ram of British diplomacy in the Far East, credited Siam with more capacity for progress than Japan, and drew the Mikado's attention to it as a country to watch.[160]

The Opening of Japan

Japan is 'an unknown lump on our earth, and an undefined line on our charts', wrote James Brooke in 1838, planning explorations in that direction before he found himself at Sarawak.[161] Since the closing of the country by the Shoguns or hereditary dictators early in the seventeenth century there had only been a trickle of information about it, through the Dutch who were permitted to trade at one port and who provided the Japanese with a peep-hole to see the world through. Perhaps their willingness to remain on humiliating terms implanted in Japan a permanent conviction that the Western soul never rose above sordid gain. As a country that Europe had once known fairly well and then been cut off from, it was the subject of much speculation, most of which turned out to be as fanciful as the Titipu of Gilbert and Sullivan. On one theory it was an

Eden, all its inhabitants 'as virtuous as Adam and Eve before the fall'.[162]

Long before the official opening the policy of exclusion was weakening, and the power of the Shoguns with it. Whether or not economy and society were moving of their own accord towards something like Western capitalism, they contained elements more akin to Europe than to China: a hereditary aristocracy, peasants half serfs, merchants and moneyed men ripened by a long peace and ready for transformation into a modern bourgeoisie. Internal pressures were growing before foreign intervention came to release them; it was a nation in movement that the West encountered here. A mounting impulse to look abroad, to learn whatever could be gleaned from the Dutch or their books, formed part of a complicated interplay among the rulers at the centre, the *daimyo* or feudal chiefs whom they had dragooned, and some of the lesser nobles or samurai, impatient of both.

Russia was creeping down the Pacific coast, Britain's activity in China made it interested in Japan too, but it was the United States that for the first time stole Europe's thunder and briefly took the lead. Americans were more interested in whales than in Japanese (though American seamen were interested in Japanese women), and wanted whaling stations on these coasts where sailors were always being shipwrecked. Commodore Perry arrived with his squadron in 1853 and 1854, while Britain and France had their eyes fixed on the Balkans, and compelled Japan – half-willing, like a lady in two minds, to be compelled – to open certain ports. Other governments followed, and treaties were drawn up. Meanwhile Japan was plunged into the political turmoil out of which a new régime and a programme of modernization emerged.

At this stage the odds looked heavy against its chances of remaining united and independent, let alone of becoming a major power. But Japan was a more manageable country than China, because it was small and because the masses, accustomed to feudal lordship, were more tractable. This docility, which as in Siam foreigners did not fail to notice, made it simpler to carry out fundamental changes once the higher classes had settled their differences. There were peasant riots, but no

Taiping rebellion. Also, in the ancient dynasty relegated to seclusion by the Shoguns, and now brought forward by the party of change as their figurehead, Japan possessed an embodiment of national tradition, a reassurance against the flood of innovation. What was really revolution could be presented to the country, and stands now in the history-books, as the Meiji Restoration.

This tranquillizing air of legitimacy, and the fact that things were always in the hands of solid men of substance and never degenerated into an affair of the populace, helped to recommend the change to the foreign representatives as well. Not many years had passed since Europe's revolutionary fever-fit of 1848; and the opening of Japan coincided with the Western backing given to the Chinese ruling class against its Taiping rebels. Only little by little, however, could foreigners groping in the fog of Japanese politics and syntax make out what was really happening, and what were the respective positions of Shogun and 'Mikado'. Civil broils of its own after 1861 put the US out of action; when the British envoy Parkes decided to lend his countenance to the party of change – thus stealing a march on his French rival – he may have exerted more influence on Japan's destiny than Perry and his squadron had done. In 1867 the last Shogun resigned.

To most Japanese, as to other peoples away from Europe, all these Westerners were the same, mostly nose and noise, and all were exposed to outbursts of anti-foreign feeling. Conservatives were as firmly convinced as in China that foreigners were barbarians, and among the unlettered strange stories were told of them, for instance that the red blankets they sold were dyed with the blood of stolen infants.[163] The social and psychological strains of the transition period could find relief in attacks on them. But by contrast with more democratic China, such attacks were less often mob riots than acts of assassination carried out by individuals of rank in the old samurai spirit of romantic self-immolation. Europeans could feel a degree of respect for them, though they demanded severe penalties. Against humbler trouble-makers retaliation was more summary. When a crowd threw stones at a party of Frenchmen the latter promptly opened fire and killed eight or nine of them :

this was 'looked upon as a wholesome lesson to the rabble'.[164] It was by way of reprisal for the murder of an Englishman that British warships bombarded Kagoshima, capital of the Satsuma clan or fief, in 1862. Soon afterwards a combined European and American bombardment of forts on the Straits of Shimonoseki gave a foretaste of the anti-Boxer combination.

The most instructive narrative of these events by any Westerner who took part in them was given by Parkes's young assistant Ernest Satow in his memoirs. A scholar by natural bent, this youth plunged into the intricacies of Japanese grammar and social life with zest; he had a taste too for *saké* and the company of geisha-girls. Later in his career, away in South America or Morocco, he always had with him a faithful old Japanese servant, and pined for Tokyo, where he came back as minister in 1890. All this only emphasizes the degree to which he shared the conventional ideas of his time about the handling of native peoples. He disliked Sir Harry's hectoring attitude, 'the overbearing language to which the chief habitually resorted'; still, one had to deal somehow with 'the bad faith which is the usual refuge of Asiatics in a difficult position'.[165] He criticized the destruction at Kagoshima, the firing of rockets into the town after its batteries had been silenced, as excessive.[166] It was one of those theatrical displays of power that the West, like a Wagnerian ruffian-hero, loved. Yet he could go on calmly: 'We had, it might be said, conquered the good-will of Satsuma' – 'the demonstrated superiority of European methods of warfare had converted our bitterest and most determined foes into fast friends.'[167] There was a touch of the overgrown British schoolboy in this faith in friendship founded on fisticuffs. His Japanese acquaintances fully understood, he believed, that 'all the English wanted was the good of the Japanese as a nation'.[168]

After one of the bombardments Satow was ashore with a pair of admirals, who wanted to inspect a Japanese battery. A sentry inquired whether they had leave. 'The answer to this astounding query was that we were not in the habit of asking leave'[169] – an answer that would have served as the motto of Westerners everywhere in the East. Yet it was hard to please these truculent foreigners, in whose eyes Asia was always either too obstinate or too soft. At one point Satow 'began to feel contempt for the weak-kneed officials who so easily allowed themselves to be brow-beaten by a few foreigners'.[170]

Parkes promoted the newly-founded Asiatic Society of Japan, and encouraged his juniors to study the country;[171] and Japan like China cast a spell over some who landed on its shores. Among these was Lafcadio Hearn, the Irish-Greek who came out from America in 1890: men of such jumbled origins find it easier than undiluted Swedes or foursquare Scotsmen to be at home in a new civilization. He married into an impoverished samurai family, became a Japanese national, translated poetry, and interpreted Japanese culture to the West. A few other foreign residents were prepared to meet the Japanese on equal terms and exchange ideas with them.[172] But most of them were there to broaden their bank-books, not their minds, and it was an observation of Satow's that when the average European settles in the East 'the mind's growth comes to a standstill'.[173]

In the ports a cosmopolitan community grew, with a good proportion of undesirables as in all the ports of Asia. At Nagasaki the Russians had a sailors' club and hospital, and looked forward to a spree when ashore with whatever women were to be got; thus giving the Japanese, as a Russian reflected ruefully after the war of 1904–5, opportunities for taking the measure of the Russian navy and its officers.[174] A French visitor in the 1880s was sorry to find that most of his countrymen were deserters, bankrupts, or ne'er-do-wells.[175] Many foreigners employed by the Japanese authorities found themselves no longer required as the Japanese learned their skills, and grumbled at their pupils' ingratitude. From such men casual visitors must have picked up such information as that 'the Japanese cannot count properly, having no head for mathematics', so that all cashiers had to be Chinese.[176] (Before the Second World War it was being said that they could not pilot war-planes, because of some peculiarity of their eyes.) An expatriate more indulgent than most said to Kipling at Yokohama: 'Well, I am very fond of the Jap; but I suppose he *is* a native any way you look at him.'[177] 'Jap' was an abbreviation as much resented as 'Chink'.

Tourism soon brought another type of foreigner, much more rare in China; Japan was becoming – except for Palestine – Asia's first tourist country. 'Murray's Handbook' first came out in 1891. It mingled warnings about inn smells with admonitions against upsetting Japanese feelings. 'Whereas the lower classes at home are apt to resent suave manners ... every Japanese, however humble, expects courtesy, being himself courteous.' Impatience should be curbed. In the dictionary *tadaima* might mean 'immediately', but in practice it meant 'any time between now and Christmas'. Travellers ought not to behave as if these islands were nothing but 'a sort of peep-. show set up for foreigners to gape at'.[178] This was indeed a delusion not easily shaken off, Japan being 'so reposeful, so full of antique grace, and soft, fair courtesies'.[179] The leisurely refinements of the old tea-drinking ceremony were written about gushingly.[180] 'The Japanese should have no concern with business,' Kipling thought: the country ought to be 'put in a glass case' and paid to go on looking pretty.[181]

Few sightseers moved away from the beaten track of temples, landscapes and peach-blossom. Isabella Bird, one of the handful of notable women travellers of that age, met with a very different Japan up in the north, full of disease and half-naked squalor. (The indifference of the Japanese poor to clothes often gave offence to sedate foreigners.) Among the Ainu aborigines, known for their hairiness, her guide Ito laughed at the idea of treating them civilly – 'they're just dogs, not men'.[182] Japanese along with Chinese, Malays, Hindus, fully shared the contempt of the European for the lower races. Mrs Bird thought the Ainu less badly treated by the Japanese government than Red Indians by the American.[183] Hirsute Europe might have been expected to meet this lowly race, possibly its own remote relative,[184] with some thrill of fellow-feeling, but gave no sign of this.

One observer who was in Japan in the first years and came back for another look twenty years later could not help regretting some of the changes: picturesque official costumes gone, manners grown free and easy, 'almost disrespectful', the people no longer, as formerly, 'contented and happy each in his own place'.[185] The indiscriminate haste to imitate everything Western that marked the first decades of modernism struck many jarring notes. Gentlemen of Japan sitting on chairs in Western suits looked unnatural, all the more when, as happened during the learning process, trousers were forgotten. From the outset it had been perceived that Japan's artificial stiffness (like Britain's) could be thawed by liquor, and diplomats like Townsend Harris took care to have plenty of Western brands in stock. Some austere officials whom he entertained on shipboard were soon plastering one another's hair with mustard.[186]

Western Opinions of the Japanese

Altogether it was difficult to make out the Japanese character; it cannot have been easy for the Japanese themselves, in those years of rapid flux. One recurrent impression was of dishonesty. Linguistic obstacles, which never ceased to be formidable, must have been partly to blame, but it was an epoch when the ethics of an old society were crumbling, those of a new one had not yet replaced them. 'They are the greatest liars on earth,' wrote Harris comprehensively.[187] Japanese traders unlike Chinese had a reputation for cheating and swindling (and Japan unlike China was taking to modern capitalism like a duck to water). It was 'the rule for statesmen to amass fortunes'.[188] A French missionary saw the Japanese as marvellously gifted with ability to assimilate anything outside the moral sphere, a realm to them unknown.[189] A Frenchwoman described them as intelligent, hard-working, brave, even honest, yet stained by disgraceful vices such as would subvert any European society.[190] This might be all very well so far as art was concerned, and Japanese painting was all the rage among collectors and a good many artists in the West. But in more important matters it was a chronic puzzle, to Britons especially, conscious of their own high moral standards, that Japan seemed to get on so comfortably without them, and without any real religious convictions. The Japanese 'will not and cannot take either life or religion *au grand sérieux*'.[191]

Sex was another thing they failed to take as seriously as

Europe thought it ought to be taken, preferring to view it as an amusement. Harris was shocked to discover that men and women shared the public bath-houses, and that even married life had features 'disgusting beyond belief'.[192] On the other hand geisha-girls were shocked at pictures of European ladies in low-necked gowns dancing with men's arms round them.[193] Not all Westerners were as strait-laced as Harris, and it was part of tourist routine to visit the Yoshiwara quarter and, in the tactful words of the Handbook, observe the 'unfortunate inmates, decked out in gorgeous raiment', from the street; Japan's solution to an old problem ran 'counter to Anglo-Saxon ideas', but avoided the 'disorderly scenes' common in Western towns.[194] The geisha was soon becoming for the West a new emblem of romance, its own having grown somewhat stale. There was nothing in Turkey or India or China like these diminutive, soft-mannered creatures, in whose company the foreigner well primed with *saké* could feel that he was really getting to know the country and entering into its life, as he never could in those vast arid expanses of Asia peopled only by men. Japan's women blended charmingly with its paintings and plum-trees, and old residents declared that their beauty stole on one by degrees, until one suddenly liked it better than any high-nosed European face.[195]

Verdicts on Japan were thus very divergent; and Japanese settling abroad, in Hawaii or California, were, like Chinese emigrants, no easier to diagnose than those at home. The safest aphorism was that Japan was different. As a French diplomat wrote, '*dans l'Extrême-Orient, on raisonne autrement qu'en Occident*'.[196] He thought the Japanese volatile, inconstant, wanting to be the Germans of Asia but having no real affinity with them.[197] They were sometimes dubbed the Frenchmen, sometimes the Spaniards, of the Far East; Europeans often tried to classify alien peoples by equating them with familiar neighbours. Until they began winning wars, the common view was that they had 'a moderate future' before them. 'The Japanese are a happy race, and being content with little, are not likely to achieve much.[198]

In the meantime they were held fast by the 'Unequal Treaties' imposed when Japan was weak, which deprived it of tariff freedom and gave foreigners extra-territorial rights. There were decades of agitation against them, while national sentiment was inflamed by talk in the foreign-language Press and at meetings of residents about Japan being still an only half-civilized country. Negotiations over revision dragged on and on. 'It is a question of the Sibylline Books,' the harassed British minister once wrote. 'Japan moves forward so rapidly, that the terms which are considered favourable in one year, are out of date in the next.'[199] As in China, it was England that had built up the biggest interests, and could be accused of exploiting Western solidarity to defend them. But newer and larger interests at home might be more flexible than the short-sighted traders in the ports, to whom a privileged status was as necessary as a rickshaw. When a Mr Reed came out to sell warships he did much buttering of the Japanese and being buttered by them, and was quite sympathetic to their demand for revision. He could sympathize even with rickshaw coolies, and 'sincerely hope they are able to bear their hard lot without too much of that pain which we must all feel in thinking of it'[200] – another characteristic attitude of the West.

The skill of the Japanese workman led a visitor to predict that the country would be 'England's most dangerous rival in commerce'.[201] But in order to convince the West that it was really in earnest and civilized enough to be treated as an equal, Japan had to fight and win a war. It was after the victory over China that Britain decided to lead the way in surrendering the old privileges. In Turkey it and France were still refusing to do this in 1914, thereby helping Germany to another ally. Britain had been teaching Japan how to run a navy, while the army owed its training to French military missions; the prestige and orders for arms that accrued were valuable, and after the Franco-Prussian War the French strained every nerve to avoid being supplanted by the victorious Germans. But the West was very slow to realize how fast its pupils were learning the science of war. A professional estimate of 1882 was that the army was quite good, for Asia, but could not stand up to European troops; its men lacked 'the true military instinct'.[202] Next year at the Mikado's birthday review an imperial prince lost an epaulette, and the war minister's horse bolted and threw him: an English journalist who was looking on reflected twenty years later that it would have been hard from these auguries to foretell the triumph over Russia.[203]

Thoughts of Japan as a very subordinate ally had cropped up a good many years before the Anglo-Japanese treaty. During the Tonking fighting France angled vainly for Japanese support against China, making overtures also to Siam. Sienkiewicz, the then French minister at Tokyo, told his government that Japan hoped to take Formosa some day (as it did in 1895), and therefore disliked seeing French forces there; nevertheless it might feel all the more respect for a France that gave a display of strength by keeping the island. The best model to follow in Asia, he went on, was Russia, which with its *'convoitises insatiables'* was not loved, but was respected, from Stamboul to Peking. As to any notion of Asiatics genuinely liking any Western country, that was mere moonshine – *'on peut en parler, il n'est guère permis d'y croire'.*[204] Both France and Britain were inclined to credit Russia with knowing best how to handle Asiatics because it was half-Asiatic itself.

Britain recommended Japan not to become France's catspaw, but itself, during an Anglo-Russian crisis of 1885, wanted an arrangement at least to enable it to use Japanese bases. Here was the first germ of the alliance of 1902, an alliance with an Asian state not against an Asian neighbour but against a fellow-European nation. Japan's performance against China in 1894–5, and again in the Boxer campaign, was greatly admired. Requiring a bastion against Russia at the eastern end of Asia such as Turkey had provided at the western, Britain first thought of China, and now turned to Japan; while to Japan's continental ambitions Russia had become the chief hindrance. Two years after the alliance came the Russo-Japanese War. Before it began the whole Russian army held its small opponents in derision. '"A Japanese? Pooh! he's a mosquito. Why, I'll stick a pin through him and send him home in a letter", was a favourite remark of the moment.'[205] In the siege of Port Arthur and the mammoth battle of Mukden the Japanese, fighting with the same bravery as the Boxers and with far more skill, demonstrated conclusively that Asia could produce as good soldiers and as good officers as Europe. One enlightened European who welcomed Japan's attainment of equal status was Bertrand Russell. 'The Japanese alliance seems to me excellent,' he wrote to a friend at the end of 1905 '– I am glad England should be ready to recognize the yellow man as a civilized being, and not wholly sorry at the quarrel with Australia which this recognition entails.'[206]

Militarism and technology Japan took over precociously: Europe's experiments on a higher plane were less easily copied. In the modernizing movement there was a liberal wing, desirous of parliamentary rule and attracted by foreign ideas like those of the Russian novels that were making a stir there. After about 1885 a reaction against Western ideas, as distinct from Western machines, set in. This was partly disenchantment with less admirable aspects of the Occident. Japanese who went abroad, it was half-seriously said, came back convinced that Europe's three chief qualities were dirtiness, laziness and superstition.[207] But it was mainly a turning away from liberalism, as the new oligarchy, backed by a partnership of military and capitalist interests, consolidated its power. Its leaders vastly admired Bismarck and his new Germany, which Ito visited, and Bismarck's German constitution was the pattern for the one inaugurated in 1889.

Few tears were shed in the more democratic countries over the failure of Japanese liberalism. No responsible Westerners, apart from some Americans, were eager to see Asia unsettled by democracy, any more than in the twentieth century by socialism. A wide-awake but authoritarian régime was the most convenient to deal with. The group of resolute men like Ito who had led Japan out of the past into the present, as nobody had come forward to do in China, were men Europe could not but applaud. 'Whatever its shortcomings, the ruling oligarchy has guided Japan with admirable skill and courage.'[208] As for tourists, those seekers of the exotic cared as little as today in countries like Spain what was in the constitution or who was in the jails.

For the new order the buttress of a popular ideology was required. As late as the 1880s it was being asked whether Japan ought to preserve its links with Asia by holding on to Confucianism. But this was too Chinese, too static, too literary a creed. Among foreigners it was quite seriously asked whether the leaders, themselves agnostics, would decide to adopt Christianity as the religion of state, and have the Mikado baptized, in order to put Japan on the same footing with Europe and strengthen its claim to equality.[209] A good many individual conversions did take place, as in China; the Far East had no religions with anything like the unshakeable hold of those of India, and converts had been numerous in the sixteenth century too. In that age the iron men of Europe had looked to Christianity for a 'mollifying of such adamantine hearts, as those of the natural people of these islands';[210] while the English factors would flog a Japanese slave 'till all the skin was beaten off, and after washed him in brine', and the Dutch cut a slave of theirs in pieces for stealing.[211]

Long after the success of the new Japan was fully apparent, it remained a Western belief that Japanese could copy everything but invent nothing, and if they were borrowing Europe's clothes and guns they might as well be expected to borrow its God too. Instead the decision of the men in power was to resurrect the old primitive local cult, Shinto. They were doing methodically what the Manchu Court did for a moment in 1900 when it patronized the cults of the Chinese peasantry. Shinto was refurbished with a patchwork of new ideas, some taken (as part of the Taiping creed had been) from Christianity. It and the Mikado-worship artificially worked up with it[212] gave the oligarchy a further hold over the masses. Japan's outward westernization was thus balanced by an opposite process within the national mind, a turning away from both Europe and China to something older, more autochthonous, than either Christianity or Confucianism.

In 1884 when the British minister was advising Japan's leaders not to join the French against China – which 'will one day be a great Power, who will then pay Japan off with interest' – they talked as if they thought it 'contrary to the rules of the game' for Japan to join hands with any Western country against an Eastern neighbour.[213] In practice solidarity with Asia would mean only ambition to dominate Asian countries lagging behind Japan. Inner forces set up pressure towards imperialism, though here too allowance must be made for the contagion of Christian example. By 1878 an American general was aware that 'Japan, no longer contented with progress at home, is destined to play an important part in the history of the world'.[214] In 1895 when Japan defeated China it might still pose as champion of Asia; a Western writer who expected the world's future to be decided in the Far East cited a speech by Okuma about the decadent West, which Japan on behalf of Asia would expel.[215] An anti-imperialist like W. S. Blunt was so sure that only Japan could save eastern Asia from European control that he could look on Japanese control of China as the necessary price.[216] With the same logic, when it came to war in 1904 Russia could pose as champion of European civilization.[217] Other Europeans, including Englishmen, wondered uneasily whether there might not be something in this. If Japan won, an Englishman at St Petersburg wrote, she might before long 'unite the yellow races and get too big for her boots'.[218] Forty years later Japan did get too big, and Europe's bastions in eastern Asia collapsed.

NOTES

1. See P. J. d'Orléans, *History of the Two Tartar Conquerors of China*, trans. Earl of Ellesmere (Hakluyt Society, 1854).

2. S. C. Brown, *Count Rumford. Physicist Extraordinary* (1964 edn), p. 164.

3. See *Le siècle de Louis XIV* (1751), Chapter 39.

4. L. Dermigny, *La Chine et l'Occident. Le commerce à Canton au XVIIIe siècle, 1719–1833* (Paris, 1964), p. 292.

5. R. Walter, *Lord Anson's Voyage round the World, 1740–1744* (1748), p. 160 (abridged edn by S. W. C. Pack, 1947).

6. ibid., pp. 185–6.

7. ibid., pp. 196, 210.

8. Boswell, *The Life of Samuel Johnson* (Dent edn, 1926), Vol. 3, p. 17.

9. *An Embassy to China* (Lord Macartney's journal), ed. J. L. Cranmer-Byng (1962), pp. 229–30.

10. ibid., pp. 128, 210.

11. ibid., pp. 68, 71, 74, 76.

12. ibid., pp. 98, 216.

13. ibid., pp. 77, 107, 186–8.

14. ibid., pp. 170, 48, 51.

15. G. E. Simon, *China: its Social, Political and Religious Life* (English edn, 1887), p. 6.

16. S. W. Williams, *The Middle Kingdom* (revised edn, New York, 1883), Vol. 1, p. 391.

17. W. A. P. Martin, *Hanlin Papers* (1880), Chapter 2.

18. W. H. Medhurst (consul at Shanghai), *The Foreigner in Far Cathay* (1872), Chapter 18.

19. Sir A. Lyall, *Asiatic Studies* (1884), Chapter 6.

20. Preface to *Hellas* (1821).

21. *Marx on China, 1853–1860*, ed. Dona Torr (1951), p. 3; cf. p. 50.

22. L. Dermigny, op. cit., pp. 290 ff.

23. Captain W. J. Gill, *The River of Golden Sand* (1883), p. 289.

24. A. Hosie, *Report of a Journey through Szechuan* ... *1883*, in Foreign Office 17. 946, Public Record Office, London.

25. A. R. Colquhoun, *Across Chryse* (1883), Vol. 2, p. 201.

26. The chief minister met by Macartney took some interest in European affairs (*An Embassy to China*, pp. 120, 127, 160).

27. J. O. P. Bland and Sir E. T. Backhouse, *China under the Empress Dowager* (1910), p. 112.

28. L. Dermigny, op. cit., p. 1,397.

29. A. Michie, *The Englishman in China during the Victorian Era, as illustrated in the career of Sir Rutherford Alcock* (Edinburgh, 1900), p. 81.

30. Tseng Chi-tse, envoy to London and Paris in 1872, and sent to Europe again in 1880.

31. F. Wakeman, *Strangers at the Gate. Social Disorder in South China, 1839–1861* (University of California, 1966), pp. 46–7.

32. ibid., pp. 174, 176.

33. Captain S. Osborn, *The Past and Future of British Relations in China* (Edinburgh, 1860), p. 2.

34. ibid., p. 5.

35. ibid., p. 10.

36. ibid., pp. 178, 59.

37. ibid., p. 169.

38. ibid., pp. 43, 15.

39. Gordon believed the rebels were bringing only misery on the country (D. C. Boulger, *The Life of Gordon* (1896), Vol. 2, p. 341). Undeniably their leadership degenerated in the later stages.

40. *The Chinese Recorder* (Shanghai), Vol. 17, editorial of January 1886. See further my book *British Diplomacy in China, 1880 to 1885* (Cambridge, 1939; reprint, New York, 1970), Chapter 18.

41. V. Chirol, *The Far Eastern Question* (1896), p. 9.

42. Masataka Banno, *China and the West 1858–1861* (Harvard, 1964), p. 308.

43. 'B. L. Putnam Weale' (B. L. Simpson), *Indiscreet Letters from Peking* (5th edn, 1906), pp. 4–5; cf. A. Michie, op. cit., pp. 261–2.

44. *An Embassy to China*, p. 113.

45. W. H. G. Kingston, *The Three Midshipmen* (2nd edn, 1873), Chapter 34.

46. A. Coates, *Prelude to Hongkong* (1966), p. 184. Such ideas must have been held chiefly by the illiterate.

47. F. Wakeman, op. cit., pp. 12, 16–17, 56. He quotes Chinese sources.

48. S. W. Williams, op. cit., Vol. 2, p. 693.

49. *Memoirs of William Hickey*, ed. A. Spencer (9th edn, n.d.), Vol. 1, p. 224.

50. W. J. Gill, op. cit., p. 39.

51. R. Coltman, *The Chinese* (1891), p. 23.

52. G. B. Endacott, *A History of Hong Kong* (Oxford, 1958), pp. 121–2, Sir John Bowring was then British Plenipotentiary in China.

53. H. W. Lucy, *East by West* (1885), Vol. 2, p. 116.

54. W. H. Medhurst, op. cit., pp. 28–9.

55. L. Giles, 'The Present State of Affairs in China', in *The Fortnightly Review*, September 1879.

56. A. J. Sargent, *Anglo-Chinese Commerce and Diplomacy* (1907), p. 309; part of his concluding warning that China's patience should not be abused too far.

57. V. Chirol. op. cit., p. 60.

58. Somerset Maugham, *The Painted Veil* (1925), Chapter 37.

59. See on this incident J. Bredon, *Sir Robert Hart* (1909), Chapter 4.

60. C. F. Gordon Cumming, *Wanderings in China* (1887), Chapter 5.

61. S. Merwin, *Drugging a Nation* (1908), p. 56.

62. C. F. G. Cumming, op. cit., Chapter 5.

63. 'B. L. Putnam Weale', op. cit., p. 7.

64. See V. Purcell, *The Boxer Uprising. A Background Study* (Cambridge, 1963), pp. 109 ff. Protestant missions often taught English; Catholics more rarely French.

65. M. Banno, op. cit., p. 244.

66. F. H. Balfour, *Leaves from my Chinese Scrapbook* (1887), p. 48.

67. Mrs A. Little, *Li Hung-chang: his Life and Times* (1903), pp. 302, 221. On Li's appetite for foreign bribes, cf. P. Joseph, *Foreign Diplomacy in China, 1894–1900* (1928), p. 161.

68. *The Memoirs of Count Witte*, trans. A. Yarmolinsky (1912), p. 94.

69. Lin Yutang, *My Country and my People* (1936), p. 11.

70. A. Coates, op. cit., pp. 180, 208. Most of the book is far more sensible.

71. *The Heathen Chinee* (1870).

72. D. C. Boulger, *Sir Halliday Macartney* (1908), p. 195.

73. *Feng-shui* ('air and water'), a system of geomancy, cropped up incessantly in disputes over land purchases. Dragons were still getting in the way late in the Second World War when my friend Squadron-leader R. H. Macintosh (now MBE) was constructing airfields.

74. J. R. Chitty, *Things Seen in China* (1909), pp. 15–16.

75. Archdeacon J. H. Gray, *China* (1878), Vol. 1, pp. 15–16. R. A. Hall, *Eminent Authorities on China* (1931), gives a selection of judgements on China, arranged into optimistic, pessimistic, and realistic.

76. *Mendoza's Historie of the Kingdome of China*, ed. Sir G. T. Staunton (Hakluyt Society, 1853), p. 32.

77. A. Michie, op. cit., pp. 263–4.

78. See G. B. Endacott, op. cit., pp. 175–7.

79. J. J. Abraham, *The Surgeon's Log. Impressions of the Far East* (1911), p. 90 (18th edn, 1933). cf. Jack London's story, 'Chun Ah Chun', about an astute but honourable millionaire, in *South Sea Tales* (1911).

80. Despatch from Shanghai, 5 January 1859, in *The Second China War, 1856–1860* (Navy Records Society, Vol. XCV, 1954), pp. 383–4.

81. J. Hutchinson, *Indian Brick Tea for Tibet* (*Report on a mission to Ssuchuan*) (Calcutta, 1906), p. 3.

82. C. F. G. Cumming, op. cit., Chapter 6.

83. W. H. Medhurst, op. cit., pp. 172–3.

84. W. D. Foulke, *Slav or Saxon* (2nd edn, New York, 1899), p. 57.

85. S. D. Gamble, *Peking. A Social Survey* (1921), p. 185.

86. R. Coltman, op. cit., p. 174; and see generally Chapter 8. On China's frightful overcrowding and poverty cf. A. H. Smith, *Village Life in China* (1899), p. 310.

87. Sir R. Alcock, *Life's Problems* (1857), p. 37.

88. C. R. Chitty, op. cit., pp. 72–3.

89. W. H. G. Kingston, op. cit., Chapter 28. On the 'Ladrones' or South China pirates see J. B. Eames, *The British in China* (1909), pp. 142–3.

90. L. Dermigny, op. cit., pp. 81–3.

91. Persia C. Campbell, *Chinese Coolie Emigration to Countries within the British Empire* (1923), p. 97. cf. p. 117: 'The abuses of the traffic had increased with the competition. In Canton they beggar

credence.' See also Chapter 12 of *An Autobiography*, by Sir E. Hornby (1929), a British judge in the Far East from 1865 to 1876.

92. W. H. Lucy, op. cit., Vol. 1, p. 174.

93. See H. C. Thomson, *The Case for China* (New York, 1933), Chapter 12. For a socialist view see H. M. Hyndman, *The Awakening of China* (1919), Chapter 13: 'Asiatic Emigration'.

94. J. Thomson, *The Straits of Malacca, Indo-China and China* (1875), p. 14.

95. H. H. Montgomery, *Foreign Missions* (1902), p. 38.

96. D. F. Rennie, cited by M. Banno, op. cit., p. 272 n.

97. *An Embassy to China*, pp. 153, 226.

98. S. Osborn, op. cit., p. 77.

99. F. Wakeman, op. cit., p. 56.

100. A. R. Colquhoun, *China in Transformation* (1898), pp. 203–4.

101. V. Chirol, op. cit., p. 41.

102. C. Bigham, *A Year in China, 1899–1900* (1901), pp. 48, 140.

103. W. F. Sands, *Undiplomatic Memories* (New York, 1930), p. 107.

104. Ven. A. E. Moule, *Half a Century in China* (1911), p. 222.

105. Ven. A. E. Moule, *New China and Old* (1892), p. 9.

106. Sir G. F. Bowen, 23 February 1885, in S. Lane-Poole, *Thirty Years of Colonial Government* (1889), Vol. 2, p. 350.

107. H. Norman, *Peoples and Politics of the Far East* (1895), p. 199.

108. R. Kipling, *From Sea to Sea* (1900), Vol. 1, p. 294. The tour he describes was made in 1887–8.

109. Mrs A. Little, op. cit., p. 246.

110. R. F. Johnston, *From Peking to Mandalay* (1908), p. 18.

111. ibid., p. 355.

112. C. Holcombe, *The Real Chinaman* (New York, 1895), p. 215.

113. Rev. J. Ross, *The Manchus, or the Reigning Dynasty of China* (1880), p. 638.

114. Mrs T. F. Hughes, *Among the Sons of Han* (1881), p. 159.

115. V. Purcell, op. cit., pp. 75 ff.

116. Rev. F. L. H. Pott, *The Outbreak in China* (New York, 1900), pp. 85–7.

117. G. N. Curzon, *Problems of the Far East* (1894), Chapter 9. cf. the episode of a bad-tempered missionary getting himself chased out of a town, in W. S. Percival, *Land of the Dragon* (1889), pp. 161 ff.

118. See on this phase M. C. Wright, *The Last Stand of Chinese Conservatism. The T'ung-chih Restoration, 1862–1874* (Stanford University, 1957).

119. Chang Chih-tung, *China's Only Hope*, trans. S. I. Woodbridge (New York, 1900).

120. ibid., pp. 41, 123, 63.
121. See·V. Purcell, op. cit., Chapter 11.
122. Antonio de Morga, *The Phillippine Islands*, trans. Hon. H. E. J. Stanley (Hakluyt Society, 1868), p. 122. cf. A. Ular, *A Russo-Chinese Empire* (Paris, 1902; English edn, 1904), Preface: 'Books dealing with China are almost without exception hostile.' One exception is the sympathetic discussion of China's awakening by Sir R. Hart, long head of the Chinese Customs service, in '*These from the Land of Sinim*' (1901), pp. 48 ff., etc.
123. C. Bigham, op. cit., pp. 2, 173, 175.
124. 'B. L. Putnam Weale', op. cit., pp. 58–9; and see generally.
125. P. W. Sargeant, *The Great Empress Dowager of China* (1910), p. 239.
126. On the looting of Peking, in which foreign officers and even, it was said, envoys took part, see 'B. L. Putnam Weale', op. cit., p. 258, etc.; W. J. Oudendyk, *Ways and By-ways in Diplomacy* (1939), pp. 106 ff.
127. V. Purcell, op. cit., pp. 260–61.
128. Sir E. T. Backhouse and J. O. P. Bland, *Annals and Memories of the Court of Peking* (1914), p. 185.
129. E. H. Parker, *China Past and Present* (1903), p. 44.
130. ibid., pp. 46, 356, 365.
131. 'Upton Close' (J. F. Hall), *The Revolt of Asia* (New York, 1927), Chapter 5.
132. Wu Yu-chang, *The Revolution of 1911* (English edn, Peking, 1962), p. 30.
133. Sir E. T. Backhouse and J. O. P. Bland, *Annals and Memories*, p. 335.
134. J. O. P. Bland, *Li Hung-chang* (1917), p. 212.
135. *The Memoirs of Count Witte*, p. 82.
136. Rev. J. Ross, *History of Corea* (n.d., c. 1880), p. vii.
137. R. Kipling, op. cit., Vol. 1, p. 277.
138. Major-General Sir N. Stewart, *My Service Days* (1908), pp. 247–8.
139. G. E. Sîmon, op. cit., p. 79.
140. A. Krausse, *China in Decay* (1900), p. 374.
141. A. Little, *Gleanings from Fifty Years in China* (1910), p. 204.
142. R. S. Gundry, *China and her Neighbours* (1893), p. 315.
143. A. Reid, *From Peking to Petersburg* (1899), Chapter 4.
144. W. D. Foulke, op. cit., p. 64; cf. p. 55.
145. C. Bigham, op. cit., p. 191.
146. A reproduction of this cartoon forms the frontispiece to *The*

New Far East, by A. Diósy, Chairman of the Japan Society of London (1898); and see Chapter 8, 'The Yellow Peril'.

147. *The Intimate Papers of Colonel House*, ed. C. Seymour (1926), Vol. 1, p. 251. All foreign military observers in China were anxious about its potential strength (S. Merwin, op. cit., p. 119).

148. See R. von Möllendorf, *P. G. von Möllendorf. Ein Lebensbild* (Leipzig, 1930).

149. A. Hamilton, *Korea* (1904), pp. 118-19. On the grinding taxation that led to repeated peasant risings, see G. D. Tyagai, *Krestyanskoe vosstanie v Koree 1893–1895 g. g.* (Moscow, 1953), pp. 7 ff.

150. W. G. Aston, report on Korea, 13 September 1882, in 'Japan No. 1': *Accounts and Papers*, 1883, Vol. 75.

151. Marquis of Zetland, *The Life of Lord Curzon* (1928), Vol. 1, p. 191.

152. Ekai Kawaguchi, *Three Years in Thibet* (Madras, 1909).

153. C. Pearl, *The Girl with the Swansdown Seat* (1955), pp. 178-9.

154. See M. Landon, *Anna and the King of Siam* (New York, 1943), founded on the two books written by its heroine, Mrs Leonowens, about her stay in Bangkok from 1862 to 1867.

155. A French translation appeared in the *Journal of the Siam Society*, Vol. 7, Part 3, 1910.

156. M. Smith, *A Physician at the Court of Siam* (1947).

157. Report by W. J. Archer, June 1885, in *Accounts and Papers*, 1884–5, Vol. 81.

158. C. Crow, *Harris of Japan* (1939), p. 100.

159. B. A. Allen, *Sir Ernest Satow: a Memoir* (1933), p. 89.

160. Dr Masao, in discussion of a paper on Siam by Mr Heide, in *Journal of the Siam Society*, 1906.

161. Captain H. Keppel, *Expedition to Borneo of H.M.S. Dido* (2nd edn, 1846), Vol. 2, App. 1.

162. R. Fortune, *Yedo and Peking* (1863), p. 38.

163. E. A. Sugimoto, *A Daughter of the Samurai* (1933), Chapter 8.

164. Sir E. Satow, *A Diplomat in Japan* (1921), p. 314. cf. the view of his colleague A. B. Mitford (Lord Redesdale) that attacks on foreigners were instigated by enemies of the Shogunate to embarrass it: *Memories* (1915), Vol. 1, p. 415.

165. E. Satow, op. cit., pp. 266, 139. cf. S. Mossman, *New Japan, the Land of the Rising Sun* (1873), p. 346: 'It was the invulnerable right hand of British valour which fought the battle of Western civilization . . .'

166. E. Satow, op. cit., pp 89–92. Allowance must be made for

strained foreign nerves. 'For nearly four years,' Mitford says, 'I never wrote a note without having a revolver on the table, and never went to bed without a Spencer rifle and bayonet at my hand.' (op. cit., Vol. 1, p. 389).

167. E. Satow, op. cit., pp. 95, 134.

168. ibid., p. 191.

169. ibid., p. 123.

170. ibid., p. 149.

171. S. Lane-Poole and F. V. Dickins, *The Life of Sir Harry Parkes* (1894), Vol. 2, p. 358.

172. One such was Baroness A. d'Anethan, wife of the Belgian minister from 1893; see her *Fourteen Years of Diplomatic Life in Japan* (1914).

173. E. Satow, op. cit., p. 28.

174. A. Novikoff-Priboy, *Tsushima, Grave of a Floating City*, trans. E. and C. Paul (1937), pp. 378–9.

175. P. de Lapeyrère, *Souvenirs et Épisodes* (Paris, 1885), p. 45.

176. J. J. Abraham, op. cit., p. 125.

177. R. Kipling, op. cit., Vol. 1, p. 411.

178. H. H. Chamberlain and W. B. Mason, *Handbook for Travellers in Japan* (4th edn, 1891), pp. 16–17.

179. Sir E. Arnold, *Seas and Lands* (1891), p. 286. Dilke, one of the few politicians who travelled beyond Europe, wrote from Japan on a world tour in 1874–5: 'I am in love with this country and people' (S. L. Gwynn and G. M. Tuckwell, *The Life of the Right Hon. Sir Charles W. Dilke* (1917), Vol. 1, p. 195).

180. See especially Okakura–Kakuzo, *The Book of Tea* (1906).

181. R. Kipling, op. cit., Vol. 1, p. 335. On Pierre Loti's similar misrepresentation of Japan as a comical Lilliput, see W. L. Schwartz, *The Imaginative Interpretation of the Far East in French Literature, 1800–1925* (Paris, 1927); pp. 131–3 (English edn). He surmises that it helped to decide Russia to risk war with Japan.

182. Isabella L. Bird, *Unbeaten Tracks in Japan* (1880), Letter 35.

183. ibid., Letter 36.

184. See S. Cole, *Races of Man* (1963), pp. 83, 94.

185. W. G. Dickson, *Gleanings from Japan* (Edinburgh, 1889), pp. 8, 15.

186. C. Crow, op. cit., p. 144; cf. p. 161.

187. ibid., p. 174; cf. p. 186.

188. A. M. Pooley, Introduction to *The Secret Memoirs of Baron Hayashi* (1915).

189. *Le Japan d'aujourd'hui. Journal intime d'un missionnaire apostolique* (Tours, 1892), Preface.

190. 'A. S. de Doncourt' (Comtesse Drohojowska), *Les Français dans l'Extrême Orient* (Lille and Paris, n.d. (?1884)), p. 113.

191. E. Arnold, op. cit., p. 175.

192. C. Crow, op. cit., pp. 176–8.

193. J. J. Abraham, op. cit., p. 141.

194. *Handbook for Travellers.*, p. 112.

195. J. J. Abraham, op. cit., p. 152.

196. Sienkiewicz to Ferry, no. 41, 18 July 1884 : *Le Japon*, Vol. 30, in Foreign Ministry archives, Paris.

197. Sienkiewicz to Ferry, no. 34, 2 May 1884, ibid.

198. *Japan Herald*, 9 April 1881.

199. F. R. Plunkett to Lord Granville, 27 September 1884, Foreign Office 46.315.

200. Sir E. J. Reed, *Japan* (1880), Vol. 1, p. xlix.

201. Colonel Strange, in 1891, cited by A. L. Sadler, *A Short History of Japan* (Sydney, 1963), p. 265.

202. Captain J. M. Grierson, *The Armed Strength of Japan* (War Office, London, 1886), p. 6. cf. a report by Major Knollys forwarded with F. R. Plunkett to Lord Granville, no. 172, Conf., 8 October 1884, Foreign Office 46.315.

203. Sir H. W. Lucy, *Sixty Years in the Wilderness* (1909), p. 173.

204. Sienkiewicz to Ferry, no. 66, 21 November 1884, *Le Japon*, Vol. 30.

205. E. K. Nojine, *The Truth about Port Arthur* (English edn, 1908), pp. 12–13.

206. Letter of 10 November 1905, in *Autobiography, 1872–1914* (1967), p. 180.

207. B. H. Chamberlain, *Things Japanese* (1905), p. 263.

208. ibid., p. 218.

209. Sienkiewicz to Freycinet, no. 115, 20 October 1885, *Le Japon*, Vol. 31. He quotes the British minister Plunkett, a Catholic, as expecting Japan to adopt Protestantism rather than Catholicism, because of the too close identification of the latter with French interests.

210. *Mendoza's Historie*, p. 299.

211. See *The Diary of Richard Cocks, 1615–22*, ed. E. M. Thompson (Hakluyt Society, 1883), Vol. 1, pp. 344, 19.

212. See B. H. Chamberlain's pamphlet, *The Invention of a New Religion* (1912).

213. F. R. Plunkett to Lord Granville, no. 258, Conf., 31 December 1884, Foreign Office 46.317.

214. Major-General E. Upton, *The Armies of Europe and Asia* (Portsmouth, England, 1878), p. 12.

215. H. Norman, op. cit., pp. 599, 322. Okuma Shigenobu (later Marquis) became premier in 1898.

216. W. S. Blunt, *My Dianes* (1932 edn), p. 496.

217. ibid., p. 500.

218. C. A. Spring Rice, secretary of embassy, 29 October 1904, in Lord Newton, *Lord Lansdowne. A Biography* (1929), p. 274. cf. W. L. Schwartz, op. cit., p. 153 ff., on the revival of Yellow Peril ideas in France as a result of the Russo–Japanese war.

6. AFRICA

Africans in Europe

In Charles II's time there was talk of an English expedition to the Guinea coast, to be led by Prince Rupert; it was abandoned, for one reason because of blood-curdling rumours about the natives, 'a hellish people' with poisoned arrows who ate their prisoners, and about terrifying monsters in the interior.[1] Africa – the Africa of the Negro, the 'black Moor' or blackamoor as Elizabethans called him by contrast with the 'white Moor' of the northern fringe – was already reputed the Dark Continent. There was a Dutch colony at the Cape, and older Portuguese settlements on the coasts chiefly exporting slaves; otherwise Africa was unknown, as most of it was long to remain, or known only by the kind of tales that Defoe wove together in 1720 in his *Captain Singleton*. The first Africans his imaginary party of castaways fell in with on their journey across the continent from east to west were 'an ignorant, ravenous, brutish sort of people, even worse than the natives of any other country that we had seen',[2] and the rest were little different. Only the white men's muskets cleared a way through them. As the slave-trade grew and prospered, it suited Europe to think Africa so unmitigatedly barbarous that no removal from it could worsen the lot of its inhabitants.

While his homeland was still unknown, the Negro himself could be met with over most of the world, nearly always as slave or freedman; over the Americas since the sixteenth century, over the Arab and Muslim world since before Islam began. Two Negroes were in Captain Cook's crew when he set out to explore the South Seas, though they perished wretchedly on the way.[3] Some of the earliest Chinese interpreters employed by the English at Canton – strange go-betweens of East and West – were African runagates from Portuguese Macao.[4] At the Mikado's first reception of foreign envoys a young prince displayed a childish eagerness to be shown a black man;

another preferred the sight of a European cat.[5] Not even the Jews have gone through such wanderings and experiences up and down the world.

Europe itself had a sprinkling of Africans, besides the many assimilated into the population of southern Portugal where their influence on the physical type still struck visitors in the nineteenth century.[6] In the eighteenth century there were believed to be several thousands in London, and sales were advertised and rewards offered for absconders until slavery on British soil was ended by the Mansfield judgment of 1772.[7] An aura of servitude clung to Africans as a race, finding such expression as the Amsterdam inn-sign on which a Negro in chains crouched at the feet of a pipe-smoking young white merchant.[8] It took a softened, stylized form in the vogue, which has left many quaint memorials in Dresden china,[9] of African flunkeys or page-boys in great houses. A multitude of black faces may at times repel white people (and equally the converse), but a black face here and there was attractively exotic, and set off the powdered hair and satin gowns of the company as the ladies' patches did their cheeks. An urbanized aristocracy wants its servants very distinctly marked off from it, as a different species of humanity, and an African in European finery met this requirement perfectly. In 1748 a Lieutenant Bemish brought home a black boy, 'a good-natured child, about ten years old', to present to Admiral Boscawen's lady, who felt she could not civilly decline, especially as the boy had been handsomely rigged out in her livery.[10] A black attendant stands behind Josephine in David's painting of her court circle.

Individuals could win esteem by more than picturesqueness. A Duke of Buckingham recorded in a polemic against Catholicism that some of its doctrinal fallacies were readily detected by a young African of his household.[11] Dr Johnson's servant Frank enjoys a modest celebrity in English literary annals. Early in the next century Mrs Cappe, widow of an Evangelical clergyman, wrote in the highest terms of her servant John Hacket, a Negro born free in Jamaica who made his own way to London; he attended her daughters through a hazardous voyage from Italy, giving proof of devoted loyalty and presence of mind. He had taught himself to read the Bible. Yet he was 'one of that cruelly treated, and unjustly despised race, of whom it has been disputed, whether they should be reckoned as beings of the same species'. 'Generous fire, and lively animation', were among the qualities Mrs Cappe ascribed to them.[12] If a torrid climate engendered torrid emotions, as was conventionally assumed, the African might be expected to have the fieriest temperament of all. Men like Hacket, unconscious missionaries of their race, must have helped to sustain anti-slavery ardour through the long struggle for abolition. They were ancestors too of a long line of African characters, sympathetically if not always flatteringly drawn, in English fiction, where there are few equivalent figures from India or China.

Africans in the Americas

Schopenhauer refuted pantheism by pointing out the absurdity of any God transforming himself into a world where on an average day six million slaves received sixty million blows.[13] In the history of Negro slavery the extraordinary thing is the ability of the race to survive, though myriads of individuals perished; it lacked the faculty which Chinese exiles owed to a more complex social evolution of mastering a new environment and rising in it. It was the endurance of the African, where other enslaved races sank under the white man's burdens, that made him so profitable; while his weakness in collective organization in his own land made him an easy prey. It warped his masters, Arab or Turk, Spaniard or Englishman, as much as it degraded him; it conditioned western Europe to think of all 'native' peoples as destined bondsmen.

Spanish and Portuguese apologists have often maintained that their forms of slavery in the Americas were softened by Catholicism, that their laws held the Negro a human being whereas those of Protestant British or Dutch treated him as a chattel. In reality what regulated the degree of exploitation was not the owner's nationality or religion but the extent to which there was a lucrative market for the products of slave labour.[14] Thus the slave code of 1840 in Cuba, still under the sway of Catholic Spain, was far harsher than the earlier one; in

Brazil conditions were often vile.[15] Much the same might be said as to degrees of exploitation of serfs in eastern Europe. It may be added that whether slavery continued in the nineteenth century did not depend in any simple way on whether areas of the New World were still under European rule or had become independent. But in all cases moral growth and idealism were required before abolition could come about.[16] Even where economic changes made slavery less profitable, it would not end automatically; any social system gathers round it habits and prejudices not merely money-grubbing. In England humanitarian agitation was a powerful agent in the suppression of the slave trade in 1807 and of slavery in the colonies in 1838. In Spain it was nearly a century slower to develop.

Opponents of slavery, like all reformers, were often portrayed as maudlin sentimentalists. What the sturdy sensible Briton thought can be gathered from *Tom Cringle's Log*, an autobiographical novel about a roistering career in the West Indies in the first decades of the nineteenth century. Slave-trading, this hard-headed Scotsman admitted, was very wrong, but slavery was what most Negroes were designed for. He thought of them with an exceedingly rough sort of good humour; a practical joke in which someone let fly with a hard apple that landed 'bash on the blackamoor's obtuse snout' made him hold his sides.[17] Having pictured Jamaican society as made up of 'a miserable, squalid, half-fed, ill-clothed, overworked race' of blacks and 'an unwholesome-looking crew of saffron-faced tyrants', he was agreeably surprised at what he found, even if he did witness 'not a few rum scenes'. It was the same in Cuba, where the slaves all looked to him 'deucedly well cared for, and fat, and contented'.[18] Conditions were not so bad there in his time as a little later, when there was a long series of slave risings ferociously suppressed by Spanish governors. An English traveller about the same time reported that planters in Demerara, one of whose daughters he married, behaved very decently, but a hundred pages later had to regret that their Negroes were rebelling.[19]

Altogether there were dozens of slave risings up and down the West Indies. The colony whose slaves, aided by special circumstances, seized freedom was Haiti. When the French Revolution started in 1789 this western division of the old Hispaniola was a French colony, the eastern (since 1844 the Dominican Republic) still Spanish. Haiti was growing sugar under pressure, and the death-rate among the slaves was exceptionally high. In 1791 they revolted, and 'the vapouring crowds of negroes', as a British historian characteristically terms them,[20] found a leader in Toussaint L'Ouverture, one of the greatest of all Africans. It swelled into one of the two greatest Black rebellions in history, the other being that of the slaves brought into southern Iraq to drain marshes for the Arabs a thousand years before; and these two along with the Spartacus rising in Roman Italy may be counted the three most tremendous slave revolts in all history.

France like England had an anti-slavery movement, and in 1793 when the Robespierrists were in power in Paris they proclaimed an end to colonial slavery – forty-five years before Britain. The planters refused to accept this, and in 1794 the idealists of the French Revolution were guillotined and replaced by the profiteers, who eventually found the boss they needed in Napoleon. In 1802 he sent an army to reconquer Haiti, with the covert intention of restoring slavery. Toussaint was defeated, treacherously sent to France, and thrown into a dungeon where he perished wretchedly in 1803. This earned him Wordsworth's sonnet, the noblest tribute ever paid by a European to an African. But it was typical of Europe that Napoleon was far less often reproached, then and afterwards, for his treatment of the Negro hero than for his hasty execution of an insignificant Bourbon princeling the year after Toussaint's death.

No savagery that has been recorded of Africans anywhere could outdo some of the acts of the French in their efforts to regain control of the island.[21] Disease helped the defenders to wipe them out. But anything like a constructive programme had vanished with Toussaint; and Haiti was starting its free life under the most adverse conditions, cut off from any counsel or comfort, hated by the colonists all round. 'Every white slave-owner, in Jamaica, Cuba, or Texas, lived in dread of another Toussaint L'Ouverture.'[22] In 1804, the year when Napoleon made himself Emperor of the French, Dessalines – an

African born – declared himself emperor of Haiti. He was the first of a set of sanguinary chiefs whom Europeans could depict as examples of innate African ferocity, but who can as plausibly be thought imitators of the white men they had known. These white men left behind them an infusion of their blood as well as of their habits, and a great deal of Haiti's anarchical feuding was a contest between Negro and mulatto.

A union with the other, mainly mulatto, half of the island, now freed from Spain, only lasted twenty years. Haiti continued to exist, a free black kingdom and then republic, but it accomplished little more, and made a standing target for satire. White visitors were apt to take the same malicious pleasure in the failure of these self-emancipated Africans to manage their own affairs, as today when they see African countries like the Congo fumbling and floundering. An early sightseer was 'Tom Cringle', who gleefully described a general dilapidation and decay, the people looking much less well off than 'the blackies of Jamaica', the once rich sugar plantations derelict.[23] He met the Counts of Lemonade and Marmalade, and made great fun of this comic peerage.[24] Nearly all the able-bodied men seemed to have been drafted into the army of the tyrant king, Henri Christophe, who reigned from 1812 to 1820. His rival Pétion, called by admirers the black Washington, made a better impression on Cringle, largely because though very dark he had European features and had lived in Europe.[25]

H. H. Prichard, a geographer who was in Haiti at the beginning of the next century, gave his book on it the title, plainly intended to shock, *Where Black Rules White*: in fact there were very few whites to be ruled. He was a man of conventional outlook for whom the French Revolutionaries, and particularly the *Amis des Noirs* or emancipationists, were the 'madmen of liberty'.[26] Slaves might have been ill-treated, but 'negroes have far duller nerves and are less susceptible to pain than Europeans'[27] – a thought that consoled many Europeans for the sufferings of Africans as well as of Chinese. He had a good word for Toussaint, but considered him no evidence for 'the pro-negro line of argument': indeed he could scarcely bring himself to believe that Toussaint was a pure Negro.[28] Other Europeans have been unwilling to believe that Jesus was a Jew;

and when Prichard wrote Africa was being partitioned, and had to be thought of as deserving its fate. He related the lurid tales of King Christophe, but had a certain esteem for him as a ruler who knew how to strike awe into his subjects: 'the will of a strong man usually holds the key to any situation'.[29] Strength of any kind was a virtue to the imperial age. In Kipling's philosophy East and West might come together at odd moments when 'two strong men' – not two good men – met.

Marmalade had risen to Duke, but there had been no similar ascent of the nation: Prichard saw only sloth, disorder, cruelty, the uniforms of a preposterous army, economic torpor. All that still lingered from his golden age of white rule was the dregs of that French culture or way of life whose spell, able to outlive the worst-hated French dominion, has often puzzled and exasperated Englishmen. 'With his whole heart ʹand soul,' Prichard wrote distastefully of the Haitian with a smattering of education, 'he admires France ... Moreover, he regards the rest of the world through French eyes.'[30] If so he saw it through a glass, darkly, for apparently Boers were imagined to be rebel blacks, and their successes against the British applauded accordingly.[31]

Not many years later Van Dongen the Fauve painter made a full-length portrait of a Haitian ambassador standing uneasily elegant in glittering costume before the allegorical figures of a ship of the old days under full sail and a small Negro carrying a load on his head; an enigmatic vision of past and present.[32] Haiti's slaves had freed themselves and become a nation, if a very poor one; those of Jamaica and other colonies were emancipated from above, like the serfs in Russia, however much in both cases revolt or fear of revolt may have helped to speed emancipation. In both cases, and in the USA, the result was legal freedom without political or economic freedom, and strife continuing on new lines. In Jamaica the whites complained of their plantations going to the dogs because Negroes would not work on their terms, and imported Asian coolie labour: race relations worsened, until in 1865 disturbances broke out, some white men were killed, and Governor Eyre retaliated vengefully. There was heated controversy in England, where Carlyle of course and other prominent men more surprisingly made Eyre a national hero. It was a fresh fit of the hysteria stirred up a few years earlier by the Indian Mutiny, but it was also one of the few occasions when England was roused to serious debate on how other races ought to be treated.

Tensions became less acute after 1865 in the British West Indies. Most of these were turned into Crown Colonies, losing the archaic self-government that meant government by the white settlers – here as in India, or later in Rhodesia, a far worse lot than officials from Britain mostly were, and slow to shed the 'nigger-driving' mentality of slave days. But this was still not an environment where Negroes could find their feet and win respect. Visitors, and readers at home, contemplated them with mild amusement, as irresponsible loafers in the sun. An easy-going Anglican clergyman who officiated out there for a while soon decided that 'Black people are nothing but children', and saw no point in being censorious about the lax unions that passed for marriage among them. An experience he enjoyed was a funeral at which he read the service with a sexton dressed in loin-cloth and top-hat.[33]

Away from British territory a Jamaican Negro like James Kempton, flogged by some ruffians in Peru during a time of anarchy, enjoyed the protection of the British flag; but only as a third-rate citizen, since he served no diplomatic purpose like Don Pacifico, the Gibraltar Jew of Palmerston's 'Civis Romanus' oration. The Foreign Office asked for £100 on Kempton's behalf; it settled for £50, and Lord Salisbury scribbled in his humorous vein: 'The negro will ask to be flogged again.'[34]

The Slave Trade and its Suppression

The Negroes whose toil laid the foundations of the New World came mostly from two regions of western Africa, the Portuguese settlement of Angola and the 'Slave Coast' or southern rim of the great westerly bulge. Along this coast Europeans, without being in occupation of it, could easily come by all the slaves they required on a basis of fair exchange, rum and gunpowder for men and women. African simplicity was not that of a garden of Eden: many of its inhabitants were as willing to sell one another for a bottle as ancient Britons or Russians once were. War-captives, or offenders condemned for crime or witchcraft, were brought down to the coast and disposed of by the chiefs there to the foreign dealers. It is a question worth asking whether this turmoil of man-hunting was the result of the foreign demand, or whether the prime cause was over-population, supply stimulating demand. In either case the merchant from Liverpool or Glasgow was no robber, not always even a receiver of stolen goods, and had a clear conscience. It was left to low Spanish, Portuguese, or half-caste slavers to go about catching their wares themselves. Reputable dealers were often on excellent terms with the coastal chiefs, arranged for their sons to go to school in England, and accepted temporary wives from them.

Behind this cordiality the true reaction of Europe and Africa to each other was different. 'The Natives are cheated ... in every possible way,' wrote the former slave-trader John Newton after his religious conversion, and the more contact they had with the white man the more 'jealous, insidious and re-' vengeful' they grew. Each race looked on the other as 'consummate villains', and a Negro taxed with dishonesty would sometimes retort: 'What! do you think I am a White Man?'[35] Baron Munchausen, some of whose most surprising adventures befell him in Africa – that 'prodigious field of discovery'[36] – once met a party of Negroes who had seized European shipping and started a trade in white slaves for work on plantations in cold latitudes. They had contracted 'a barbarous prejudice ... that the white people have no souls!'[37]

That black people had only second-rate souls, and that they were better off as slaves, even in Turkey, than in their own land, was a conviction that faded very slowly from the European mind. Albert Smith strolling about the slave-market at Constantinople felt it must be a blessing to these poor degraded creatures to be provided with a master and regular work.[38] He himself might have blinked and gibbered after being marched for a month in an Arab slave-gang. Thackeray was shocked here, less so at Cairo where he fell back on the comforting stereotype of Africans as happy, carefree creatures, shackled in body but spared the heavy load of thought and doubt,[39] the real white-man's-burden as it felt to those who suffered from it and envied the artless classes or races that had never eaten of the tree of knowledge. He was heartened by a holiday festivity in the swarming black suburb of Alexandria. 'Every one of these jolly faces was on the broad grin.'[40]

But officially England, and emotionally many Englishmen, were committed to regarding the slave trade as the world's deepest abomination, which England's duty was not merely to renounce but to persuade or compel others to renounce. Burton stood in the slave-market at Mecca and silently vowed to strike the death-blow at the traffic in eastern Africa.[41] To Ruskin the greatest painting of the greatest artist of the age was Turner's *Slave Ship*, exhibited in 1840. It showed an enormous Atlantic swell at the end of a storm, littered with bodies thrown overboard, and lurid sunset colours falling 'like the shadow of death upon the guilty ship ... its thin masts written upon the sky in lines of blood'.[42]

Pressure of humanitarian opinion was important here too. There was no reason of pure economics why slavery should not continue, hitched on to capitalism. The US gave up the slave trade only a year after Britain, but John Bull's European competitors, who never believed him to be quite so transparently honest as he liked to be thought, suspected that his aim was to deprive them of an advantage which he himself no longer needed. Through most of the nineteenth century British diplomacy was entangled in vexatious disputes arising out of its attempts to make effective the pledges to abandon slave-trading obtained at the end of the Napoleonic wars. Anti-slavery societies in England kept on prodding the Foreign Office, which would have liked to forget about the matter, to prod the worst backsliders, Spain and Portugal.

Britain, France and the US worked out measures for patrolling the western coasts of Africa, and British tax-payers plumed themselves on the part played by their ships; the navy's popularity owed much to this. Kingston's midshipmen threw themselves with enthusiasm into the work, and held in horror the degenerate Spanish or Portuguese traffickers. 'To an Englishman no class of men are more hateful.'[43] All this could make for self-righteousness, and a belief, not quite extinct today, in Britannia's right to 'police the seas' anywhere. It gave John

Bull a sort of treasury of merit, which he felt able to draw on whenever assailed by qualms about items like opium or misgivings about his moral supereminence.

As late as 1888 *The Times* alleged that slave-running still flourished along eastern Africa and across the Indian Ocean, under French as well as Arab auspices.[44] All round Africa the hunt for the slaver led to closer acquaintance with the continent; it also paved the way for occupation of parts of it. Formerly the argument in defence of the trade, that removal from Africa was the Negro's only chance of redemption, had been repeated by men as prominent as Nelson: now that he was no longer to be carried off to civilization, it might be right that civilization should be carried to him. Sympathy, which he now received, seldom implied respect. Progress was Europe's watchword, and Africa far more even than Asia appeared incapable of it. Its stagnation at a low material level was a fact, which can be tentatively explained in terms of a slow drift of population from north to south, away from the Mediterranean and its culture, over an unwelcoming land-mass where it was too thinly spread to develop a technology equal to some of its arts.[45] These arts found few to appreciate them among Europeans in Africa, one of whom spoke for nearly all when he dismissed its music as 'those unearthly noises which in Africa pass current for song'.[46] Only late in the nineteenth century did artistic Europe begin to discover Africa, its sculpture first and foremost.

Meanwhile African backwardness was accounted for in sundry ways. One was to think of the black man as descended from Ham, the black son of Noah; Europeans were still reading their Old Testaments, and deriving from that ancient oriental source notions as bizarre as any they met with in Dahomey or Swaziland. Missionaries were often advocates of annexation. They were sometimes mixed up with trade; but what weighed more was the desire to see the weak protected against the strong, above all against the slave-raider. They showed best when denouncing the evil done by lawless European enterprise. Once European government was established, and with it a more orderly exploitation, they usually felt obliged as in India to acquiesce in whatever its policies might be.

Europeans in Western Africa

Those who talked of the descendants of Ham had in mind the pure Negro type they were familiar with in America; that is, the West African, less modified by admixture of northern or 'Caucasoid' blood than the other two main families, the Nilotic and the Bantu.[47] He was the African they thought they knew best, but thanks to the distorting slave-relationship may really have understood least. Physically he was the darkest of hue among the main African races, the one most unlike themselves and therefore most readily assumed to be inferior to themselves. This was enough to give West Africa a 'darker' look than most of the continent. Its crocodiles and jungles, its fatal diseases and steaming heat, strengthened the impression. Our feelings about a country are always coloured by its climate; English weather has given the Englishman much of his reputation for sullenness. Mungo Park, it is true, having returned in 1799 to his native Scotland after his first search for the Niger, thought better of it, and decided as he told Scott that 'he would rather brave Africa with all its horrors' than stay here.[48] He went back to perish.

There were well-established kingdoms along the Guinea coast, but none of an inviting aspect. What did most to bring Ashanti, Benin, Dahomey into the news were their annual rituals of human sacrifice, and the king of Dahomey's regiment of Amazons. West African life was permeated too by the activities of secret societies with their weird *ju-ju*, harder to fathom and easier to shudder at than the secret societies of China. But amid all that was fearsome or grotesque in the region, the after-effects of the slave trade were the worst. It was the missionaries who felt most concern about them, and who had a big share in forming opinion in Europe because few other white men except desperadoes ventured out here.

The evil that the slave-dealers had done lived after them, as the first pioneers of the Church of Scotland Mission found when they started work in 1846 at Calabar. A Parliamentary committee had been told that this port, where trade with Europe was three centuries old, was the most barbarous spot in Africa; human skulls were kicked about in the streets.[49] Coastal chiefs who had been thrown up by the slave trade, and ruled and robbed by virtue of their Western fire-arms, went by such Haitian-flavoured names as Adam Duke or King Eyo Honesty. The West has displayed a perverse talent for making friends with the worst scoundrels of other lands. 'These African Nabobs drank champagne copiously', we read,[50] but older habits of royalty were kept up too. One that it cost the missionaries long years of effort to check was the killing of scores of slaves at the funerals of great men, to attend them into the next world.[51] Slaves were still being brought down the rivers from the interior, and since they could no longer be exported except by stealth they were perhaps slaughtered more wastefully than in former times. To the missionaries all African women seemed to be treated little better than slaves. In the Calabar area female circumcision was the rule, widows were virtually outcasts, all twin children were destroyed. A long struggle had to be waged for the right of women converts of the poorer class to appear in public decently clothed.[52] In Europe women were starting their long struggle in the opposite direction.

European contact was still for the most part making things worse rather than better. Low-grade gin and rum, the chief imports, circulated far inland and led to 'wild excesses'.[53] Life was very wild along the rivers when 'Trader Horn' went out, about 1871, a young fellow fresh from peaceful Britain, to sink or swim among slave-raiders, ivory-hunters, and cannibals. Of the lot he found the cannibals the most respectable, the men good trackers and workers and the women exceptionally faithful – whereas many of the headmen who sold him rubber would 'trot out' their wives and bid him help himself.[54] Winwood Reade's book on Africa came out in 1872; three years earlier he was exploring the Niger. About its people he was in one sense a pessimist, in another an optimist. Africa as it was, thrown on its own resources, he thought frightful; Africa as it might be, with civilizing influence from outside, full of promise. To him the more romantic features of native life were only varnish, the reality beneath was terror. 'It is impossible to describe, or even to imagine, the tremulous condition of the savage mind; yet the traveller can see from their aspect and manners that they dwell in a state of never-ceasing dread.'[55]

Even he could look back on the slave trade as a painful kind of escape from this darkness, and he thought it would be no bad thing if Turkey, banished from Europe, came to reign over Africa instead, for Turkish rule was 'perfection itself' compared with any in Africa.[56] Given a chance, Africans could go ahead. 'The negroes are imitative in an extraordinary degree, and imitation is the first principle of progress.' Whether their endowments were in all respects equal to those of Europeans was a question 'idle and unimportant'; there was no lack of useful things they could do well.[57] Reade thought highly of the progress being made, with the help of missionary schools, in Sierra Leone, the settlement for freed slaves. Its people called themselves Englishmen, and he welcomed them as such. 'However ludicrous it may seem to hear a negro boasting about Lord Nelson and Waterloo . . . it shows that he possesses a kind of emulation.'[58]

How much of the terror of daily life in West Africa was a shadow-play projected by the European mind can only be guessed; but the aptitudes Reade found in the Negro must have been moulded by traditional African society. Anthropologists were to piece together a picture of this as an existence with its own normality, not one of insensate violence. More recently African writers still close enough to the lingering past have begun bringing it more vividly to life for us. A remarkable novel by Chinua Achebe carries us into one of those Nigerian villages that the missionaries were peering at through jungle glooms. It is a place where a boy can be murdered as an act of revenge against another village; a woman whose twin children have been taken from her is one of the first to join the Christians when they come. Yet it is also a place with orderly standards of good and ill, cordial neighbourship, athletic sports, music, palm wine and democratic self-rule, all knit together by clan spirit and by a strange, sometimes cruel, religious cult. When this guardian cult is desecrated by a rash convert the community is plunged in horror. 'It seemed as if the very soul of the tribe wept for a great evil that was coming – its own death.'[59]

All over Africa there was a twilight of old gods who had served men faithfully enough in their time. The friendly Bushman who guided Laurens van der Post to the shrine in the Slippery Hills said to him mournfully when it was time to leave: 'The spirits of the hills are not what they were, Master ... Ten years ago they would have killed you all for coming.'[60]

France was the country promptest to occupy territories in West Africa. Besides completing the conquest of Algeria, Napoleon III built up some old coastal settlements into the colony of Senegal, with Dakar for its capital and a force of native auxiliaries who helped French power to expand by stages into other regions. Dahomey was taken in 1894. It was in the first stage that France was most deliberately setting out to transform a part of the Dark Continent, to bring it into the charmed circle of civilization. Mid-century Europe was more enlightened in some ways than either the earlier Europe of the time when British conquest in India began, or the later, when the general scramble for Africa took place. Senegal's first governor, Faidherbe, won praise for his work, not from Frenchmen alone. The French ideal, inherited from the Revolution, was of equality of rights and laws for all subjects of France, incorporation in a single commonweal. In Senegal, as half a century before in the Rhineland, France looked with the courage of this conviction for men capable of being developed to the highest human level, in other words of being turned into Frenchmen.

It was a new version of an old optimism about the perfectibility of man; but this called for something like perfection in the teacher, and it has been part of France's history to alternate more widely than its neighbours between exalted ideal and cynical realism. In 1848 and 1870 citizenship was conferred on the Senegalese so far brought under French rule, with the right to send a deputy to the Assembly in Paris. Subsequently tests were imposed, which very few Africans were able to pass.[61] For this small minority the price of initiation into French culture might well be loss of any real contact with their own people.[62] Unlike Hindus or Muslims they had no religious anchor strong enough to hold against the tides of the new age. For the majority French rule meant in practice an administration like that of other empires, more straightforwardly authoritarian as time went on and the dream of assimilation faded. A type of district officer that Englishmen could admire grew up: 'paternal towards the natives, strict yet benevolent, reactionary yet understanding.'[63]

Africans without citizen rights were liable to *corvée* labour, and all, educated or not, were reckoned fit for the highest duty and honour of the nineteenth-century European, compulsory service in the army. France after 1870 was short of manpower to face Germany with, and conscripted Africans to fill the gap. Conscription was one of those new forms of slavery that Europe was inventing for itself and others in place of the old. It took a heavy toll of health and family happiness in more backward European countries like Spain or Russia, and in Africa the toll must have been far heavier.[64] Senegalese and other Negro troops were put to good use on the western front in 1914–18; they were sometimes unsteady under heavy fire, but their habit of killing prisoners on the spot helped to unnerve the Germans.[65]

Frenchmen in their colonies, unlike Britons, have prided themselves on knowing how to get on cordially with their subjects. A good deal of mingling, on diverse levels, did develop. A factor that promoted it was language; African languages, not in French colonies alone, changed bewilderingly from district to district, so that a lingua franca was now necessary, and French or English pidgin could provide it.[66] As to the quality of the mixing, there may be some general truth in the surmise of a novelist in search of copy, at a party at Libreville, that what he was seeing was 'the worst whites mixing with the worst blacks'.[67] Possibly there is always an attraction between the best elements of two races, and between the worst. This intercourse is another thing we have begun to learn about in late years from the African side. Oyono's novel about the French Cameroons gives an extremely unpleasant picture of it, and of sexual relations between the races in particular. He can easily be believed when he says that the rulers knew their subjects far less than they were known by them. 'The eyes that live in the native location strip the whites naked. The whites on the other hand go about blind.'[68] An uneasy awareness of this, an irritated impulse to turn the tables, must have helped to push European colonists into a great many arbitrary acts of force.

From 1844 there was a British protectorate over the Niger coast, and missionaries favoured extensions of it. Mary Slessor served as vice-consul as well as missionary at her river station. The government was not desirous of going further, because prospects of gain were limited. Penetration inland was left to business enterprise, chiefly to the chartered company that in 1886 became the Royal Niger Company. Englishmen trusted mightily in legitimate trade, as Frenchmen did in culture, to bleach the darkness out of Africa; and the substitution of palm-oil for slaves was an improvement, even if commerce and civilization did not prove so exactly congruent as earlier Victorians thought them. What roused most interest at home was always a spirited campaign, with some well-known regiment taking part. There could be no effective resistance by village republics, but only from the kingdoms, which therefore caught the eye and were regarded as more typical of West African life than they really were.

The first Ashanti war, in what is now Ghana, was fought in 1821, the most spectacular in 1873, when the Ashantis put fifteen or twenty thousand men in the field who were admitted to be 'brave and warlike', though savage – whereas the Hausa auxiliaries whom the British were trying to lick into shape were at first so timid and superstitious that they would hang their guns up in trees and pray to them.[69] Not all races have been equally eager to accept the white Prometheus's gift of gunpowder. There were Highlanders in the fight, and a Scots town honoured their commander with a banquet at which the Provost held forth on 'the spread of civilization and the prevention and prohibition of slavery and cruelty'.[70]

The Gold Coast was annexed in 1874, the Ashanti state inland not until 1896. King Prempeh was then removed; he had swelled in British minds into an ogre, an image of all African barbarism. Many years later he came back briefly into the limelight when the Prince of Wales was touring Africa soon after the Great War. The illustrated book of the tour dwelt on 'the indescribably abhorrent condition of Kumasi', the Ashanti capital, in former days, and introduced to its readers a

Prempeh who had seen the light and been allowed to return on a comfortable pension, a good Christian now and 'an active participant in Church and municipal work'.[71] This was as good as Nero or Bluebeard turning deacon, and if a Prempeh could be so marvellously changed by British influence, surely all Africa could. But the book was careful to explain that while the 'white man's burden in West Africa' included the duty of training its people for self-government, that goal was still far off : they had 'accepted the superficial attributes of civilization, but would straightway shed them and relapse and revert to primitive savagery if their white mentors withdrew'.[72]

In 1900 the British government stepped into the Niger Company's shoes, and modern Nigeria took shape. Achebe's novel is a reminder that the coming of European authority to a Nigerian district might be a painful intrusion, the worse for being accompanied by African policemen of alien tribes, inclined to make the most of their power. The irreconcilable who kills one of these and takes his own life is a truly tragic figure. To the well-meaning commissioner he is simply a paragraph for a book to be written on 'The Pacification of the Primitive Tribes of the Lower Niger'.[73]

Village democracy and unity was Africa's most valuable social heritage, though by itself it fostered as in Asia an over-rigid conservatism. It was something unfamiliar to Westerners, who did not know how to work with it or through it. Instead there was much recourse in British Africa to 'indirect rule', widely under discussion by this date among all colonial administrators. It meant delegation of authority to native notables, even if chiefs or headmen had to be manufactured for the purpose as landlords had been in parts of India. The system made for inertia just as the old village did, but lacked its compensating virtues.[74] In northern Nigeria, where it went furthest, there were petty autocrats ready to be taken under the British wing. There as in the Soudan, Islam had been carried down into middle Africa by better-armed invaders. Their chiefs, the Fulani emirs, were colourful personages who could be collected, with their horsemen in antique chain armour, to grace durbars, small imitations of those held in India. Always fond of ceremonial, Englishmen shared with their Indian subjects an old-world taste for such displays, and adopted the Hindi *tamasha*, spectacle, into their language.

Europeans in Eastern Africa

One of Burton's journeys, in 1854–5, carried him inland from the north-east coast through Somalia to the capital of another small Muslim despot, Harar. He was the first European to reach it, and he lay down for his first night's sleep rejoicing in the thought that he was 'under the roof of a bigoted prince whose least word was death; amongst a people who detest foreigners ... and the fated instrument of their future downfall'.[75]

He had travelled through an abode of bloodshed and rapine, of mixed population – Galla, Harari, Somali – and clan vendettas. On this side of Africa too slave-raiding was rampant, Arab dealers foraging far afield or buying captives from the more warlike tribes who seized them. Even warfare had grown sordid, brutal, unchivalrous. '"Conscience", I may observe,' wrote Burton, 'does not exist in Eastern Africa, and "Repentance" expresses regret for missed opportunities of mortal crime.'[76] There were few Noble Savages in Burton's world. He thought archaic peoples in the mass more mercenary than civilized man. It was no use punishing them for outrages by killing a few of them: 'The fine is the only true way to produce a lasting impression upon their heads and hearts.'[77] These denizens of Somalia were as little refined in body as in soul. 'The men were wild as ourang-outangs,' he says of a Danakil caravan, 'and the women fit only to flog cattle.'[78]

A man like Burton roved for the sake of adventure, and because he was out of place in a Europe where the thrill of danger was being standardized into wars of mass armies, as it were gigantic Cook's Tours where the tame citizen felt adventurous at the word of command. It is revealing of his distaste for his homeland, and especially for its plebeians, that when he occasionally lets fall an indulgent remark about savages he is comparing them with his fellow-countrymen. He got a better reception from the wild inhabitants of one place than he would have expected in a mining district in England, or in 'enlightened Scotland' where any stranger was a target for hoots or brickbats. 'The ridiculous Somali peruke of crimsoned sheepskin' was a shade less 'barbarous' than the headgear of Wales.[79] But to lend his rovings and his disgusts with mankind a meaning – over and above his genuine hatred of the slave trade – he had to cultivate the semi-mystical creed of empire; he had to convince himself and his readers that Britain somehow needed colonies, and that there were races all over Asia and Africa that needed Britain. Somalis were a case in point: they were not incapable of progress, but had 'lapsed into barbarism by reason of their political condition – the rude equality of the Hottentots'.[80] A democratic state of society thus became for Burton a positive vice, not unconnected with another cardinal failing, a 'worse than Asiatic idleness'.[81] This remark may be set beside one by an administrator in an African colony later on : 'The natives think we are lazy dogs, but very clever at making the black man do our work.'[82]

Harar, which Burton looked forward to seeing under the British flag, forty years later was absorbed into Abyssinia, that still half-mythical country, or confusion of petty principalities. It was an old outpost of Christendom, but its outlandish Church, like the related Coptic Church in Egypt, awoke little feeling of kinship in Europe. To Shakespeare the word 'Ethiopian' meant African, black, as 'Habshi' or Abyssinian had done for ages in India, and the usage was current in the US as late as the Civil War. Bruce the explorer was there in 1769; closely pressed by Boswell about the inhabitants' colour he defined it as 'tawny copper'. Abyssinia he called 'a barbarous, mountainous country'.[83] It survived a British punitive expedition in 1868, a sort of African Afghanistan no one was sufficiently foolish to want until in 1896 Italy proved hungry and rash enough. By then a new ruler, Menelek II, was strengthening the country and expanding it into an Amhara empire; it was he who reduced Harar to a vassal position. (In 1964 Arnold Toynbee was shown the house there where Haile Selassie was educated as a boy by French missionaries.[84]) W. S. Blunt was disgusted at the sight of mushroom Italy, only just freed from

Austria, attacking 'the oldest free people and kingdom in the world . . . and there was not a voice in Europe to cry shame! All the English papers applauded.'[85] European approval did not save the Italians from a resounding defeat at Adowa, one of Africa's very few victories over Europe.

In 1857–8 Lieutenant Speke, in quest of the sources of the Nile, penetrated into Uganda. Down here he was in the midst of a population which he regarded as inferior to the Hamitic races of northern Africa. Two boys he met were 'of the common negro breed . . . such as no one could love but their mothers'.[86] He was very much aware that conquering migrants had come down from the north, and was on the look-out for faces showing evidence of racial differences. Englishmen listened from the cradle to nonsense about Norman blood and Normal noses, and Speke was prepared to feel some faint affinity with an African aristocracy, a crude precursor of the European. He was never better pleased on his journey than in Karague, the territory of a well-featured king named Rumanika. 'The farther we went in this country the better we liked it, as the people were all kept in good order', and the ruler and his brother were 'as unlike as they could be to the common order of the natives . . . They had fine oval faces, large eyes, and high noses, denoting the best blood of Abyssinia.'[87] At the equator Abyssinian blood looked comparatively blue.

Other travellers were struck by this superimposition of 'higher' stocks on 'lower', Africa's substitute for higher and lower classes; Grogan, for instance, who crossed Africa from south to north at the end of the century. He contrasted the tall, well-built Awemba of one district with their Mambwe neighbours, 'the ordinary, dirty, stunted, cringing or insolent, ill-fed type of Central Africa'. He saw the ruling Watutsi of Ruanda as 'descendants of a great wave of Galla invasion' from the north, and in Uganda the upper class of Galla origin shone by contrast with 'the coarse, squat, ape-like appearance of the rabble'.[88] All this implied that the mass of Africans deserved to be ruled by men of higher race, and that European conquest would only mean for them a change to a better set of masters. In all these impressions there must have been a subjective bias. One of the best authorities on central Africa, Sir Harry Johnston, could detect no general variation of skin colour between 'higher' and 'lower'.[89] Europeans came from a society so permeated by class consciousness, and were so conditioned to the need of having social inferiors to look down on, that they were likely to magnify any analogous divisions in Africa, or to imagine them.

The Africans whom Speke saw most of, and who probably inspired many of his large generalizations, were the sort he picked up on the coast as porters: slaves, or vagrant ex-slaves, men torn from home and family and thrown on a callous world where to survive from day to day was the best they could hope for. A foreigner might have generalized in similar terms about the British character after employing a gang of Irish navvies. Speke gave the African of this type good marks for strength and endurance, but for no higher qualities. 'Economy, care, or forethought never enters his head ... A wonderful amount of loquacity, great risibility, but no stability – a creature of impulse – a grown child, in short.' 'Great forbearance, occasionally tinctured with a little fatherly severity', was required in managing him.[90] What Speke understood by this we learn when we find that he often ordered a porter a hundred or more lashes.[91]

It would be interesting to know what his men thought about him. Ten of them ran away early on because they supposed white men to be cannibals and thought they were being taken into the bush to be devoured.[92] This notion of the white man coming to eat up the black was widespread,[93] and may be allowed a degree of poetical truth at least. Livingstone found that many Africans believed the white man to come not from across the sea but out of the sea depths.[94] Even Rumanika, who turned out very sensible, was alarmed at Speke's approach, thinking his visitors might be 'some fearful monsters that were not quite human'.[95]

Speke's prescription for Africa was the same as Burton's – British rule. Black men were improvident because they were 'lazy', and they were lazy because they lacked 'a strong protecting government'.[96] The logic is equivocal, as if what Speke really meant was a strong coercive government, ready for fatherly severity. But any such distinction he would have called hair-splitting. After ages of stagnation the time had come when 'the African must soon either step out from his darkness, or be superseded by a being superior to himself. Could a government be formed for them [*sic*] like ours in India, they would be saved; but without it, I fear there is very little chance.'[97] In Buganda he saw and much disliked the most pretentious government this part of Africa had produced for itself. It was a state founded on conquest, and now degenerate. Mtesa, the *kabaka* or king, was a pampered youth of twenty-five, too feather-pated to want to hear any news of the outside world, but eager to borrow a pair of trousers too short for him, so that 'his black feet and hands stuck out at the extremities as an organ-player's monkey's do'.[98] He was delighted to get his hands on some guns, and set about shooting his subjects for sport. Ministers or attendants were liable to be flogged or executed at any moment, for any reason or none. Mtesa's wives stood in most danger of all:[99] he was a lady-killer in the most literal sense, but vacancies were quickly filled with new brides presented by fathers seeking his favour.

No doubt it was only a few years since adolescents were hanged in England for petty theft. Soldiers' costumes in Buganda that Speke found absurd[100] were not more so than Europe's busbies and shakoes; the lion-step or royal gait cannot have been more grotesque than the goose-step. Tyranny like Mtesa's, moreover, was felt chiefly in a limited sphere round the royal hut. But this was the sphere that foreigners would draw most of their conclusions from. As everywhere in Afro-Asia they would be strongly affected by the sexual pattern they found, and this was bound to be most repulsive in the royal harems they saw or heard about, which all over Afro-Asia were mere private brothels. Speke pitied Mtesa's women, and was amused or disgusted by the custom he met with here and elsewhere of royal wives being fattened to such dimensions that some could not stand unaided. One such beauty he was enterprising enough to take measurements of.[101]

Speke came home northward, by way of the Soudan, where Turk–Egyptian power was still expanding. It seemed hardly distinguishable from brigandage. He encountered it first in the shape of 'a very black man, named Mahamed, in full Egyptian regimentals', at the head of 'a ragamuffin mixture of Nubians,

Egyptians, and slaves of all sorts', who insisted on embracing him.[102] Before long the Soudan or its most warlike tribes, led by the Mahdi, rebelled. This might appear natural and laudable, but about the same time the British were occupying Egypt, and General Gordon's death at Khartoum in 1885 gave a generation of Englishmen an emotional symbol of civilization stabbed by savagery. Mahdism, this 'new power emerging out of the African darkness',[103] was indeed very far from angelical, but Europe treated it as purely diabolical, one more witches' brew of African primitivism and Muslim fanaticism. Kitchener's conquest of the Soudan at Omdurman in 1898 was set down as the close of 'a chapter which, even in the history of the Soudan, is unparalleled for horror and human depravity'.[104] The moral was that any African land cutting loose from the outer world was bound to relapse instead of advancing. Civilization was learning something from barbarism, as well as the other way about; the Mahdi's tomb was desecrated and his skull carried off by General Kitchener, who in young Winston Churchill's opinion 'behaved like a blackguard'.[105]

When Speke set out, the travels farther south in eastern Africa of the greatest of all African explorers had just been published, and were making a stir. Livingstone first went to Africa in 1841, and died still on the march in 1873. In 1857 he gave up his connection with the London Missionary Society for an official commission to explore, with the rank of consul. He is a more enigmatic figure than any of the others. What drove him on through the wilderness was in part the same thirst for discovery that carried Mungo Park to his death; but with this went an equally overmastering desire to discover ways of saving the land, African bodies still more than African souls, from destruction. Throughout the area of his wanderings the slave trade was still growing, with Zanzibar under its Arab ruler and the Portuguese possessions, themselves expanding, as the chief sources of infection. Livingstone denounced them more and more openly, and also made enemies by his criticism of the Boers who were spreading desolation from the south. To prevent worse things he came to favour occupation of territory by Britain, and African nationalists of a later day have sometimes reckoned him among the empire-builders.

Most of his Africa was a chaos of warring peoples, and it would be astonishing if his private estimate of the human race in the end was very high – whatever his secret opinion of Divine Providence may have been. Africans were preyed on by white men and Arabs, but also, as in West Africa, by one another. And he was at a loss for words to convey to readers at home 'the degradation to which the people have been sunk by centuries of barbarism and the hard struggle for the necessaries of life'.[106] At times he seemed to be of the commonest way of thinking about Africans. 'They are mere children, as easily pleased as babies.'[107] Even the best Christians forgot that on Sundays they prayed to become as little children themselves. But what set Livingstone apart was that his estimate of African capabilities rose as time went on, or at all events he was more willing to suspend judgement. He was baffled by the contradictions he saw among the Makololo. 'They perform actions sometimes remarkably good, and sometimes equally the reverse ... On the whole, I think they exhibit just the same strange mixture of good and evil as men do elsewhere.'[108]

Livingstone was proud of his Highland descent. His Scotland lay on Europe's verge, and knew the hard struggle for survival, and a Scotsman with imagination – Robert Louis Stevenson in the Pacific was another – might gain an insight into the workings of untutored minds denied to the average Westerner. Besides this, he took account of the African outside Africa as well as at home. What he had read of slavery in the US inspired the hatred of slavery that he brought with him to Africa; and he was impressed by what he heard of the bearing of Negro soldiers in the Civil War, in which his son Robert lost his life.[109] He was spared the knowledge of how meagre were the fruits of the war for Negro progress.

Twenty years after Livingstone's death the Australian missionary Booth came out to the same part of Africa. He had more democratic views than most preachers from England, and held that Africa could only be redeemed in the end by Africans.[110] Lawlessness still reigned. Yet his ten-year-old daughter Emily was to remember the black men among whom she lived, and who carried her over long journeys on their shoulders, for their almost invariable friendliness and goodness. 'I had absolutely no fear of them.'[111] White men she knew of who got into trouble with them usually brought it on themselves:[112] they were often quite as wild as any of the inhabitants. 'The bottle, the bullet, and the Bible' were the companions of Europeans of very distinct species.[113] Grogan, an explorer with no evangelical nonsense about him, saw some of these species at a boozing party where he met 'the most cosmopolitan crowd imaginable ... animal-faced Boers, leavened with Jews, parasites, businessmen, nondescripts, and every type of civilized savage'.[114]

As in other parts of the world the spectacle of native oppressing native helped the outsider to feel that he might as well join in and do the same. In Nyasaland the dominant Ngoni or Angoni, of warlike Zulu stock, exploited as well as protected the Tonga peasantry. The Ngoni also practised cruelties like witch-hunts and ordeal by poison on themselves, as the Zulus and other fighting peoples of Africa often seem to have done; the habit of violence against their neighbours reacted on their own relationships. Imperial Europe was to undergo the same experience.

Missions like that of the Church of Scotland at Blantyre were acquiring a degree of informal control over their spheres of influence, and here and outside them concern for the safety of their converts made them advocates of intervention by their governments. Christianity had always boasted its martyrs, and there were new ones in this age in many far-off lands. A persecution in Madagascar had attracted a good deal of attention. Preachers and pirates arrived there about the same time, the latter according to Trelawney plundering and murdering 'whenever they wanted a salad, or a fresh egg'.[115] Missionaries got a footing because the Hova people were building up their power over the island, and wanted Western arms and training. Under Queen Ranavalona (1828–61) there was a sharp anti-Christian reaction, after which her successors reversed her policy and adopted Christianity. Ballantyne prefaced a novel about Madagascar by calling it 'one of the most interesting and progressive islands of the world'.[116] But his story, founded on mission records, was of the persecution by Ranavalona, and painted her as a most bloodthirsty despot, a female Prempeh;

it was bound to turn readers' thoughts to other areas where similar troubles might be threatening.

One of these was Buganda, where regular mission work started in 1877, but where King Mwanga, the son of Mtesa, fell foul of the converts and killed a number of them. He was only taking the same view as European kings in the age of religious wars, that a subject who chose to differ from his ruler in religion was a rebel. In Madagascar the Christians had been left to rough it, but in Uganda there were other motives for intervention: interests of strategy, and of an East Africa Company, and a growing inclination to annex territory in general. Good and bad arguments reinforced each other, and in 1890 a protectorate was declared over Zanzibar, in 1893 over Nyasaland – which brought the Tonga peasantry relief from the Angoni – and in 1894 over Buganda. Next year the French took Madagascar, and its last sovereign, another queen, was deported to Algeria. Even an English onlooker was willing to put the blame on native tyranny and corruption, rather than French greed.[117] Hova rule had alienated many of the other inhabitants; Protestant groups now formed a national resistance, and were persecuted again, this time by the French.

Southern Africa : the Conflict of Races

It was the misfortune of the Dutch settlers in Africa's deep south, which they have never outgrown, that they came at a time when slavery was in European eyes a natural institution. They were then cut off from their homeland by the advent of the British at the beginning of the nineteenth century. The British too were there for three decades before the abolition of slavery in the empire; but they had a home country to keep them from complete stagnation. Any enlightenment they received from it they failed to pass on to the Boers. Whatever successes it may have had with native races, Britain made a poor job of the two European stocks it became responsible for, Boers and French Canadians.

This southern tip of the continent held a medley of the most primitive races, Bushman and Hottentot, which had been pushed down into it, along with some of the most energetic Bantu tribes still pressing down from farther north. Hottentots were a cross between Bushmen and some earlier invaders. Winwood Reade expressed the common view when he called them 'a dwarfish race who have restless, rambling, ape-like eyes';[118] and their name entered the English vocabulary as an equivalent for idiot or underling. They were little able to defend themselves against the Boers, whose predatory instincts were deepened by having a population easily enslaved to work on. Along the frontiers of the gradually expanding colony were Bantu tribes of another mettle, and a series of 'Kaffir wars' against them went on for a hundred years. During one of these, in 1850, Hottentots inside the colony seized the chance to rebel. Kaffirs too came under the Boer yoke, and there is a glimpse of how they were regarded in Olive Schreiner's first novel, written in the 1870s: when family prayers were held on the farm the Kaffir workers were not present, 'because Tant' Sannie held they were descended from apes, and needed no salvation'.[119] Darwin may have met with obstruction in some Christian quarters, in others he had been anticipated. 'Kaffir' or 'Caffre', a corruption of the Arab term for pagan, was itself an index of the gulf between the races. Africans considered it 'an insulting epithet'.[120]

In 1836 a section of the Boers set out on their trek northeastward to found two little independent republics. They were actuated both by a noble love of freedom and by an ignoble grudge at the British action in emancipating their slaves. Their descendants would look back on this migration in terms borrowed from later empire-builders, as civilized society imposing order on anarchy.[121] At the time these Boers were not much concerned with phrases, and plunged into the anarchy as one set of savages among others, the most destructive because the best equipped, with guns and horses. One of their stratagems was to go on raids driving a crowd of Africans in front of them as a screen, and open fire on a village over their heads; they then carried off their victims' cattle, women, and children.[122] They were not above employing bands of armed Hottentots and other Africans; like all European territories on the continent this was conquered with the aid of Africans under the white man's orders, as India was with that of Indians.

Likewise the Cape Dutch had indulged freely in native women, and fathered a large mixed or 'Coloured' community. Some of these, the 'Griquas', established a small border republic of their own, under an able leader who won Livingstone's praise by forbidding raiding expeditions.[123] The Boer trekkers had white wives with them, who in harsh pioneering conditions had to be treated as partners, and white offspring had to be multiplied; black women had therefore to be discarded, except as menials. There was no native aristocracy to be conciliated and made use of, as in Indonesia. Here in south Africa the Dutch were following their natural line of development, the same as that of the British in India, towards racialism, sexual taboos and apartheid.

Of the peoples they overran, those whose labour could be exploited were reduced to servitude, the rest got rid of. Bushmen were among the chief sufferers. They were 'looked upon as vermin and exterminated on contact', as General Smuts's son and biographer tells us, and by Zulus as well as Boers.[124] Both complained of pilfering; but these hunters when expelled from their lands had no recourse but to steal cattle. Boer and Bantu between them turned the veld into the scene of carnage pictured – with it may be hoped some overstatement – by Laurens van der Post.[125] Britons coming up later from the Cape joined in the *mêlée*, while the British government looked the other way. When Sir J. Campbell asked in Parliament in 1881 whether it approved of the plundering or destruction of crops and property in the fighting against the Basutos, that model of a Victorian under-secretary M. E. Grant Duff replied that the responsibility lay with the Cape Colony authorities: Her Majesty's Government 'expresses neither approval nor disapproval'.[126] Three years later, however, Basutoland was taken out of the Cape's jurisdiction, and Bechuanaland was also made a protectorate, with a Scottish missionary for its first deputy-commissioner.

Of all the southern Bantu the most striking were the Zulus. Their tribes were being welded into a nation, and conquering far and wide, at the beginning of the nineteenth century, under Tchaka, a leader as remarkable in his very different way as that other great African of the same epoch, Toussaint. Zulus in the south, Mehemet Ali's Turk–Egyptians in the north, were forging empires in Africa before any of the Europeans joined in. Egypt was set going by the stimulus of Western contact, and there are hints of this, slighter and more devious, in the Zulu case too. Tchaka's predecessor, Dingiswayo, had been a wanderer, and in touch with a white man; he opened trade with Delagoa Bay and began to create the regiments that made the Zulu army famous. Tchaka was interested in the white man's weapons, and though he seems to have concluded that his own were better he did employ a detachment of European and Hottentot musketeers.[127] More generally he was eager to learn about the white man's arts and teach them to his people, and therefore avoided conflict with the English; he toyed with the idea of sending young men to England for training.[128]

A trading party that visited Tchaka in 1824 was impressed by 'the order and discipline maintained in the country'. It was impressed in a different way when Tchaka, conversing genially as he took his bath, all of a sudden decided to have one of his attendants killed, and the man's neck was wrung on the spot.[129] Europe's picture of Zululand shared this contradictoriness. No other African people caught the Western, especially the British, imagination so powerfully. Besides their splendid physique they were 'shrewd, energetic, and brave', wrote Livingstone, and except for colour and hair 'would take rank among the foremost Europeans'.[130] To the generations of English boys who had the luck to grow up on Rider Haggard's novels they shared the heroic aura of the Red Indians. But all that was heard of them apart from their fighting prowess – their bloody witch-hunts, their devastating raids, their despotic rulers surrounded by executioners – had a repulsive flavour, like Red Indian torture or Aztec human sacrifice.

Tchaka was murdered in 1828. He could scarcely have led his people further. Like the Asiatic monarchs of that century who tried to equip their kingdoms for survival, he was too much embedded in the past to be able to enter the future that he descried from afar. Superstition, ferocity, a vast harem, weighed him down. But the nation he welded with blood and iron outlasted him, came through a defeat by Boer fire-arms in 1838, and showed signs of a capacity to evolve further. Left to itself Zululand might have grown into a country both modern and African, a more original, more intriguing facet of mankind's total experience that any now likely to be produced by southern Africa. Unfortunately the *impis* were still armed with spears when the last Kaffir war brought them into collision with the British in 1879. Their victory over one British force at Isandhlwana was another of Africa's few triumphs, and the superlative courage they displayed was second to none that Europe was ever confronted with. A war correspondent at the final battle at Ulundi watched them charge under 'pitiless showers of death' from the Gatling guns; those Zulus, he wrote, 'could dare and die with a valour and devotion unsurpassed by the soldiery of any age or of any nationality'.[131]

In the white conquest of southern Africa gold and diamonds were the strongest lure; the search was directed by men like Rhodes, of the same stamp as the Morgans and Rockefellers who were rearing empires of another sort in America. In London the interested section of the Stock Exchange came to be known as the 'Kaffir Circus'. To this holy of holies of Europe financial racketeers flocked together from all quarters, men to whom all flags were flags of convenience, among them a number of Asiatic Jews.[132] These men, rootless and emancipated, gained a welcome in the highest circles by their skill in manipulating stocks and shares, and by helping their patrons to shake off old-fashioned prejudices. About the end of the century moralists as well as socialists were complaining of a moral degeneracy among Europe's upper classes, now far on in their metamorphosis from aristocracy into plutocracy: rampant materialism, worship of wealth and luxury, contempt for moral scruples.[133] 'The Stock Exchange had become the centre of the national life';[134] high society was bewitched by prospects of new Eldorados, and the cheap newspaper reader was taught to revel in them too, at least in fantasy. Ideas of civilizing the backward native were overlaid by the frank philosophy of the giant in the old rhyme:

> Be he living or be he dead
> I'll grind his bones to make my bread.

In Kipling's *Recessional* of 1897, his finest poem and one of the few great English poems of that time, the misgivings of more responsible men of empire perhaps found expression. The corruption of English society by the Nabobs with their Indian loot was being repeated a century later on a European scale. Despite the lamentable record of the old English and Dutch East India Companies in the treatment of native peoples, 'development' was again being entrusted very largely to chartered companies of private speculators. Rhodes and his South Africa Company received their charter in 1889, and organized more systematically the methods that were already being used in southern Africa. Like the British North Borneo Company it set up its own force of mercenaries; one of Olive Schreiner's stories was about an English recruit and his change of heart on the subject of nigger-shooting.[135] 'The Chartered Company never cared a snap of its fingers for the Colonial Office,' wrote E. D. Morel, a stalwart defender of African rights: it was too well-connected to bother about mild protests. 'The Rhodesian outrage is an intolerable national disgrace.'[136]

One incident in the scramble for Africa was the Boer War of 1899–1902. This conflict between white men had all the bitterness of civil war, but neither serious cause nor serious result so far as the basic problem of race relations was concerned. As a young Boer of the Cape, Smuts had advocated partnership of Boer and Briton under Rhodes's direction. 'Unless the white race closes its ranks,' he said in a speech in 1895, 'its position will soon become untenable in the face of the overwhelming majority of prolific barbarism.'[137] Only the reckless impatience of the Kaffir Circus for quicker profits precipitated the struggle with the Boer republics. Before this was over Boers who experienced the 'methods of barbarism'[138] for which the British Liberal leader censured the British army had time to wonder whether Europe was really much less barbarous than Africa. A habit of treating troublesome natives as 'vermin' was bound to brutalize white men's treatment of one another when they fell out. In the wild and whirling propaganda in England against the Boers an assortment of the clichés accumulated in Western dealings with coloured men were now turned against fellow-whites. Boers, exactly like Chinese, could be impressed only by

strength. 'There is not in the whole world,' solemnly pro-
nounced the *Scotsman* of Edinburgh, 'a man more ready than
your Dutch Afrikander to understand the argument of force'.[139]

Belgians and Germans

With the scramble for territory went the humbug of 'treaties',
scraps of paper that chiefs were cajoled or bullied into signing, and with them signing away lands that did not belong to
them. The black man scrawling his mark on a document, as he
hugged his bottle of rum, became a stock figure of fun. Frontier lines were drawn on maps in distant capitals, tribes and
nationalities were split up as slave families had been by the
auctioneer, populations were bandied about from flag to flag –
'disloyalty' to any of which was a capital crime. Africans were
being disposed of as Europeans were by their princes not long
before, when the Congress of Vienna reckoned them up and
distributed them in lots of so many thousand 'souls'.

When Blunt was in Rome to attend a peace conference in
1891 he was repelled by the Italian attitude to native peoples:
they could not even, as Englishmen could, speak of them with
any decency.[140] The brutalism that was reviving in Europe was
displayed most grimly in the 'Congo Free State' sanctioned by
the Berlin Conference on Africa in 1885, and from then until
1908 a private empire of King Leopold of the Belgians. Here
could be seen private enterprise at its worst, free from all public inquiry or check, and the new plutocracy at its glossiest,
with a royal manager. Its devious origins show how missionary
zeal, like all Europe's better impulses, could be exploited by
money-grubbers. A titular Archbishop of Carthage launched
with papal approval a campaign for stronger action against
slave-trading; he invited Christian soldiers to volunteer, and
dreamed of a new order of knights-errant.[141] Leopold encouraged the idea, and when his 'Free State' was set up humanitarians rejoiced.

His agent for the preliminary spadework or collection of
'treaties' was H. M. Stanley, the Anglo-American explorer
whose chief performance in Africa was his expedition to find

Livingstone in 1871–2. Those who saw him at the Berlin Conference were puzzled: he 'spoke with real affection of the natives', but there was something about him that belied his words.[142] He may have been speaking more from the heart when he inspected an early model of the Maxim gun and declared that it 'would be of valuable service in helping civilization to overcome barbarism'.[143] It has been said that his newspaper sponsors really wanted him to find not Livingstone but sensational stuff for them to print, and that he manufactured excitement by moving with a huge retinue that could only feed itself by plundering.[144] North America and Europe were indeed avid for blood-and-thunder yarns about Africa, as an outlet maybe for repressed blood-and-thunder impulses of their own.

In the Congo it was as easy as elsewhere to employ Africans of one tribe against another. Leopold assembled a mercenary army with, by 1905, 360 officers from up and down Europe, and 16,000 natives. Its business was to ensure quick profits in rubber, ivory, or palm-oil collected as tribute or by forced labour. The consequences were of a sort and on a scale not seen again in the world until the Nazi epoch, when they were seen in Europe itself. Africa, or this part of it, now became very truly a Dark Continent, but its darkness was one the invaders brought with them, the sombre shadow of the white man. Revelations of what was happening percolated very slowly through Europe's self-complacency, before the Belgian government at last in 1908 assumed responsibility for the Congo. Inevitably in a colony where Africans had been instigated to torment and kill one another for so many years, the new régime adopted the policy, which was never relaxed, of treating them all as a race of juvenile criminals.

Indirectly the Belgian public was responsible all along for its king's misdoings; as the French public was more directly for the not much better state of affairs in the French Congo, where in spite of De Brazza the first governor, a man of an older and better school, get-rich-quick syndicates were given a free hand.[145] Their nemesis came to both Belgium and France in 1914. But all the talk in Allied countries was now of German atrocities in Belgium, instead of Belgian or French atrocities in the Congo; which led on easily to a belief that Germany's conduct in Africa, where most of its few colonies were, must have been equally atrocious. This was erected into a dogma of Allied war propaganda, and paved the way for the confiscation of all German colonies by the treaty of Versailles.[146]

Before 1914 Englishmen had usually thought of German colonial methods with respect; the same kind of respect for efficiency that they felt for the Dutch, whose system the Germans were in some ways emulating though without their financial success. Grogan admired all that he saw of German work in Tanganyika. He liked the freedom of action allowed to officials, 'not cramped by the ignorant babblings of sentimentalism'; he gave less questionable praise to their thoroughness in learning languages.[147] This empire too was brought into being partly by well-meaning missionaries, of whom Germany since the eighteenth century had been a nursery. By 1870 there were eight strong mission societies, 'active centres of agitation for national expansion'.[148] But Europe had two selves, further apart than ever before in human history because this new Europe was more complex and altering more rapidly; and the discordance was revealed most of all in the encounter with Africa, the region most opposite to it. And within Europe it was Germany that had the most deeply divided soul. Until the nineteenth century much of it was like Russia a land of lord and serf; Germans for a very long time had consoled themselves by looking down on Slavs as inferiors; German nationalism, unlike French, had from the start a racialist tinge; German respect for Culture easily bred contempt for the uncultivated, in or out of Europe.

When Germany suddenly entered the colonial field in 1884 imperialism in its virgin fields was sinking towards its lowest moral level. This country which for centuries had watched others act while it theorized, and was now free to act at last, displayed with increasing violence down to 1945 an impulse to push action, as it had formerly pushed metaphysical speculation, to its furthest and maddest extreme. The worst episode in German Africa was the suppression of the Herero rising in the south-west in 1904, after which many of the tribesmen were driven off their land into the desert to perish and make way for culture. 'The German ideal of colonisation,' writes Smuts's son, 'was ... extermination', and not 'straightforward extermination, but sadistic ill-treatment, flogging, interference with women and brutality'.[149] Such a charge does not come best from an Afrikaaner; it does all the same apply exactly to German behaviour in occupied east Europe after 1939. Here again happenings in Africa and other colonial regions were a rehearsal for what was to happen in Europe.

The fate of the Hereros was not unknown to other governments. A report to the British Foreign Office in 1909 said that German policy with the native was 'to reduce him to a state of serfdom, and, where he resists, to destroy him altogether. The native, to the German, is a baboon and nothing more.'[150] With relations worsening between the two countries it may seem odd that propaganda was not made out of this long before 1914. But on the one hand, German admistration, under criticism at home from the Socialist and Catholic parties, was improving:[151] it became, as in Prussia, orderly and legalistic, if severe. A new Colonial Secretary, Dernburg, worked to give the natives protection, in spite of 'endless odium' heaped on him by those who did not want natives protected.[152] On the other hand, to denounce another government's colonial methods would have invited obvious retorts. Even in South-West Africa human rights were scarcely more blatantly ignored than they had lately been in some British territories, in Rhodesia, for instance, as Morel pointed out.[153] The difference was that in one case German troops carried out the orders of German officers, in the other Britain shuffled responsibility on to its colonists, much as Belgium left the Congo to Leopold.

White Settlers

It was in areas where colonists from Europe were settling in numbers that the native population was likely to fare worst. Failure to foresee this was another missionary miscalculation. Livingstone was eager to see Europeans coming out, and was always looking for healthy uplands where they could live. He wanted immigrants who would not themselves farm, but would guide and superintend Africans; that African use of the land was inefficient and wasteful was a commonplace. He had left Britain soon after the abolition of colonial slavery, when feelings kindled by the long campaign were still warm, and he seems to have gone on conjuring up in fancy a settler community public-spirited and philanthropic. In fact, wherever settlement took place the African would be exchanging the risk of kidnapping into slavery for the certainty of reduction to peonage.

Most of Asia was preserved from white immigrants by its climate or its teeming population. Regions where mixed colonies could grow, with big European minorities among native majorities, were virtually confined to Africa and to that overseas Africa, the southern United States. One such was Algeria. France had found no other colony of settlement since losing Canada; it had its eye for a while on New Zealand, but was forestalled there by Britain. In Algeria the newcomers got control of the most fertile land, reducing its former communal possessors to tenants or labourers, a situation destined to end in one of the most atrocious of all colonial wars. Of the settlers who compelled France for years to go on fighting it, about one quarter are said to have been authentic Frenchmen: the rest were flotsam and jetsam of the Mediterranean, hardened into a distinctive amalgam by pride in their sole original asset, white or near-white blood. A pauperized European, like a decadent aristocrat, is proud of his 'blood' because he has nothing else to be proud of.

In such a society dividing lines of class and race coincided and deepened each other. Traditional Africa itself had many precedents for this, and in many parts of Europe class and nationality coincided. Croat peasants lived under Magyar landlords, Czech under German, Irish under English. In Ireland religion aggravated the division still further, as colour did in Africa, and between Protestant Ascendancy at Dublin and White Supremacy at Cape Town the analogies are close. Wherever the future of a large white community depended in this way on the permanent subjection of Africans, it had the strongest inducement to believe that they were inferior by nature, and therefore must always be at the bottom, and ought to be grateful to their betters for keeping them there. A regular body of doctrine was emerging; it drew on both science and divinity, pseudo-Darwin and pseudo-Bible harnessed together. It was flattering to the white man to think that inalienable higher qualities, not merely better weapons, had brought him to the top. A flight of fancy in a recent book on the Zulus, the more startling because most of the book is quite rational, illustrates this mystical tendency. Tchaka's amicable reception of some English visitors is taken to prove that the white men possessed an 'indefinable aristocratic ascendancy', 'some dominant quality even in rags which compelled the black men to regard them as their superior'.[154] By an exactly parallel convention of late-feudal times in Europe, Shakespeare's young princes and gentlemen, even when brought up in ignorance among churls, have an innate nobility of soul which lifts them above their fellows, and which their fellows recognize. Livingstone, who saw no sovereign virtue in either white or blue blood, observed that to the black man the first sight of a white man was apt to be 'frightfully repulsive'.[155]

Mystique of race was Democracy's vulgarization of an older mystique of class. It gave white settlers an agreeable sensation of being one large family, as an aristocracy always is, a counterfeit of the equality that western Europe had dreamed of for so long, and to so little avail. This had an insidious attraction for muddle-headed plebeians arriving from Europe, where on a larger scale classes were being drawn together in brotherly harmony by a common sensation of superiority to the lesser breeds outside; above all to plebeians from England, accustomed to breathe an air composed of oxygen, nitrogen, and snobbery. To keep up the family feeling an exclusiveness like that of caste was necessary. 'The system of Government in Kenya,' wrote Jomo Kenyatta in his rebel days, 'is based on strict racial discrimination ... The white man looks upon his own authority and prestige as of the greatest importance': all male Africans had to carry a certificate with their fingerprints, and resented it as 'a mark of their virtual serfdom'.[156]

They resented it all the more because Indians in Kenya were exempt. As in Asia, European power brought with it an influx of other aliens. There was a brief, unpleasant experiment with Chinese labour in the gold mines of South Africa; Indian immigrants were more numerous in the south, and also in east Africa which had always had links with India. Many of them were or became shopkeepers, traders, professional men, and their desire was to be as close as they could to the white man's level and as far as they could above the black majority. They began to find their way into Mozambique too. Portugal's growing colonies needed more educated men, and were free from racialism of the doctrinal kind; ultimately this allowed the few Africans who could get an education to be assimilated into the dominant minority, but Indians found it much easier to pass the tests. For the ordinary African in Livingstone's day the term current in Mozambique was *bicho*, animal; in Angola he was addressed as 'devil', or 'brute'. 'In fact slave-owners come to regard their slaves as not human.'[157] Whatever Shakespeare had in mind when he drew Caliban, it is understandable that some modern readers outside Europe have seen in him a personification of the races crushed down and exploited by the white man.

In South Africa the foundations of racial antagonism were being laid deepest. The Boer War called forth some talk in Britain about protection of the African against the Boer; but when it was over the two white peoples very soon came to terms at the expense of the black peoples.[158] The Liberal conscience hit on one of its happy compromises by keeping the three protectorates of Bechuanaland, Basutoland and Swaziland, but doing nothing to develop them, so that their inhabitants had no choice but to migrate into the Union and work for whatever wages the white employer chose to pay. In the Union itself Boer and British outlook differed chiefly in the way they were expressed.[159] Isolation from the world, religiosity, and now a humiliating defeat in war that had to be wiped out by louder self-assertion, all led the Boers towards a Teutonically elaborate and obsessive philosophy of race, a forerunner of Hitler's. Englishmen smiled at the verbiage but copied the behaviour. 'The settler,' said a guidebook for British immigrants, in plain practical language, 'will not find much difficulty in handling the natives, provided he and his wife avoid familiarity with them, exercise close supervision and enforce strict discipline ... The native despises the employer who is slack and lenient.'[160]

Cheap labour, the same oracle pointed out, ensured plenty

of leisure for the white woman, who would have a native maid to bring her tea in bed in the morning.[161] Very few European women would be proof against temptations like this; it would scarcely be fair to expect women, not yet admitted to a full share of higher responsibilities in Europe, to uphold Europe's higher values in Africa. They have on the contrary, like other underprivileged Europeans, been prompt converts to apartheid. The least regrettable consequence has been to inhibit white men still further from relations with black women, which if allowed would almost always be unedifying. In an area like the Congo where white women were few the white man continued to make do with black women; he might even come to prefer them.[162] It does not appear that this in any way improved his attitude to the black race. Men in general have always lived with women in general, and have always treated them as inferiors.

The 'Child-Races' and their Reaction

Rider Haggard's mysterious white queen made a symbol of the white race ruling over the black that caught Western fancy, and had a brood of bastard imitations.[163] All over Africa the same pattern was emerging – 'a handful of Europeans in command, directing, watching, while the African men run and stumble, robbed of dignity'.[164] That Africans must be prepared to labour for their new rulers seemed too obvious for discussion. It still comes naturally to white men to speak of someone 'working like a black'. Never tired of inveighing against 'sentimental balderdash' about Africa, Grogan was typical in recommending a 'good sound system of compulsory labour', which he said would do more to improve the native in five years than missionary effort in fifty: 'a little firmness would transform him from a useless and dangerous brute' into a useful being.[165]

Africans were no longer taken away to America to produce commodities for Europe, but instead they were to perform the task at home. Various modes of compulsion were brought to bear, and backed by a robust labour discipline. 'The nigger is a lazy beast,' said Sir Rudolph Slatin of the Soudan, 'and must be compelled to work – compelled by Government.' Asked how, he replied: 'With a stick.'[166] Europe was only practising on others what it formerly practised on itself – that is, on its poorer classes, educated in the early days of capitalism by much flogging, branding and jailing. An English historian critical of Hohenzollern despotism in Prussia admitted that 'personal guidance – even forceful guidance – may be necessary in early stages, as we have found it necessary among the child-races of Africa'.[167]

This notion of the African as a minor, endorsed at times even by a Livingstone, took very strong hold. Spaniards and Boers had questioned whether natives had souls: modern Europeans cared less about that, but doubted whether they had minds, or minds capable of adult growth. A theory came to be fashionable that mental growth in the African ceased early, that childhood was never left behind. Johnston lent his authority to it, and conjectured that obsession with sex was what arrested mental development at puberty.[168] The white man's smothered impatience with his own tediously decent conventions, his sneaking envy of the more untrammelled sexual life of the less civilized, often peeped out through disguises like this. Johnston found much to like in Africans, not least a habitual cheerfulness; they were always ready to laugh, 'and laughter lights up their faces to advantage, making them quite like a man and a brother'.[169] Others less charitably saw in this jolliness another symptom of childishness. The infantilism, real or pretended, of the human being reduced to hopeless dependence provided confirmation; and many Africans were in a state of dependence on the will of others before men like Speke or Grogan first saw them.

Grogan's picture of the African was that of the average middling European, neither idealist nor blackguard, at the end of a century of exploration and conquest. He was a worshipper of Rhodes, a frank believer in Africa for the white man, but also in orderly rational government for black men, so abject a race in his view that to hew wood and draw water for Europeans would be a blessed advance for it. Here and there on his long march he could not help reflecting that some African peoples left to themselves got on quite well, so finely adjusted to their environment that it would be a pity to see them disrupted.[170] And no one described more ghoulishly the vast horrors of the Congo under Leopold's régime, 'a vampire growth, intended to suck the country dry'.[171] But overwhelmingly his sense was of a total inaccessibility of the African mind, if indeed there was any mind governing the motions of African limbs and tongues. The African was 'fundamentally inferior in mental development and ethical possibilities (call it soul if you will)'; he stood at a point of evolution 'but slightly superior to the lower animals'; he was destitute of qualities prized in Europe like pity and gratitude.[172]

Grogan arrived at the conclusion which the strong always arrive at about the weak whom they cannot understand – that Africans only understood force, and positively enjoyed being ruled 'with a rod of iron' by Arabs, far better than by easygoing Britons.[173] In principle his advice was 'to let the native see that you respect him in his own line, but take your own absolute superiority for granted', while treating him with scrupulous justice.[174] In practice he felt that fist and boot might serve better; under stress of irritation 'one is often tempted to think that the Boer method of treating natives is, after all, the only one they deserve'.[175]

A more academic writer, at ease in England, summed up the matter by saying that Europe's duty was to train Africa to industrious habits, without brutality but equally 'without pretending to treat the African as the equal of the white man in any way'.[176] Even outside the white settlement areas where black inferiority was the law and the prophets, few Europeans had any real faith in an ascent of the African masses to a civilized level. If there was disagreement, it turned rather on whether or not a few African individuals were capable of the ascent. It had its counterpart at home in disagreement between conservatives who held the working class to be congenitally unfit for higher education, and liberals ready to welcome a few clever members of it into universities. As a Fabian pamphleteer was to lament, proposals to raise standards of living were derided by those who professed to know the African. 'An overwhelming barrage of evidence on the "laziness", "imbecility", "unreliability" of the native workman is produced which is not easily disposed of.'[177] The African's first steps in his new world were bound to be halting. He was left morally shelterless by the crumbling of the old clan and its ways, his eternal verities. A mass of uprooted villagers huddled in shanty-towns made as dismal a sight as Europe's derelicts in the slums of New York; the Zulu who was never known to tremble on the battlefield cut a poor figure as the white man's servant, wearing his master's old clothes. It was a fact often observed in ancient as well as modern times, a classical scholar pointed out, that 'enslaved people lapse into a state of extreme degradation and immorality'. He instanced the Africans locked up in their compounds at Kimberley.[178]

As in the Americas, what determined the treatment of Africans was their profitability. Where there were no assets like diamonds to attract men like Rhodes, men like the Scottish missionaries at Blantyre, the heirs of Livingstone, had more room. Their self-governing Kirk gave converts a new framework in place of the old clan democracy, and round it a Malawi nation could gradually come into being.[179] 'Now he's talking like a real Nyasa,' says someone in a story by an African writer, 'a real Brak Scosh' – or black Scot.[180] Yet Nyasaland was not immune from the reaction against Europe that Africa, more sluggishly than Asia, was experiencing by the early years of the twentieth century. Political movements could not grow quickly, and African protest took a negative form, a turning back to traditional values, good or bad, or else, more positively, a religious form. Here, as in Taiping China, Christianity fused with local cults to produce new sects often of a messianic cast, somewhat as Islam in the Soudan had engendered Mahdism. 'Ethiopianism', the impulse towards separatist churches run by Africans instead of by white men, was appearing from 1884. It was an African minister, John Chilembwe, who headed the small rebellion of 1915 in Nyasaland, a milestone of modern African history.[181]

Africa was no longer existing in isolation. Some years before this a Nyasalander called on his people to emulate 'our fellow country Japan';[182] Chilembwe, a convert of Booth, was taken by him to America, and got his education there. Many new

African ideas were being worked out first by Africans in Europe, especially Britain, and in America. These ideas, among men drawn from many corners of Africa, veered almost at once towards Pan-Africanism. It was a repudiation of the old fatal mosaic of tribe and clan, in a continent where few elements of the European nation-state existed; it was also a reflex of the solidarity of white men against black. Thus Africa was ahead of Europe in catching at least a glimmering vision of continental union. In 1900 the first Pan-African Congress was held in London,[183] a year after Europe had held its first Hague Peace Conference with the less ambitious but not less unsuccessful aim of limiting war.

What was for Africans a rosy dream might be for Europeans a gloomy spectre. A Black as well as Yellow Peril floated at times before them. Occasionally, half-seriously, there was a notion of the Negro having mental endowments that would one day render him formidable. 'They have marvellous abilities, that strange race,' says a lawyer in Hilaire Belloc's most entertaining fantasy.[184] As a rule it was Negro muscle, the Negro as a fighting-man or fighting-machine, that aroused misgivings. Years before 1914 Europe was beginning to be frightened by its own weapons; and if war was destined to grow more murderous year by year, the most primitive race might prove the best adapted to it. More than in the case of the Yellow Peril, the fear was mainly of some European Power adding a vast native army to its own, for use against its neighbours. This formed one of the gravest accusations against Germany after 1914, and was worked up sensationally in the Allied Press.[185] German apologists could argue that Germany had not in fact sought to militarize its colonies, but had only armed a few thousand natives for police duties.[186] Whether this abstention owed more to respect for native rights or to fear, or contempt, of native capabilities, may be less clear. It was the French who had really been training a black army and were using it in Europe, and at the end of the War Clemenceau insisted on the right to raise forces even in mandated territories. Lloyd George gave way with a perfunctory proviso that France should not 'train big nigger armies for the purposes of aggression'.[187]

Hazier but still more upsetting to weak nerves was the

thought, an emanation of the white man's uneasy conscience, of a rising of black against white, a race war of revenge. Grogan talked darkly of 'dusky Napoleons', reminding his readers how formidable Zululand and Ruanda had proved that Africans could be once they merged their tribalism in large entities.[188] The Mahdi and his largely Negro or Arab–Negro army of 'Fuzzy-Wuzzies' in the Soudan were not forgotten. In 1910 the popular novelist John Buchan, one of many Scotsmen who have earned a good living by supplying upper-class England with spectacles to look at the world through, wrote a tale about an educated but atavistic African uniting his people for a crusade against the white man.[189]

What was really about to erupt was the first of Europe's two great internecine wars, its own relapse into savagery. When white men in the most desolate parts of Africa recoiled from scenes of massacre and ravage, they were in a way recoiling from something lurking in their own souls. Caliban, the African, was the baser self that Christendom with its dualistic philosophy of soul and flesh had always been conscious of; he was the insecurely chained Adam of the Puritan preachers, the Hyde of Stevenson's novel,[190] the *id* of the Freudians. When he was let loose the same devastation that Africans or invaders had inflicted on Africa would fall on Europe.

NOTES

1. A. Hamilton, *Memoirs of the Count de Grammont* (1713), pp. 285–8 (English edn, 1906).
2. Defoe, *The Life, Adventures and Piracies of the Famous Captain Singleton* (1720), p. 18 (Everyman edn).
3. *Captain Cook's Voyages of Discovery* (Everyman edn), pp. 16–17.
4. A. Coates, *Prelude to Hongkong* (1966), pp. 4, 13.
5. Sir E. Satow, *A Diplomat in Japan* (1921), pp. 371–2.
6. See Lord Carnarvon, *Portugal and Galicia* (3rd edn, 1848), p. 10; W. E. Baxter, *The Tagus and the Tiber* (1852), Vol. 1, pp. 27, 64.
7. See E. Williams, *Capitalism and Slavery* (1964), pp. 44 ff.
8. 'Multatuli', *Max Havelaar* (1860), pp. 77–8 (English edn, New York, 1927).
9. There are some good specimens in the china collection at Fenton House, Hampstead, London.

10. C. Aspinall-Oglander, *Admiral's Wife (Life and Letters of Mrs Edward Boscawen)* (1940), p. 124.

11. Duke of Buckingham, *Works*, Vol. 2, pp. 179–80 (1775 edn).

12. *Memoirs of the Life of the Late Mrs Catherine Cappe*, by herself (2nd edn, 1823), pp. 333–8. cf. her account of an unfortunate mulatto girl from Jamaica, who had 'all the genius, generosity, and fire, united with all the eccentricity of a native West-Indian' (pp. 236–9).

13. 'Some Words on Pantheism', in *Selected Essays of Schopenhauer*, ed. E. B. Bax (1888).

14. See E. Williams, op. cit., generally; he is followed by H. Hoetink, *The Two Variants in Caribbean Race Relations* (English edn, Oxford, 1967), pp. 23 ff.

15. See e.g. *Cook's Voyages*, p. 14, on the mortality among Negroes in Brazilian gold-workings in 1768 – 'Who can read this without emotion!'

16. Neglect of this fact by E. Williams, op. cit., was criticized by R. Anstey and J. D. Hargreaves in a seminar on the slave trade at the Centre of African Studies, Edinburgh, June 1965.

17. M. Scott, *Tom Cringle's Log* (1836), p. 249 (Everyman edn).

18. ibid., pp. 125, 289.

19. C. Waterton, *Wanderings in South America* (1825), pp. 80–81, 208–9 (1906 edn).

20. J. H. Rose, *The Life of Napoleon I* (6th edn, 1913), Vol. 1, p. 359.

21. See e.g. the episode described in R. Korngold, *Citizen Toussaint* (1945), pp. 256–7.

22. E. Williams, op. cit., p. 202.

23. M. Scott, op. cit., pp. 413, 421.

24. ibid., p. 420.

25. ibid., p. 424.

26. H. H. Prichard, *Where Black Rules White* (revised edn, 1910), p. xi.

27. ibid., p. 200.

28. ibid., p. 359.

29. ibid., p. 259.

30. ibid., p. 327.

31. ibid., p. 297.

32. Portrait of Auguste Casseus at Nice; exhibited at the French Institute, Edinburgh, August 1966.

33. A. Goldring, *Some Reminiscences of an Unclerical Cleric* (1926), pp. 100–104.

34. Minute on a memorandum by P. Currie, in Foreign Office 61.359 (1884), Public Record Office, London.

35. J. Newton, *Thoughts upon the African Slave Trade* (1788), pp.

22–4, 31. I owe these references, and some of the foregoing detail on the trade, to my colleague Mr C. Fyfe, of the Centre of African Studies at Edinburgh University.

36. E. A. Raspe, *Baron Munchausen* (1785), Sequel, Chapter 21.

37. ibid., Chapter 24.

38. A. Smith, *A Month at Constantinople* (1850), pp. 128–30.

39. W. M. Thackeray, *Notes of a Journey from Cornhill to Grand Cairo* (1845), pp. 126–7, 293–5 (1888 edn).

40. ibid., pp. 260–61.

41. R. F. Burton, *A Pilgrimage to Al-Madinah and Meccah* (1855), Vol. 2, p. 252 (Bohn Library edn).

42. J. Ruskin, *Modern Painters*, Part 2 (1846), Sec. 5, Chapter 3, paras. 39–40.

43. W. H. G. Kingston, *The Three Midshipmen* (2nd edn, 1873), Chapter 8 ff.

44. *The Times*, 14 September 1888, p. 3, col. 4.

45. B. Davidson, *The African Awakening* (1955), pp. 38 ff. I am glad to have been able to discuss this problem with Mr Davidson.

46. E. S. Grogan and A. H. Sharp, *From the Cape to Cairo* (1900), p. 183 (Nelson edn, n.d.).

47. 'Hamitic' has confusingly come to denote the northern language-group akin to Semitic (Berber, Egyptian), and then their speakers, with reference to their Caucasian affinities. cf. C. G. Seligman, *Races of Africa* (revised edn, 1939), p. 18: 'The history of Africa south of the Sahara is no more than the story of the permeation ... of the Negro and Bushman aborigines by Hamitic blood and culture.' Whether the stress should be laid on *blood* or on *culture* is today a controversial issue.

48. J. G. Lockhart, *The Life of Sir Walter Scott* (1838), Vol. 2, p. 169 (Edinburgh edn, 1902).

49. D. M. McFarlan, *Calabar. The Church of Scotland Mission 1846–1946* (Edinburgh, 1946), pp. 2–3.

50. *Trader Horn. The Ivory Coast in the Earlies* (reminiscences, ed. E. Lewis, 1927), p. 30 (Penguin edn).

51. See, for much horrid detail on this, D. M. McFarlan, op. cit., pp. 32–3, 52–3, 163.

52. ibid., pp. 49, 62–3, 66.

53. ibid., pp. 63–4, 97.

54. *Trader Horn*, pp. 25, 167, 94–5.

55. W. Reade, *The Martyrdom of Man* (1872), pp. 227–9 (Thinker's Library edn).

56. ibid., pp. 242–3.

57. ibid., pp. 316–17.

58. ibid., p. 303. There is a lesson for today on p. 317: 'Experience has shown that, whenever aliens are treated as citizens, they become citizens, whatever may be their religion or their race.'

59. Chinua Achebe, *Things Fall Apart* (1958), p. 168 (1966 edn).

60. Laurens van der Post, *The Lost World of the Kalahari* (1958), p. 187 (Penguin edn).

61. In 1939 only 0·5 per cent of the inhabitants of French West Africa had full citizenship: D. K. Fieldhouse, *The Colonial Empires* (1966), p. 315.

62. P. Worsley, *The Third World* (1964), pp. 119–20.

63. R. Maugham, *The Slaves of Timbuktu* (1961), p. 73 (1964 edn).

64. There is much on this in G. E. S. Gorer, *Africa Dances* (1935).

65. A. Horne, *The Price of Glory. Verdun 1916* (Penguin edn, 1964), p. 308.

66. See R. B. LePage, *The National Language Question* (Oxford, 1964).

67. Graham Greene, *In Search of a Character* (1961), p. 93 (the time referred to is 1946).

68. F. Oyono, *Houseboy* (English edn, 1966), p. 81.

69. W. Baird, *General Wauchope* (Edinburgh, 1900), pp 39, 41.

70. ibid., pp. 49–50.

71. See A. St J. Adcock, *The Prince of Wales' African Book* (1926).

72. ibid.

73. Chinua Achebe, op. cit., pp. 176–87.

74. cf. A. J. Hanna, *European Rule in Africa* (1961), pp. 22–3, on how the new science of Social Anthropology fostered the preservation of tribal society as if in a museum, until educated Africans protested.

75. R. F. Burton, *First Footsteps in East Africa* (1856), p. 205 (Everyman edn).

76. ibid., pp. 127–8.

77. ibid., p. 18n.

78. ibid., p. 65.

79. ibid., pp. 50, 85.

80. ibid., pp. 13–14.

81. ibid., p. 96, n. 2; cf. pp. 316–17, 323. cf. Trotsky's indignation at the 'extreme Oriental laziness' of Stalin (*Stalin*, English edn, 1969, Vol. 1, p. 210).

82. Cited by G. A. Shepperson, 'Church and Sect in Central Africa', in *Rhodes–Livingstone Journal*, No. XXXIII (October 1963), p. 83.

83. *Boswell for the Defence*, ed. W. K. Wimsatt and F. A. Pottle (1960), p. 274.

84. A. J. Toynbee, *Between Niger and Nile* (1965), p. 39.

85. W. S. Blunt, *My Diaries* (1932 edn), p. 217.
86. J. H. Speke, *Journal of the Discovery of the Source of the Nile* (1863), p. 438 (Everyman edn).
87. ibid., p. 168.
88. E. S. Grogan and A. H. Sharp, op. cit., pp. 96, 145, 227.
89. Sir H. H. Johnston, *British Central Africa* (1897), p. 394 (3rd edn, 1906). But Uganda had legends clearly indicating 'the advent from the north of a "white", i.e. Hamitic aristocracy' (C. G. Seligman, op. cit., p. 210).
90. J. H. Speke, op. cit., p. 14.
91. ibid., p. 222.
92. ibid., p. 30; cf. p. 397.
93. G. A. Shepperson, 'Myth and Reality in Malawi' (Herskovits memorial lecture; Northwestern University, 1966), pp. 6–7; P. Worsley, op. cit., p. 25.
94. D. Livingstone, *Missionary Travels and Researches in South Africa* (1857), p. 206 (1912 edn).
95. J. H. Speke, op. cit., p. 173.
96. ibid., pp. 3–4.
97. ibid., p. 8; cf. p. 45.
98. ibid., pp. 236–9, 281, 288.
99. ibid., pp. 289, 306, 315, 328, 358.
100. ibid., pp. 334, 237.
101. ibid., pp. 212–14, 189.
102. ibid., pp. 453–4.
103. W. Baird, op. cit., p. 89.
104. Sir A. Colvin, *The Making of Egypt* (1906), p. 250 (Nelson edn).
105. W. S. Blunt, op. cit., p. 684.
106. D. Livingstone, op. cit., p. 113.
107. J. I. McNair, *Livingstone the Liberator* (1940), p. 99.
108. D. Livingstone, op. cit., p. 349.
109. I owe these details of Livingstone's interest in America to Professor G. A. Shepperson's lecture on him to the Historical Association conference at Edinburgh in April 1967.
110. G. A. Shepperson, 'The Politics of African Church Separatist Movements in British Central Africa, 1892-1916', in *Africa*, Vol. XXIV (1954), p. 237. Joseph Booth was a Baptist, who became a leading member of the Watchtower movement, often regarded by officialdom in Africa as subversive.
111. Emily Booth Langworthy, *This Africa was Mine* (Stirling, 1952), p. 27.
112. ibid., p. 124.

113. ibid., p. 15.

114. E. S. Grogan and A. H. Sharp, op. cit., p. 21.

115. E. J. Trelawney, *The Adventures of a Younger Son* (1831), p. 156 (World's Classics edn).

116. R. M. Ballantyne, *The Fugitives* (1887).

117. E. F. Knight, *Madagascar in War Time* (1896), pp. 20 ff., 92 ff.

118. W. Reade, op. cit., p. 222.

119. Olive Schreiner, *The Story of an African Farm* (1883), Chapter 5.

120. D. Livingstone, op. cit., p. 145.

121. J. C. Smuts, *Jan Christian Smuts* (1952), p. 10.

122. D. Livingstone, op. cit., p. 30.

123. ibid., p. 78.

124. J. C. Smuts, op. cit., p. 5.

125. Laurens van der Post, op. cit., Chapter 2. He had family traditions about how the Bushmen were got rid of. They seem to have survived in larger numbers than he supposed.

126. *Hansard*, 3rd Series, Vol. CCLVIII (1881), Col. 1, 652.

127. E. A. Ritter, *Shaka Zulu* (1958 edn), pp. 236, 292.

128. ibid., pp. 244, 307, 310.

129. ibid., pp. 231, 235.

130. D. Livingstone, op. cit., p. 72.

131. A. Forbes, *Memories and Studies of War and Peace* (1898), p. 43.

132. See F. W. Hirst, 'Imperialism and Finance', in *Liberalism and the Empire*, by F. W. Hirst, G. Murray and J. L. Hammond (1900).

133. There is a good deal on this theme in *Collections and Recollections* (Series 2) by the Right Hon. G. W. E. Russell (1909; first published 1902).

134. A. G. Gardiner, *The Life of Sir William Harcourt* (1923), Vol. 2, p. 367.

135. Olive Schreiner, *Trooper Peter Halkett of Mashonaland* (1897). On the conventional whitewashing of Rhodes cf. T. Ranger, 'The Last Word on Rhodes', in *Past and Present*, No. 28 (1964).

136. E. D. Morel, *The Black Man's Burden* (Manchester, ?1920), pp. 45, 52.

137. J. C. Smuts, op. cit., p. 31.

138. Campbell-Bannerman, speech on 14 June 1901 and in Parliament on 17 June. On the resulting uproar see J. A. Spender, *The Life of the Right Hon. Sir Henry Campbell-Bannerman* (1923), Vol. 1, pp. 323 ff.

139. *The Scotsman*, 4 October 1899, third leader.

140. W. S. Blunt, op. cit., p. 60.

141. Comte L. de Lichtervelde, *Leopold of the Belgians* (English edn, 1928), p. 199.

142. Sir J. Rennell Rodd, *Social and Diplomatic Memories 1884–1893* (1922), Chapter 2.

143. A. Bott, *Our Fathers, 1870–1900* (1931), p. 122.

144. This charge was repeated by E. S. Grogan in old age, in a talk on the BBC on 11 December 1964.

145. E. D. Morel, op. cit., Chapter 10.

146. W. R. Louis, *Great Britain and Germany's Lost Colonies, 1914–1919* (Oxford, 1967), pp. ix, 16.

147. E. S. Grogan and A. H. Sharp, op. cit., pp. 121, 378.

148. M. E. Townsend, *The Rise and Fall of Germany's Colonial Empire* (1930), p. 43.

149. J. C. Smuts, op. cit., pp. 149–50.

150. W. R. Louis, op. cit., p. 31.

151. A. H. H. Schnee (former Governor of E. Africa), *German Colonisation Past and Future* (English adaptation, 1926), p. 71.

152. W. H. Dawson, *Industrial Germany* (1912), p. 261.

153. E. D. Morel, op. cit., pp. 56–7.

154. E. A. Ritter, op. cit., p. 242.

155. J. I. McNair, op. cit., p. 238.

156. Jomo Kenyatta, *Kenya: the Land of Conflict* (Manchester, n.d.), pp. 5–6. When some white skins were first seen there they were thought to be the result of some pitiful disease (p. 7).

157. D. Livingstone, op. cit., p. 311.

158. See on this J. A. Hobson, *The Crisis of Liberalism* (1909), p. 243.

159. cf. J. C. Smuts, op. cit., p. 306: 'The British outlook is one of goodwill and tolerance, however misguided and over-emphasized ... The Boer, after centuries of fighting for a foothold in this country, takes a sterner view of things.'

160. C. Norton, *Opportunity in South Africa* (1948), pp. 69–70.

161. ibid., pp. 94–5.

162. B. Davidson, op. cit., p. 18.

163. H. Rider Haggard, *She* (1887). cf. the unpleasant film-star in F. Scott Fitzgerald's novel *The Last Tycoon* (1941), who 'modelled herself after one of those queens in the Tarzan comics who rule mysteriously over a nation of blacks' (Penguin edn, p. 63).

164. B. Davidson, op. cit., p. 16.

165. E. S. Grogan and A. H. Sharp, op. cit., pp. 65, 369–71.

166. F. W. Hirst, etc., op. cit., p. 135.

167. L. Ragg, *Dante Alighieri, Apostle of Freedom* (1921), p. 34.

168. H. H. Johnston, op. cit., p. 408.

169. ibid., p. 407.

170. E. S. Grogan and A. H. Sharp, op. cit., pp. 136, 337.

171. ibid., p. 251; cf. pp. 185–9.

172. ibid., pp. 356, 361, 363.

173. ibid., p. 365.

174. ibid., p. 296.

175. ibid., pp. 255–6.

176. J. S. Keltie, *The Partition of Africa* (1893), p. 514.

177. L. Silberman, *Crisis in Africa* (1947), p. 7.

178. Gilbert Murray, 'The Exploitation of Inferior Races in Ancient and Modern Times', in F. W. Hirst, etc., op. cit., p. 148.

179. See G. A. Shepperson, 'Myth and Reality in Malawi'.

180. A. Hutchinson, 'Machado', in *Modern African Stories*, ed. E. A. Komey and E. Mphahlele (1964), p. 102. My colleague the Rev. A. C. Ross, who knows Malawi well, tells me that the expression is widely current there and in South Africa; a fact of which his native Scotland may be proud.

181. See G. A. Shepperson and T. Price, *Independent African; John Chilembwe* (Edinburgh, 1958).

182. G. A. Shepperson, 'African Church Separatist Movements', p. 240.

183. See I. Geiss, article on 'Pan-Africanism', in *Journal of Contemporary History*, Vol. 4, No. 1 (1969).

184. Hilaire Belloc, *The Mercy of Allah* (1922), p. 117 (1932 edn).

185. W. R. Louis, op. cit., pp. 2–3, 94–5, 85–6.

186. A. H. H. Schnee, op. cit., p. 79.

187. W. R. Louis, op. cit., p. 137.

188. E. S. Grogan and A. H. Sharp, op. cit., p. 361.

189. John Buchan, *Prester John* (1910).

190. R. L. Stevenson, *The Strange Case of Dr Jekyll and Mr Hyde* (1886). Hyde is the lurking evil within Jekyll's personality, which assumes a separate existence and comes to dominate him.

7. THE SOUTH SEAS

Free Love on Tahiti

Remote as they were, the Pacific islands were more accessible than most of Africa or much of Asia; from the mid-eighteenth century they were coming to be known to explorers, and then, less happily, to traders, whalers, and other rough customers of many nations. Tahiti or Otaheite, with its cluster of 'Society Islands', was from the first 'the focal point of Pacific exploration'.[1] It lies roughly half-way between South America and Australia, and after an early Spanish visit was re-discovered in 1767 by the English expeditionary ship *Dolphin*. By contrast with almost every other corner of the world it gave its visitors a breathtakingly warm welcome, which was to launch Europe on some warm day-dreams about the South Seas. At first the islanders may have indulged in still rosier illusions about Europe. To a race of navigators the sight of a huge sailing-ship must have been dazzling.

Two dominant notes in the *Dolphin*'s reception were repeated many times later here and at other islands. One was the instant and boundless amiability of the women. So far as good taste is concerned, one may wonder at their being attracted to suitors emerging from the noisome, verminous ships of that age; the people of the Pacific were perpetually bathing, and their personal cleanliness drew 'peculiar attention'.[2] But the sailors' white skins, when washed sufficiently to be visible, seem to have had an appeal. As regards morality marriage is a lax affair on Tahiti to this day, and before wedlock young people do as they like. On some islands the custom prevailed of their living together in one big communal house. It is clear besides from the early narratives that the girls who came tumbling out in their canoes with open arms wanted not only love but trinkets, and iron nails presumably to hand over to their men. Polynesia was starved of metals, and jumped at this chance to enter the Iron Age – as the coming century was to be for it in more senses than one. It may be reasonable to guess that the canoe-maidens belonged to the inferior social class whose existence was not at first suspected.

Willingness to offer strangers, for a consideration, the temporary use of women was displayed by many peoples, as far apart as Eskimaux and Australian blackfellows, though what was offered was seldom as tempting as here. And the rude seafarers now moored off Tahiti's charmed shore were not unused to having women flock out in boats to greet them: the same happened at Portsmouth, except that there guineas were the love-tokens instead of nails. But the other note in the procedure was less harmonious. If Tahitians were free in offering their women, they were equally free in helping themselves to anything that could be pilfered. Very likely in their minds the two things went together. An indistinctness of ideas about *meum* and *tuum* was again something that Europeans met with in many lands, where simple folk led a semi-communal life. It always upset them; they might admire a Noble Savage, but they wanted him to have the solid bourgeois virtues as well. The note struck in reply by the *Dolphin* was a thunderous one. A light-fingered islander or two were shot, and cannon discharged. The result, as reported, was miraculous. So far from showing any resentment the Tahitians promptly 'did everything they could to be friendly and hospitable'.[3] It was just like a miniature rehearsal for the bombardment that made Japan so friendly a century later.

Legitimate commerce now flourished, nails and love exchanging briskly. When Captain Wallis was departing a 'queen' came aboard to try to dissuade him, and only left at last in a flood of tears, a Dido of the Antipodes. Next year two French ships arrived and again the eager canoes darted out, laden with girls who, if Captain Bougainville was not mistaken, were being undressed by their men or old women, to save time.[4] These sailors must have felt like Mahomedans, or Frenchmen, arriving in paradise, though they too were pestered by thievery. Captain Cook's first coming was in 1769. He was a worthy representative of his country, and of European enlightenment, a man who had risen in the service by talent, and an officer mindful of a duty to keep his men under control. Western superiority he nevertheless took for granted, and expected the 'Indians' to be equally conscious of. He wanted them not merely friendly but 'tractable and submissive'.[5] When he and his party among some natives whose language was unknown repeatedly caught the word *tut, tut,* they took for granted that this must be 'an expression of astonishment and admiration'.[6] Possibly natives who heard the same expression in English conversation interpreted it in the same way. Cook went about the ocean hoisting flags and 'taking possession' of this island or that for George III: any lands not protected by guns were for any European to take who chose. His death in the Sandwich Islands was, his lieutenant thought, the result of an error of judgement in shooting a man to disperse a hostile crowd which might otherwise not have molested him.

By 1769 the white man's prestige apparently stood very high on Tahiti, for when a party went ashore the first man who approached 'crept almost upon his hands and knees'.[7] It may be presumed that he was of low rank, and accustomed to kotow to his own grandees. Some girls were 'the most beautiful the gentlemen had ever seen'.[8] It was odd for Europe to be finding the physical type closest to its own standards of beauty here at the other end of the world. Some of the crew immediately absconded, to live with native brides, and Cook felt obliged to get them back at all costs, for fear of his whole crew melting away. But his worst embarrassment was the chronic stealing. It grew serious when a Tahitian tried to snatch a musket away, and he was shot dead. Next day trading recommenced as usual, as it did after another contretemps in which four natives were killed.

It is not easy to know how to take this apparent callousness of the Tahitians to the fate of their companions; it may suggest that they were often as summarily dealt with by their chiefs. To Cook's credit he was always ready to punish theft by his own men, who stole in a more civilized spirit. One culprit proving 'very refractory . . . thinking an Englishman had a right to plunder an Indian with impunity, was flogged out of his opinion with six additional lashes'.[9] His opinion was to be that of countless Europeans in the Pacific who had no one to teach them better.

A good family man, of unpretentious origins, Cook was un-romantic, even censorious, about Tahitian life. He could not bring himself to admire erotic dances, and he saw that women were frequently beaten, and used with great 'harshness or rather brutality', made to do all the hard work 'as if they were pack-horses'.[10] Explorers like Cook regularly inquired into the religion of those they moved among, and gathered information that must often have been garbled. There was in their Europe much piety troubled by doubt, which would be reassured by learning that 'natural religion' led in the same direction as revelation. He satisfied himself that the islanders had an instinctive belief in 'the existence of a particular providence'. On the other hand some Tahitian notions about God were 'extravagantly absurd'; they had no inkling of divine justice in the form of 'permanent punishment after death'.[11]

On one of his later visits he had with him Omai, the celebrated Tahitian who had been taken to England in 1774, and heard from him of 'human sacrifices to the Supreme Being'; on a neighbouring island he was able to study a sacrificial ceremony. When any chief felt that Heaven required an offering he simply told off a plebeian to be offered. On Omai informing them that in England the greatest man would be hanged for killing the meanest, a chief was very indignant to hear of such a monstrous custom, but the commoners 'seemed to listen with great attention'.[12] Pacific life was not often democratic; there was a recurrent pattern of societies founded on conquest, and controlled by an oligarchy of chiefs, pampered loafers with few duties except in war and few scruples about the use they made of their exorbitant rights. This must have favoured the cannibalism practised in certain island-groups and in New Zealand, another aspect of Pacific life that kept Cook from Utopian illusions. 'Few consider what a savage man is in his natural state,' he wrote.[13]

Baron Munchausen, who ran into Omai after his return home, reported that he was setting up Sunday-schools all over the ocean;[14] in fact, not surprisingly, his fabulous journey had turned his head, and to Cook's regret he behaved imprudently.[15] In London society he had been the rage, as another Tahitian youth brought to Paris five years earlier was there. He was presented to King George at Kew, and caressed by the nobility and gentry – much in the same fashion as Burns a few years later at Edinburgh. A well-mannered 'Indian' or a talented ploughman, dressed up as a gentleman, was equally a refreshing novelty. Like his compatriot in Paris, Omai was attentive to the ladies; and what invested him with a special interest, and fascinated the reading public, was the sex life of Tahiti, as seen by the West through its own spectacles. About this, the appetite for information was insatiable.[16]

Cook's news that Tahitians did not marry, but came together and separated at will,[17] might well sound like a flourish of an angelic harp to readers in lands where 'one to one was cursedly confined', and where social change and ferment were giving old clogs a fresh irksomeness. Just as China seemed to offer freedom from war and unreason, the Orient from toil and fret, the South Sea waves murmured of freedom from holy matrimony. Like China too, Tahiti afforded a meeting-ground for fantasies of an aristocracy now drooping and of a bourgeoisie ready to rise and shine. Aristocracy in its last frivolous years practised a kind of free love within its own ranks as well as ranging at large among women of the humbler classes; the bevy of female attendants round a Tahitian chief was something it could appreciate. Middle-class romantics could indulge the thought of love as free choice, not shackled by convention or convenience. Female readers in Europe doubtless had their own day-dreams about splendid brown men, free-limbed and athletic instead of paunched and bewigged. Tahitian men doubtless speculated about the white women whom in those early days they never saw. Captain Bligh discovered that they had formed a soaring idea of the beauty of English ladies from the large wooden figure-head of the *Bounty*, 'which they greatly admired'.[18]

In the great age of expansion that followed, Britain and Europe drew back from matrimonial freedom because, for one reason, it seemed the hallmark of primitive peoples. They had to pick their way between the laxity of Tahiti and the jail-like strictness, a mark of backwardness of another sort, of Turkey.

It may have struck some feminists that the South Sea husband and the Mahomedan, despite their opposite principles, were of one accord with the African in leaving their women all the hard work. In later days when Westerners were too far ahead in wealth to care about being ahead in virtue, Tahiti, or the Tahiti of the cinema, helped anew to guide them into an easier climate of love. It could not, unfortunately, lend their amorous sports an accompaniment of music or dancing on anything like a level with its own.

If the West learned something from its magic island, the island learned from the West far too much. Its degeneration was astoundingly rapid. Before the end of the eighteenth century the old handicrafts were in decay, and if estimates made about that time were anything like correct, population was fearfully reduced. Drink worked much evil, and fire-arms were given or sold indiscriminately by traders. Venereal disease, which Westerners were carrying with them about the globe, made heavy inroads. There was no close-knit family unit like those of Europe or Asia to protect the islanders against the corrosive forces they were exposed to. And the old gods had no more strength than Africa's to protect the old ways against deities with nails and bullets to bestow.

Decorum on the Lewchew Islands

There could not be a more striking contrast than between the Tahitian encounter and the earliest formal meeting of the West with another group of Pacific islands, not very far away to the north but morally in a much cooler latitude. This was the Lewchew or Ryukyu chain, stretching from the southern tip of Japan towards Formosa. It was mainly Chinese in manners, but politically a dependency of the daimyo of Satsuma, a kind of Japanese Lord of the Isles. Here courteous reserve on the one side, self-restraint on the other, brought about a more decorous intercourse than any among the atolls and lagoons of the luscious south.

In 1816, the year of Lord Amherst's mission to China, two naval vessels under Captain Maxwell were detached to reconnoitre other areas. They found Korea very forbidding, and were all the more gratified by a 'remarkably friendly' reception, with boatloads of provisions brought them as a free gift, when they arrived for a stay of several months at 'Great Loo-choo Island'[19] – known to the world today as Okinawa. With them was Basil Hall, another Scottish officer, who recorded their proceedings. In his narrative Maxwell stands out as an ideal commander for such an expedition – patient, good-humoured, receptive, and like Cook firm though kindly with his own crew. Language was as usual a difficulty, but a Chinese servant was of some use, and one officer set about learning the dialect: two Lewchewans caught his enthusiasm and started learning English. One of these, Maddera, won all hearts, and in the end turned out to be a young man of rank in disguise.[20] He picked up European ways as quickly as Omai had done, including the science of eating with knife and fork which Europe had come to reckon a *sine qua non* of civilization – and which India and all middle Asia have persistently rejected.

Hall knew how easily travellers scribbling down impressions could be misled,[21] but on many points the evidence of their eyes seemed to warrant a highly favourable verdict. Relations between men of position and commoners always appeared smooth, those between grown-ups and children delightful. No poverty or distress were discernible, scarcely a trace of disease. More astonishing yet, no weapons of any kind were ever seen, and the art of war seemed unknown.[22] Later travellers too were to comment on the good manners that prevailed.[23] Their all behaving so well to one another, as well as to strangers, must have helped to make the latter feel bound to behave well to these people. 'Our hardy seamen were softened by such gentle intercourse', and 'treated the natives at all times with the greatest consideration and kindness'.[24]

Good feeling was assisted by an entire absence of pilfering. These islanders could be allowed a free run of the two vessels, and nothing was ever missing. Yet they took the keenest interest in everything they saw, and Hall reflected, as other travellers did, that it was the most benighted nations that showed least surprise or curiosity about Western wonders.[25] One of the race; some incredulous spectators rubbed his skin with a damp cloth to make sure its colour was genuine.[26] There was another wholesome absence, of women. Prudently reluctant to test the virtue of these foreigners too far, the inhabitants made great difficulties about letting them go ashore at all, and then warnings went ahead so that women could hide from their approach, and their only glimpses were of shy creatures peeping from a safe distance.[27]

South Sea orgies were very far away. Instead there were sociable dinner-parties in Captain Maxwell's cabin, where tobacco and wine, often in propitious circumstances the best mediators between Europe and the world, could do their beneficent work. As Hall sagely remarks, 'a single whiff of tobacco-smoke often blows away much misunderstanding and ill-will', and with the aid of 'that universal interpreter, the bottle', linguistic problems melted or seemed to melt away.[28] So did the constraints of formality. When a guest clapped Dr M'Leod's cocked hat on his head the jolly doctor responded by donning his friend's hatchee-matchee.[29] Each side laughed good-humouredly at the other's peculiarities; Hall noticed that Lewchewans had fewer prejudices than some of his own shipmates 'who, in true John Bull taste, had no conception that anything could possibly be good which was not English'.[30] Before long all Europe was making up its mind that its own ways were the only rational ones; but Hall belonged to a more inquiring generation, and (like Dr M'Leod) to a Scotland whose last hundred years had been spent in learning new ways from England, as well as teaching new ideas to England.

Politically as well as morally the Lewchewans drew a precise line. All Maxwell's polite perseverance failed to penetrate the mystery of what or where the government of this land was, or how he could get in touch with it. It lay, though he could not guess this, within the sphere of Japan's self-isolation. He did not argue the point with his cannon, as others would have done (and as he himself did at Canton on the way back), but ended by being willing to take no for an answer. Today when this idyllic island where no weapon could be seen has been turned into a vast foreign military base, it may be agreed that both sides showed good sense.

White Savages and Brown in the Pacific

Tahiti was stumbling painfully into a new world. In the process of adjustment a leading part was played by the missionary, soon joining the explorer and the buccaneer as the third type of white man in the Pacific. A group sent out by the London Missionary Society reached Tahiti in 1797.[31] There were many obstacles, including the fatal beauty of the women that even men of religion were not always proof against. When progress began to be made it was by taking a hand in local politics and backing the paramount chief in his endeavours to exalt his authority over the lesser ones. 'King' Pomare may have felt the benefit of foreign prayers, and was certainly alive to the value of foreign guns. In alliance with the missionaries he regained power in 1815, and there was a series of contests between autocracy and Christianity on the one side, aristocracy and paganism on the other.

In Tahiti's demoralized condition a drastic reformation may have been essential. Darwin judged the banning of liquor wise, and took a very favourable view of the inhabitants as he saw them in 1835, by which time nearly all had a smattering of English. 'There is a mildness in the expression of their countenances which at once banishes the idea of a savage.' He and his companions attended a parliament held by Queen Pomare and her notables to debate a British claim for damages. 'I cannot sufficiently express our general surprise at the extreme good sense, the reasoning powers, moderation, candour, and prompt resolution, which were displayed on all sides.'[32] History since then has scarcely given Polynesia adequate opportunity for developing these qualities. One way in which they could be applied to new purposes was in the service of the new religion.

By now many other islands were well known, or becoming familiar. It was being realized by degrees that the Pacific contained a medley of races, at diverse levels of development, sometimes superimposed on one another by conquest; so that, as in parts of Africa, the white man's arrival only added a new top layer. Of the three main stocks, Polynesian and Melanesian and Micronesian, it was the first, scattered from Hawaii through Tahiti to New Zealand nearly five thousand miles away, that appealed most to Europeans, by its fine physique and light complexion, and sometimes though not always by the quality of its life. Everywhere skill at swimming and boating, dances and decorative arts, won admiration. This was outweighed on the whole by gloomier impressions, partly because these served to palliate European conduct, so that as in China the bad came to be as much exaggerated as originally the good had been.

Instead of troops of poetical lovers, bands of savages were now seen perpetually at war. A collection of South Sea curios in Scotland included 'a formidable-looking weapon for battering skulls. How grand they must look,' wrote a home-keeping young lady, 'a set of wild, fierce Indians with their feather crowns and their long spears in battle array.'[33] At closer quarters they were less attractive. Fijians in Melanesia had a gruesome reputation, as 'cunning, cruel, and vindictive', and 'among the vilest and most ruthless cannibals'.[34] Not always were strangers welcomed as they had been at Tahiti, and vessels that made land incautiously or were driven ashore might be attacked and plundered. Probably few sufferers paused to reflect that the same fate might have befallen them not many years before on the coast of Cornwall. Some argued that the islanders' natural disposition was revealed in such behaviour, and that any friendliness they might put on was only a mask to deceive strangers or wheedle presents out of them.[35] A more charitable view was that they were naturally amicable, and only attacked strangers when they had been molested by previous visitors.

This was the situation Herman Melville found in the Marquesas, a Polynesian group that was coming under French suzerainty when he got there in 1842. The 'Typees' of his autobiographical novel had been exasperated into 'deadly hatred' by an onslaught thirty years before, of foreigners allied with an enemy tribe, and the destruction of their villages and shrines.[36] On warships some discipline was maintained: on other ships the beastly riot of debauchery that Melville describes, when the fair mermaids flocked on board, must have been common.[37]

Seamen thus introduced to island ways might well suppose they were at liberty to make up to any women they saw, and fights and murders would be the result. More than any other region the Pacific refutes any hypothesis of race relations being improved by free sex relations. If respect and esteem between two races do not grow by daylight, they will not grow by moonlight.

Melville and a friend, disgusted with their swinish shipmates, took the risk of deserting, though the Marquesans were more warlike than most Polynesians, and were occasional cannibals. From what he saw of them in an unspoiled condition, leading an elysian life in an idyllic climate, they had nothing to gain from intercourse with white men, even with missionaries. There would be at least as much point in sending Marquesan missionaries to America, for Western life was tainted and feverish, its offspring 'the most ferocious animal on the face of the earth'.[38] As for talk of the spread of civilization, let the 'once smiling and populous Hawaiian islands, with their now diseased, starving, and dying natives answer the question'.[39] It merely meant that chiefs were screwing more tribute out of serfs in order to ruin themselves with new-fangled luxuries.[40] Something like this was happening all round the world, as Western luxuries became available to Russian landlords, Indian princes, Malay chiefs. Melville described King Kamekameha of Hawaii, or the Sandwich Islands, as 'a fat, lazy, negro-looking blockhead', 'a most inveterate dram-drinker'.[41] Native potentates of this stamp made poor representatives of their people when they went abroad and Western potentates pretended to regard them as brothers. In 1881 another Hawaiian monarch, Kalakaua, was in London, and the Germans were indignant because he was given precedence over their crown prince. The Prince of Wales put the matter in its proper perspective. 'Either the brute is a King or else he is an ordinary black nigger, and if he is not a King, why is he here at all?'[42]

A German merchant-shipping officer, A. Tetens, with a good record, came out in 1862 to the Pelew (Palau) islands in Micronesia, and unlike most rovers left an account of his experiences. He unsuspectingly went into partnership with an English scoundrel named Cheyne, whose method was to foment disputes

between clans, sell fire-arms to both sides, and set everyone against other white men in order to monopolize the trade.
He bullied and cheated, and when cornered threatened the
natives with a British warship. Finally they killed him, as he
richly deserved; a British warship did then come, and the chief
was executed.[43] All this corroborated the view that islanders
were vicious when white men made them vicious. But even in
remote, almost untouched areas life seemed to Tetens anything but idyllic. He spent eight months on Yap, whose 'king'
was an unpleasant character and whose customs repelled him,
only consoled by the charming young princess who fell madly
in love with him when he gave her a necklace of glass beads.
He made another perilous sojourn at Koror in the Pelews,
where it was the king's young sister who became his 'house-
keeper'.[44] Subsequently he operated on a bigger scale, setting
up trading posts for a firm in Germany. He wanted to be
humane, but came to believe that in dealing with savages 'an
unequivocal sternness', 'an evidence of strength', was indispensable.[45] To supply this he recruited one of the small private
armies of that age – a few Europeans, some Malays, fierce Yaps
– and with this advance-guard of civilization took part in
native wars, rather like Gulliver in the war between Lilliput
and Blefuscu. Every collision made things worse, and his once
liberal philosophy fell away.

Robert Louis Stevenson sailed from San Francisco in search
of health in 1888, three years before Gauguin came to Tahiti.
'Few men who come to the islands leave them,' he wrote, and
he never did. 'No part of the world exerts the same attractive
power upon the visitor.'[46] It is our good fortune that the South
Seas drew from Europe and America some men of genius
worthy of them, and Stevenson had the advantage of belonging
to Europe's Celtic fringe, not separated by a barrier of centuries from a primitive past. In the Marquesas, now pacified by
the French, he was at once struck by analogies with the Scottish
Highlands,[47] and like a good Lowlander saw both picturesque
and barbaric in the old order that was passing away. The
Samoans among whom he settled struck him as 'knotless,
rather flaccid' – 'like other folks, false enough, lazy enough,
not heroes, not saints – ordinary men damnably misused ...'[48]

In general, like Melville he blamed most of the friction on white men, such as those who went philandering in the Gilbert islands, 'an archipelago of fierce husbands and virtuous women'. When natives did commit outrages they usually had white men for instigators.[49]

A more cosmopolitan collection of white men gathered in the Pacific than in any other region, and kindred spirits from Asia flocked after them. Roebuck Bay, the pearl-fishing station on the west coast of Australia, came to have about four hundred whites and four thousand Asiatics. Of the two 'the coloured were a trifle the whiter', thought a tenderfoot.[50] What was heard of these white men, their ferocity and their sordid greed, anticipated the Congo events of a few years later. One evil was the kidnapping of 'Kanakas' – *men*, the term current for natives – to work, virtually as slaves, on plantations in the South Seas and in Queensland. A milder form of 'blackbirding' was to inveigle natives into binding themselves to perform a number of years of indentured labour, from which there was no escape.[51] It sounds very much like, and possibly borrowed something from, the time-honoured trickery by which rash or tipsy young men were inveigled into the British army.

On some islets a planter might establish himself as a petty despot, thanks to his guns and to the white man's fearsome reputation, and perhaps to ready-formed habits of submission to native chiefs. Some of these were taking a leaf out of the white man's book, like the king of Butaritari in the Gilbert islands where Stevenson made a stay, a beastly figure squatting among his women and rifle-armed guards, 'his nose hooked and cruel, his body overcome with sodden corpulence'.[52] Another was Tembinok', a spryer sovereign and a crack shot who kept his subjects in awe with his own rifle, and engrossed the trade of three islands.[53]

Missionary Influence and Western Rule

Protests about white misconduct multiplied. Relics of old notions of the South Seas as an Eden lingered on, and stirred self-reproach at the thought that the white race had poured its foulest scum into this happiest realm ever discovered. Tourism was inevitably coming in, aided by the pidgin English that Stevenson found in use as the lingua franca of much of the Pacific, and put some check on white violence. But the strongest voice in rousing opinion was that of the missionaries, a more important influence here than anywhere except in parts of Africa. They were controversial figures, attacked by believers in a native culture entitled to respect as well as by devotees of the divine right of the white man to do whatever he liked. They stood for root-and-branch destruction of old cults. In the earlier, more hazardous times only zealots would cross the world to harvest souls instead of profits, and there were martyrs among them like John Williams, who went out in 1816 and was killed in the New Hebrides in 1839. And the standing, and funds, that enabled them to condemn white savagery effectively were secured by condemnation of heathen savagery. They were apt, as Melville complained, to paint its darker features, even the most harmless superstitions, in the darkest possible colours. They made cannibalism appear far more widespread than it really was, until a semi-comic association of ideas between *missionary* and *cannibal* grew up. All this could have the opposite effect to what they intended, by making brutalities against natives look venial.

Their way of thinking is reflected in a novel, *Coral Island*, that must have helped to spread it among English readers. Three young castaways who have been happy on an uninhabited island discover that in the seas round about there is only an unhappy choice between foreign pirates and native savages. Their first sight of the islanders is a war-band rushing on shore from its canoes to hunt down its fleeing enemies and close a hideous massacre with a more hideous feast.[54] A native heroine appears – a stock character in such tales – a convert persecuted by a ruthless chief; she and they are saved in the nick of time when this Fijian Nero is himself suddenly converted by a *deus ex machina* in the shape of an English missionary, and the scene closes with chief and people piously burning their wooden idols.[55]

With all their lack of humour and their other deficiencies, Stevenson declared, and their wives' preoccupation with getting their flocks to wear clothes, 'the missionaries are the best and most useful whites in the Pacific'.[56] Those who vilified them were the ruffians bent on keeping the Pacific open for robbery and debauchery, wrote Bullen,[57] himself sufficiently case-hardened by life in the floating hell of an American whaling-ship. He liked 'the lovable, lazy, fascinating Kanakas' as they were, without bell, book or candle, so happy with so little, 'even a lounge in the sun'. All the same, some Wesleyans from Vau Vau who joined the ship proved highly reliable, and so well-behaved as to be 'quite a reproach to some of our half-civilized crew'.[58]

A frequent criticism was that missionaries worked through or took over the authority of native despots, and they did sometimes acquire an undue combination of spiritual and secular power. Another was that they imposed an absurdly austere code of morals, as if Eden could be turned into Geneva at one trumpet-blast. They aspired to cure sexual laxity, the taproot of evil, by cutting off all its social accompaniments, as the Kirk had endeavoured to do in Scotland, in the long run with the same lack of success. 'No song, no dance, no tobacco, no liquor, no alleviative of life – only toil and church-going',[59] wrote Stevenson, who saw Kirk discipline at close quarters on one island.

It was an over-zealous native preacher that was in charge there. An important feature of the spread of Christianity was its being largely the work of converts, which gave it from the first the same vitality as in African provinces like Nyasaland. It is likewise the clearest proof of how much social injustice existed in the old Pacific that some of its ablest men were so ready to adopt a new faith, and so rigorous in their championship of it. It may be guessed that a good many converts came, as in other mission fields, from the humbler classes on which the abuses of the old society pressed: their iconoclasm was a revolt against the chiefs and priests, their erstwhile masters. They might rationally feel, too, that their people's best chance lay in accepting Christianity and thus gaining the protection of more civilized Westerners against Western criminals.

One further charge the missions were open to was of sectarian rivalry. On various islands animosities of Protestant and

Catholic sprang up; the religious strife that Europe was leaving behind was being re-enacted outside, like a good deal of Europe's past. Discord started on Tahiti in 1835, with the advent of French Catholic missioners who were naturally looked on as poachers, and who invoked, as they always did, the active support of their government. France was in search of colonies, and Tahiti was one of many lands where real or alleged ill-usage of Catholics and their converts made a pretext for intervention. Queen Pomare appealed to Britain, and in 1843–4 a serious crisis broke out, as of Mars and Vulcan wrangling over Venus – though Pomare herself was 'a large awkward woman'.[60] Britain withdrew, and after some small-scale fighting French control was established.

Western opinion came to favour such annexations, for the same two-fold reason as in Africa: commerce scented profits, humanitarians saw in public control the only remedy against the ravages of private enterprise. In 1874 Britain took over Fiji: Gladstone called this 'sadly deluded philanthropy', but it was urged that these islands were falling into the clutches of a gang of slave traders.[61] Colonies were coming back into fashion, and three foreign countries squabbled over Samoa during Stevenson's last years. He thought the Germans were behaving badly, and wrote bitterly of a 'dance of folly and injustice and unconscious rapacity'.[62] A short time before his death in 1894 he made a speech to the chiefs, advising them to seek their country's salvation through building roads rather than armed resistance, and warned them of the fate of depopulated Scotland and Ireland.[63] In 1899 Samoa was partitioned between Germany and America. Hawaii had long since been losing any real autonomy, as foreign trade and immigrants poured in; it lost its last sovereign – another queen – in 1894, and became an American possession four years later.

In these waters, where the French flag had arrived early, an older French amiability persisted. 'The French are certainly a good-natured people, and make easy masters,' wrote Stevenson, though he heard unpleasant stories of some gendarmes;[64] no one has ever thought French policemen amiable. All Tahitians were given French citizenship in 1880 as a special compliment, to the women perhaps as much as to the men. French tutelage is described as having become strikingly popular,[65] and relations between the races have seemed to visitors in recent times very cordial. Among British administrators the young Arthur Grimble who began his career in 1913, and who was to write fascinatingly about the South Seas and their people,[66] was less typical than the one met by Somerset Maugham. This man looked at everything in life like a boy in a public school, and viewed the natives as 'wilful children, unreasonable and only just human, who must be treated without any nonsense but not unkindly'.[67]

In general, Western administration behaved moderately well in the absence of compelling motives for behaving badly; proof maybe for a philosopher that human nature is fundamentally, or fifty-one per cent, good. Sea-shells and sea-slugs gave lone traders pickings, but to Western economies were negligible. On some bigger islands there was enough room and soil for plantations, which required labour. Few islanders showed much turn for steady work, particularly work for the benefit of foreigners, who therefore considered them scandalously idle. Africans too were 'idle', yet could be got to work, and so apparently could Kanakas when similar compulsion was applied. Broadly speaking the docility of any native race set to work for the white man depended on how far it was already accustomed to be made use of by rulers or higher classes of its own. The fact that Africans and Chinese, unlike Red Indians, could survive in servitude and exile, was proof that old Africa as well as China was familiar, though in simpler ways, with exploitation of man by man.

So was the Pacific, if in yet more rudimentary forms. But it was not necessary to experiment very far with its propensity to work. Once settled rule superseded anarchy, the limited quantities of labour required could be more easily got from outside than by blackbirding. Chinese coolies were being brought into Tahiti from 1864; their dialect of pidgin-Polynesian is an odd by-product of the shuffling up of peoples that was going on. In Fiji half the population came to be Indian. This created the same tension as in many other colonies, but had the effect, as in Malaya, of making the original population look to the white ruler for protection against the immigrant.

Foreign rule brought protection at a price that sometimes seemed likely to be heavier than any of the evils it averted. The Marquesans whom Cook had called the finest race in the ocean,[68] and Stevenson thought the handsomest in the world, were in his day dwindling in numbers, and morbidly conscious of a doom hanging over them, 'a shadow of mortality awful to support'.[69] They were a dying people, said a Frenchman, and should be allowed to die peacefully.[70] Stevenson showed insight in recognizing that the warfare of the old days was a kind of sport, not often very destructive, a stimulus and outlet for energy, and that deprived of any such excitement life was growing vacuous.[71] War, dread of ghosts, bloody rituals, all the darker sides of Pacific life, were doubtless linked with the interests of ruling groups; but they may also have given it a depth and shadow, an admixture of pain without which existence is insipid, and which human beings will invent if natural conditions do not force it on them. If so, the austerities of the early converts can be reckoned as a substitute for them.

Hawaiians as a pure stock were being absorbed into an amalgam of immigrant groups. Elsewhere the island races at whose bedside Europe sat, watch in hand, did not after all prove so moribund. New generations acclimatized themselves to a new epoch, and numbers began to recover. Today some of the smaller islands are overcrowded, and there are Samoans earning a living in New Zealand. Something may none the less have really been dying, and nothing adequately took its place after the transitional years to which Christian conversion and ardour belonged. When Rupert Brooke toured the South Seas in 1913 Honolulu was 'a dreadfully American place', and Fiji, whose name breathed wildness, contained an English town with a big jail, two banks, and several dentists.[72] Away from all this the old fabled existence of the children of the sun was still wonderfully in being – 'heaven on earth, the ideal life, little work, dancing and singing and eating; naked people of incredible loveliness, perfect manners, and immense kindliness ...'[73] It horrified him to think of these oases becoming, like Hawaii, merely another annexe to a stereotyped modern world.

But he felt pessimistic about their spiritual vitality as Europeans had been not long before about their physical survival.

This paradise regained was a bowdlerized one, well suited to tourist appreciation, whose people might be doing no more than live a play-acting imitation of life. If Brooke was drawn so strongly to it, it must be said that his own class and culture in western Europe were in some ways by this time simulating life instead of living. He tore himself reluctantly away from Tahiti to return home by way of America, that abode of 'harshness and hideous sights, and ugly people, and civilization, and corruption, and bloodiness, and all evil'.[74] But this was April 1914, when his Europe was about to show itself at least as far gone as America along the road of progress. Tahiti may have deepened in him a sense of emptiness, an obscure self-disgust, shared by many of the European intelligentsia, that made them rush into the War with exultation, as a deliverance. Some Tahitians he had known may have been among those the French brought to die with them on the western front.

New Zealand and the Maoris

The Maoris or Polynesians of New Zealand, for whom a comparatively bright future was in store, in early days met with unanimous disapproval. They were among the 'inveterate savages' and cannibals of the Pacific.[75] New Zealand like Australia was not naturally fertile, but they might have lived contentedly on such plain fare as its edible fern had they not been plagued with a set of chiefs as turbulent as any European baronage, who regarded any useful activity as beneath them, and owned slaves. This must have been what kept them fighting, for prisoners could serve either as slaves or as food. 'I might have extirpated the whole race,' Cook wrote after a visit, 'for the people of each hamlet or village, by turns, applied to me to destroy the other.'[76] So little, here as in most parts of the world, did the arrival of the European induce neighbours to unite against him. One virtue Cook did grant them: they could be 'as modest and reserved in their behaviour and conversation as the most polite nations of Europe'.[77] It was the quality most often admired in the Malays; as in Europe, aristocratic rule produced good manners, if nothing better.

A chief named Shongi who was brought to England early in the next century seemed incapable of any idea except to collect weapons for his next round of fighting at home. Sixty years after Cook, Darwin read 'cunning and ferocity' in the Maori's horridly tattooed visage, and comparing him with the Tahitian declared: 'One is a savage, the other a civilized man.'[78] The single bright spot in his visit was a mission settlement, a smiling corner of England in the wilderness, all the work of ransomed Maori slaves who learned quickly under tuition. They were learning cricket too. He was moved to a 'triumphant feeling at seeing what Englishmen could effect'.[79]

But 'the greater part of the English are the very refuse of society', he added.[80] They were runagates and ruffians who were polluting so many Pacific beaches, and while missionaries endeavoured to restrain tribal warfare these men fomented it by selling guns and rum. When the British government abruptly annexed the islands in 1840 it was not to bring these pests under control, but to forestall the French. At this date there were only about three thousand whites, perhaps fifty times as many Maoris. Conciliation was therefore expedient, and in the same year the treaty of Waitangi with a number of chiefs recognized tribal land rights. This was to benefit the Maoris in later days, but as immigrants multiplied land was bought from the tribes, often by trickery, until in the South Island they lost it all.

In the North Island they fought a dogged series of wars against white encroachment, the fiercest of them between 1861 and 1871. Their tactics remained primitive, and some clans were prepared to fight for the invaders against their brethren. They had the mountains for shelter, however, and their old warlike habits stood them in good stead now; adversity generated something like a national spirit, which took shape as a fanatical religious cult, Hau-Hau. Britain tired of the expense, and in 1863, a time when the humanitarian feeling roused by the anti-slavery movement had slackened, insisted on transferring responsibility for native affairs to the colonists, who had been given self-government in 1854.[81] There was always something of Pilate washing his hands in Britain's grants of autonomy to white settlers. In this case the effect was not so bad, since the natives were not defenceless and the colonists also grew tired of the cost of fighting them, and willing to try conciliation instead of extermination.

'What will you all say if I marry a Maori?' asked Samuel Butler, a sheep-farmer on South Island from 1860 to 1863, in a letter home. 'Unfortunately there are no nice ones in this island. They all smoke and carry eels and are not in any way the charming, simple-minded innocent creatures which one might have hoped.'[82] On his voyage home he was nearly wrecked on the northern coast, where as a biographer points out he might have been eaten;[83] he would thus have gone the way of all flesh prematurely. In the less warlike south the same insidious influences were at work as in Tahiti or Hawaii. Numbers went on dwindling until near the end of the century, and by the time of the Great War only about one in twenty of the population was Maori. Nevertheless the resistance in the north had earned respect for the race, and a not undignified position in its transformed homeland: one of the careers it has found open to it is the army. Ceasing to be a menace to the colonists, Maoris became an object of interest, even pride, like the Highlanders after their defeat in 1745 to the rest of Scotland – from where many New Zealanders came – and of Britain. They were a link with the past for a new nation with no history, and lent a picturesque touch to its humdrum provincial life.

Relations between the races improved so much that New Zealand became one of the few regions where intermarriage attained, in spite of Butler, a more or less respectable status. Usually it was white men marrying brown women. Bullen got to know a Captain Gilroy who had a squad of Maori relatives by marriage on board his whaler; several of its officers and harpooners were Maoris, and white men were quite content to serve under them. They all made such a happy family that seamen deserted from English and American ships to join them.[84] Intermarriage brought with it the prospect of this small minority ceasing to exist as a separate community. Few are now left with pure blood, and their culture can scarcely achieve much independent growth. Their musical language has begun to be taught in colleges, and to be learned by other New Zealanders. It may be hoped that this will do more than provide white men with a hobby, and will help to perpetuate memory of things gone by and the leavening influence of a coming together of races, a humanizing quality of New Zealand that Australia has lacked.

Australia and the Aborigines

That undeveloped races could not adapt themselves to 'civilization', and were bound to die out, had come to be taken for granted by many pioneers. From believing this to expediting their departure to another world was no great step. Since the Spanish descent on the Caribbean islands no cleaner sweep had been made of any primitive people than was made in Tasmania. Its inhabitants, happily never numerous, stirred none of those qualms that Europeans sometimes felt about wiping out handsome Polynesians. They were very dark, having come here in fairly recent times from nearer the equator[85] – a long journey only to be exterminated – and are thought to have been still in the Old Stone Age rather than the New. Cook found them 'mild and cheerful, without reserve or jealousy of strangers', but dull and torpid.[86]

Their open-heartedness had a rude shock when British settlement started early in the nineteenth century. A high proportion of the newcomers were convicts, thanks to the system of transportation to Australia adopted when the American colonies ceased to be available. Criminals who committed fresh offences in New South Wales were got rid of to Tasmania, and the boldest of these, the cream of the cream, escaped and took to the bush. Thus the kind of ruffians who were finding their own way into the Pacific were deliberately brought here by the British government. Escaped desperadoes must have been responsible for many of the outrages that turned the Tasmanians against all white men, and set them burning farms and committing murders. Ordinary settlers who wanted them out of the way then made these acts of retaliation the pretext for wholesale reprisals.

In 1835 all the 210 survivors were rounded up and confined to an islet, where their number rapidly dwindled. Darwin was in Tasmania soon afterwards, and was well aware that 'this train of evil and its consequences originated in the infamous conduct of some of our countrymen'. As a result the colony now enjoyed 'the very great advantage of being free from a native population'.[87] Only fourteen were alive at the census of 1858, and these soon disappeared. Civilization, in whose name far more crimes have been committed than in that of Liberty, continued for some time to be represented chiefly by convicts, and, more permanently, by sheep. It was to make room for sheep that the Scottish Highlands were being cleared of their superfluous inhabitants during the same years, sometimes not much less roughly.

On the mainland a similar process was unfolding, though it failed to arrive at the symmetry of a *final solution* because the area was vaster and because a section of the old population was worth keeping as a helot class. Here too the lamentable convict system may have had a lasting effect on attitudes to natives. Nearly five thousand were sent out in one year, 1834, and when New South Wales jibbed at taking any more after 1840 they were sent farther afield, to Western Australia until 1867. From first to last 137,161 convicts were shipped out, a figure that may have been more than half as large as the total original black population. No doubt many of them were far better men than the judges who sentenced them, but even some of these might be corrupted by evil company. In colonial situations everywhere poor whites consoled themselves by looking down on coloured men, and released criminals struggling towards citizenship would be aptest of all to do so. Gangs of convicts were hired out to big farmers, and employers with fellow-countrymen working for them under armed guard would have no sympathy to spare for 'blackfellows'. Convict labour also accelerated development by providing cheap roads, and Darwin's first impression was of fine progress, but his later ones were less cheerful. Staying on a ranch worked by forty convicts, he felt that the system was poisoning the social atmosphere.[88] And warped habits of mind were likely to persist and be handed on to later comers.

White men found it far easier to look down on the inoffensive natives here than on the savage but brave and well-mannered Maoris; a fact that reveals how little Europe's instinctive judgements owed to Christianity. Australia even more than New Zealand was a country that could yield a comfortable living only to men who brought a developed technology with them. Lacking this, the aborigines had done well to survive at all, and it can be said that they had made the utmost of their meagre resources.[89] They were hunters of phenomenal skill, and white Australia has invented nothing so remarkable as the boomerang, now its plaything. Warfare was not unknown, but it was mild, if only because tribes were thinly spread. Unafraid of one another, these people were unafraid of the white man when they first sighted him, though they might be terrified of his horses or camels. He was a fellow-man; one tribe indeed is said to have hailed him as the spirit of an ancestor returned to life.[90] He, however, was very far from recognizing a brother in the blackfellow.

Near the townships, by the time of Darwin's visit, natives were earning shillings by displays of skill at spear-throwing, and they seemed to him 'far from being such utterly degraded beings as they have usually been represented'.[91] At King George Sound, the south-west tip of the continent, he and his friends in return for rice and sugar were entertained to a corroboree, a rude but merry affair.[92] So quickly does tourism make its way. Explorers groping more slowly into the vast interior likewise found most of the tribesmen they met unsuspicious and helpful. They were happy to barter fish for matches, and embarrassingly willing to offer their women, either out of the goodness of their hearts or in hope of a return. As in the Pacific, this community spirit often led to pilfering of the white man's property, which fired that sturdy individualist's resentment as much as the sharing of wives aroused his contempt.

As the natives were so poorly armed he had no need to hide his feelings. At the outset of an expedition in 1860 the leader, Burke, instructed one of his men 'if they annoyed me at all to shoot them at once'.[93] It was characteristic of the white man to be angry when black men showed fight, as they occasionally did, but to despise them when they were scared away by a few shots. In difficulties these explorers sometimes had cause to be grateful for their friendliness. Stray white men must have been looked on as helpless children, just as native peoples baffled by a new environment looked to Europeans. A man named King, alone and famishing, was kept alive for two months by the charity of a group itself badly off for food. His account, a recent writer has said, is 'one of the most moving tributes ever written to the kindness of the primitive people of Australia, and it makes perhaps the best epitaph for the now vanished blacks of Cooper's Creek'.[94]

Behind the explorers came the settlers, in the interior often big ranchers, men who had gone round the world to better themselves, and who were out of sight of any restraining authority. Unlike the relatively strong Maoris the Australian natives were not recognized as having any title to the land, and only a few were wanted for employment as stockmen: these, split off from their tribes, became the 'tame' natives, while the 'Abos' were left to fend for themselves. Women have always something to offer, and however much these settlers might look down, like the Boers, on an 'inferior' race, they had no objection to sleeping with it when nothing else was available. Today a good part of the coloured population is of mixed ancestry. Men might have no recourse when pushed off their hunting-grounds but to steal, which entitled the invaders to destroy them by bullet or poison or whatever means were quickest. Here as in other continents the argument was heard that natives had no souls, so that killing them was nothing like murder.[95] Like any killing, it could come to be viewed as a sport. Late in the century Gilbert Murray's brother stayed with a man in Queensland 'who showed him a particular bend of a river where he had once, as a jest, driven a black family, man, woman, and children, into the water among a shoal of crocodiles'.[96]

In England there were protests, by the sort of people who make a fuss about such things, and in the earlier stages they found hearers. In 1837 a parliamentary committee of which Gladstone was a member expressed horror at what was going on, as 'dreadful beyond example'.[97] Some further remonstrances were made in London and ignored by the colonists, until the grant of self-government in 1855–6 put an end to them. England reserved no right and recognized no duty to protect the native population, and was free to collect its dividends or eat its frozen mutton without looking too closely into how they were being produced. Tacit agreement was spreading in Europe with the doctrine of the men on the spot that primitive races were bound to be displaced, even to die out, very much as a large annual crop of accidents in mines and mills at home was accepted. Progress has to be paid for, preferably by someone else. Lord Rosebery, the converter or perverter of the Liberal party to imperialism, was translating this thought into the mirror-language of statesmanship when he told a responsive audience at Adelaide in 1883: 'It is on the British race ... that rest the highest hopes of those ... who seek to raise and better the patient masses of mankind.'[98]

In Australia there could be no national policy, for native affairs were not transferred to the federal government formed in 1901; and no national opinion, for the new colonists continually arriving from Europe were too busy finding their own feet to care what was happening to a few black scarecrows on the outskirts. Once more missionaries, including Lutherans, were the first to try to improve things. They had a more up-hill task even than in the Pacific islands, where at least things happened under the eyes of the world. Thinning out or reduction to serfdom of the aborigines went on into the twentieth century. There was some irony in Australia being given the mandate of German New Guinea after the Great War when Germany was deprived of all colonies on the ground of bad treatment of native peoples.

While the settlers were still spreading across their 'own' continent they had been badgering the government in London to annex Pacific islands for them, and establish a sort of Monroe Doctrine for Australasia. The impetus came from capitalists and planters who, having lost their convicts, wanted to get their hands on a supply of native labour more suitable to their requirements than the blackfellow could be. One British minister spoke of these demands as 'mere raving', and the Aborigines Protection Society denounced the seizure of Kanakas for work on Queensland plantations.[99] It was the Australian labour movement that put a stop to the import of Kanaka or Chinese or Indian coolies; but less from opposition to exploitation than from fear of competition. Many immigrants were radicals, and they built a strong organization and kept alive an ideal of social equality. But they could only do this by subscribing to their employers' ideas of racial inequality. Dislike of Asians as blacklegs turned to dislike of Asians as aliens; instead of a brotherhood of man there was growing a brotherhood of white Australia.

In New Zealand too import of Chinese coolies was restricted in 1881, in spite of protests by employers at this 'depraved pandering' to the working class.[100] Ill-will between classes was left to subside into ill-will between races, but less perniciously than in Australia where it was fostered by the atmosphere of contempt for their own native race that all white folk breathed. Australian clerks whom Rupert Brooke saw in Fiji seemed to him to be 'uncertain whether they most despised a "haw-haw Englishman" or a "dam nigger"', and he wrote them down as 'secret devil-worshippers, admirers of America'[101] – with some poetic licence, but also with some prophetic vision of an alliance of Australia with America against Asia. Yellow Peril ideas found a fertile soil, and at the peace conference in 1919 it was Australia that frustrated Japan's proposal for a statement of the principle of equal rights of all races.

Only since the Second World War has the plight of its aborigines touched a public conscience in Australia. Today it gives rise to much discussion and some heart-searching, and there is a tentative policy of bringing them into the national life. Yet even now their remaining lands are still being taken from them.[102] We have lately had a pure-blooded tribesman's narrative, as told to a white friend, of his boyhood in the old conditions, harsh but enriched by many skills and values, followed by education at a mission settlement and rise to a respectable position.[103] Whether most of his people can be brought into the fold like this, or want to be, is another matter. Their dominant feeling, white Australians sometimes regretfully say, is hatred of all white men. In a world threatened with monotonous uniformity it would be a pity if the special experience of life that such a race has had should vanish. Yet life in a protected reserve like the one at Arnhem Land must be artificial; while scattered about the country the aborigines have hardly any

badge of identity except colour to unite them: unlike the
Maoris they have no single language and oral literature, and
unlike the American Negroes they have no culture formed by
a long epoch of collective existence under white power.
Stranded uneasily between the two races, as happens in such
situations, are the half-castes.[104]

NOTES

1. R. Langdon, *Island of Love* (1960 edn), p. 38.
2. *Captain Cook's Voyages of Discovery* (Everyman edn),
p. 40.
3. R. Langdon, op. cit., p. 13.
4. ibid., p. 17.
5. *Cook's Voyages*, p. 56.
6. ibid., p. 86.
7. ibid., p. 20.
8. ibid., p. 45.
9. ibid., p. 62.
10. ibid., pp. 326, 193. Impressions varied, however; cf. p. 151, about
another island : 'The women were found to be the merriest creatures
they ever met with . . .'
11. ibid., pp. 51, 327.
12. ibid., pp. 145, 301–3.
13. ibid., p. 157.
14. E. A. Raspe, *Baron Munchausen* (1785), Sequel, Chapter 32.
15. *Cook's Voyages*, pp. 296 ff.
16. R. Langdon, op. cit., pp. 23, 26.
17. *Cook's Voyages*, p. 42.
18. Rev. T. B. Murray, *Pitcairn: the Island, the People, and the
Pastor* (1857), p. 22.
19. Captain B. Hall, *Voyage to Loo-Choo and other places in the
Eastern Seas in the Year 1816* (Edinburgh, 1826), p. 144.
20. ibid., pp. 204–5, 250–51.
21. ibid., p. 139.
22. ibid., p. 213.
23. E. Satow, 'Notes on Loochoo', in *Transactions of the Asiatic
Society of Japan*, Vol. 1 (1872–3), pp. 1 ff.
24. B. Hall, op. cit., p. 223.
25. ibid., p. 219.
26. ibid., p. 244.
27. ibid., pp. 167, 180. In near-by Korea too women proved hard

to see; an early party of visitors were thrilled by the sight of a few (W. R. Carles, *Life in Corea* (1888), p. 19).

28. B. Hall, op. cit., pp. 133, 232.
29. ibid., p. 164.
30. ibid., p. 186.
31. R. Langdon, op. cit., pp. 68 ff.
32. C. Darwin, *A Journal of Researches* (1839), pp. 384, 392–3 (1910 edn).
33. *Parties and Pleasures. The Diaries of Helen Graham, 1823–1826*, ed. J. Irvine (Edinburgh, 1957), p. 190.
34. T. B. Murray, op. cit., p. 36.
35. A. Tetens, *Among the Savages of the South Seas* (memoirs of 1862–8; English edn, Stanford University, 1958), p. 25.
36. Herman Melville, *Typee* (1846), p. 31 (Collins edn).
37. ibid., p. 18.
38. ibid., pp. 164–5.
39. ibid., p. 163.
40. ibid., p. 255, n. 1.
41. ibid., pp. 255–6.
42. S. L. Gwynne and G. M. Tuckwell, *The Life of the Right Hon. Sir Charles W. Dilke* (1917), Vol. 1, p. 415.
43. A. Tetens, op. cit., pp. 6, 28, 61–2, 103.
44. ibid., pp. 10 ff., 27 ff.
45. ibid., p. 94.
46. R. L. Stevenson, *In the South Seas* (Edinburgh, 1896), p. 10.
47. ibid., pp. 19 ff.
48. R. L. Stevenson, *Vailima Letters* (Edinburgh, 1895), pp. 249, 72.
49. R. L. Stevenson, *In the South Seas*, pp. 305, 14.
50. L. Kornitzer, *Pearls and Men* (1935), p. 96 (Penguin edn). cf. pp. 94–5, on the vicious exploitation at an earlier date of the aborigines at Roebuck Bay. The author was there about the beginning of this century.
51. Various of Jack London's *South Sea Tales* (1911), in particular 'Mowki', give lurid pictures of this racket.
52. R. L. Stevenson, *In the South Seas*, p. 250.
53. ibid., Part 5.
54. R. M. Ballantyne, *The Coral Island* (1857), Chapter 19. This was his most popular novel, and ran through innumerable editions.
55. ibid., Chapter 34.
56. R. L. Stevenson, *In the South Seas*, p. 90.
57. F. T. Bullen, *The Cruise of the 'Cachalot'* (1898), pp. 140–41 (Penguin edn). His picture of Pacific conditions is the common one of white men's crimes, orgies, and beastliness.

58. ibid., pp. 143–4.
59. R. L. Stevenson, *In the South Seas*, p. 270.
60. C. Darwin, op. cit., p. 95.
61. W. Page (ed), *Commerce and Industry, 1815–1914* (1919), Chapter 8.
62. R. L. Stevenson, *Vailima Letters*, pp. 69–70.
63. ibid., pp. 282–5.
64. R. L. Stevenson, *In the South Seas*, pp. 74–5.
65. R. Langdon, op. cit., pp. 187–9. My friend Dr W. A. L. Collier, who spent six months on Tahiti in the 1930s, felt that relations were very good. Today there is a movement for local autonomy, but still not a very strenuous one.
66. See Sir A. Grimble, *A Pattern of Islands* (1952); e.g. Chapter 6, for a balanced account of missionary zeal and iconoclasm.
67. Somerset Maugham, *A Writer's Notebook* (1949), p. 110; cf. p. 120 (Penguin edn). He is referring to 1916.
68. *Cook's Voyages*, p. 166.
69. R. L. Stevenson, *In the South Seas*, pp. 35, 38.
70. ibid., p. 74.
71. ibid., p. 48.
72. *The Collected Poems of Rupert Brooke: with a Memoir* (1918), pp. lxxxix, xc.
73. ibid., p. lxxxix.
74. ibid., p. cxvii.
75. R. L. Stevenson, *In the South Seas*, p. 99. On the Maori question generally see P. Mason, *Patterns of Dominance* (1970), p. 112 ff., with bibliographical references.
76. *Cook's Voyages*, p. 242.
77. ibid., p. 68.
78. C. Darwin, op. cit., pp. 398–9.
79. ibid., p. 403.
80. ibid., p. 407.
81. D. K. Fieldhouse, *The Colonial Empires* (1966), pp. 260–61.
82. P. Henderson, *Samuel Butler, the Incarnate Bachelor* (1953), p. 49.
83. ibid., p. 55.
84. F. T. Bullen, op. cit., pp. 222–3.
85. S. Cole, *Races of Man* (1963), p. 21.
86. *Cook's Voyages*, p. 240.
87. C. Darwin, op. cit., pp. 422–3. The disappearance of the Tasmanians has lately been studied by R. Travers in *Story of a Doomed Race* (Cassell, Australia, 1969).
88. Darwin, op. cit., pp. 408, 416, 419–20.

89. G. Parsons, *Black Chattels* (?1946), pp. 7 ff.

90. M. Durack, Foreword to C. Johnson, *Wild Cat Falling* (1965).

91. C. Darwin, op. cit., p. 410.

92. ibid., pp. 425–6.

93. A. Moorhead, *Cooper's Creek* (1963), p. 156 (1965 edn).

94. ibid., p. 141. Of another vanished tribe we read that 'they were more sinned against than sinning' – described by pioneers as '"a fine, stately, well-formed race"', and useful to them at first–'but they rapidly disappeared before the onward march of civilization ... a fact worthy of note – and, it should be added, of some reflection' (Hon. A. Morgan, 'The Darling Downs', in *Queensland Geographical Journal*, 1901–2, pp. 106–7).

95. G. Parsons, op. cit., p. 11.

96. G. Murray, 'The Exploitation of Inferior Races in Ancient and Modern Times', in F. W. Hirst, etc., *Liberalism and the Empire* (1900), p. 154. He details other horrors, of which he had family knowledge.

97. G. Parsons, op. cit., p. 10.

98. Lord Crewe, *Lord Rosebery* (1931), Vol. 1, p. 187.

99. P. Knaplund, *Gladstone's Foreign Policy* (New York, 1935), pp. 48–9, 107.

100. Persia C. Campbell, *Chinese Coolie Emigration* (1923), p. 80.

101. *The Collected Poems of Rupert Brooke*, p. xciii.

102. According to information in the *New Statesman* (London), 2 February 1968.

103. See D. Lockwood, *I, the Aboriginal* (1963). My friends Dr and Mrs J. Legge of Melbourne gave me this very interesting book, and much information.

104. C. Johnson, op. cit., is a fictionalized statement, by a young man of mixed blood, of his community's predicament.

8. LATIN AMERICA

Independence: White Man and Indian

In the eighteenth century Spain was trying to tighten its control over its transatlantic colonies, the same attempt that had lost it Holland two centuries earlier. Colonists of the higher classes, wanting more management of their own affairs and more freedom to trade with other lands, began to call themselves 'Americanos' and the officials or merchants who came out from Spain 'Peninsulares'. As a preface to rebellion there sprang up 'one of the most extraordinary systems of organized smuggling which the world ever saw',[1] mainly with Britain and, like its successor the opium trade to China, employing a swarm of well-armed coastal craft. Political separation was hastened, prematurely perhaps, by the Napoleonic occupation of Spain between 1808 and 1814. This was followed by years of sporadic effort to restore Spanish authority: ragged campaigning with small armies but much destruction, and barbarous executions or massacres on both sides, very much like a rehearsal for the Carlist civil war that soon followed in Spain. Europe as represented by Spain was showing itself at the end in the worst light. One of the heroes of independence, Páez, never spoke of Spaniards in his memoirs except as 'Goths'.[2]

Most of the ambitious leaders who emerged on the rebel side were not much less gothic, and their disorderly followers found the habit of fighting hard to shake off. Conspicuous among these were the wild irregular horsemen, the gauchos of the Argentinian pampas and the *llaneros* of the Venezuelan prairies, men with a strong tincture of Indian blood, innocent of any political prejudices but fond of plunder and ready to follow a chosen leader anywhere. There were at first vast schemes of federal union, and one in Central America lasted for some years. But distances and communications were difficult, and already under Spanish rule provinces had acquired their own personalities and indulged in border disputes. While other outgrowths of Europe like the USA, or later Australia, arrived at freedom as federations, here a whole congeries of new countries reproduced on a feebler level the State-system or international anarchy of Europe. For the most part the old boundary lines remained, enclosing what were in a recognizable sense nations. These did not often break down into smaller units, and the continent was not Balkanized nearly so far as might have been expected; but they were nations of a sort unfamiliar to Europe, all with the same official language but all with a varying proportion, some with a majority, of non-Spanish inhabitants. Wedged in among them was Brazil, the giant in size, which drifted more gently away from Portugal in the same period with one branch of the royal family settling at Rio de Janeiro as emperors.

When Basil Hall, the philosophic Lewchew voyager, arrived on this very different scene in 1820 as captain of HMS *Conway*, to cruise along the Pacific coast, it struck him that both the ardour and the benefits of Chilean independence were confined to the small upper classes.[3] But there and in other regions he saw hopeful signs of a spirit of progress kindled by the struggle: the slave trade was being abolished, slavery was under attack, bull-fights going out of fashion.[4] Idealists were few, however, and forces of inertia strong. In Chile liberalism was nipped in the bud in 1829 by a conservative *coup d'état*. Landowners with their wealth and their retainers and semi-servile peasantry, and generally having a good understanding with the Church, were coming out on top nearly everywhere, and the weak commercial and professional classes trailing behind them.

A feudal cast of society, which was being prolonged in Spain and Portugal by the backwardness of the peasant masses, was preserved more fully in Latin America where all the literate groups were cut off still more completely from their Indian masses. Population altogether was still scanty, and strung out chiefly round the coastal areas; the vast jungles of the interior were still almost unknown when the nineteenth century began, and the most absurd tales about them, picked up from Indians, were current.[5] Racially the situation might be compared with that of India after the Aryan conquest, but with the same wide diversity between one region and another. Down in the south,

Argentina had a solidly white population in the settled tracts near the sea: the plains far inland were scoured by wild Indians, and in between lay the mixed race of gauchos. In neighbouring Chile, west of the Andes, the south was still Indian, the rest a fairly complete and unusually successful amalgam of Indian and Spanish. In what had been in Spanish days the wealthier provinces farther north, Bolivia and Peru, small white ruling classes lived on the back of a degraded peasantry, Indians or, towards the coast, mestizos or half-breeds on much the same level. Brazil was the most multifarious, because its vast area included scattered tribes of many types, and because some of its provinces had the heaviest concentration of those African slaves who were to be found nearly everywhere on the continent. Every kind of cross was taking place, each with its special name. 'Mameluco' meant a blend of white and Indian, 'Cafuzo' – regarded as 'the most evilly disposed' – of Indian and Negro.[6]

English prisoners forced to work on a Spanish warship in 1745 along with some warlike Indians captured near Buenos Aires saw the Spaniards 'beat them most cruelly on the slightest pretences', until they mutinied and seized control of the ship: they held it for two hours before their 'great and daring chief' Orellana was killed.[7] A hundred years later Indian resistance had been pushed back into the interior, but there on the slowly-moving frontiers of white settlement, as on the North American prairies, it went on through the century. Thanks to the horse, multiplying and running wild on the plains, the Indian gained mobility, and a new lease of life. Bands of horsemen, riding in a great semi-circle in a cloud of dust, would descend on Argentinian outposts, drive off cattle and girls, and leave nothing else alive.[8] No wonder that when Darwin was out on the pampas he found the settlers full of praise for the army organized by the dictator Manuel Rosas; it was a wild enough horde of gauchos, but efficient in Indian warfare – 'the most just of all wars, because against barbarians', as they called it.[9] No doubt the Indians called it something very similar. Not until 1878–9 did the decisive campaigns against these Indians in the south end in their subjugation or massacre.

Easier to admire were the Araucanians of southern Chile,

whose resistance to the conquerors had inspired an epic poem by a Spaniard of the sixteenth century.[10] While the Chileans were fighting their own war of independence from Spain they were making a fresh attempt to destroy the freedom of the Araucanians, who fought as doggedly as ever. At Valdivia on the marches Darwin was impressed by the undaunted bearing of the Indians he saw, the legacy of centuries of resistance, in contrast with the ordinary native abasement.[11] It was only in the last decades of the century that more modern weapons overcame them, and their tribal lands were carved up, and even then their spirit remained unsubdued.[12] There are some resemblances between their history and that of the Maoris. Today they are probably being assimilated even more rapidly, into a Chilean population in which their blood has always been an important element.

In most areas fighting was more desultory. At the close of the nineteenth century a traveller found a massacre of Spaniards in the Orinoco basin in 1776 still remembered with dread. 'It was concerted in a most profound secrecy, and executed with that spirit of unity which the natives of America, skilled in concealing their hostile passions, well know how to practise.'[13] But so sinister an atmosphere was unusual. Warlike tribes of the tropical interior were more a menace to peaceful Indian settlements than to the white men gradually making their way inland along the river channels, who seem as a rule to have been attacked only when they invited trouble. H. W. Bates the naturalist found that 'the first impulse of the Brazilian red-man is to respect Europeans', if they did not meddle with him, and that episodes of violence were often provoked by lawless 'traders',[14] the same kind of men who made so many Pacific islands too hot to hold them.

Very different from these migrant hunters were the stationary masses of Indians, long since subdued by the Spaniards, to be found all over Mexico and Central America and a broad western fringe of the southern land mass, where there was more upland and less jungle than in most of Brazil, and across it through Bolivia to Paraguay. Here there were analogies with those parts of Africa where white and coloured populations lived side by side, or rather one on top of the other, in the days before racial segregation came in. As in Africa also, some of the larger Indian nationalities had been cut up by the white man's frontiers, meaningless to them, and the continent was a palimpsest with the boundary-lines of two ages superimposed. They kept their own languages, some of them remarkably widespread, notably the Quechua of the vanished Inca empire and the Guaraní of Paraguay and its borderlands.

To the white man there was a more than Oriental impenetrability in these subject races, and a fatalistic apathy that must have been induced in them by ordeals of recent centuries was frequently regarded as an innate Amerindian quality. They might seem created by Providence on purpose to serve as hewers of wood and drawers of water for the white man, though incapable of learning many new kinds of service. 'Nine tenths of the population,' said a consular report from an interior province of the Argentine, 'are of Peruvian origin and speak only the Quichoa language and possess all the docility and passive obedience which now characterizes and indeed always did characterize the race.'[15] Whatever their original nature may have been, they had been broken in by Inca rule and were ready for the yoke before the Spaniards arrived; but for this, the first epoch of Spanish rule could scarcely have been (like the first epoch of British rule in Bengal) so atrocious. Their subjugation was completed by the new religion imposed on them. Unaccompanied by any appreciable material advance, this had a sterilizing effect, reducing them to a sort of infantilism. There was something symbolic of their enslavement in the annual procession at Chorrillos in Peru in honour of the patron saint, where the hero of the day was the Indian who could carry the huge wooden crucifix on his back longest.[16]

It was in Paraguay that the 'infantilizing' of the native masses had gone further than anywhere else in Latin America, possibly in the history of the world. On the Jesuit 'Reductions' or settlements they were protected from the ordinary rapacious colonists, drilled into an orderly communal life, and employed to produce a revenue for the Order. They were kept 'in such submission', the Jesuit-hating Portuguese dictator Pombal wrote to the Pope in 1759, 'as had never been acquired over rational creatures'.[17] Before Spanish rule ended the Jesuits had been ousted, but the habit of unquestioning obedience to paternal authority they had instilled was preserved by Paraguay's isolation. Thanks to this conditioning the country was predestined to fall under the series of dictators who first built it up and then destroyed it. C. A. López, the second of these, got his brother made bishop, thus restoring in a new form the old dovetailing of religion and authority. In neighbouring Bolivia after its defeat by Chile in 1879 the discredited government was heard calling on the Church 'to use its influence with the Indians in order to inspire them with patriotic feelings',[18] in other words to get them to submit quietly to further levies for the army.

Towards the end of the Spanish régime there were Indian rebellions in the old settled areas, the fiercest in Peru. There the leader was a mestizo, a man of some substance, who professed to be attacking only administrative injustice but who by taking the old Inca name of Tupac Amaru appealed to Indian memories of the past. Spain was roused into taking some measures to protect the natives against their white masters, whereas Creole officials were 'notoriously harsh' in their attitude to the Indians.[19] For a home government to try to protect a native population, however half-heartedly, is always the surest way to stir disaffection among colonists. Spanish authority came to be resented by the white settlers for its better as well as its worse qualities, even if charges against it of cruelty to natives were added hypocritically to other grounds for shaking it off.

During the wars of independence and the feuds that followed, Indians mostly failed to seize their opportunity, or assert themselves as a distinct force. In some countries like Peru with a dense native population, fear of setting Indians a bad example may have helped to keep the ruling minority fairly quiet. When San Martín came from Chile to liberate a hesitant Peru and his lieutenants recruited bands of Indians, 'savage and undisciplined troops', the wealthier citizens of Lima were highly apprehensive of these allies.[20] Far away from any towns Indians could be more safely employed. Páez in Venezuela recruited a wild troop armed with bows and arrows, who when well primed with brandy fought fiercely.[21] Spanish generals also mobilized Indians to swell their scanty ranks, chiefly with infantry. But on both sides the gaucho horseman, with Indian blood but no Indian consciousness, was a more important factor.

Independent America's false dawn of idealism and progress included some reforms for Indians as well as white men. Burdens like the special poll-tax many of them had paid and the labour services they owed were abolished by several of the new régimes. But this was the impulse, partly perhaps the prudence, of the moment, and like Negro emancipation in the USA was not followed up by constructive programmes to better the condition of the Indians and draw them into real citizenship. A century later Bryce was to note the absence of any civic bond between the races, and the fact that in the once-imperial Inca city of Cuzco there was scarcely an Indian of higher status than a labourer.[22]

In general the old race was being shifted away from the coasts into the sluggish interior, as new immigrants and foreign techniques came in to replace it. This saved it from some forms of exploitation, but left it to stagnate in backwater towns like La Paz, or antediluvian villages, or an semi-feudal estates. Indians had little part to play in the urban life now expanding round the coasts, but could only drift into it as casual labourers or paupers. Even before independence a demoralized sediment of mixed race was collecting in the towns. This went on, and contact with the often more rebellious African might stir a mutinous spirit, even if it could only express itself in occasional rioting and looting. Dread of this sort of mob outbreak, more than of the rural Indian mass, was a permanent feature of South American life. When the Spanish authorities were forced to withdraw from Lima in 1821 Captain Hall found the citizens in panic fear of a slave rising within the capital, as well as of attack by San Martín's Indian auxiliaries from outside.[23] There was extensive looting when Lima fell to the Chileans in 1881, and the British legation was afraid that Chilean withdrawal would leave the city again 'to the mercy of the communistic mob'.[24]

Docility and endurance made peasant Indians good cannon-fodder, and in countries that had plenty of them they were being saddled with a new burden, conscription. Armies like the

Peruvian had a marked resemblance to colonial forces raised by conscription. This 'blood-tax' was a worse misery for them than any other they had suffered since the days of forced labour in the silver-mines. It could be said by way of palliation that army service was the only school most of these benighted creatures could ever enter, and gave them some sort of acquaintance with the modern world – even if it often expedited their departure from it. The army was also a ladder by which an individual could sometimes rise, aided by the fact that service was less attractive to white men than an officer's career in Europe. In 1865 we hear of a Peruvian general being entrusted with the command against a rebellion because of his influence with the Indians who formed the bulk of the rank and file. 'From his appearance he seems to have himself a good deal of Indian blood, – and therefore probably the perseverance and tenacity, especially in soldiery, of the indigenous Peruvians.'[25] War and politics going as closely together as they did in South America, such a man could attain a position in the State, like the Andrés Santa Cruz who for a short time united Peru with Bolivia. But these men rose as individuals, not as leaders of their people, whom their removal may have left even more inert.

Mexico was the only one of the mainly Indian or mixed countries (the purely white population at the start of this century was reckoned no more than a fifth of the total) where Indian or mestizo leaders rose to prominence during the independence struggle.[26] It was also the only one where the superficial change brought by independence was followed by a second, more thorough-going revolution, long drawn out and with many reversals but leading by degrees towards at least a partial social transformation. Its greatest leader, Benito Juárez, president from 1858, who defied both reactionary opposition and foreign intervention, was an Indian, a sort of Mexican Toussaint. Today Mexico can take pride in regarding itself as a nation both modern and truly American, with roots far older than the Conquest, not a mere extension of Europe. Cortés remains a Spanish hero, he is no longer a hero for Mexico.

Imitation Europe or New World ?

A good many foreigners took part in the wars of independence, chiefly British: enthusiasts such as Lord Cochrane who went out in 1818 to organize a Chilean fleet, like Byron a few years later going to Greece, and adventurers or mercenaries including a flock of English and Irish soldiers demobilized in 1815. Hall was captivated at first, as many liberals at home in Europe were, by the spectacle of 'such a prodigious political and moral experiment' as the continent seemed to display;[27] the romantic chiefs of the freedom movement, particularly San Martín, fascinated him. But like Byron he discovered that such patriotic struggles were more impressive at a distance than at close range, where 'the fictitious representation of pure, disinterested, public spirit' was marred by a thousand pettinesses.[28] Out of these wars an opinion was already forming that Latin Americans were a pretentious, undisciplined, shiftless lot, alternating between ferocity and cowardice.

When the continent was still closed against them Britons had occasionally thought that Indian discontent might be turned to good account. Planning an attack on the Isthmus in 1741 Commodore Anson hoped for support from local Indians 'who were greatly disposed in our favour'.[29] Subsequently such hopes were fixed on the white colonists instead. When the British occupied Buenos Aires in 1806 they took pains to assure the citizens that there was no intention either of liberating their African slaves or of playing on Indian thirst for revenge.[30] Europeans had no wish to see the non-white races fighting for freedom; they themselves were not yet ready to renounce slavery. Conservative Europe had equally little sympathy with the colonists, and there was talk among several governments, headed by Tsarist Russia, about 1820 of a combined expedition across the Atlantic to help the King of Spain to quell them. Britain was to the fore in frustrating this design. But even Britons might be illiberal enough to think white rebels little better than their native drudges. 'Tom Cringle' considered Latin America a better place before it ever felt 'the pestilent breath of European liberalism' : Bolívar ought to have known that despotism was 'your only government for the savages he had at one time dignified with the name of fellow-patriots'.[31]Republicanism sprouting in this new soil had an unpleasantly Yankee and democratical look. Europe, and England with it, would have had a more indulgent eye for the new nations if they had felt their nakedness, like Adam and Eve, and covered it with decent monarchical institutions. Preferably they should have borrowed pedigree princes from Europe, as Brazil did, but even crowned upstarts would have been better than elected presidents. Various individuals did try to crown themselves, like Itúrbide in Mexico, but all failed. Balkan experience later in the century scarcely suggests that a supply of monarchs, however authentic, would have done Spanish America much good, except to soften European disapproval.

In 1806 London was all agog at the news from Buenos Aires. 'Nothing less than the conquest of South America was envisaged.'[32] This bubble was quickly pricked, but after the wars of independence the idea revived in the less extravagant form of a British political leadership, or guardianship. Even now there was a reluctance to think of the New World as anything like an equal, or its governments (with the grudging exception as time went on of the one at Washington) as really responsible entities. The nationalism that Europe admired in itself was only an affectation in outsiders, or a superfluous luxury. In 1828 a British envoy cautioned the government of Argentina against 'the doctrine set up by some crude theorists "that America ought to have a political existence separate from the political existence of Europe"': economic ties would always bind them together, and Europe would always know how to protect its interests and assert its rights.[33] In Paris the Hispanic scholar Mazade, reviewing a book about the gauchos, treated them as more or less typical of the whole population, and exclaimed against the *Americanism* that some South American writers were beginning to canvass: word and idea were equally repulsive, an aberration of raw, rootless peoples, '*illusion d'un patriotisme étroit, inintelligent et brutal!*'[34] They ought not in short to look for any identity of their own, but be content to see their hemisphere as an outpost or a dependency of the Old World.

Endless quarrels among the republics and faction-fights within many of them lent colour to thinking of this kind. Meanwhile for four decades after Waterloo Europe was astonishingly peaceable at home, and so had some right to lecture these rowdy pupils on their foolish bickerings. An official British memorandum of 1841 deplored the disturbances and lawlessness that were paralysing trade or imperilling property over a great part of Latin America: even in relatively stable Brazil there was 'great insecurity for our merchants'. The writer put forward a far-reaching scheme of intervention by Britain to bring order out of chaos. An expert on Colombia agreed that the confusion there might well be remedied by judicious British action, and another who was consulted believed that several countries were disposed 'to look up to England ... in their opinion the only Power sufficiently interested in their welfare, capable of affording them protection against unjust aggression on the part of their neighbours; and to give them honest advice against the effects of their own errors and wilfulness'. Britain should above all teach them 'the important truth, that honesty is the best policy'.[35]

In 1842 intervention in the River Plate estuary to protect Montevideo from the Argentinian dictator Rosas seemed to herald the adoption of an active policy. It saved the city in the nick of time, Proconsul Dale reported, from 'the cruel, grasping despot of Buenos Aires', whose myrmidons would have 'cut throats right and left'. 'I glory more than ever in the name of Englishman ...'[36] France was acting with Britain, and it was only in partnership that these two could hope to police South America effectively. Had they been better friends they might have drawn other interested European governments along with them and established something like a joint tutelage, less burdensome very likely in the long run than the one exercised in the next century by the USA, a single Power closer at hand and more overwhelming.

There remained a possibility of Latin America becoming civilized, or Europeanized, without political pressure, simply by the flow of goods and ideas from Europe accompanied by troops of immigrants. Montevideo was for a time a European enclave, with an actual majority of Frenchmen, Italians, or

Britons in its population. But this was a small place, and in general immigration altered the pattern less than it was expected to do. Settlers from the more advanced parts of Europe tended to form compact groups and keep to themselves, like the German community in Brazil, 400,000 strong by 1914 and still leading as German a life as the Germans settled since Catherine the Great's time on the Volga. Newcomers from southern Europe, who were far more numerous, were on the contrary absorbed into their new environment only too readily. They might be accustomed to conditions not much less primitive, and some brought reactionary political ideas with them. A battalion of Carlists, defeated in the Spanish civil war just ended, took part in the assault on Montevideo,[37] while Garibaldi and his redshirts took part in the defence. Most of the steady trickle of Portuguese into Brazil consisted of illiterate peasants who seemed to Bates as simple-minded and superstitious as the Indians they settled among.[38] Italians and Irish were to be found everywhere, and Catholicism helped to merge them with the older white population; individuals who climbed into the ruling circles of the more feudal countries like Peru, as a good many with humble beginnings in Europe did, were absorbed likewise into their aristocratic mode of living. On the whole the continent South-Americanized its immigrants instead of being Europeanized by them.

Englishmen left it mostly to Irishmen to settle in the country, but they took the lead in the floating community of foreign businessmen, who in many ways exerted more influence than the settlers. They congregated in the big ports, and Buenos Aires especially grew, after the fall of Rosas, into a cosmopolitan metropolis, with an English as well as Spanish Press, in which a mineral-water advertisement might wind up impartially: '*Viva el Presidente!* God save the Queen! Hail Colombia!'[39] It was from the foreign residents (as from those at Shanghai) that visitors and the public in Europe acquired most of their impressions. These were as a rule highly unfavourable. Yet the wealthier classes with whom foreigners came chiefly in contact, and with whom they shared a nervous distrust of the local 'mob', could not be accused of failing to appreciate European models. In 1877 an Italian tragedian named Rossi was giving applauded performances of Shakespeare at Lima.[40] More often European culture meant European costume. One of the first, contradictory impulses of independence was to abandon traditional dress: Chilean ladies cast off their old, 'almost savage costumes', men their 'slovenly cloaks'.[41] Fashion could induce rich Brazilians to grunt and sweat under a load of furs or frock-coats in the tropical sun. In such attire white men with no vital spark of European culture, or without pure European ancestry, could carry themselves as legitimate sons of Europe.

These were fopperies that could only make an isolated upper class still more alien to its own fellow-countrymen. Yet the ideal of a Europeanizing of South America could appeal in the earlier decades of independence to some of its best minds. To this mood Sarmiento, the Argentinian writer, polymath, statesman, gave the most uncompromising expression.[42] Born in 1811 at the foot of the Andes, in the remotest hinterland of Argentina, he grew up glimpsing the light of Europe as it were very far away at the end of a dark tunnel. He came naturally enough to picture Civilization and Barbarism as two things antithetical instead of interwoven, and this made the dominant image of his intellectual life. It translated itself all too easily into racial terms. Wild frontier Indians, or the gaucho hordes welded by Rosas into the force that enabled him to set up his terroristic régime at Buenos Aires, were barbarism : white men with their European languages and books were civilization, and the way to expand this was not to educate backward peoples but to push them out of the way. Visiting Algeria during the French conquest he felt no qualms about the harsh measures explained to him by Marshal Bugeaud;[43] Moors, like his own Indians, were savages who could not be reclaimed, only driven into the desert where they could do no harm except to one another. In most parts of Argentina Indians were few enough to make this programme of the survival of the fittest race practicable; for most of Latin America it made no sense.

If aboriginal Americans were irreclaimable, their white successors did not always appear to Sarmiento much better. They came from an Iberia itself doomed to stagnation and tainted by a barbarian ancestry, half Moorish or African.[44] In the bitterness of exile from his native land he sometimes wrote as if he – like Tom Cringle – believed independence had done more harm than good. Spain had been a link with European civilization, though it selfishly tried to keep its colonies shut off from other, more enlightened European centres. He wanted to see French, English, German books, ideas, goods, flowing in, and immigrants with them, a strong dose of new blood to revitalize a degenerate stock. When in Europe he wrote a pamphlet urging Germans to go to South instead of North America. He taught himself English, devoured English literature, wrote an article entitled 'England for ever!'[45]

Such tributes were flattering, and Europe then, as the US now, liked flattery laid on with a trowel; it was quite content to be the world's fountain of honour. Disillusionments were bound to come on both sides. Sarmiento himself was quick to discover that western Europe did not stand on such a pinnacle of perfection as he had fancied. His tour was made in 1846–7, just before the 1848 revolutions whose tremors he already detected. He saw Italy divided and downtrodden. In the industrial districts of England and other countries he saw wretched poverty and class bitterness. France, whose culture held most charm for Latin Americans, disappointed him the most; and having always thought of Spain as a second-rate part of Europe he was irked to find Spaniards looking down their noses at South America. He liked the US and its democracy better, though there too he was aware of many evils, from slavery downward.[46]

Sarmiento turned away, as others were doing, towards the thought of South America as a new world with a soul of its own to discover. Resentment at Europe's airs of superiority strengthened this. A British representative reported indignation in Chile because foreign residents were accused of thinking that 'the people of South America, like the Blacks, are to be governed only by the lash', that they were 'semi-barbarians'.[47] There was dislike too of the economic stranglehold that these outsiders were clearly bent on acquiring. A German report of 1876 spoke of 'extraordinary animosity' against powerful British banks that were crushing native rivals and threatening to engross all the business.[48] At Ciudad-Bolívar, 240 miles up the

Orinoco, most of the leading firms were German or Corsican, and 'monopolised the trade of this part of Venezuela'.[49] 'We have the *whole of Peru Boots and Breeches,*' said a complacent businessman from North America, brother of the great railway-contractor Meiggs.[50]

Of all jolts to Latin American feeling the sharpest came from foreign use or misuse of superior armed strength. France's quarrel with Rosas in 1838 and blockade of the River Plate only fortified his power by rallying national sentiment round him. There was little to choose here between Europe and the United States, which in 1846 went to war with Mexico and annexed New Mexico and California. In the 1860s there was the Anglo-French-Spanish pressure on Mexico leading to the disguised attempt of Napoleon III to get control of the country. In 1864 Spain, still hankering for any bits of its old empire it might get back, picked a quarrel with Peru and Chile and occupied Peru's valuable Chincha islands. This event revived advocacy of closer ties among the republics, not for mutual protection alone. It had been part of the idealism of the first era of independence – Africa years later was to feel a similar aspiration – to think of making the New World a new one morally as well as geographically, free from the old plagues of strife and aggression. Since the breakdown of the early projects of federation strife had been only too common, and made it easier for foreign States to interfere and bully. It was high time for a fresh effort at creating a new international order, not merely equalling that of Europe but going beyond it.

A conference met at Lima, though not many governments were represented; treaties of arbitration and friendship were drafted, and a joint protest was addressed to the Spanish admiral. Having been left (in the Spanish style) without any instructions, he fell back on rhetoric about the bonds between South America and Spain – Spain, that with a handful of men had opened a whole hemisphere and bequeathed to it two cornerstones for great nations, Catholicism and love of liberty...[51] Other Europeans watched the conference with a scepticism tinged with dislike. As soon as this issue was settled, the British representative at Lima thought, the republics 'would probably soon relapse into their former indifference towards each other', and he like Mazade disliked as anti-European the outlook expressed in the term, still gaining currency, *Americanismo*.[52]

Subsequent events warranted his scepticism. At the Lima Congress the Argentinian spokesman was Sarmiento, and he took a vigorous anti-Spanish line. But his president, Mitre, did not share his enthusiasm for South American unity; to his way of thinking these republics were not sisters but rivals, like all States in a competitive world where the devil took the hindmost. Before long Sarmiento was coming round to much the same opinion, and from having been first a citizen of the world, and then of Latin America, was turning into an Argentinian patriot. War helped to fan his ardour. From the Crimean War of 1854 Europe had been embarking on a new round of conflicts, and the example was contagious. In 1865 war broke out between small Paraguay and a vast combination of Brazil, Uruguay and Argentina, and when Sarmiento became president of Argentina in 1868 he inherited this conflict and fought it to its fearful end, the almost complete destruction of the male population of Paraguay.[53]

In 1879, eight years after the German annexation of Alsace-Lorraine, the War of the Pacific broke out; Chile defeated Bolivia and Peru and annexed the provinces containing their nitrates and guano, in demand in Europe as fertilizers and enveloped in an odour of international high finance nearly as strong as their own.[54] Thoughts of Latin American fraternity were roused afresh, but chiefly, as was to be expected, on the beaten side. Peruvians and Bolivians expatiated on the danger of the continent sliding into the same fatal system of armaments, alliances, conquests, as unhappy Europe, caught in 'a circle of iron from which she cannot escape': the New World ought to be setting an example to the Old, as intelligent Europeans were praying it would do, instead of slavishly imitating it.[55] These noble precepts fell on deaf Chilean ears, and proposals of mediation by neighbour countries came to nothing.

Debate continued about how Latin America might achieve harmony, and this can be thought of as part of the wider current of ideas from which the League of Nations was to come. But there was also an opposite inclination to borrow the ideology of power that was growing fashionable in Europe. A Peruvian writer expressed reluctant admiration for Chile as a conquering nation like Germany, and subscibed to the classification of peoples as 'virile' or 'decadent'.[56]

Spanish America through European Eyes

From the distance of Europe all Latin America was apt to look much the same, and much oftener decadent than virile. Argentina and Uruguay stood somewhat apart, as racially the whitest countries and commercially the best customers. Little Uruguay enjoyed a place in European esteem from the first. 'The Monte Vidian republic,' an English visitor wrote in 1842, 'is making unparalleled progress in wealth and political importance'; he thought it might well become the leader of the whole region.[57] Argentina was much slower to win confidence. As late as 1874 the British minister answered an inquiry from the Emigration Commissioners with a gloomy 'Memorandum on the insecurity of life and property in the Argentine Confederation'.[58] It was in the 1880s and 1890s that the big expansion of British enterprise took place. All industry was passing into foreign, mostly British hands, a reporter of *The Times* wrote. He went on to predict 'a new and more energetic race of Argentines', predominantly of Anglo-Saxon blood but Spanish-speaking and anti-British: 'the children of English parentage born in Spanish-speaking countries are almost invariably passionately fond of their native soil'.[59] One of the closest economic relationships that have ever linked a nation in Europe with one outside was developing. Their indifference to each other in our own day testifies how little real feeling such a relationship leaves behind it.

Paraguay stood apart in an opposite way, as the most Indian of all the countries, and for a long time the most inaccessible. At the time when Spanish rule was ending it was believed to contain much wealth awaiting development, and its people were understood to be – as a US survey described them in 1818 – peaceful, docile, industrious.[60] But four years before this the reign of the first dictator, Dr Francia, had begun, and after a plot against him in 1820 he enforced the strictest isolationism. It gave rise to much curiosity about this forbidden land, and a prevalent belief that Francia was a monster exercising a reign of terror.[61] He was reducing the country to 'desolation and slavery', two Scots who had been there wrote.[62] Two Swiss who had been interned there were willing to admit that its 'mild, hospitable, and generous' people had some things to thank their terrible master for.[63] Modern historians have given him some credit for saving Paraguay from being swallowed up by its bigger neighbours. He treasured a library of three hundred books, including a Rousseau, and perhaps liked to think of his realm as a sequestered Arcadia. South Americans were restless, frivolous creatures, he declared, whom he alone knew how to govern.[64]

A US diplomat who was there after the opening of Paraguay, looking back on Francia's regimented economy through the spectacles of free enterprise, asserted that it made the country 'poorer and more ignorant, less frank and hospitable, and less fit for self-government'.[65] A judicious Paraguayan historian points to the essential fact: the régime was virtually one of State socialism, with all important commercial products such as tobacco and *maté* tea government monopolies; and it was based on a largely communal system of land-holding, far better for the cultivators than the big private estates that replaced it after Paraguay's defeat. And this 'socialism' was part of what incited the three enemy countries against Paraguay in the war provoked, no doubt, in good measure by the reckless conduct of Solano López, last and worst of the three dictators. Foreign capitalism, with the British minister at Buenos Aires as one of its spokesmen, warmly approved the crusade, and when it was over the syndicates fell hungrily on the prostrate country.[66]

President Sarmiento, erstwhile Utopian socialist, tried to believe that he was waging war not against peasant socialism but against some nameless evil, some lurking poison in South America's blood that made it prone to 'Asiatic despotism', or dictatorship, and recalcitrant to civilization.[67] It was a race war as well as a social war, and Sarmiento was fighting over again the conflict of Civilization and Barbarism that haunted his mind in youth. He was still obsessed with the racial problem when in old age he wrote his last book, rambling and bewildering though with flashes of insight. He complained that some of the bigger Indian peoples were too fierce and intractable, others too crouching and spiritless, all equally unfit for rational political life.[68] Possibly ages of war and empire had, indeed, eliminated intermediate types of character and left too little of a psychological mean between the two extremes, not only here in the Americas but in other realms such as India.

Chile scored better marks. Its land-owning oligarchy, controlling both economic and political life, maintained an unusually stable system as well as a parliamentary façade, while its long coastline and commercial opportunities kept it from standing still. It was an amiable habit of Europe's to be prepared to recognize affinities between good qualities (seldom bad ones) in outsiders and in itself; and Englishmen who admired the solid Chilean governing class were obliquely complimenting themselves on their own. An Anglophil diplomat from Washington bracketed the two: 'Like the English aristocracy that of Chile is truly representative, wielding its power with a keen sense of its responsibility to the nation.'[69] To complete the resemblance, the Chilean *inquilino* like the English farm-labourer was very poor and very firmly taught his place.

The ability of Chile's leaders in 1879 to plan and win a profitable war gave them a further strong claim on European respect. Their triumphs in the War of the Pacific earned them the title of 'the Prussians of South America', another example of how Europe liked to pigeonhole strangers. Their naval commander Patricio Lynch was accused of callous attacks on the Peruvian coast, in which foreign property suffered; but British critics might have recollected that besides his Irish origins Lynch had spent eight years in the British navy and served in the first Opium War. Chileans retorted that Britain and France had behaved worse when they bombarded Nagasaki and Kagoshima.[70] Mixed with respect for Chile after the war was a feeling, shared by Europeans with North Americans, that this small republic's success had gone to its head, that it was getting too big for its boots. A British envoy at Santiago who had a strong distaste for South America at large and Chile in particular drew a satirical picture of an election in progress. There was not a little loss of life', he reported, 'revolvers, knives, and stones, having been freely used', while each side affected 'the utmost moral indignation' at the other's behaviour; really there was nothing to choose between them.[71] His French colleague commented on the election in the same spirit. Which party won mattered little, he wrote, so far as foreign interests were concerned, for all Chileans had the same defiant attitude towards Europe, and the same ambition – '*la formation d'un grand empire maritime sur le Pacifique*'. They disliked France, and their newspapers dwelt maliciously on any breaches of public order in Paris. It took him three months to get any satisfaction over a scandalous case of ill-treatment of a French immigrant family.[72]

Peru displayed to perfection a degenerate élite battening on a helpless mass, mostly Indian or mestizo, and chronically squabbling over the spoils of office. In such a ruling class the surviving aristocracies of Europe, which prided themselves on moving with the times and were compelled to move by middle-class criticism, saw a disgusting parody of themselves, such as the Prince of Wales saw in the King of Hawaii. These Peruvians had an ever-open hand for bribes, which a foreign businessman like Meiggs learned to supply ungrudgingly. 'By that means,' as his biographer says, 'he managed the men who managed Peru.'[73] Wealth from guano intensified corruption and profligacy, and when the Chilean attack came the ruling class made a sorry showing. Its other main prop, its sugar-plantations, had been built on Negro labour: the Indians, however downtrodden, had a stubbornness of their own and were less easily drilled into labourers than into soldiers. When African slaves ceased to be available some Hawaiians were kidnapped and tried out, but they all disobligingly died. Chinese coolies were then imported. A long train of abuses gave the traffic an evil name, and the government's half-hearted efforts to check them were of no avail against the planters. Most of the coolies were shipped out from Macao, so the Portuguese felt some responsibility. Their envoy at Lima protested that most planters looked upon a labourer 'not as a man, but as an instrument and less than a slave', and that in the city could be seen an 'immense number of Chinese mutilated in the service of their masters and abandoned by them'.[74] Yet here too many Chinese, inured to the harsh demands of life in their own country, managed to survive their contract term and set up as traders or shopkeepers; though here as in their other new homes they were in danger of mob violence at any breakdown of order. They were intelligent, an Englishman wrote, and those who prospered were more civilized and better company than his own brandy-swilling compatriots.[75] As for the native Indian, he according to this witness had been too lazy to be useful ever since he was freed from the old poll-tax. 'He is perhaps the slyest of animals – more sly than a fox, more obstinate than an English mule, and as timid as a squirrel.'[76]

Neighbouring Bolivia, seen through respectable European eyes, was 'little removed from a state of semi-barbarism'.[77] Clearly this impression was coloured by the fact of Bolivia being a 'native State', with only a small white upper class, one that could scarcely pass muster – as Peru's by some stretch of language might – as an aristocracy. Political life was a travesty, partly because the supply of cheap Indian manpower was an invitation to disgruntled politicians to take to arms. Between 1826 and 1898 there were sixty army risings and ten new Constitutions.[78] Colombia and Ecuador too were easy to dismiss as beyond the pale. Their scanty population was mostly Indian or mixed, and their capitals like Bolivia's were high up in the mountains. Whymper the mountaineer, who traversed Ecuador about 1880, agreed with other observers that its people had an 'inveterate habit of procrastination, and use of the word *mañana*', and he considered them an untrustworthy lot.[79] At Quito he was struck by the 'extreme timidity' of the Indians, but in this they only shared 'the universal mistrust of each other and of everybody that is exhibited throughout the country'.[80] He was told that there was not a single family of pure Spanish descent in the country, and he found 'revolting' a practice that many of mixed blood had inherited from the natives of picking vermin out of one another's hair and eating them.[81]

Venezuela, next door to Colombia on the west, was if anything still less attractive, until its dowry of oil lent it charm. At the end of the century a botanist travelling in the interior found life exceedingly rude and primitive. In one settlement nobody could read or write; an itinerant scribe came round occasionally. In parts of the Orinoco basin civilization seemed to have been receding, and the natives to have 'reconquered the country from the Spaniards'.[82] Townships along the rivers were kept in a state of wretchedness by civil broils, on top of the government's ordinary torpor and obstructiveness. In the past five years there had been three principal revolutions, besides minor risings.[83] Here again a reservoir of cheap soldiery that any faction could draw on helped to keep the country in turmoil. On one river trip this explorer found himself on a steamer crammed with raw recruits collected to put down a revolt, 'a wild lot' only interested in the free beef and drink they were looking forward to.[84] It was an indication of the state of society out on the rolling plains, the jumbling of class and race, that any man of position, whatever his colour, was called a 'Blanco'.[85]

A small country making good looks all the better, a small one making a mess of things looks all the worse; and the diminutive republics of Central America were looked on as the acme of futility. Mexico was a different matter, but it evoked far more hostility than esteem from Europe – as every nation struggling to throw off the yoke of oppression all through modern times has done. In the protracted social conflict between the feudal ruling class and Church, mainly Spanish, and the peasant mass, mainly Indian or mestizo, respectable sympathies lay with the conservative side; just as in the US civil war English conservatism sympathized with the genteel South against the democratic North. Juárez's long years of guerrilla struggle began while the Mutiny was raging in British India, and to many Europeans must have looked a revolt of the same stamp, of benighted natives against civilized rule. Napoleon III no doubt felt he could count on their approval when he tried to set up a Hapsburg emperor of Mexico; and when this Hapsburg was caught and executed Europe was duly shocked. It failed to perceive the fine touch of historical retribution in this fate of a prince of the same lineage under whose banner Mexico was conquered four centuries before. Manet painted a picture of Maximilian before the firing-squad. A few years later, after the

Paris Commune, he painted a picture of soldiers shooting prisoners,[86] and put these French soldiers into exactly the same attitude as Juárez's men, as if to symbolize his discovery that a Mexican Indian revolution was no more savage than a European counter-revolution.

Brazil and the Democracy of Races

Brazil had until 1889 a more legitimate emperor. Real power belonged to the sugar-growing plantocracy, but the presence of a *bona fide* court at Rio de Janeiro gave this capital a tone that for well-bred Europeans all the others lacked. 'The state of Brazil has afforded so bright a contrast,' the British minister wrote in 1868, 'to the wretched condition of anarchy, of ruin and of civil warfare exhibited by nearly all the South American Republics, that her well-wishers view with unfeigned regret any occurrence that may tend to add strength to the republican party, already forming in the Empire, and furthered in every possible manner by the Press of the United States.'[87] Brazil nevertheless, like Mexico, though by a less revolutionary route, was to find its way towards a fusion of races and cultures. This amalgam would not have as in Mexico a solidly Indian foundation, for instead of two compact racial and social elements confronting each other there was a diversity of Indian and European ingredients and a third big contingent from Africa.

In all the coastal regions of northern Brazil and the Guianas the original Indians had been for the most part peaceful and easy to get on with. 'The temper of the Indian of Guiana is mild and gentle, and he is very fond of his children,' wrote the English explorer Waterton early in the nineteenth century.[88] Forest-dwellers near the white settlements would display their dances and blowpipes for visitors, and seemed 'a poor, harmless, inoffensive set of people' whom it would be a kindness to Christianize and make useful.[89] But he began to see that these Indians, though 'laid low in the dust' by conquest, were still 'very jealous of their liberty' and had 'no inclination to become civilized'. Some who were taken to Europe threw off their clothes and disappeared into the woods as soon as they got back.[90] This need not have surprised Waterton so much, considering that what white men offered the Indian as civilization was hard labour on their estates for their profit. Too lazy to jump at this opportunity of self-improvement, the natives were pushed back into the jungles to make room for workers with more energy, African slaves and later, in British Guiana, coolies from the East Indies.

Multitudes of Negroes were brought into Brazil, down to 1851, chiefly for the coastal plantations. There a mixed white and black population grew up, while inland the blend was of white and Indian. Slavery made coastal Brazil, with its wealth and urbanity, unpleasant to visitors of less aristocratic leanings, like Darwin for whom it was a land of servitude 'and therefore of moral debasement'.[91] Whether or not such feelings are natural to men of science, their researches also led them to prefer the interior, with its raw but less corrupt life; that immense unknown Brazil which was Conan Doyle's natural choice as the setting for his fabulous plateau and its pterodactyls and iguanodons.[92] H. W. Bates went out to Amazonia in 1848 and spent what he called 'eleven of the best years of his life there,[93] collecting insects but also observing men and manners. He liked the colonists whom he got to know in their unpretentious townships in the backwoods. Even the lower classes were 'light-hearted, quick-witted, communicative, and hospitable', if also 'indolent and sensual' as such a climate was bound to make them; there was nothing but their 'incorrigible nonchalance and laziness' to keep them poor.[94]

There were tame Indians, called *caboclos* by the Brazilians, often debased by having lost their old skills and acquired no new ones. Bates sojourned for long spells among the more or less wild tribes. Like all other travellers he admired their skill at tracking, and at managing their frail boats on perilous rivers. But even those who practised agriculture and had some social organization showed 'no aptitude for the civilized life of towns', and seemed to him 'incapable of any further advance in culture'.[95] Through almost all the history of the Old World urban life and civilized life had been one and the same thing, and wherever Europe spread by conquest this pattern was intensified, the gulf between city and countryside widened. The aversion of the Amerindian to urban life helped to convince Bates, and many others, that his ruling trait was an apathy, an inertia, which must 'infallibly lead to his extinction':[96] that is, his absorption into more active racial compounds. Bates saw nothing in this to regret.

Racial assimilation was indeed going on, often as in other parts of the world by the will of the stronger. White men in the interior, Bates found, 'cannot comprehend why they are not allowed to compel Indians to work for them, seeing that they will not do it of their own accord'[97] – the white man's simple logic wherever he went. At Ega, and doubtless not there alone, the authorities winked at the practice of buying, or as it was called 'ransoming', children to be brought up as servants; this encouraged the more warlike tribes to raid their neighbours for the purpose of carrying off children for sale.[98] The resemblance to slave-trading in Africa was close. Women thus became available, and by other means too Indian wives were secured by the pioneers, themselves mostly half-breeds, who were gradually pushing back the frontiers. Portuguese women, even if they could be got, were less fit for the hard life of the clearings, and now as in earlier days the fewness of the pioneers helped to incite them to multiply their kind by interbreeding freely. A settler taking to himself a native wife, or two or three, has been regarded as a contributor to amicable relations; the corollary that in each case a native husband, or two or three, have been displaced, is often lost sight of. As districts came to be opened up, intermarriage on less uequal terms could spread. Conversion of Indians to the newcomers' faith, or to a low common denominator between tribal and rustic Catholic cults, was no arduous task.

Turmoil followed the fall of the monarchy exactly as conservative Europeans had foretold. But it led on to more rapid development. Slavery had lately been abolished, capital and immigrants were flowing in from Europe. Discussion of racial questions was lively, with the Darwinian ideas now in vogue to stimulate it. Brazil was becoming an 'intricate labyrinth of race', as Da Cunha said.[99] This army engineer and radical republican was born in 1866, half a century after Sarmiento, to wrestle with the same problems and come at last to very different conclusions. At the outset Da Cunha thought like his fore-runner in terms of a struggle for survival among stronger and weaker races; and he felt compelled by the weight of 'scienti-fic' opinion to believe that any grafting of one race on to an-other was likely to do harm, producing at best a gifted but unbalanced mentality.[100] What altered his outlook was an emo-tional response to a happening, trivial in itself, in a remote corner of northern Brazil.

Here was another breed of cowherds, like the *llaneros* of Venezuela and the gauchos of southern Brazil and Argentina, but with an archaic character of its own, rich in folk-lore and songs and a medley of religious notions derived from white and Indian forbears long since laid to rest. Somewhat as in the Soudan of the Mahdi, that backwater of Islam and meeting-point of races, elemental discontents and hopes found a vent in wild millennarian prophesyings. Towards the end of the cen-tury a half-crazy fanatic, Antonio 'Conselheiro' – *the Coun-sellor* – formed a sect at Canudos which drew down on itself the government's displeasure. In 1896 a force was sent to crush it; Da Cunha was with the troops as an observer. He saw a terribly dogged resistance, and the sectaries brutally wiped out. From the official standpoint this was one more milestone in the conquest of Barbarism by Civilization; but Da Cunha had a revulsion of feeling at the spectacle of these ignorant men, with their physical vitality and fanatical heroism, destroyed by a civilization whose only argument was the machine-gun. His great book on the rising, published in 1902, can be thought of as a confrontation of Sarmiento's great book on the gaucho hordes sixty years earlier. He was advancing beyond Sar-miento's too narrow and rigid categories; and he was writing a book for the world, not for his own continent alone, a world where the juggernaut of power-politics was rolling over one weak people after another.

In the years since then Brazil, with his book in its hand, has moved towards its now proclaimed ideal of 'ethnic democ-racy'. Freyre, the best-known expounder of this ideal, very ex-plicitly regards the society and culture taking shape in Brazil as 'predominantly European', but not solely European.[101] No-where else, he can declare, has European life adapted itself so well to a tropical environment;[102] it has done so by incorporating many exotic elements, and it must learn to incorporate more.

Decadence and the Dictators

When Latin America began to find its feet and move forward its achievements were often, as those of Spain and Portugal had been, cultural and artistic rather than political or economic. By the early twentieth century a good deal had been accomplished, and Brazil was leaving Portugal behind. By contrast North America, stemming from the technically expansive northern half of Europe, was about to leave its parent behind in technology, but had not begun to catch up with it in artistic or intellectual culture. Europeans and North Americans of the nineteenth century, however, when they took stock of Latin America set little value on music or poetry; the Anglo-Saxon businessman, that double-dyed philistine, least of all. By and large their attitude was growing more captious, not to say contemptuous. A symptom of this may be seen in the first hints of a change of viewpoint about the pre-Columbian cultures. Europe was making the acquaintance not only of alien peoples but of silent kingdoms of the past, disinterred by the antiquarian; and beside the noisy chatter of Lima or La Paz the silence of the Incas had an impressive dignity. Formerly it had been taken for granted, even by an Adam Smith who condemned the brutality of the Conquest, that it represented the first step forward of a continent incapable of advance by itself.[103] Before the close of the century there were Europeans who thought that the Spaniards, in Peru above all, destroyed more than they brought.[104]

Energy and hard work stood high among Europe's ten commandments; the European overseas, it is true, preferred to display energy by getting other people to work hard. Everywhere in the New World south of the Rio Grande these virtues seemed unknown, and sloth and slackness reigned undisputed. In countries where the Church kept its hold there was an inordinate calendar of saints' days when all work came to a halt

Ruling classes fostered an anti-work psychology by trying to improvise disciplined labour forces out of Indian gangs, African slaves, Chinese coolies, all working under compulsion, so that work became a thing to be avoided by all who could avoid it. Climate helped them. 'Life seemed too easy for the lower orders', Whymper felt at Guayaquil; they could sleep out and live on bananas, instead of having to exert themselves.[105] Indian porters supplied to him by the authorities made haste to decamp.[106] To a few eccentric foreigners this lolling and loafing atmosphere had its appeal, the more persuasive when Europe saw its own brisk bustling ways outdone and caricatured by the Yankee. That aristocratic radical with a Venezuelan grandmother, Cunninghame Graham, enjoyed the leisurely, free-and-easy tone of social intercourse, an inheritance he said from Indian as well as Iberian tradition, which he found everywhere in the New World except in 'the great gold-standardized republic of the north'.[107]

Stay-at-home notions about South America were likely to be comic or derisive. Sydney Smith suggested that poisoned arrows instead of duelling pistols would be 'the weapons of gentlemen in the New Republics'.[108] Knowledge of these was hazy, sometimes even in quarters supposed to be better informed. When a bundle of departmental reports reached London from the Chilean capital Santiago, a Foreign Office pundit scribbled on it: 'I feel sure that the Home Off. and the Treasury wd. not care to read a pack of lies about the Govt. and finance of Venezuela.'[109] British diplomacy had a loungingly South American style of its own: Bismarck and his well-drilled team were setting a stiffer professional standard, which others, grumblingly, had to emulate.

British businessmen, for their part, were drifting into a habit of blaming their customers for all their failures, especially customers in godforsaken places who ought to have been grateful for any notice taken of them; while German businessmen in South America, newcomers with their way to make and no great colonial empire to feel haughty about, were buckling to their work differently. All the same there really was a good deal to complain of : a demand on every side for bribes or commissions, red tape uncoiling itself *ad infinitum* as though out of

Latin America

a conjurer's hat, chronic disorder. One frequent grievance was the American propensity (not confined to south of the Rio Grande) to borrow money and not pay it back. What caused most embitterment here was that a good many loans were frauds rigged up between Stock Exchange swindlers in Europe and irresponsible governments in Latin America, to empty the pockets of investors on one side of the Atlantic and tax-payers on the other. A classic instance was the series of Honduras loans floated in London from 1867, so unblushingly fraudulent that it led to an investigation of Stock Exchange doings.[110]

Sir Harry Parkes, who was often angry with the Japanese, once relieved his feelings in the strongest language he could resort to by saying that Japan would never be anything better than 'a South American Republic'.[111] The phrase conjured up a fantasia of political incapacity, humbug, rodomontade, and an interminable wrestling match between Tweedle-dum and Tweedle-dee, a succession of revolutions sometimes bloody but always resounding with empty proclamations. An eye-witness at Lima in 1872 gave a typical description of a 'dreadful four days' of bloodshed throughout which the dictator of the moment went on pouring out manifestoes in 'the most ridiculous style of falsehood, rant, and bombast'.[112] Similar affairs happened every now and then at Lisbon and Madrid, not to speak of Paris, and Anglo-Saxons were confirmed in their opinion of Latin excitability or childishness. Freyre cites as a specimen of such prejudice a US commentary on Italian immigrants in Brazil depicting them as little better than so many criminals at large.[113] It may be that Latin America's annual crop of *pronunciamientos*, made the most of by the conservative press in Europe as an object-lesson in revolutionary folly, did something to discredit the Socialist revolution that the Second International was pledged to.

Englishmen were still suspicious of the professional stage, and of anything 'theatrical' except what was enshrined in their own national customs. It was when dressed up as a general or generalissimo, in dazzling spurs and self-bestowed medals, that the South American looked most histrionic, and South American rhetoric, always exuberant, excelled itself in time of war. An obscure Peruvian commander of a ragamuffin army promised his men 'the admiration of the universe, which will contemplate you with stupefaction as it resounds to the echoes of your imperishable prowess'.[114] Cries of 'national honour', 'war to the last drop', and so on, which thrilled Europe's own blood, sounded absurd in this setting. Army service being a less elevated career than in Europe, 'officer' and 'gentleman' did not fit so closely together. This was due partly to the Indian or mestizo military element being so strong; and in fighting ability too Europeans were not likely to rate a 'native' or half-native army very high. In the War of the Pacific British military observers were uncomplimentary to both sides. Many of Peru's conscripts, they reported, had no idea what the war was about. Chile's troops they admitted to be fierce in battle, but too fond of drink and only kept in order by flogging;[115] very much what Wellington thought about his own British troops.

That Latin America's ills were at bottom the exploitation of the people by selfish bosses and property-owners was a fact that respectable Europe grew less willing to look in the face, as time went on and the Paris Commune made its flesh creep and socialists denounced its own ruling classes. Other explanations were more congenial. Anti-clerical Frenchmen or Presbyterian Scots readily convinced themselves that it was all the fault of Roman Catholicism. Undeniably the Church was for the most part as little friendly to the light of reason as to social progress. Hall heard a Mexican priest, 'a rational man on some points', regaling his credulous congregation with 'the wildest absurdities' about miracles he believed himself to have witnessed.[116] Brazilians and Paraguayans in those early years of the century conceived heretic Englishmen as demons escaped from the abyss, with webbed feet and trailing an odour of sulphur.[117] One such demon showed its malignity by professing to know a bishop in Peru with more bastard children to his name than years to his life.[118]

There hung on into the nineteenth century, as one expression of Europe's self-complacency, an old notion that all animals and men deteriorated when removed from the Old World to the New. In the tropical south it had a more plausible air than in Boston or New York. An enervating climate where wood, metal, clothes were so speedily eaten away by heat, damp,

insects, might well explain human decay (and Catholicism) as
well. Unrestricted racial mixing might have further deleterious
effects. Instincts acquired by the British and others in Asia or
Africa, and by North Americans at home, were bound to prejudice them against the alloys forming in this melting-pot of
races. All its crossings came indiscriminately into the category
of 'Dagoes'. They were, too often, warped by a morbid social
environment, and Darwin himself had misgivings at the sight,
for instance, of the 'villainous, banditti-like army' of Rosas,
mostly an amalgam of white, black and Indian. 'I know not
the reason, but men of such origin seldom have a good expression of countenance.' He noted that in a gaucho camp all
labour was left to women, whose duty was to be, 'like the
wives of all savages, useful slaves'.[119] At Lima and its port of
Callao the inhabitants, of 'every imaginable shade of mixture', looked to him 'a depraved, drunken set'.[120] Bates spoke
of 'the mongrel population' of Brazil.[121]

As usual women were more indulgently viewed, by European men, than their husbands or brothers. European nations
after all were 'virile', others mostly 'effeminate', so these
others might well breed fascinating, if ill-regulated, women.
Novelists had a weakness for fiery, temperamental creatures
from Latin America. Travellers were fond of saying or hinting
that in their experience female virtue was lamentably lax.

The prescription most often favoured as an antidote for
Latin American ailments was firm, authoritarian rule. Most of
Europe down to 1914 was very firmly ruled, and the countries
proudest of their free institutions were equally proud of the
firm rule they bestowed on their colonies. Latin Americans
seemed to them hardly more fit for parliamentarism than Bengalis or Tunisians. Businessmen, always at least as short-
sighted as hard-headed, failed then as now to comprehend that
conservative government in Latin America meant conservation
of ignorance and misery, and of the poor market they were
always grumbling about. From the first there was a willingness
to admire the strong men who emerged amid the wreckage of
the Spanish empire. If Rosas and Francia came in for vitupera-
tion, it was more because they were anti-European than because they were tyrants. Rosas had his apologists who argued

that the first need of new countries was order. Carlyle sang Francia's praises in 1843;[122] it was a good text for a diatribe against democracy and an exercise in hero-worship. Francia was for Paraguay 'the one veracious person', as Cromwell had once been for England. 'All South America raging and ravening like one huge dog-kennel gone rabid' – and Paraguay, under his firm hand, at peace, its natives taught the virtues of obedience and toil.

'A little shooting and hanging of these disturbers of the public peace would produce a salutary effect,' wrote a disgusted visitor to Brazil.[123] As foreign investments mounted, labour agitators came to rank with bandits and politicians as disturbers of the peace, and governments were judged according to their zeal in holding them in check, by shooting or hanging or other means. Meiggs was accused of getting local officialdom to round up Indian labour for his daring railway projects in the Andes;[124] in a speech at the opening of one line in 1863 he paid unctuous tribute to his well-behaved Chilean workers, by contrast with the refractory Irish navvies who were 'capable even of assaulting those who direct them'.[125] Conditions in his camps were such that numbers of Chinese and other labourers died. He may be supposed to have felt, as Frederick the Great did about his soldiers, that they had to die some time; they may be supposed to have seen railway-building in a different light. Business interests operating in a restricted area might need no more from the government than a blind eye turned on their own enforcement of discipline. In Peru the 'London Pacific Petroleum Company' between 1889 and 1914 was allowed to behave virtually as a sovereign power, and to exercise an 'absolute and harsh authority over the labour force'.[126]

After the strong men of the early decades of independence came a procession of transient dictators intent on little but quick profits for themselves and their factions. To these adventurers native or foreign businessmen might have to pay blackmail or protection-money merely to be left alone. This was what the mine-owner in Joseph Conrad's *Nostromo* had to submit to, a taciturn Englishman ready enough to pay but impatient at having to listen as well to a flood of 'deplorable balderdash' about the patriotic sentiments of the great man or his local satrap.[127] But by the end of the century a third era was being reached. There were regions now where investments were big enough and labour problems grave enough to call for a new kind of régime, and a new type of boss. He was a leader with a genuine function again, as in the early epoch, but one of partnership with Europeans instead of bolting the door against them. Porfirio Diaz, who reigned over Mexico from 1884 to 1911, was the grand example of a species that is still with us. Mexico had resources to be tapped by foreign capital, and a popular revolutionary movement to be damped down. Under Diaz the impetus of national growth continued, but diverted from social reform to material construction benefiting chiefly the foreign investor and the native ruling class. Pearson the great contractor was the leading foreign capitalist (as well as a Liberal M.P.), and he and Diaz took to each other amazingly. Diaz understood and handled human nature 'superbly', said Pearson – he might have paid the same tribute to the dictator's police – and the 'highly-cultured officials' he met were always most obliging.[128] There were anti-foreign riots when Diaz was overthrown at last, and Pearson was accused of having made himself *de facto* ruler of the district of Tehuantepec.

It was in Latin America that Europe was making its first serious acquaintance with dictatorship, little guessing how this exotic growth was to transplant itself on to its own soil, where it had only been seen in Spain and Portugal or the Balkans. A few months before Hitler came to power a student of the *caudillo* in the politics of the New World remarked that while there was a vast Spanish American literature on the subject, in Britain and North America there had been 'an almost complete lack of intelligent discussion'.[129] It was one instance among a thousand of how much less the 'West' learned than it might have done from its intercourse with the rest of the world.

NOTES

1. Captain B. Hall, *Extracts from a Journal written on the coasts of Chile, Peru, and Mexico, in the years 1820, 1821, 1822* (Edinburgh, 1826), Vol 1, p. 253. It was this smuggling business that brought the *gaucho* into prominence: see M. W. Nichols, 'The Historic Gaucho', in *Hispanic American Historical Review*, Vol. 21 (1941), pp. 417 ff.

2. R. B. Cunninghame Graham, *José Antonio Páez* (1929), p. 75 n.

3. B. Hall, op. cit., Vol. 1, pp. 16, 20.

4. ibid., Vol. 1, p. 88.

5. C. Waterton, *Wanderings in South America* (1825), p. 27 (1906 edn).

6. H. W. Bates, *The Naturalist on the River Amazons* (1863), pp. 17 n, 114 (1915 edn). cf. the blend of races described in D. A. G. Waddell, *British Honduras* (Oxford, 1961), pp. 64–5.

7. R. Walter, *Lord Anson's Voyage round the World 1740–1744* (1748), pp. 32 ff. (abridged edn by S. W. C. Pack, 1947).

8. R. B. Cunninghame Graham, op. cit., pp. 67–8.

9. C. Darwin, *A Journal of Researches* (1839), p. 130 (1910 edn).

10. A sixteenth-century English prose translation of part of the epic by A. de Ercilla y Zúñiga, *The Historie of Araucana*, has been edited by F. Pierce (Manchester, 1964).

11. C. Darwin, op. cit., p. 291.

12. See G. M. McBride, *Chile: Land and Society* (New York, 1936), Chapters 11 and 12.

13. E. André, *A Naturalist in the Guianas* (1904), pp. 269–70 (Nelson edn, 1912).

14. H. W. Bates, op. cit., pp. 159–60; he recounts an instance.

15. Report by Vice-Consul Gordon at Cordova, with Hon. W. Stuart, British minister at Buenos Aires, to Lord Clarendon, no. 89, Conf., 22 July 1869, Foreign Office 6.283; Public Record Office, London.

16. D. F. Sarmiento, *Conflicto y armonías de las razas en América* (Buenos Aires, 1883), Vol. 1, pp. 319–20; he watched the procession in 1864.

17. J. Smith, *Memoirs of the Marquis of Pombal* (1843), Chapter 9.

18. A. St John, British minister at Lima, to Lord Granville, no. 134, 13 December 1883, Foreign Office 61.348.

19. J. H. Parry, *The Spanish Seaborne Empire* (1966), p. 336.

20. B. Hall, op. cit., Vol. 1, pp. 189–90.

21. R. B. Cunninghame Graham, op. cit., p. 125.

22. Lord Bryce, *South America. Observations and impressions ...* (1912), p. 114.

23. B. Hall, op. cit., Vol. 1, p. 187.

24. Consul J. R. Graham, in charge of the British legation at Lima, to Lord Granville, no. 52, 8 July 1882, Foreign Office 61.340.

25. Hon. W. S. Jerningham, British chargé d'affaires at Lima, to Lord Russell, no. 38, 8 April 1865, Foreign Office 61.226.

26. J. H. Parry, op. cit., p. 380.

27. B. Hall, op. cit., Vol. 1, p. 101.

28. ibid., Vol. 2, p. 216.
29. R. Walter, op. cit., p. 132.
30. H. S. Ferns, *Britain and Argentina in the Nineteenth Century* (Oxford, 1960), pp. 30–31.
31. M. Scott, *Tom Cringle's Log* (1836), pp. 267–8 (Everyman edn).
32. H. S. Ferns, op. cit., p. 36.
33. ibid., p. 194.
34. C. Mazade, in *Revue des Deux Mondes*, 1846, p. 631. He was reviewing Sarmiento's masterpiece, *Facundo* (1845), on the gauchos and on the tyranny of Rosas; it was translated by M. Mann, as *Life in the Argentine Republic* (New York, 1868). In 1847 the *Revue des Deux Mondes* (Vol. 1, pp. 57–80), had a more liberal article, by M. Radiguet, who saw a new culture stirring in Chile and hoped that it would emancipate itself from French and English influence.
35. Foreign Office memorandum by J. Murray, 31 December 1841, with comments by Adams and Wilson, August 1842, in Foreign Office 97.284.
36. J. P. Dale to Bidwell, Private, 21 September 1842 and 29 December 1842, Foreign Office 51.20.
37. D. F. Sarmiento, *Viajes por Europa, Africa i América* (1849), p. 52 (Paris edn, 1909).
38. H. W. Bates, op. cit., pp. 114, 264.
39. *The Standard and River Plate News*, 25 September 1868.
40. T. J. Hutchinson, *Two Years in Peru* (1873), Vol. 1, p. 324.
41. B. Hall, op. cit., Vol. 1, p. 78.
42. See my article 'Sarmiento and Europe', in Vol. 1 (pp. 119–50) of the commemoration volumes of *Humanidades* issued in 1961, the 150th anniversary of Sarmiento's birth, by the National University of La Plata; and A. W. Bunkley, *The Life of Sarmiento* (Princeton, 1952).
43. D. F. Sarmiento, *Viajes*, pp. 217–18.
44. ibid., p. 63; cf. *Conflicto y armonías de las razas*, p. 155.
45. In Vol. 42 of his Works: *Obras de D. F. Sarmiento* (Paris, 1889–1909).
46. See the *Viajes*.
47. H. W. Rouse, acting consul-general at Santiago, to Lord Russell, no. 6, 17 May 1864, Foreign Office 16.129.
48. A. S. J. Baxter, *The International Banks* (1935), p. 134.
49. E. André, op. cit., p. 89.
50. W. Stewart, *Henry Meiggs – Yankee Pizarro* (Duke University, 1946), p. 96.
51. Copies of the protest and reply with Hon. W. S. Jerningham

to Lord Russell, Private and Conf., 28 November 1864 Foreign Office 61.219.

52. Hon. W. S. Jerningham to Lord Russell, no. 68, 12 September 1864, and no. 87, 28 October 1864, Foreign Office 61 219.

53. See R. B. Cunninghame Graham, *Portrait of a Dictator, Francisco Solano Lopez, Paraguay, 1865–1870* (1933).

54. See my article on 'Foreign Interests in the War of the Pacific', in *Hispanic American Historical Review*, Vol. 35 (1955).

55. See V. M. Maurtua, *The Question of the Pacific* (English edn, Philadelphia, 1901), pp. 74 ff., 124, 263.

56. J. M. Valega, *Causas i motivos de la Guerra del Pacífico* (Lima, 1917).

57. Sir G. Sartorius to Lord Aberdeen, private, 1 November 1842, Foreign Office 51.21.

58. Hon. L. S. Sackville West, minister at Buenos Aires, to Lord Derby, no. 90, Conf., 13 October 1874, Foreign Office 6.321.

59. M. H. Hervey, *Dark Days in Chile* (1892), p. 18. cf. H. S. Ferns, op. cit., p. 134: 'Between 1860 and 1914, Argentina grew into one of the cornerstones of the British economy.'

60. W. R. Manning, *Diplomatic Correspondence of the United States concerning the Independence of the Latin-American Nations* (New York, 1925), Vol. 1, pp. 418–19. A sympathetic writer fifty years later spoke of the 'sobriety, industry, and obedience to law' inculcated by the Jesuits as still prevailing (Anon., *Paraguay. A Concise History* . . . (1867), p. 10; cf. p. 38).

61. See my article on 'Britain's First Contacts with Paraguay', in *Atlanta* (London), October 1955.

62. J. P. and W. P. Robertson, *Letters on Paraguay* (2nd edn, 1839), Vol. 1, p. 92, Vol. 2, p. 29. Woodbine Parish, British representative at Buenos Aires, believed the whole population to be 'under such a terror of Francia as to be reduced to the lowest state of servile subjection' (Parish to Canning, no. 23, 8 April 1825, Foreign Office 6.8).

63. J. R. Rengger and M. F. X. Longchamp, *The Reign of Doctor Joseph Gaspard Roderick de Francia* (English edn, 1827), pp. 188 ff.

64. J. P. and W. P. Robertson, op. cit., Vol. 2, p. 277.

65. C. A. Washburn, *The History of Paraguay* (Boston, 1871), Vol. p. 334.

66. See H. Sánchez Quell, *Política internacional del Paraguay* (2nd edn, Buenos Aires, 1945), pp. 170 ff., 239–41; he follows the French geographer E. Reclus.

67. Presidential message to Congress, May 1869.

68. *Conflicto y armonías de las razas*, pp. 19 ff.

69. T. C. Dawson, *The South American Republics* (London and New York, 1904), Vol. 2, p. 229.

70. Hon. F. J. Pakenham, British minister at Santiago, to Lord Granville, no. 68, 2 October 1880, Foreign Office 16.208.

71. H. Fraser to Lord Rosebery, no. 65, Conf., 31 July 1886, Foreign Office 16.242.

72. P. Duprat to J. Ferry, no. 88, 12 February 1885, and no. 90, 9 March 1885: *Chili*, Vol. 26, in Foreign Ministry archives, Paris.

73. W. Stewart, op. cit., p. 47. cf. pp. 242–3: 'The morals of the dominant class of Don Enrique's day were on a par with the sanitation of their capital city.'

74. W. Stewart, *Chinese Bondage in Peru* (Duke University, 1951), pp. 148–9.

75. A. J. Duffield, *Peru in the Guano Age* (1877), pp. 41–2, 48–9; cf. E. Romero, *Historia económica del Perú* (Buenos Aires, 1950), p. 412.

76. A. J. Duffield, op. cit., pp. 12–13. Sir C. R. Markham, who had a sympathetic interest in the Indians, considered that apart from conscription their lot had improved (*The War between Peru and Chile 1879–1882* (1882), p. 62, etc.).

77. Hon. F. J. Pakenham to Lord Granville, no. 50, 11 September 1881, Foreign Office 16.213, quoting the Dutch consul-general in Chile.

78. T. F. Rippy, *Historical Evolution of Latin America* (Oxford edn, ?1932), pp. 199–201.

79. E. Whymper, *Travels amongst the Great Andes of the Equator* (1892), p. 178 (Nelson edn, 1908).

80. ibid., pp. 179, 183.

81. ibid., pp. 179, 113.

82. E. André, op. cit., p. 137.

83. ibid., pp. 69–70, 243.

84. ibid., pp. 141–2.

85. R. B. Cunninghame Graham, *José Antonio Páez*, p. 281.

86. See plates 30 and 38 in the Phaidon Press volume, *Edouard Manet, Paintings and Drawings* (1958).

87. G. B. Mathew to Lord Clarendon, no. 53, Secret, 23 July 1868, Foreign Office 13.454.

88. C. Waterton, op. cit., p. 143.

89. ibid., pp. 3, 21. He is speaking of Dutch Guiana, under British occupation during the Napoleonic wars.

90. ibid., p. 139.

91. C. Darwin, op. cit., p. 469.

92. A. Conan Doyle, *The Lost World* (1912).

93. H. W. Bates, op. cit., p. 1.

94. ibid., pp. 79, 138.

95. ibid., p. 225.

96. ibid., p. 39.

97. ibid., cf. p. 227.

98. ibid., pp. 256–7, 259–60.

99. Euclides da Cunha, *Revolt in the Backlands* (trans. S. Putnam, 1947), p. 53.

100. ibid., pp. 61–2.

101. G. Freyre, *New World in the Tropics* (New York, 1959), p. 7. Lord Bryce was one of many visitors who felt that Brazil knew nothing of racial prejudice (op. cit., p. 471). This picture can easily be made too rosy. Brazilian friends – in exile – tell me that Negroes really may be treated as equals if they have money and education, but this is very seldom the case. As to Indians, during 1968 there were revelations of gross ill-treatment of some tribes in the interior, driven off their land or even wiped out to make room for development.

102. G. Freyre, op. cit., p. 6.

103. Adam Smith, *The Wealth of Nations* (1776), Vol. 2, pp. 165–6 (World's Classics edn); cf. B. Hall, op. cit., Vol. 1, p. 257.

104. e.g. A. J. Duffield, op. cit., pp. 1 ff.

105. E. Whymper, op. cit., p. 29; cf. p. 256.

106. ibid., p. 82.

107. R. B. Cunninghame Graham, *José Antonio Páez*, p. 104.

108. S. Smith, review of C. Waterton, op. cit., in *Edinburgh Review*, 1826.

109. Minute on enclosures with Hon. F. J. Pakenham to Lord Granville, no. 5, 13 January 1883, Foreign Office 16.223.

110. See Report of the Committee on Foreign Loans, 1875; cf. A. K. Cairncross, *Home and Foreign Investment 1870–1913* (Cambridge, 1953), pp. 90 ff.

111. S. Lane-Poole and F. V. Dickins, *The Life of Sir Harry Parkes* (1894), Vol. 2, p. 359.

112. T. J. Hutchinson, op. cit., Vol. 2, pp. 1 ff.

113. G. Freyre, op. cit., p. 164 n. 1.

114. Proclamation by General Montero; text in *Bulletin de la Guerre du Pacifique* (Santiago), 1880, no. 29.

115. Reports in Foreign Office 61.337.

116. B. Hall, op. cit., Vol. 2, p. 236.

117. G. Freyre, op. cit., p. 4.

118. A. J. Duffield, op. cit., pp. 14–15.

119. C. Darwin, op. cit., pp. 85–6.

120. ibid., p. 351.

121. H. W. Bates, op. cit., p. 17.

122. 'Dr Francia' (1843), in T. Carlyle, *Scottish and Other Miscellanies*.

123. W. Hadfield, *Brazil and the River Plate, 1870–76* (1877), p. 29.

124. W. Stewart, *Henry Meiggs*, p. 202.

125. ibid., pp. 30–31.

126. E. Romero, op. cit., pp. 421 ff.

127. Joseph Conrad, *Nostromo* (1904), Chapter 7.

128. J. A. Spender, *Weetman Pearson, First Viscount Cowdray 1856–1927* (1930), pp. 94, 97; cf. p. 188, on Pearson's 'unbounded admiration and affection' for the dictator. Spender's admiration for Pearson is equally unbounded.

129. C. E. Chapman, 'The Age of the Caudillos', in *Hispanic American Historical Review*, Vol. 12 (1932), p. 281.

9. CONCLUSION

In 1914 the world had an orderly, well-policed appearance, by comparison with a hundred years earlier. Under the surface things were more in a state of flux than at any earlier time. Political and economic relations between Europe, which had wrought the transformation, and the rest of the world, might seem fixed for good, but were really very unstable; their feelings about each other were a chaotic medley. Europe itself had been rapidly altering, partly through its involvement with the world, and had become a stranger to itself. Contradictions in its nature had always been more strongly marked than in any other, less complex, civilization; they were intensified by the advent of perpetual change as a condition of its life, and were often shown on a magnified scale in its behaviour outside its own borders. Whole healthy races were wiped out, while at home, as if by a compulsive atonement, morbid humanitarianism spurred doctors and hospitals to keep alive deformed infants or idiots.

Europe's estimate of its fellow-continents was sinking, on the whole, as the nineteenth century went on and knowledge of them grew more realistic, or seemed to because new distortions of vision went unnoticed. Its estimate of its own effect on these others showed signs of drooping too. Colonizing countries did their best to cling to a conviction that they were spreading through the world not merely order, but civilization; which implied that other peoples were not civilized yet, but were capable of becoming so. Speke's diary of 1855 in Somaliland closed on a note of faith that human nature there did not gainsay 'the hope entertained by every Englishman – that of raising his fellow-man in the scale of civilization'.[1] Shortly after writing these words he was nearly murdered in a mob attack on his camp. Such an attack threw doubt on the willingness of backward peoples to accept the blessing offered them. So in another way did the bomb thrown at the Viceroy of India at Delhi in 1911; the only difference was that Somalis were rejecting British medicine without trying it, Indians after lengthy dosing with it. Doubt crept in also about whether European civilization really was good for those exposed to it. Burton saw the Arabs corrupted by contact with Aden;[2] the least objectionable inhabitants of British India, in British eyes, were those least touched by the white man's learning There remained a final stage, to be reached by 1918, of doubt whether European civilization was much good even for Europe.

At home Europe was shuffling away from forms of society based on compulsion towards new ones founded on assent. Abroad it was acting in the opposite spirit. Whether empires were agencies of civilization or of exploitation, they rested on power, and all attitudes towards backward countries or 'native' peoples were deeply imbued with the sensation of power, of imperial dominion. It was Britain's mission, said the writer of a book on the North-West Frontier who styled himself 'a man of peace' by preference, 'to spread amongst these savages the power of that great civilizer the Sword'.[3] Here was another lurking contradiction. It was very often argued that possessions like India could only be safely governed by the methods they were already accustomed to: by personal authority, the will of the strong man. One must 'stand on the ancient ways, the ways familiarised to the natives of India by centuries of use', Colonel Malleson wrote: abandonment of these for an impersonal rule of Western law led straight to the Mutiny.[4] But for Europeans to reign as despots, however benevolent, was more likely to bring them down to the political mentality of their subjects than to raise these to a Western plane.

Not only individuals but whole groups of conquerors, or administrations, might be perverted in this way, from the first Europeans who issued forth to their latest successors or supplanters, the Americans. Europe habitually looked on its clashes with Afro-Asia as a distinguished Anglo-Indian saw the scrimmage with the Malays of Perak in 1875 it was a clash between civilization and 'wild aborigines'.[5] Viewed from the other side things might look exactly the reverse. It was thus that the American seizure of the Philippine islands appeared to the patriot leader President Aguinaldo when he called on his countrymen to resist 'the dominion of force, accompanied by the repugnant barbarity of primitive times . . . Do not hope for compassion or consideration.'[6] 'The innate cruelty of the southern Latin races,' says the historian of Chittagong, writing of the Portuguese expansion, 'and the inflamed lust of seamen in foreign ports, made the entire Feringhee race a terror and abomination to the people of lower Bengal.'[7] There were always some Europeans, from Las Casas onwards, who thought that these men were right, and Europe wrong. Diderot asked himself what made the Spaniards treat their new-found brothers in the Americas like wild beasts. *'Est-ce la soif de l'or, le fanatisme, le mépris pour les mœurs simples? ou est-ce la férocité naturelle de l'homme renaissant dans ces contrées éloignées . . .?'*[8]

Panic fear of those myriads of alien beings must have been the chief cause, Diderot charitably concluded. But similar cruelties were often repeated against men like the Australian blackfellows, too few and ill-armed to inspire fear. Herbert Spencer collected many testimonies of them, and pointed out how self-flattering was the bent of mind that had led Europe to attach the meaning 'cruel and bloodthirsty' to the word *savage*, originally signifying only 'wild or uncultivated'. Ferocity was now 'always thought of as an attribute of uncivilized races', whereas oftener than not it was European ferocity that provoked them to retaliate.[9] Things that could not be done in Europe under any government calling itself civilized went on being done in colonial territories. A British governor in the West Indies, Sir Thomas Picton, was removed in 1803 on a charge of allowing torture to be used; but torture, more or less abandoned in Europe until well on in the twentieth century, lingered clandestinely if not openly in Western practice outside, or was always liable to recur. It was noted by a social psychologist as a proof of how weak are men's acquired habits of self-restraint, in unfamiliar circumstances, compared with their instincts, that American soldiers fighting their first Asian war in the Philippines were so ready to torture prisoners.[10]

'The old century is very nearly out,' W. S. Blunt was writing in his diary in December 1900, 'and leaves the world in a pretty pass ... All the nations of Europe are making the same hell upon earth in China ... So ends the famous nineteenth century in which we were so proud to have been born.'[11]

It was through warlike encounters that Europeans and others formed their vividest conceptions of one another, and colonial armies were among the principal meeting-points of European officers and men with native troops. Out of such experiences grew the maxim laid down by Malleson: 'There is only one true method of fighting Asiatics. That mode is to move straight on.'[12] By attacking at once, always, against any odds, the European would convince both himself and his opponent of his superiority, and undermine the will to resist. It would not be hard to trace a connection between this thesis and the military doctrine of 1914–18, especially among the grand colonizers the French and British: the insensate faith in the offensive *à outrance*, to hypnotize and paralyse the enemy by asserting the firmer will and higher morale of the attacker. It began then to dawn on infantrymen that machine-guns and barbed wire were not so easily hynotized as half-armed Asiatics. Their generals in the rear, many of them with minds still farther away in the Asian or African campaigning-grounds of their youth, could not be got to see the point.

A rough and ready but tenacious habit grew up of classifying peoples, not in India alone, as 'martial' or 'non-martial', and of paying more respect (or less disrespect) to the first. Townsend Harris thought a parade of the Siamese army a very ludicrous sight;[13] Westerners saw many like it round the world, which were too apt to put burglarious thoughts into their heads. In the presence of other peoples nearly all Europeans tried to look martial; though Asia learned that some Western countries were too small to be truculent, and Siam employed a number of Danes among its foreign advisers. Japan was demonstrating before 1900 that a nation long unused to war could learn quickly enough to fight. Fifty years later China and Israel, more surprisingly still, were to do the same. But at the beginning of this century the roll seemed to have been called and closed: there might be some peoples everywhere who could fight bravely, but most of these had been shattered, like the Zulus; there were none outside Europe except Japan and the US that could fight a modern war effectively.

'Oh, the difference of man and man!' cries Goneril, comparing dull husband with dashing lover. In the nineteenth century mass armies and mammoth cities and pseudo-democracy were blurring individual features, but the European could console himself by exulting in the differences of race and race. What these precisely were was not easy to state, and races even more than nations melted into one another by every gradation. Hence the importance given to the crudely obvious distinctions of colour. 'The European in considering the Chinese character should recollect that the Aryan and the Yellow races are physically and mentally distinct.'[14] But behind all this lay the fundamental criterion of strength or courage, of which war was the grand test. Generally speaking, the lighter the skin the sharper the sword. Warlike prowess had been a cardinal virtue of other societies too, though very seldom so exaggeratedly as in Europe, and intercourse with Europe heightened regard for it, and for the freedom that it might preserve. Nations that remained independent, however precariously, could look down on their fallen neighbours, as Persians were inclined to do on Indians. Armenia was partitioned between Turkey and Russia, yet an Armenian in England could boast to George Borrow that his countrymen were less debased and spiritless than the Jews, because they still had a homeland, and sometimes still took up arms.[15]

In Rolfe's perversely brilliant novel of 1904, *Hadrian the Seventh*, a new pope arranges the affairs of mankind by promoting a redivision of the world among the virile peoples, those capable of conquest and government. He allots a good share to Japan, and all the western hemisphere to the US, while France and Russia are blotted out.[16] This being a Catholic work Italy figures among the chosen; more often Anglo-Saxons or Teutons thought of it and other southern countries as an inferior part of Europe, shading off into Afro-Asia. In Conan Doyle's novel of 1913, *The Poison Belt*, a table of ranks among the races, an order of fitness to survive, is implied in the sequence in which they succumb to the mysterious etheric poison that the planet has swum into. Africa and the Australian aborigines are speedily extinguished, followed by India and Persia, while in Europe the Slavs collapse sooner than the Teutons, and southern France sooner than the north, after 'delirious excitement' and a 'Socialist upheaval at Toulon'.[17]

In Aryan India 'varna' meant both colour and caste, or the main four-fold division of society; and in the European mind the affinity between race and class is equally palpable. If there were martial races abroad, there were likewise martial classes at home: every man could be drilled to fight, but only the gentleman by birth could lead and command. In innumerable ways his attitude to his own 'lower orders' was identical with that of Europe to the 'lesser breeds'. Discontented native in the colonies, labour agitator in the mills, were the same serpent in alternate disguises. Much of the talk about the barbarism or darkness of the outer world, which it was Europe's mission to rout, was a transmuted fear of the masses at home. Equally, sympathy with the lower orders at home, or curiosity about them, might find expression in associations of ideas between them and the benighted heathen far away.

Aymará Indians in Bolivia seemed to Bryce to be existing in conditions 'no more squalid than that of the agricultural peasantry in some parts of Europe'.[18] When Robert Blatchford and his friends inspected a workhouse school in England and the children crowded round them, fascinated by their clothes and watch-chains, 'It made me think of what I had read about savages crowding round white men who have landed on their shores.'[19] Higher up the scale the relative positions, the social intervals, were the same. There is an exquisite scene in Proust where the Comte de Bréauté-Consalvi meets the highly polished but middle-class young narrator in a grand salon, and is all agog at this extraordinary novelty of a meeting with a plebeian, which will furnish him with a brilliant topic of conversation in his own circle – and fixes him with a beaming monocle and encouraging exclamations, 'just as if, in fact, he had found himself face to face with one of the "natives" of an undiscovered country on which his keel had grounded, and from whom he hoped by a display of friendly interest to obtain ostrich eggs and spices in exchange for his glass beads'.[20]

Empire widened the real gulf between the classes at home, but also provided them with a spurious fraternity. Mrs Rapkin the Cockney landlady in Anstey's novel, *The Brass Bottle*, asked whether she had 'an Oriental gentleman – a native, you know', lodging with her, was indignant at the thought of a 'blackamoor' in her house. A relative of hers let rooms once to 'a Horiental – a Parsee *he* was, or *one* o' them Hafrican tribes – and reason she 'ad to repent of it'.[21] She as well as the natives she looked down on was being laughed at by Anstey's educated readers. In England the educated as a rule felt less fear of their lower classes than in most Continental countries, and could afford to be tolerantly amused by them; to see the Cockney feeling superior to the Horiental was very diverting. In public, amusement had to be smothered, as time went on and official nationalism fostered the myth of all Britons, or all Germans, being brothers; class superiority was then transformed into patriotic, or still better into racial superiority, that all could share in. The more democratic Europe became or pretended to become at home the more supercilious it was abroad.

Another connection of ideas might be traced between Europe's simple notion of the right way to rule natives, or to fight them, and some of its less liberal notions about the right way to impress on women the superiority of men. All such elements in social psychology evolve in clusters, in continual association and interaction. Sex in any case formed an important area of contact between societies. Impressions of foreign lands owed much to men's impressions of their women, and vice versa, and also of the way their men and women behaved to each other. But in many regions women were invisible, or at any rate inaudible. This veil of secrecy hanging over the domestic life of a great part of the world helped to invest all life there with a forbidding quality. It could also conjure up speculations about mysteries of sex better known to old, exotic, vice-haunted races than to enlightened Europe. Sex being for Englishmen especially a thing that respectable folk ought not to know too much about, they were willing to credit foreigners, Frenchmen in Europe and *a fortiori* Hindus or Japanese, with secret lore probably acquired from nameless orgies.

In an analogous fashion Europe prided itself on having the

only reputable religion, just as it had the only decent kind of family life, but it might credit lower religions with access to abnormal realms grotesque or depraved. Indian fakirs *might* be able to throw ropes into the air and climb up them, with what purpose in view was never asked. With all his disdain for the Negroes of Haiti, Prichard was half-prepared to believe that some of them might have occult powers beyond the white man's ken; but only evil powers, only black magic.[22] In general Christianity was closely woven into the fabric of European ascendancy. It was the creed of the white man, of the conqueror, and doctrines of Election led easily towards a philosophy of chosen nations or a chosen race, a Herrenvolk. It might be bestowed on men of other colours, and it was indeed part of Europe's beatific vision of itself that it was the bearer of the true faith to the heathen; but all bishops and nearly all priests would continue to be white, as officers in colonial armies were. A man should be grateful to Heaven, Richard Hopkins had written in 1586, for making him a Catholic 'and not a Jewe, Moore, Turke, or Heretike', free from infection of Lutheranism and 'all other damnable Sectes, and opinions'.[23] Sects and opinions mattered less now, but to be grateful to Heaven for making him a white Christian was still an obvious duty.

All the other religions, like nearly all the kingdoms they gave their blessings to, were in a more or less decrepit condition when Christian Europe came on them like the strong man of Scripture ready to run his race. Islam was sunk in superstition or dogma, Buddhism venerated a Dalai Lama. The spectacle of their degraded state filled all Europeans with the complacent sense of betterness that Protestant countries felt in a lesser degree over Catholic. Their own priests had been put in their place: mullah and lama and Brahmin had not, and it is priestcraft, not doctrine, that makes a religion ridiculous. Europe could feel that it stood alone in combining piety with good sense. 'Is it not marvellous,' a Victorian wonder-book asked after detailing the sloth and greed of Burmese monks, 'that a whole people should ... submit to be thus scandalously cheated?'[24]

Towards the end there were hints of a shift of view. For one thing native priestcraft might in some cases be enlisted as a supporter against colonial nationalism – just as Christian bishops and patriarchs in the Ottoman empire, when French Revolution ideas spread there, were made to exhort their flocks to loyal obedience to the Sultan.[25] In a less calculating way, when events like the Indian famines brought home to Europe the excruciating poverty of so much of the world it was consoling to think that India or Tibet in their rags and misery enjoyed a fund of spiritual comfort withheld from the affluent West. It is always a symptom of qualms of conscience when the rich like to be assured that the poor are more blessed than they are. Here and there in the West, as reason and religion drifted apart, there was a stirring once more of something akin to the fascination of Asiatic deities for Hellenistic Greeks.

If in most ways the West found less and less to praise, as time went on, outside its own boundaries, others found more and more to hate, if also to admire or envy, in the West. Europeans through whom Europe manifested itself to the world were a motley throng: elegant diplomats, buccaneers, hymn-singing missionaries, drunken seamen, and alongside them all the faceless soldier in uniform, the human machine marching in step that Afro-Asia had never known before. To a people like the Chinese it must have seemed as if a band of freaks had broken loose from some bizarre madhouse. (To William Hickey at Canton the Chinese were 'the best pickpockets in the world',[26] and not much else.) Europe's great deeds in the world, like the African slave trade, must be placed to its corporate responsibility: they were acts of historical necessity, given the line of social and economic advance to which Europe was committed. A vast number of smaller, random crimes, as well as good actions, were the work of individuals whom Europe merely turned loose, gratuitous insult or injury to other races. One way or the other, contact with these was rude and forcible, and was setting them at odds with one another as well, for Europe was throwing the other continents together, sending Indian sepoys to China, Chinese coolies to South Africa, African slaves to Brazil. In one sense these peoples were being brought closer, in another sense more deeply divided.

All the drowsy syrups of the world could not restore it now, any more than Othello, to the old unthinking tranquillity. A mood of resentment against the all-powerful Westerner was spreading everywhere; things happening in one corner might set up vibrations in another far away. King Theebaw of Burma is said to have heard one day when deep in his cups of the battle of Isandhlwana in Zululand, and to have wanted to order a march on Rangoon forthwith.[27] Many others who longed for the downfall of the West were dreaming of a simple expulsion of the trespasser, a return to the past, as Theebaw was or as most of the rebels of 1857 in India were. Early in this century a Frenchwoman travelling in Mongolia was astonished by an outburst from a quiet lama working as a merchant's clerk about the coming return of Gesar, the invincible hero of Mongol and Tibetan legend, to 'lead the millions of Asiatics who, to-day, are drowsing ... we shall throw back into the sea those insolent Whites ... we shall invade their countries in the West, and everywhere the cleansing army will have passed nothing will remain, no, not even a blade of grass!'[28] It would be ironical if this hero's name was indeed, as has been conjectured, derived from Caesar's; but such apocalyptic visions of revenge, clothed in ancient myth, haunted many lands, and men with no flesh-and-blood leaders as yet looked back to shadow-figures of the past.

In more awakened lands and minds another ambition was stirring, of taking over Western knowledge and acquiring Western power, as Japan was already doing. The two stages were analogous with the two that Europe itself had been going through: first the peasants and artisans turning their backs on capitalist industry, then the working class trying to take it over and socialize it. In both cases the second threat was the more alarming one. Japan's rise was a portent, watched with uneasiness by the West even though down to 1914 European predominance seemed secure and still growing. Twenty years before, Curzon was warning the Japanese against national vanity and dreams of stepping into Britain's shoes in the Far East.[29] But Europe could not close its ranks against this threat, as it could do against the earlier, more primitive one. In 1900 its troops marched side by side to crush the Chinese peasantry; in

1902 Britain signed an alliance with the Japanese militarists in order to baffle a European rival, Russia. As 1914 approached Germany was cementing a similar alliance against the same rival with Turkish militarists, and laying plans to stir up colonial revolt against Britain, beginning with India. Meanwhile violence outside Europe was about to come home to roost. In 1911 General Bernhardi cited the bombardment of Alexandria in 1882 among instances of the British ruthlessness and contempt for international law that Germany must be prepared to encounter in Europe.[30]

Hitherto the earth's peoples had not on the whole learned much from one another, except in very material matters. Europe had found new things to eat, and taught new ways to fight. Relationships had been too arbitrary, too dependent on force. Muslims and Hindus for similar reasons had not learned much from their thousand years of living together in India, or men and women from their still longer cohabitation. Nor had Europe, with all its exploring of the world, learned much more about itself. It was a long time now since 'the completely developed "Europeanism" of Montesquieu',[31] but the deepening of a surface uniformity into a real common consciousness had made little progress. A multitude of fresh impressions and sensations crowded what may be called Europe's mind, but from the majority of Europeans they were shut out by prejudice, stupidity or ignorance.

Englishmen more than others insulated themselves when abroad from both what was bad and what was good in their environment. On his eastern travels Byron found that he had to wait hand and foot on his servant Fletcher, and ended by sending him home, tired of 'the perpetual lamentations after beef and beer, the stupid, bigoted contempt for everything foreign, and insurmountable incapacity of acquiring even a few words of any language'.[32] At home Englishmen preserved through all their national doings up and down the world an impregnable insularity. English literature reflected this in an indifference, nearly as complete as Mrs Rapkin's, to everything beyond the British Channel and St George's Channel, those natural frontiers of civilization. A tiny handful of Englishmen tried to follow Indian affairs and lend a helping hand to their Indian fellow-subjects;[33] the man in the street was satisfied with such items of interest as the 'wild Indian' exhibited in 1824 at Bartholomew Fair.[34]

'If only,' Ruskin exclaimed in one of his tirades against John Bull's absorption in his own comforts and profits, 'we English, who are so fond of travelling in the body, would also travel a little in the soul!'[35] Exploration of this kind was at least growing less rare by the end of the century, and with it interest, which had never been altogether lacking, in the arts and ideas of other regions, recognition that Europe and civilization were not one and the same thing. One symptom was the first appearance in 1904 of the popular series of translations entitled 'The Wisdom of the East'; it was edited by an English translator of Chinese poetry and an Indian scholar, and had for its object 'to bring together West and East in a spirit of mutual sympathy, goodwill, and understanding'. In 1911 a Universal Races Congress was held in London, another faint prelude to the quest for world harmony. Three years later the wisdom of the West was abruptly and violently called in question. Between its two great wars Europe passed through a long crisis of doubt and self-distrust that owed much to declining confidence in its position in the world, and deepening uncertainty about what the world thought of it. Fascism was in one aspect a convulsive effort to shake off this mood, to restore the legend of virility by hysterical and suicidal violence. Loss of empire has set Europe free to begin finding a better confidence, inspired by a new consciousness of itself and a new relationship with its neighbours, and to recollect in tranquillity its adventures across the seven seas.

NOTES

1. In R. F. Burton, *First Footsteps in East Africa* (1856), p. 333 (Everyman edn).
2. ibid., p. 308.
3. W. P. Andrew, *Our Scientific Frontier* (1880), pp. 54, 74.
4. Colonel G. B. Malleson, *The Indian Mutiny of 1857* (1892), p. 59.
5. Sir R. Temple, *India in 1880* (3rd edn, 1881), p. 418.

6. Proclamation of 13 February 1899; English text in R. B. Sheridan, *The Filipino Martyrs* (1900), p. 183.

7. S. Murtaza Ali, *History of Chittagong* (Dacca, 1964), p. 56.

8. Diderot, 'Sur les cruautés exercées par les Espagnols en Amérique', in *Fragments* (1772).

9. H. Spencer, *The Study of Sociology*, p. 211 (15th edn, 1889).

10. Graham Wallas, *The Great Society* (1914), Chapter 5.

11. W. S. Blunt, *My Diaries* (1932 edn), p. 375.

12. G. B. Malleson, op. cit., p. 249.

13. C. Crow, *Harris of Japan* (1939), pp. 79–80.

14. C. Bigham, *A Year in China, 1899–1900* (1901), p. 214.

15. G. Borrow, *Lavengro* (1851), Chapter 50.

16. F. Rolfe, *Hadrian the Seventh* (1904), Chapter 21.

17. A. Conan Doyle, *The Poison Belt* (1913), Chapter 2.

18. Lord Bryce, *South America. Observations and Impressions . . .* (1912), p. 123.

19. *Dismal England. By the Author of 'Merrie England'* (R. Blatchford) (1899), p. 209.

20. M. Proust, *The Guermantes Way*, trans. C. K. Scott-Moncrieff (Phoenix edn, 1930), Vol. 2, pp. 169–70.

21. 'F. Anstey' (T. A. Guthrie), *The Brass Bottle* (1900), p. 38 (Penguin edn).

22. H. H. Prichard, *Where Black Rules White* (revised edn, 1910), Chapter 9.

23. R. Hopkins, *An Exhortation to Good Life* (1586), p. 227.

24. Anon., *Ten Thousand Wonderful Things* (n.d.), p. 266.

25. See an article in *Middle Eastern Studies* (1969) by R. Clogg on the *Dhidhaskalia Patriki*, or 'Paternal Teaching', of Patriarch Anthimos (Stamboul, 1798), with translation of text.

26. *Memoirs of William Hickey*, ed. A. Spencer (9th edn, n.d.), Vol. 1, p. 220.

27. Colonel W. F. B. Laurie, *Our Burmese Wars and Relations with Burma* (1880), p. 397.

28. Alexandra David-Neel, translation of *The Superhuman Life of Gesar of Ling* (1933 : 1st edn, Paris, 1931), Introduction, pp. 34–5. On the derivation of 'Gesar' see Preface by Sylvain Lévi.

29. G. N. Curzon, *Problems of the Far East* (1894), Chapter 12.

30. F. von Bernhardi, *Germany and the Next War* (1911), p. 236 (trans. A. H. Powles).

31. D. Hay, *Europe, the Emergence of an Idea* (Edinburgh, 1957), p. 122.

32. Letter of 14 January 1811, in *The Letters of Lord Byron*, ed. R. G. Howorth, pp. 38–9 (Everyman edn).

33. A good proportion of them were Quakers. See J. H. Bell, *British Folks and British India Fifty Years Ago: Joseph Pease and his Contemporaries* (Manchester, n.d. (1891)).

34. *Oxberry's Dramatic Biography and Histrionic Anecdotes* (Vol. 3, 1825), p. 31.

35. A lecture of 1857, in *A Joy for Ever*, p. 100 (1906 edn).

INDEX

Note: Names in notes have not generally been included. A few of especial interest are; in these cases the number given first is that of the page on which either the note itself or the reference to it occurs, and is followed by the number in parentheses of the note in the list at the end of the chapter.

Abdul Hamid II, Sultan, 116
Abdul Mejid, Sultan, 120
Abd-ul-Qadir, 124–5
Aborigines Protection Society, xxi, 280
Abyssinia, 27, 222–3
Achebe, Chinua, *Things Fall Apart*, 216, 220
administration, *see* civil service, colonial administration *and* government
Adowa, battle of, 223
Afghanistan, 34, 126
Africa, 26, 27, 67–8, 203, 213; in 17C., 16; East, 221–9; North, 122–6; South, 229–35, 240–42; West, 214–21; Congo, 235–7; Berlin Conference on, 235, 236; chartered companies in, 234; Germans in, 236–8; Pan-Africanism, 246; white settlers in, 238–42; *see also* countries
Africans, 226–7; racial difference among, 223–4; and whites, 239–42; white's view of, 242–7; East, 222–25; South, 229–33, 240–41; West, 214–17; Bushmen, 229–30, 230–31; Hausas, 219; Hereros, 237; Hottentots, 229–30, 230; Ngoni (Angoni), 228–9; *see also* Zulus; in the Americas, 205–10, 332; in Europe, 203–5, 246; in Portuguese

colonies, 241; in Turkey, 211; *see also* Negroes *and* slavery
Agha Khan, the, 50
Aguinaldo, Emilio, President, 327
Ahmad, Sir Saiyad, 41, 54
Akbar, 18, 19
Albania, 119–20, 142
Alexander I of Russia, 23
Alexandria, Egypt, 122, 334
Algeria, 125–6, 217, 229, 239, 298
Ali, Mrs Meer Hassan, 59, 70
Ali Pasha of Janina, 119–20
America, *see* Latin America, United States of America, *and* West Indies
Amherst, Lord, 153–4
André, E., 306–7
Annam, *see* Vietnam
annexations, 26, 81, 270; in Africa 213; in India, 45, 47
Anson, Lord, 153, 294
'Anstey, F.', *The Brass Bottle*, 137, 331
apartheid; in Africa, 231, 242; in China, 162–4, in India, 60; *see also* race
Arabi Pasha, 124
Arabia, 126, 135–43, 143–5
Arabian Nights, The, 136, 137
Arabs, 7, 126, 207, 221, 326
Argentina, 288, 290, 295, 300, 301–3; gauchos, 286, 288, 292, 295, 316

aristocracy, 240; Chilean, 304; Chinese, 174, 259; Dutch, 93; English, 22, 37–8; Indian, 45–7 54–5, 59, 93–4; Indonesian, 93–4 Tahitian, 259

Armenians, 104, 167, 329

armies; mercenaries, 294, in Africa, 236; native, 178, 218, 246–7, 272; private, 328; Asian, 266; 137–8; British, 60–61, 83, 96, 234; Chinese, 177–8; Dutch 92; Egyptian, 122; European, 14–15, 328; French Foreign Legion, 96, 100; India, 43–4, 48–9, 55–6; Indian sepoy officers, 43, 46, 55, 162; Japanese, 189; Latin American, 292–3, 314–15, 316; Maori soldiers, 274–6; Russian, 101–2; Scottish soldiers, 219, 275; Turkish, 115, 116, 145; *see also* conscription

arts; African, 213; Chinese, 157; Indian, 70; Islamic, 7; Japanese 187; Maori music, 275; Persian, 173; of South America, 312; of Tahiti, 260; *see also* literature

Ashanti Wars, 5, 219

Asia; ancient, 1–8; through Middle Ages, 8–12, 14; in *17C.*, 16–19; *18C.*, 21–2; *19–20C.*, 23–30; resentment against Europe, 334–5; *see also* countries

Asiatic Society, 70, 88, 185

Assam, India, 63, 80–81, 82, 85

Auckland, Lord, 44–5

Aurangzeb, 19, 33

Australia, 191, 267, 273, 276–82; aborigines of, 278–9, 280–82, 327; convicts in, 276–7; half-castes, 281–2; settlers in, 279–81

Aztec empire, 10–11; Aztecs, 232

Bage, Robert, 23 (34)

Balkans, the, 28, 182, 295, 1820's risings, 114–5; *see also* Albania *and* Greece

Ballantyne, R. M., 228; *Coral Island*, 268

Basutoland, 231, 241

Bates, H. W., 289, 296–7, 309–10

Bechuanaland, 231, 241

Beckford, William, *Vathek*, 136

Bedouins, 120, 126

Belgium, 236; and Africa, 235–7

Bengal, India, 20, 34, 40, 47, 51–3, 60; 'Bengal Army', 73–4; Bengali literature, 42, 70; 'Young Bengal', 42, 46, 50

Bengalis, 34–5, 52–3, 55, 62, 71

Berbers, 7, 125

Bernard, Commissioner of Burma 82

Bernhardi, F. von, 335–6

Besant, Annie, 69

Bird, Isabella, 186

Bismarck, 128, 191, 313

Blantyre, mission at, 228, 245

Blatchford, R., 330

Blavatsky, Mme, 69

Bligh, Capt. William, 259

Blunt, Wilfred Scawen, 97, 130, 134, 193, 235, 328

Boer War, 48, 71, 234–5, 241

Boers, 24, 226, 229–31, 232, 241; Great Trek, 230–31

Bokhara, 104–5, 106

Bolìvar, Simon, 294

Bolivia, 288, 291, 301, 306, 316, 330

Bombay, India, 43, 56, 59, 71

Boole, Mary, 69

Booth, Joseph, 227, 245–6

Borneo, 89–90; British North Borneo Co., 91, 109 (56), 234; Murut tribe, 90

Borrow, George, 89, 329

Boswell, James, 140, 222

Bowring, Sir J., 122

Boxer rebellion, 28, 159, 173, 174–6, 178–9

Brazil, 11, 23, 287, 289, 295, 296; dress in, 308–12, 297–8; races in, 288, 308–12, 316, 205; slavery in, 308, 309

Brazza, Count de, 236
Bright, John, 116
Britain; and Africa, 238; and
China, 153–5, 158–60, 160,
161–4; and Egypt, 225–6; and
Europe, 22–3, 28, 129–30; and
France, 17, 27, 29, 95–6, 132,
274, 296; industry in, 167; and
Japan, 182, 183, 189, 190; and
Latin America, 294, 295, 296,
299, 300–301, 302, 304, 313–14;
and New Zealand, 273–5; and
Pacific, 269–71; and Persia, 133;
and Russia, 26, 28, 72, 105–6,
133; and Turkey, 115–18; see
also England, Ireland, Scotland
and Wales
British, the; in Burma, 81–5; in
Ceylon, 79–81; in Indonesia,
91–3; in Malaya, 85–91; and
N. Africa, 124, 125; in Persia,
134–5; and Russia, 105–6; in S.
Africa, 229–30, 232, 232–5,
240–42; see also Boer War; see
also Englishmen
British army, 267; in Burma, 83;
in India, 43–4, 59–61; in S.
Africa, 234
British empire, 26, 30, 33, 57, 64,
91, 92, 96, 30–31; creed of,
222; see also countries
British Indian Association, 42
British navy, 67, 92, 212
Brooke, J., 181
Brooke, Rajah, 89–90, 91
Brooke, Rupert, 272–3, 281
Browne, E. G., 130–31, 133
Browning, Robert, 125
Bruce, James, 222
Bryce, Lord, 292, 323 (101), 330
Buchan, John, 247
Buddhism, 332; in Burma, 83, 84;
in Ceylon, 80
Buenos Aires, 294, 296, 297,
303
Buganda, E. Africa, 224–5, 229
Bugeaud, Marshal T. R., 298

Bullen, F. T., 269, 275
Burke, Edmund, 114, 116
Burma, 81–5, 87, 96, 156, 332;
Shans and Karens, 84–5
Burnaby, F., 105
Burton, Richard, 221; in Africa,
221–2, 326; in East, 117, 121,
124, 125–6, 138, 141–2, 144, 212;
in India, 47–8, 71
businessmen, 27; in Africa,
218–19; in Latin America, 299,
314, 316, 317–18; in Pacific,
265–6; see also companies,
finance, industry and trade
Butler, Samuel, 275
Byron, Lord, 74 (43), 115, 119–20,
141, 142, 294, 335; Don Juan,
141
Byzantium, 5, 8; Byzantine
Empire, 4, 6, 7

Cairo, Egypt, 123, 141; slave-
market at, 211–12
Calabar, W. Africa, 214–15
Calcutta, India, 35, 42, 45, 60, 66,
71, 78, 82; education in, 40, 41
Cambodia, 95, 97
Cameroons, the French, 218
Campbell-Bannerman, Sir H., 234
Canada, 20, 239; French Canad-
ians, 229
cannibalism, 135, 224, 258, 268
Canning, George, 38, 49
Canning, Stratford, 118
Canton, China, 153, 154, 158, 162,
172, 175, 203, 262, 333
capitalism, 97; 'feudal', 15; in-
dustrial, 13, 334; British in
India, 62–3; Dutch in Indo-
nesia, 91–3; Japan and, 187;
Latin America, 291, 303; see
also finance
Carey, W., xxix, 34, 40, 41, 61,
65, 66, 69
Carlyle, T., 143, 209, 317
Carthage, 4, 37; Archbishop of,
235

caste, in India, 2, 35, 37, 40, 44, 53

Castelar, E., 125

Catherine the Great, 14, 134

Catholicism; in Brazil, 310; 'Chinese Rites', 164; and slavery, 205; in S. America, 312

Catholics, 332; missionaries, 195 (64); in Indochina, 99; in Japan, 201–2 (209); in Latin America, 201–2 (209); 291, 297, 315; in Pacific, 269–70; *see also* Jesuits

Caucasus, the, 102–3, 120, 125; Trans-caucasia, 103

Celebi, Katib, 112

Ceylon, 62, 79–81

Chang Chih-tung, 174

Chaudhuri, Nirad, 71

children; in Brazil, slavery of, 310; twins in Calabar, 215; Chinese girls, 169; in India, 60, 66, marriage of, 39

Chile, 287, 288, 289, 291, 299, 304–5; Araucanians, 289; armies of, 315; dress in, 298; and Peru, 280, 291, 292; in War of Pacific

Chilembwe, John, 245–6

China; ancient, 1, 2, 4, 5; history of, 9, 11, 21–2, 152–60; *19C.*, 25, 27, 28, 112, *20C.*, 328; Manchu conquest, 18, fall 177; opening of, 158–60; Boxer rebellion, 174–6; reprisals, 176; Taiping rebellion, 159–60, 174, 183; Foreign Office, 165; foreign residents in, 161–5; religion of, 164–5; and Europe, 16, 17, 18, 19; and Japan, 181–3, 192–3; Western view of, 259

Chinese, the, 71; and British, 162–4; business and labour of, 166–9; conversion of, 164–5; family life, 168; governing classes, 174; numbers of, 177–9; opinions of other nations,

early, 155–8; xenophobia of, 171–6; Western view of, 158–60, 165–71; abroad, 170–71, 205, 271, 305–6; in Africa, 240; in Indochina, 98; in Malaya, 88; in Peru, 305; in Singapore, 85; and Vietnam, 96; *see also* 'coolie' labour

Ch'ing dynasty, the, 152, 155, 158

Christianity; early, 5–6, 6–7, 7–8; schism, 12, 15; in Africa, 229, 245; in Burma, 85; in China, 164, 172; and imperialism, 11, 15, 24, 64, 332; in India, 40, 64–9; and Islam, 6, 143–5; in Japan, 192–3; in Latin America, 10, 290; 'muscular', 67; in Pacific, 269; *see also* Catholicism, missionaries *and* Protestants

Christophe, King Henri, 208, 209

Churchill, Winston S., 226

civil service; in Ceylon, 80; in China, 154; in India, 37, 42, 53, 58, 94

Clarke, Sir A., 86, 87

class structures; in Africa, 220, 223, 238–42; in Britain, 97; in Chile, 304; in China, 259; in Europe, 1, 2, 12; in France, 98; in India, *see* caste; in Indonesia, 93–4; in Japan, 157; in Tahiti 259; and race, 60, 239–40, 330–31; *see also* aristocracy *and* feudalism

Clemenceau, G. F., 246

Clive, R., 161

Cochrane, Lord, 294

Colombia, 296, 306

colonial administration, 33, 327; and home government, 291; Belgian, 235–7; British xxxi, 87, 124, 159–60, 210, 219–21, 240–42, 273–5, 276–7, 279–81; in India, 33, 37–9, 43–7, 48, 52–7; Dutch, 91–5, 229–31; French, xxxi–xxxii, 96–100, 125, 206–

207, 217–18, 229, 236, 210–11; German, 236–8; Portuguese, 10, 205, 241, 287; Russian, 102–3, 104–5; Spanish, 10, 206, 186–9; Turkish, 115, 117–18, 123–4
colonial armies, 218, 246, 328
colour, 15, 102, 162, 329, 332; in Africa, 223, 238–40, 253 (156); in India, 35; *see also* race
Columbus, 10
Colvin, Sir Auckland, 124
Connolly, James, 30
Combermere, Lord, 43
companies, chartered; in Africa, 218–19, 220, 234; British North Borneo Co., 91, 109 (56), 234; *see also* East India Co. *and* London Stock Exchange
Confucianism, 156, 192
Congo, the, 242, 267; Belgian, 235–37, 244; French, 236
Conrad, Joseph, *Nostromo*, 317
conscription, 14, 218; in Africa, 218; in Central Asia, 106–7; in Latin America, 292–3; in Turkey, 115
'Conselheiro', Antonio, 311
Constantinople, 8, 118· *see also* Stamboul
Cook, Capt. J., 256–8; in Pacific, 92, 203, 256–9, 261, 272, 273, 276
'coolie' labour; in Africa, 241; in Australia and New Zealand, 280–81; in India, 63–4, 67; in Indochina, 98; in Jamaica, 209; in Malaya, 88, 90; in Pacific, 271; in South America, 305, 317; Chinese 'coolie trade', 169–70
Crimea, 141; war in, 28, 113, 115, 116, 125, 301
Crusades, the, 7
Cuba, 206; *see also* West Indies
Cunninghame Graham, R. B., 313
Curzon, G. N. (Lord), 131–2, 133, 135, 136, 144, 174, 180, 334
Cyprus, 113, 117

Da Cunha, E., 311
Dahomey, W. Africa, 214, 217
Dale, J. P., 296
Dalhousie, Lord, 38
d'Anethan, Baroness A., 200 (172)
Darwin, C.; in Africa, 230; in Australia, 276–7, 278; in Latin America, 288, 289, 309, 316; in Pacific, 263, 274
Das, Sarat Chandra, 52 (76)
Daudet, Léon, 125
Davis, Sir John., 157
de Lanessan, J. L., 99
Defoe, Daniel, *Captain Singleton*, 17, 203
Delhi, India, 85, 127, 326
democracy, 191, 240; African village, 220; Greek, 2; parliamentary, 118; *see also* liberalism
Derozio, 42
Dessalines, 207
Diaz, Porfirio, 318
dictatorship, 318
Diderot, D., 327
Dilke, Sir C. W., 76 (85), 200, (179)
Dingiswayo, 232
Disraeli, Benjamin, 43, 116
Doyle, Sir Arthur Conan, 309; *The Poison Belt*, 229–30; Sherlock Holmes, 131, 139
dress; in Africa, 225; of European women in tropics, 93; in Latin America, 298; in Turkey, 121
Dryden, John, 33
Dunsterville, General L. C., 135, 137, 160
Dutch, the; in Africa, 203; 'Griqua' half-castes, 231, *see also* Boers; in Ceylon, 79; in Japan, 19, 181, 192; in Indonesia, 12, 85, 91–5; and slavery, 205; and Spain, 11, 13; Dutch forces, 92; *see also* Holland

Dutch empire, 91–3, 97
Dutt, R. C., 54 (78)
Dyaks, 89, 90

East India Co., British, 11, 20, 25, 34, 38–9, 42, 45, 47, 49, 61, 234
Eastern Question, the, 26, 112, 114
economy; in Burma, 84; in Ceylon, 79; in Egypt, 122; in India, 49, 62–3; 'Culture System' in Indonesia, 92; of Paraguay, 303; in Turkestan, 106; see also capitalism, finance, trade and usury
Ecuador, 306
Eden, Emily, 44 (36), 40
education; in China, 164–5; in England, 38, 50; in India, 40–42, 49–50, 52, 59, 66, 70; in Indonesia, 95; in Russia, 41
Edward, Prince of Wales (later Edward VII), 265, 305
Egypt; ancient, 2, 3; and Britain, 225–6; Coptic Church, 222; under Mehemet Ali, 122–4; and N. Africa, 225–6, 232; slavery in, 211–12; and Turkey, 114, 117–18, 225; women of, 141
Elgin, Lord, 167
Elliott, C., 79
empire, see British empire and imperialism
Engels, F., 137
England; in 16C., 13, 19C., 37, 48, 50, 118, 299, 331; and Australia, 280; class in, 331; and culture, 97, 311, 335; and Japan, 189; and slavery, 206, 211, 212–13; see also Britain
Englishmen, 22, 97, 314, 335; in Africa, 219–21; in Ceylon, 79–81; in China, 153–5; 158, 162–5, 171; in India: first period, 33–7; after mutiny, 47–60, 100–101; aloofness of, 43–7;

aristocracy, 22, 37–8; missionaries, 64–9; Nabobs, 35, 37, 39, 58; reformers, 37–42; settlers, 61–4; soldiers, 59–60; in 20C., 71–2; in Japan, 184–5., 186, 192; in New Zealand, 273–4; in Persia, 128–34; in S. America, 297; see also British, the, and missionaries
Erzerum, 7
Eurasians; in Ceylon, 80; in Dutch East Indies, 93
Europe; ancient, 1–8; late Middle Ages, 8–12; 15–16C., 12–16; 17C., 16–19; 18C., 20–23; 19C., 21, 23–30, 217; 20C., 237, 238, 325; community of, 15, 28–9, 161, 239–40; wars in, 16, 20, 218, 247, 273, 328; attitude to other countries, 325–8; insularity, 335–6; civilizing mission of, 24, 25, 98, 277; fear of retaliation, 246–7, 333–4; method of rule, 326–31; religion, 331–3; and S. America, 294–302
    view of S. America, 302–307, 312–18; see also countries
European; financiers, 233–4; pioneers, 24–5, 333; in Africa, 238–42; East Africa, 221–9; West Africa, 214–21; African view of, 224–5; view of African, 242–7; in Australia, 277–81; in Ceylon, 79–81; view of East, 136–43 ; in India, see Englishmen; in Pacific, 255–67, 273–5; see also nationalities, missionaries and settlers
Everest, Sir G., 69
Eyre, E. J., Governor, 209

Faidherbe, L. L. C., Governor, 217
family, the, 332; Chinese, 168–9; in Pacific, 260; see also children and marriage
Fath Ali Shah, 143

feudalism, 12, 14, 63, 287; early, 5; and colonialism, 94–5; and serfdom, 14; in Malaya, 87–8

Fiji islands, 264, 270, 271, 272, 281

finance; banks and loans, 299, 314; moneylenders, 36, 84, 99; stocks and shares, 79, 233–4, 314; *see also* capitalism, companies, economy *and* taxation

Forbes, A. K., 70

Formosa, 25, 190

Forster, E. M., 72

France, 8, 13, 16, 20, 329; in *18C.*, 20; *19C.*, 26, 29, 299; *1789* revolution, 20, 23, 24, 152–3, 207; *1830*, 41; and Britain, 17, 26, 28, 95, 132, 296; and China, 153–4, 156, 164–5, 172; and Egypt, 122; and Japan, 183, 189, 190, 202 (218); and native troops, 218, 246, 272; and slavery, 207, 212; and S. America 296, 300–301, 305

Francia, Dr J. G. R. de, 302–3, 316–17

French, the, 20, 96; in Africa: East, 229; North, 125, 239; West, 217–18, 219; Congo, 236; in Indochina, 24, 95–100; in Japan, 184, 185, 187; and New Zealand, 239, 273; in Orient, 141; in Pacific, 264, 267, 270, 271, 272, 273; and West Indies, 207, 209; *see also* Jesuits; French imperialism, 96–100, 328; nationalism, 97

Freyre, G., 311, 314

Fuchow, China, 172, 173

Fulani emirs, in Nigeria, 220

Gandhi, xxxi

Garibaldi, 297

Ganbil, Antoine, xviii

Gauguin, 266

Geary, G., 83, 18, 19

Gell, Sir W., 119

Germans, the, 96; abroad, 163; in Africa, 237–8, 246; in Brazil, 296–7; in India, 66; in Pacific, 265, 270; in S. America, 299–300; businessmen, 313; missionaries, 237; in Australia, 280; in India, 66; Nazis, 103, 236; German army, 26, 218

Germany; in *18C.*, 12; *19C.*, 142, 191; *20C.*, 179, 236–7, 335, 173, 176, 179; loss of colonies, 280–81

Ghalib, xix, xxxi

Gilbert islands, 267

Gladstone, W. E., xxx, 91, 116, 270, 279

Gobineau, Count, xvi

Goethe, 127, 136

Goldring, Rev. A., 201

Goldsmith, Oliver, 21

Gordon Sir A., xx

Gordon, C. G., General, 143, 160, 164, 226

government, methods of; impersonal, 56–8; 'indirect rule', 220; puppet rulers, 54–5; 99; by white settlers, 210, 274; in Africa: native, 225, British, 220, French, 217; in Australia, 280; in British West Indies, 210; Chinese, 154; Eastern, 137; European, 98; in India, 37–9, 43–7, 52, 53–5, 56–8, police, 71; in Indochina, 99; in Indonesia, 92–3; in Latin America, 287, 294–5, 317; in Malaya, 86–7; in New Zealand, 274; in Persia, 133; in Tahiti, French, 270–71; Turkish, 116, 117–18; *see also* civil service, democracy *and* feudalism

Graham, Helen, 33 (1), 264 (33)

Grant Duff, M. E., 231

Gray, J. H., Archdeacon, 167

Greece; ancient, 1, 2–3, 4, 5; *1820s* rising, 114–15, 119, 121–2, 294; *see also* Balkans

Greek Orthodox Church, 5, 102, 115
Grey, Sir C., 81
Grey, Sir G., xx
Grimble, Sir A., xv, xx, 271
Grogan, E. S., 223, 228, 237, 242, 243–5, 247
Guinea, 203, 214; 'Slave Coast', 210–11; German New Guinea, 280

Hacket, John, 204
Haggard, Rider, 232; *She*, 242
Haiti, 28, 206–9, 332
Hall, Capt. Basil; in Latin America, 287, 292, 294, 315; in Lewchew, 261–2
Hall, H. Fielding, 82, 83, 84
Hapsburg Empire, 8, 29, 98
Harar, E. Africa, 221, 222
Hare, D., 41
harems; African, 225; Oriental, 139–42
Harris, Townsend, 181, 187, 188, 327
Hart, Sir R., 198 (122)
Hawaii (Sandwich Islands), 257 265, 270, 272; Hawaiians, 272, 305; monarchs, 265, 305
Hearn, Lafcadio, 185
Heber, Bishop, xxix, 44
Henry, Prince of Prussia, 172
Herbert, F. W. von, Capt'., 116(18)
Hickey, William, 333
Hinduism, 37, 51, 68; and social reform, 68
Hindus, 26, 35, 37, 51, 53, 67, 69, 71, 132; and missionaries, 64–6, and Muslims, 27, 34, 54–5, 58–9, 335
Hitler, Adolph, 16, 26, 318
Holland, 11, 13, 93, 95, 204, 286; *see also* Dutch, the
Honduras loans, the, 314
Hopkins, Richard, 332
Horace, 4
Hottentots, 229, 230

Huns, the, 6, 113

immigration; Chinese, 170–71; to USA, 28, 170–71; admission to India, 62; shuffling-up of peoples, 10–11, 271, 333; *see also* settlers *and* slave trade
imperialism, 9–12, 24, 25, 26–7, 54, 64, 81–2, 161, 237, 325–6; Belgian, 235–7; British, xxvii–xxviii, 26, 33, 34, 68, 91, 96, 133, 134, 223, 224–5, 280, 330–31, *see also* British Empire; Dutch, 12, 91–5, 97, 231; French, 95–100, 270; German, 236–8; Japanese, 192–3; Portuguese, 9, 24; Russian, 107; Spanish, 10–11, 23, 286, 290–91
Incas, the, 37, 290, 312; Inca empire, 10
India, 17, 22, 98, 336; ancient, 1–2, 4, *16C.*, 10; *17C.*, 19; *18C.*, 20; British conquest of, 25–6, 33–7, 161, 326; reform of, 37–42; rule in, 43–5; annexation, 45, 46–7; 1793 settlement, 47; Mutiny, 47–9, 94, 334, effects of, 48–53; since independence, 85; Anglo-Indian relations, 55–61, 70–72; Brahmins, 22, 34, 45, 69; civil service, 37–8, 63; education in, 40–42, 50–52, 59, 67; European life in, 45–7; European attitude to British in, 28, 105–6; landlordism, 47, 51; landowners, 45–6, 47, 54, 63; Muslim rule in, xxv, 27, 34, 39, 55; 'Nabobs', 35, 36, 39, 58; newspapers, 40, 61, 62, 63, 71, 82; princes, 45–7, 53–5, 59, 93–4; racialism in, 35, 59–60, 63; religion, 39, 64–9; European settlers, 61–2
Indian army, 55–6, 102; 'Bengal army', 43–4; sepoy officers, 28, 43, 46, 55; in China, 161–3; mutiny of, 47–9

Indian National Congress, 38, 52
Indians; in Africa, 240–41; in
Burma, 82, 84; in Ceylon, 80;
in Malaya, 88; Bengalis, 71;
Bhils, 44; Chettis, 99; Jats, 56;
Marathas, 34; Nagas, 85; Raj-
puts, 55, 71; Sikhs, 34, 48, 55,
56; *see also* Hindus
Indians, Americans, 73 (16), 287–
93, 298, 304, 305, 316, 330; of
Brazil and Guianas, 308–10
Indochina, 95–100; Moi tribes, 98
Indonesia, 11, 36, 41, 54, 59, 85,
91–5
industrialism, 13, 15, 17, 96, 334
industry; in China, 167–8, 177;
Egypt, 122; England, 67, 167;
India, 63–4; Latin America,
299–300, 314, 317, 318; *see
also* labour, plantations *and*
trade
Ionian islands, 117
Iraq, 134, 207
Ireland, 28, 29–30, 60, 101, 131,
239–40, 270
Irish, the, 29–30, 239; in Brazil,
297, 317; soldiers, 294
Isfahan, Persia, 127, 132
Islam, 2, 5, 9, 27; in Africa, 220;
in Arabia, 126; and Christianity, 6, 7, 9, 143–5, 332; in India,
19; in Indonesia, 93; in Russia,
14; *see also* Muslims
Israel, 328
Italy; in *18C.*, 12; *19C.*, 29, 125,
299; *20C.*, 329; and Abyssinia,
222; and Tripoli, 124
Italians, the, 18, 235; in Brazil,
297, 314
Ito, Prince Hirobumi, 191
Itúrbide, Agustín de, 295
Iyeyasu, first Tokugawa Shogun,
18

Jamaica, 35, 206; slavery in, 207,
208, 209–10
Jamaicans, 204, 210, 248 (12)

Japan, xxvi, 17, 18, 157, 256, 281,
314, 328, 329; alliance with, 26,
190, 192–3; and China, 156,
160, 173, 175; and Lewchews,
260, 262; Meiji Restoration,
183; modernization of, 17, 27,
119, 334; opening of, 181–7;
war with Russian, 28, 71, 176,
185, 190
Japanese, the; ideology of, 191–2;
forces, 189–91; Western views
of, 168, 187–90
Java, 93, 94, 169, 176
Jesuits; at Peking, 17, 19, 21, 152,
155, 164; in Paraguay, 290–91
Jews, 204, 233, 329; in Europe,
16, 84; in Spain, 7, 9; in Turkey, 117
Johnson, Dr, 16, 27, 140, 153,
204
Johnston, Sir H. H., 223, 243
Johnston, R. F., 173 (110, 111)
Jokai, M., *Timar's Two Worlds*,
142
Jones, Sir William, 40
Juárez, Benito, 293, 308

Kabyles, the, 125, 147 (60)
'Kaffir Wars', 230, 233
Kalakaua, King of Hawaii, 265,
305
Kamekameha, King of Hawaii,
265
Kashgar, 127
Kashmir, 66–7
Kataev, V., 104
Kaye, Sir J. W., 48 (58)
Keltie, J. S., 244 (176)
Kempton, J., 210
Kenya, 240–41
Kenyatta, Jomo, 240–41
Keppel, Capt. Hon. H., 89
Ketteler, Baron von, 176
Khiva, 104–5, 106
Kiernander, 39
Kinglake, A. W., 117, 120, 136,
137, 138, 140

Kingston, W. H. G., *The Three Midshipmen*, 122, 161, 169, 212
Kipling, Rudyard, 56, 134, 173, 177, 185, 186, 209, 234
Kitchener, H. (Lord), 108, 226
Korea, 96, 156, 179, 261; women in, 284 (27)
Kuang Hsü, Emperor, 174
Kumasi, Ashanti capital, 219

labour, forms of; *corvée*, 218; debt-slavery, 86; 'indentured', 62, 267; in Asia, 98; in Australia, 280; in China, 168; in India, 63; in Latin America, 312, 316, 318; shifted between countries, 11, 341, 271, 333; *see also* conscription, 'coolie' labour, serfdom *and* slavery
Lane, E. W., 123, 139, 141
languages, 2, 22, 41–2; in Africa, 218; Asian, 81; Chinese, 155, 163; Indian, 22, 41–2, 50; in Latin America, 290; in Pacific, 261, 268; Persian, 127
Langworthy, E. Booth, 227
Las Casis, Bartolomé de, 10, 20, 39, 327
Latin America, 1; Spanish conquest of, 10, 20; rebellion against Spain, 23, 286–7; after, 287–8; business in, 313, 316, 318; European view of, 302–8, 312–18; forces, 314–15; government of, 294–5, 298, 314–18; immigrants in, 296–8; Pan-American ideal, 300–301; races in, 287–90, 308–12, 316; religion in, 312, 315; subjugation of Indians, 290–93; women in, 316; *see also* countries
Lenin, V. I., 106
Leonowens, Anna, 180
Leopold, King of the Belgians, 25, 235
Lewchew Islands (Ryukyu), 260–262

Li Hung-chang, 165, 177
liberalism; in Chile, 287; Japan, 192; Latin America, 294
Lima, Peru, 291, 298, 314, 316; 1864 conference at, 300; and Indians, 291
literature; Chinese, 163; Eastern, 139, 336; English, 335; European, in India, 41–2, 49–51, 52; Indian, 70; Persian, 127, 138
Livingstone, D., xix, 61, 224, 226–7, 231, 232, 236, 238, 240, 243
Lloyd George, David, 246
Lockwood, D., 285 (103)
London Missionary Society, 226, 263
London Stock Exchange, 233–4, 314
López, C. A., of Paraguay, 291
López, S., of Paraguay, 291, 303
Loti, Pierre, *Vers Ispahan*, 132, 138, 200 (181)
L'Ouverture, Toussaint, 207–8
Lynch, Admiral P., 304

Macao, China, 162, 203, 305
Macartney, Lord, 153–4, 157, 158, 161, 171
Macartney, Sir Halliday, 166
Macaulay, Lord, 34–5, 38, 41, 50
Madagascar, 228
Magyars, 6, 15, 98, 239
Mahmud II of Turkey, 113, 118
Mahdism, 226, 245, 247, 311
Malawi, 245, 254 (180)
Malaya, 85–91, 271
Malays, 25, 86, 88–9, 273, 326
Malcolm, Sir John; in India, 46–7, 53–4, 87; in Persia, 128
Malacca, 86
Malleson, Col. G. B., 326, 328
Manchus, the, in China, 152, 156, 157–8, 169, 177, 192
Mandalay, 81, 82
Manet, E., 307
Markham, Sir R C., 322 (76)
Marquesas islands, 264–5, 266, 272

marriage; child-, 39; inter-; in Brazil, 310–11; in China, 162; East Indies, 93; in Europe, 16; in India, 59–60; in New Zealand, 275; polygamous: in Muslim countries, 139–42; 255–6; in Tahiti, 259–60; *see also* harems
Martyn, H., 65
Marx, Karl, xxiv–xxv, 49, 119, 155
Maugham, Somerset, 56, 59, 163, 271
Maxwell, Capt. Murray, 260–61, 262
Maxwell Sir P. B., 87
Mazade, C., 295, 301
Mecca, 33, 126, 131, 212
Medina, 144
Mehemet Ali, 122, 136, 232
Meiggs, H., 300, 305, 317
Melville, Herman, 264–5, 267, 268
Menelek II of Abyssinia,, 222
Mexico, 10, 37, 289, 293, 295, 300, 308; and Maximilian, 307; under Diaz, 318
Mill, James, xix–xx
missionaries, Christian, 10; in Africa, 213, 214–15, 216, 218, 227, 228, 245; in Asia, 6, 18; in Australia, 280; in Burma, 84–5; in China, 164–5, 174; German, 66, 237, 280; in India, 39–40, 61, 64–8, 144; in Japan, 18; and Muslims, 144; in New Zealand, 274; in Pacific, 263, 267–271; *see also* Christianity *and* Jesuits
Mitford, A. B. (Lord Redesdale), 199 (164)
Mohamed, Duse, xxxvi
Mollendorf, R. von, 179
Mongkut, King of Siam, 180
Mongolia, 19, 334
Mongols, 6, 7; Buryats, 103; Golden Horde, the, 6, 101, 103
Montevideo, 296, 300; Republic of, (Uruguay), 302

Montgomery, H. H., 66 (113), 171 (95)
Morel, E. D., 234, 238
Morier, J., *Hajji Baba of Ispahan*, 128–9, 131
Morocco, 125, 135
Mtesa, King of Buganda, 225
Multatuli, *Max Havelaar*, 94
Munchausen, Baron, 141, 211, 258
Muslims; in 19C., 143–5; in Asia, 103, 127; and Europe, 7–8; in India, 34, 37, 39, 54–5, 58–9, 65, 67 70, 71, 144, 335; in *Maghrib*, 124; pilgrims, 34, 130, in Soudan, 106, 226, 245, 311; *see also* Islam
Mwanga, King of Buganda, 229

Nagasaki, Japan, 18, 304
Napoleon, 5, 16, 23, 26, 71, 114, 122, 123, 136, 207, 208, 286
Napoleon III, 217, 300, 307
Nasr-ul-Din, Shah of Persia, 128, 131
Nasrullah Khan, Emir of Bokhara, 104–5, 100
nationalism, 5, 295, 333; in Balkans, 114; in Burma, 83; in China, 172–3; European, 12, 13, 331; in Far East, 27, 30; French, 97–8; German, 237; Indian, 41, 50–54, 68, 70, 133–4; in Indochina, 100; in Indonesia, 94–5; in Latin America, 287; Persian, 133; Spanish, 70–71; Turkish, 27
navies, 14, 92, 170; British, 67, 212; Japanese, 189; naval war, 8, 9–10; steamboats, 119, 161, 167
Negroes, 203–5, 214, 216, 246, 261; in Brazil, 309; in Haiti; 207–8; rebellions of, 207; slavery, 205–7, 210–13, 309, after abolition of, 209–10, 292, as soldiers, 219, 229, 246, 247, 272; *see* also Africans

Netherlands, *see* Holland
New Zealand, 239, 258, 272, 273–
76, 281; Hau-Hau, 274; Maoris,
273–6
Newton, John, 211
Nigeria, 144, 215, 216, 219–20
Nivedita, Sister, 68
Noble Savage, the, 22–3, 256
Northwood, J. D., 90
Nubar Pasha, 118–19
Nyasaland, 228, 229, 245, 269

O'Donnell, General Leopoldo, 125
O'Donovan, E., 129
Okuma Shigenobu, 193
Omai, 258–9, 261
Omar Khayyam, 127
Omar Pasha, 113
opium, 25, 100, 171; trade in, 155,
161, 286; Opium Wars, the,
153, 159, 161, 171
Orwell, George, 76 (88) 108 (27)
Osborn, Capt. S., 158–9, 161, 171
Ottoman Empire, *see* Turkey
Oudh, India, 45, 47, 54, 58
Outram, General Sir James, 44
Oyono, F., *Houseboy*, 218

Pacific Islands; Europeans in:
xx, 263–7; missionaries, 267–
70; Western rule in, 269–73;
native rulers, 263, 265, 266, 267,
see also Lewchew Islands *and*
Tahiti
Pacifico, Don, 210
Páez, J. A., 286, 291
Paine, Tom, 36
Pakistan, 55; since independence,
xxiii, xxxiv–xxxv
Palmerston, Lord, 26, 122, 139,
209
Pan-Africanism, 246
Panjab, India, 48, 53, 55, 66, 71
Paraguay, 290–91, 301, 302–3,
315, 317
Parish, Woodbine, 66, 303, 321
(62)

Park, Mungo, 214, 226
Parkes, Sir Harry, 181, 183, 184,
185, 314
Pearson, W., Viscount Cowdray,
305, 318
Peking; Jesuits at, 17, 19, 21, 152,
153, 160; looted, 198 (126);
ministers at, 160, 172, 173
Pelew (Palau) islands, 165–6
Penang, 71, 86
Perak, Malaya, 87
Perry, Commodore M. C., 182
Persia, 1–2, 3, 4, 5, 6, 19, 27, 34,
128–9, 137–8, 330; Babi sect,
131; Bakhtiari tribe, 134; nat-
ional movement, 133–5
Peru 210, 288, 305–6, 317; of
Incas, 10; army of, 293, 314–
15; and Bolivia, 293; Chincha
Islands, 300; Indian rebellion
in, 291, 292; religious proces-
sion in, 290; in War of the
Pacific, 301, 304, 315
Pétion, A. S., 208
Philippine Islands, 169; and
Americans, 95, 327, 328; and
Spaniards, 11, 95
Picton, Sir T., 327
pirates, 9, 18–19, 20, 24–5, 86,
112–13, 169
Pitt, William, the younger, 114
plantations; in Brazil, 309; Cey-
lon, 79, 80–81; 62–3; Indo-
china, 99; Indonesia, 91–3;
Malaya, 88, 90–91; Pacific, 267,
271, 280; Peru, 305; Turkestan,
106; West Indies, 16
Plunkett, Hon. F. R., 201 (209)
Pogodin, M. P., 101, 110 (79)
Polo, Marco, 6
Pomare, Queen of Tahiti, 263, 270
Pombal, Marquis of, 290–91
population; Chinese, 178–9;
French, 98; Persian, 131; white,
28; over-, 179
Portugal, 10, 16, 24, 29, 204, 287,
312

Portuguese, the, 11, 18, 33, 79, 95, 162, 205, 212, 305, 327; early expansion by, 9–11; African colonies, 203, 210, 227, 241; and Brazil, 11, 287, 297, 312
Prempeh, Ashanti king, 219
Prichard, H. H., 31 (40), 208–9, 332
Protestants, 11, 12, 13, 116, 195 (64), 239, 331; in Africa, 229; in Pacific, 269
Proust, M., 330
Pushkin, 101

Quakers, 64, 161, 338 (33)
Quiller-Couch, Sir A., 64

Rabelais, 8
race, 329, 330; and class, 60, 238–42, 331–2; in Europe, 16; racial mixture in Brazil, 308–12; relations: in Africa, 211, 218, 229–31, 238–46; in Australasia, 280–81; in Tahiti, 270–71; and revenge, 246–7, 333–4; Races Congress, *1911*, 336; *1919* proposal, 281; racialism: 97; in China, 162–3; in India, 35, 49, 59–60, 67, 94–5; in Indonesia, 93–4; *see also* colour
Raffles, Sir Stamford, 85, 88
Raleigh, Sir Walter, 17
Ram Mohun Roy, 41, 42, 50
Ranavalona, Queen of Madagascar, 228
Rangoon, 81, 82, 85
Reade, Winwood, 24, 145, 215–16, 230
Reed, Sir E. J., 189
Reformation, 12, 14
religion, xxviii–xxx, 331–3; and class, 239–40; and nationalism, 5; strife in, 15, 269–70; of Abyssinia, 222; in Africa, 245; in China, 164–5; 'Ethiopianism', 245; in India, 39–40, 64–9; in Indochina, 99–100; in Japan, 191–3; of Pacific Islands, 258; in Persia, 130–31; in Turkey,

115–16; *see also* Buddhism, Christianity *and* Islam
Renaissance, 12, 15
Rhodes, Cecil, xl, 233, 234, 245
Rhodesia, 67, 234, 238; Southern, 210
Ripon Lord, xxviii
Robespierre, 48, 207
Roebuck Bay, Australia, 267
Rolfe, F., *Hadrian the Seventh*, 329
Rome, 3–4; Roman Empire, 4, 207
Rosas, Manuel, 288, 296, 300, 316
Rosebery, Lord, 280
Rousseau, 22, 50, 303
Rumanika, Ugandan ruler, 223, 224
Rumford, Count, 152
Ruskin, John, 25, 212, 336
Russell, Bertrand, 191
Russell, Lord John, 57
Russia, 6, 23, 26, 28, 72, 175, 178; education in, 41; serfdom in, 15, 209; and China, 17, 161, 178; and Europe, 13–14; and India, 28, 72, 105–6; and Japan, 28, 71, 177, 185, 189, 190, 193; and Latin America, 294; and Persia, 131, 132–5; and Turkey, 26, 115
Russian Empire in Asia, 101–7
Russians, the, 101, 107; Cossacks, 70, 102, 103; soldiers, 101–2; in Japan, 185

Saigon, 96
Salisbury, 3rd Marquess of, 29, 210
Samarkand, 104, 105
Samoa, 270; Samoans, 266, 272
San Martín, José de, 291, 292, 294
Sandwich Islands, *see* Hawaii
Santa Cruz, A., 293
Santiago, Chile, 304, 313
Sarawak, 89–90, 91
Sarmiento, D. F., 298–9, 301, 303, 310, 311

Satow, Sir E., 184–5
scholarship; Arabian, 7; European, 29; re China, 163; re India, 70; *see also* Asiatic Society *and* education
Schopenhauer, 142, 205
Schreiner, Olive, 230, 234
Schuyler, E., 106
Scotland, 45, 60, 126, 214, 222, 227, 259, 262, 266, 270, 277; Church of, 269; missionaries, 214, 228, 245; Highlanders, 15, 219, 275
Scott, M., *Tom Cringle's Log*, 206 (17, 18), 208, 295 (31)
Scott, Sir W., 139, 141, 214
Secret Societies; African, 214; Chinese, 85
Seeley, Sir J. R., 57, 84, 71
Ségur, Comte P. de, 101
Senegal, W. Africa, 217–18
Serampore, India, 40
serfdom, 5, 14, 206, 209
settlers, European, 17, 80, 210, 239; government by, 210, 274; in Africa, 239–42; Australia, 276, 279–80, 280–81; Brazil, 309–10; India, 61–4; Latin America, 291, 297; New Zealand, 274; *see also* immigration
Sex, 331, 225–6, 243; Cameroons, 218; Chinese, 170–71; in Indonesia, 93, 99; Japan, 187–8; Orient, 139–41; Pacific Islands, 255–6, 264–5; *see also* marriage *and* women
Shakespeare, 17, 113, 127, 222, 240; studied in India, 50, 52; performed in Peru, 298; Caliban, 241
Shamil Bey, 103
Shelley, 155
Shinto, 192
Shongi, Maori chief, 274
Shuster, W. H., 134, 149 (114)
Siam, 27, 85, 86, 95, 180–81, 182, 328

Siberia, 17, 24, 102
Sierra Leone, 216
Singapore, 85–6
Skobolev, General, 111 (97)
Slatin, Sir R., 243
slave trade; in Africa, 203, 210–12, 215–16, 226; 'Slave Coast', 210–11; in the Americas, 205–10; Chinese 'Coolie trade', 170; in India, 35; in Pacific, 267, 270; by Russians, 106; suppression of, 212–13; *see* 'coolie' labour
slavery, 10–11, 16; in Brazil, 309, 309–10; in Britain, 204; in Indochina, 99; in West Africa, 215; abolition of, 79, 209, 239, 292; slave revolts, 206–7; *see also* 'coolie' labour
Slessor, Mary, 219
Smith, Adam, 20, 29, 91, 312
Smith, Albert, 121, 143, 211
Smith, Sydney, xxiii, 313
Smuts, J. C., Field-Marshal, 234
socialism, 30, 334; in Paraguay, 303
Somalia, 221–3, 325–6
Soudan, 106, 122, 144, 175, 226, 247; British conquest of, 226; Dervishes in, 143; Mahdism in, 226, 245, 247, 311
South Africa, *see under* Africa
South America, *see* Latin America
South Seas, *see* Pacific Islands
Spain, 112; Arab, 7, 9, 10, 11, 13, 15; in 19C., 23, 24, 28, 29, 69, 95, 287, 288, 297; and N. Africa, 125; and slavery, 205–6, 211, 212; and S. America, 10, 20, 23, 205–6, 286–7, 288, 299, 300–301
Spaniards, in America, 10, 73 (16), 286, 288, 289, 290–92
Speke, J. H., 223–6, 243, 325–6
Spencer, Herbert, 327
Spice Isles (the Moluccas), 92

Stamboul (Constantinople), 8,
118–19, 129, 138, 143; Dervishes
of, 143; the seraglio, 141, 142
Stanhope, Lady Hester, 137, 158
Stanley of Alderley, Lord, 145
Stanley, H. M., 235
Stepniak, S., 30 (19)
Sterne, Lawrence, 22
Stevenson, R. L., 3, 227, 266, 269,
270, 271
Stewart, Major-Gen. Sir N., 177
(138)
Straits Settlements, 86
Sulaiman the Magnificent, 8
Sulaiman Pasha (Sève), 122
Sumatra, 95
Suttee, 37, 39, 40, 69
Swaziland, 241
Swettenham, Sir F., 87, 88
Swift, Dean, *Gulliver's Travels*,
18, 19, 266
Syria, 137

Tagore, Rabindranath, xxxviii,
42, 50
Tahiti, 255–60, 263–4, 266; and
the French, 269, 270, 272
Tanganyika, 237
Tartars, 7, 14, 113
Tasmania, 102, 276–7
Tchaka, Zulu King, 231–2, 240
technology, 4, 23, 27, 50; African,
213; American, 312; Austra-
lian, 278; Chinese, 154; Euro-
pean, 15, 20; Japanese, 191;
Turkish, 119; *see also* industri-
alism
Teheran, 129, 131, 134
Tennyson, Lord, 127, 142
Tetens, A., 265–6
Thackeray, W. M., 35; Eastern
travels, 120–21, 122–3, 138, 141,
142, 211–12; *Vanity Fair*, 141
Theeban, King of Burma, 82, 334
theosophy, 69
Thompson, E., *An Indian Day*,
66 (121)

Tibet, 52, 69, 156, 180, 333
Timor, 95
Tonking, 97, 172
Torrington, Lord, 79
torture, 67, 129, 168, 327
tourists, 203; in Australia, 278;
Egypt, 122–4; Japan, 186, 191;
Near East, 119–22; Pacific Is-
lands, 268
trade, 4, 9, 24, 85; in China, 167;
with China, 153–4, 155, 159–60;
in India, 61; *see also* East India
Co.; in Japan, 187, 189; in
Latin America, 289, 299–300,
313–14; in Pacific Islands, 256,
257, 260, 265–6, 270–71, 274;
see also businessmen, companies, plantations *and* slave
trade
Tradescant collection, the, 17
Trelawney, E. J., 35, 86, 96, 228
Trevelyan, C. E., 38, 40
Trevelyan, G. O., 48–9, 51, 62,
71
Tripoli, 124
Turkestan, 135; Eastern, 19, 127,
160; Russian, 104
Turkey, 139, 216, previous history of, 8–9, 19, 112–13; *in 18C*.,
20, 114, *in 19C*., 26, 27, 103,
114, 119; *20C*., 189; and Balkans, 114–15; British support of,
115–16; and Russia, 103, 106,
107, 115, 144; tourists in, 120–
21; women in, 140–42, 259–60;
Turkish administration, 114,
117–18; nationalism, 27, 103,
114; *see also* Stamboul
Turkomans, 101, 105, 130
Turks, early conquests by, 7; in
Middle Ages, 7–9, 11; European
view of, 112–14, 116–19, 138–
9; and Egypt, 123; Young Turk
party, 118–19
Turner, M. J., *Slave Ship*, 212
Tyndale-Briscoe, Canon, 66–7
Tzu Hsi, Empress, 165, 174, 178

Uganda, xxii–xxiv, 223, 229, 251 (89)
Unesco, xxxix
United States of America, 27, 28, 64, 299, 329; Southern, 239; Civil War, 227, 307; colonizing by, 27, 95, 326, 327–8; slavery in, 205–10; abolished, 209, 212, 292; and the Far East, 160, 175, 182; and South America, 296, 300, 308
Uruguay (Montevidian Republic), 302
Uzbegs, 104

Vambéry, A., 95 (65), 104, 111 (91), 148 (88)
Van der Post, L., 217, 231
venereal disease, 119, 260
Venezuela, 291, 300, 306; *llaneros* 286
Verne, Jules, 31, 73 (15)
Vietnam (Annam), 24, 81, 95, 98–100
Vivekananda Swami, 68
Voltaire, F., 99, 144, 145, 149 (125), 152, 155

Wales, 41–2, 145
Wallace, A. R., 89, 91, 95
Walmsley, H. M., 125 (58, 60, 61)
warfare; in Pacific, 272; methods of military technology, 8, 9, 14–16, 155, 160, 273–4; *see also* armies *and* navies
Waterton, C., 206 (19), 308

Wauchope, A. G., 117
Wellington, Duke of, 115, 315
Wen-hsiang, 165
West Indies, the, 16, 79, 276, 327; British, 210; slavery in, 205–10; *see also* Jamaica
Whittall, J. T., 121
Whymper, E., 306, 313
Wilhelm II, Kaiser, 176, 179
Williams, John, 258, 268
Wilson, Sir A., xxxi, 72, 133
Witte, Count, 106
women, 331; African, 215, 225, 242; of Australia, 278; of Burma, 83; of China, 168; rape of, 162, 172; of England, 67, 69; European women, 58, 67; in Africa, 2, 230–31, 242; in China, 162, 171; in India, 58–9; in Pacific, 259, 268; in tropics, 93; of India, 36, 58–9, 61, 63, 67; of Indonesia, 93; Japanese geisha, 188; of Latin America, 310, 316; of Lewchew Islands, 262; of Muslim countries, 139–43; of Persia, 132; of S. Pacific, 255–6, 257, 258, 259–60, 263, 265
Wordsworth, 207

Yaqub Beg, of Kashghar, 127

Zanzibar, 226, 229
Zenzinov, V., 102
Zulus, 228, 231, 231–2, 245, 247, 329, 334

An independent publishing house, Serif publishes a wide
range of international fiction
and non-fiction

If you would like to receive a copy of our current
catalogue,
please write to:

Serif
47 Strahan Road
London E3 5DA

or

1489 Lincoln Avenue
St Paul
MN 55105

also published by Serif

THE CROWD IN HISTORY
A STUDY OF POPULAR DISTURBANCES IN FRANCE AND ENGLAND, 1730–1848

George Rudé

Who took part in the widespread disturbances which periodically shook eighteenth-century London? What really motivated the food rioters who helped to spark off the French Revolution? How did the movement of agricultural labourers destroying new machinery spread from one village to another in the English countryside? How did the *sans-culottes* organise in revolutionary Paris?

George Rudé was the first historian to ask such questions and in doing so he identified 'the faces in the crowd' in some of the crucial episodes in modern European history. An established classic of 'history from below', **The Crowd in History** is remarkable above all for the clarity with which it deals with the full sweep of complex historical events. Whether in Berlin, Beijing or Soweto, crowds continue to make history, and Rudé's work retains all its freshness and relevance for students of history and politics and the general reader alike.

'It may seem incredible that nobody tried before to discover what sort of people actually stormed the Bastille, but Rudé is the first to have done so ... Like all his work this book is concentrated, simple and clear, and admirably suited to the non-specialist reader.'
Eric Hobsbawm, *New York Review of Books*

George Rudé's numerous books include *Wilkes and Liberty*, *The Crowd in the French Revolution* and, with Eric Hobsbawm, *Captain Swing*. One of the most innovative social historians of the twentieth century, he died in 1993.

paperback